P9-DHB-597

ARISTOTLE
ONASSIS

ARISTOTLE
ONASSIS

by
Nicholas Fraser
Philip Jacobson
Mark Ottaway
and Lewis Chester

J. B. LIPPINCOTT COMPANY
Philadelphia and New York

B
On 1 f

PG BT

Printed in the United States of America

Grateful acknowledgment is made for the use of the following:

From *Billy Baldwin Remembers* by Billy Baldwin, published 1974. Reprinted by permission of Harcourt Brace Jovanovich, Inc.: quotations on pages 303–5.
From *Churchill: Taken from the Diaries of Lord Moran*. Copyright © Trustees of Lord Moran. Nutley Publications Ltd. 1966. Reprinted by permission of Houghton Mifflin Company, Boston, and Constable Publishers, London: quotations on pages 169, 170, 171.
From *House Arrest* by Helen Vlachos. Copyright © 1970 by Helen Vlachos. Reprinted by permission of Gambit, Boston, and Andre Deutsch, London: quotations on pages 236–37, 263.
From *Margot Fonteyn: Autobiography*. Copyright © 1975, 1976 by Margot Fonteyn. Reprinted by permission of Alfred A. Knopf, Inc.: quotation on page 167.
From *Onassis* by Willi Frischauer. Copyright © 1968 by Willi Frischauer. Reprinted by permission Hawthorn Books, New York, and The Bodley Head, London: quotation on pages 5–6.
From *Onassis, Mon Amour* by Ingeborg Dedichen and Henry Pessar. Copyright © 1975 by Editions Pygmalion. Reprinted by permission of Editions Pygmalion, Paris: quotations on pages 32, 43–45, 49–50, 62, 64, 67, 68.
From *Princess Grace* by Gwen Robyns. Copyright © 1976 by Gwen Robyns, published by David McKay Co., Inc., and W. H. Allen and Co. Ltd. Reprinted by permission of the publishers: quotation on page 191.

U.S. Library of Congress Cataloging in Publication Data

Main entry under title:

Aristotle Onassis.

Bibliography: p.
Includes index.
1. Onassis, Aristotle Socrates, 1906–1975.
2. Merchant marine—Biography. I. Fraser,
Nicholas, birth date
HE569.05A74 387.5′092′4 [B] 77-24417
ISBN-0-397-01218-7

To
JEAN ALICE DAY
born April 21, 1930
Washington, Pennsylvania

C. 2

Contents

Photograph sections follow pages 116 and 244.

ACKNOWLEDGMENTS

THE MAIN SOURCE MATERIAL for this book was acquired in some two hundred interviews conducted in ten different countries. Except for a few people who requested anonymity, those who provided us with information are named in the text. Most of the interviews were conducted by one or other of the co-authors, but we were also able to call upon the expertise of correspondents of *The Sunday Times* throughout the world. We are most grateful to Mario Modiano in Athens, whose intimate knowledge of Greek affairs was an unfailing help. Others who readily assisted us on particular inquiries were Peter Pringle and Laurie Zimmerman in New York, Tony Terry and Françoise Braud in Paris, Robert Lindley in Buenos Aires, Arvid Bryne in Oslo, Lars Persson in Stockholm, Peter Ward in Ottawa, Benjamin Pogrund in Johannesburg, Dalbert Hallenstein in Verona, and Ritchie McEwen in Vienna.

Among the writers and journalists who gave us the benefit of their time and particular knowledge were Nicholas Gage in New York, Jack Anderson in Washington, Stephen Aris in London, and Maurice Denuzière and Sam White in Paris. We are especially indebted to Willi Frischauer in London and Henri Pessar in Paris, both of whom have written books about Onassis. Of Onassis's closest friends, we are most obliged to Costa Gratsos in New York, Professor Yanni Georgakis in Athens, and Dr. Kurt Reiter in Hamburg.

For assistance in combing through the mass of magazine and newspaper coverage of Onassis we are beholden to Fred Sayer and his staff in the *Sunday Times* library, Bob Fowlow and the staff of the *New York Times* morgue, Armin Sellheim, the head of archives for *Der Spiegel* in Hamburg, and Walter Macauley, the librarian for the *Belfast Telegraph.* In Washington, the officials in charge of the archives of the Justice Department, the Federal Bureau of Investigation, the State Department, and the Central Intelligence Agency provided us with a wealth of previously unpublished information.

For translation of key documents and/or assistance as interpreters we relied on Gudrun Dalibar, Alexandra Fiada, Alasdair Gordon, Vickie Leonard, Renata Nash, Graham Paterson, Susan Reynolds, Sheila Walsh, Martin Warsoe, and Andrea Whittaker. Lynda Poley helped us with picture research. Mimi Day Chester and Janet Fraser gave us forceful advice on the text in its embryo stages. Dr. Elizabeth Whipp helped us interpret some medical aspects of the story. Gillian Mawer and Christine Walker expertly typed the manuscript.

Our enterprise placed considerable extra strain on the staff of the New York office of *The Sunday Times* where the manuscript was completed. Georgetta Moliterno, Joe Petta, James Timmons, and Dianne Condon made agreeably light work of our requests for help.

The suggestions of Ed Burlingame, Jake Ross, and Tom Voss at Lippincott were invaluable. Ruth Pickholtz dealt admirably with the problems imposed by a tight production schedule.

We thank Harold Evans, the editor of *The Sunday Times*, who patiently allowed us to get on with it. Robert Ducas, the president of Times Newspapers of Great Britain in New York, who had the original idea for this book, gave us continuous help and support.

For the errors that remain after so much expert assistance, we alone are responsible.

"Be rich or be an enemy of the rich.
I understand both. But never envy
the rich and try to please them."
ARISTOTLE ONASSIS
in Monte Carlo, 1954

1
Infidel Smyrna

Aristotle Socrates Onassis was born in the Greek quarter of Smyrna on the west coast of Turkey on January 20, 1906. For much of his life he remained diffident about his origins, choosing not to correct the rags-to-riches myth that came to surround him. It was suggested that his father had "hawked homemade trinkets around Smyrna" and his mother "had swept offices and taken in washing."

He was, in fact, the second child but the first son of a wealthy merchant and banker. The names he received expressed the tenuous but deeply felt connection with mainland Greece and with antiquity which the Anatolian Greeks, separated from their homeland and its culture, habitually strove for.

His father, Socrates, was one of the richest citizens of Smyrna, which in those days was one of the richest cities of the eastern Mediterranean. Although the Greeks of Smyrna were a subject race dominated by the Ottoman Turks, their linguistic and entrepreneurial skills had become indispensable to the Ottoman Empire. They were a commercial elite connecting the Turks to the West, and for that reason they were permitted to prosper. Since the promulgation of the *Rum Mileti*— the "Greek Nation"—the Anatolian Greeks were allowed a high degree of autonomy. Legal proceedings involving Greeks alone were tried by Greek

1

courts, and the Greeks established, organized, and financed such institutions of their own as schools and hospitals, all on the basis of voluntary contributions. Socrates Onassis was chairman of the local bank and hospital.

Greeks have inhabited the Mediterranean coastline of present-day Turkey since almost a millennium before Christ. Their civilization preceded that of ancient Athens. Ionia, as that area was called, was once the measure of all that was fashionable, elegant, and enlightened. Although Ionia lost its autonomy before the birth of Christ, its Greek population remained the dominant cultural group in the region. They were able to assimilate successive waves of invaders without losing their ethnic identity. When Aristotle Onassis was born, there were 165,000 Greeks and only 80,000 Turks in Smyrna. The Turks called the city *ghiaour Izmir*—"infidel Smyrna."

The Anatolian Greeks were not a homogeneous people. On the coast were recent immigrants from mainland Greece. In the north, on the shores of the Black Sea, were isolated communities which had guarded their Greekness since Byzantium and earlier. And in the interior were Greeks who had become Turks in all but their religion and, oddly, their writing—their Bibles were in the Turkish language but written in the Greek script. A subtle brand of snobbery existed among Anatolian Greeks with respect to those "Karamanli Christians," as they were called. In some circles, mostly those with social pretensions, they were not regarded as real Greeks.

The Onassis family were of Karamanli stock. Aristotle Onassis would sometimes tell the story of the curious Bible his grandmother used, but in the end he always preferred to avoid discussion of his origins. He led most people to believe that his family had recently come from Greece to Anatolia. The documentary evidence indicates that the Onassis family's association with Turkey went back several generations and that it was his father's generation that began to assert its Greekness, partly because of their improved economic status.

Socrates Onassis's life was a genuine rags-to-riches story. He was born in 1878 in the village of Moutalaski, deep in the interior of Asia Minor in the region of Cappadocia. The Turkish name for Moutalaski was Talas, and since only Turks now live there, that is its name today. It was a sizable community, not quite large enough to warrant description as a town, and the population was more or less evenly divided between Turks and Karamanli Christians of Greek origin. The Greeks had their own church dedicated to Saint Savvas, the patron saint of the district,

2

and their own school, but otherwise—to the outsider, at least—they were indistinguishable from the Turks. Turkish was their mother tongue, and some knew no Greek at all. The Onassis family were sufficiently numerous and well established to have the quarter where they lived named after them, as was the Turkish custom. It was called Onassi Mahlesi, and the census for 1924, the last year in which there were still Greeks in Moutalaski, records four separate Onassis households in the quarter.

Life in Moutalaski was hard, the soil stony and infertile. It was only with the advent of the railroad that an alternative to subsistence agriculture readily presented itself. Enterprising Greek merchants arrived from the coast to set up agencies for their wares with news of the renaissance of the Greek spirit in Smyrna and beyond, and young men from the interior departed in search of fortune and their national identity. Socrates was one of eleven children, though some must have died young since the names of only six have survived. They were (in order of age) John, Socrates, Basil, Alexander, Homer, and Maria. All of them ultimately left for the coast.

In Smyrna the brothers prospered. The railways made the produce of the Anatolian interior accessible to the affluent West and in turn provided a new export market. Smyrna became a boom town, with its Greek traders sending the produce of the Ottoman Empire—cotton, hides, tobacco, opium, figs, raisins, barley, olive oil, and carpets—throughout the world by means of the growing Greek merchant marine. Socrates worked with brother Homer in Smyrna, while brother Alexander returned inland, shipping raisins and olive oil to Smyrna and selling the products which his brothers sent him.

The family "office" was in Vezir Hane, a long, curving street in the *bedesten*—a covered oriental market which was the hub of Smyrna's teeming merchant quarter and which lay between the Greek Orthodox church of Ayia Fotini and the prosperous quarter of Yalyadika. It was not exactly a warehouse in the Western sense since the goods were on full display, spilling in their profusion out into the streets—sacks of raisins and currants, tobacco, figs, balls of raw opium, and piles of hides. There was never enough space in the large, square, ground-floor room for all of Socrates' wares in addition to Socrates himself and his three helpers. Nor was it precisely a shop since none of the goods were for retail sale. It was what today would be called an export-import agency, dealing only in wholesale but relying to some degree on attracting the passing trade of foreign importers.

3

By 1904, Socrates' place in the world was sufficiently assured for him to contemplate marriage. He took the traditional Greek step of returning to his village in search of a bride. Penelope Dologlou was eighteen years old, demure, and beautiful, and she and Socrates were married in Smyrna.

The couple moved to Karatassi, a mile along the coast to the south, only a short ride from the business district of Smyrna by regular ferryboat or horse-drawn trolley. Both the trolley and the ferry stopped at the bottom of the steps of Karatassi—the community, which had developed before the advent of the automobile, climbed away from the sea up the flank of a steep hillside, and most of the houses could be reached only up several flights of steps. The house Socrates chose reflected his unassuming and thrifty nature. It was a substantial but unostentatious one-story affair, with a porch and a small garden surrounded by iron railings. There were Greek, Armenian, and Jewish neighbors. The Armenians clustered around their church at the top of the steps, and the Jews occupied villas strung out along the shoreline. In its cosmopolitan nature the neighborhood reflected the social composition of the growing Smyrna merchant class. If the different groups did not mix very much, they nonetheless lived side by side without apparent disharmony.

Firstborn of the Onassis children was a daughter, Artemis. Next, two years later, came Aristotle, whom they all called Aristo. Then, tragically and suddenly, Penelope died of a kidney operation. All Aristotle Onassis ever conveyed about his mother was that she was beautiful and that he lost her. Perhaps, at six, that was all he could be expected to know. When Socrates married again, eighteen months after Penelope's death, Aristo was not reconciled to the new arrangement. He regarded his stepmother, Helen, as a usurper.

Socrates never developed the passionate symbiosis with Aristo that normally characterizes the relationship of a Greek father with his only son. He was a disciplinarian, a self-made man who carried with him the stern traditions of the peasant community from which he had sprung. Even when he was old and ill, he continued to inspire awe in those who met him. A contemporary described him as "dynamic, stern, upright and unbending." He had a strong concept of duty, both civic and personal, but he was not a warm or openly affectionate man. As a small and lonely boy, Aristo was often afraid of the father who exacted so much deference from those around him.

Aristotle and Artemis were brought up by Socrates' mother, Gethsemane, who had come from Moutalaski to help out after Penelope's death

4

and had stayed on. She spoke only Turkish though she could read and write. She had evaded the Turkish law barring girls of Greek descent from attending school by learning the Greek alphabet secretly in a cave as the teacher drew the characters in the sand. Her love for little "Aristo" was equaled only by her piety, which was prodigious.

Each Easter she went on a pilgrimage to the Holy Land and returned loaded with relics and mementos of all kinds. She was particularly fond of outsize lithographs depicting heaven and hell—above there was a meadow with flowers and lambs, laughing children and benign parents, while below was the devil's face in the shape of a furnace, grimacing and spitting forth fire. There is an engaging description of the impact of Gethsemane's religiosity on her grandson in Willi Frischauer's book, *Onassis:*

> Year after year Gethsemane would frame the lithographs as if they were works of art and hang them on the wall over Aristo's bed.
>
> "Grandmother," he asked with a small voice, "what's that? What does it mean?"
>
> "You must look at it every day," Grandmother replied sternly. "If you are a good boy you will go up to Heaven; if you are a bad boy you will go down to Hell."
>
> Every day early in the morning he walked to the school attached to ... the Greek church only a hundred yards or so down the road. Gethsemane was always in and out of [the church] and very close to the deacons whom she gave many tokens of her devotion. For their benefit she raided the larder of flour, butter, sugar, wine and oil, all of which owing to the war were in short supply and Socrates Onassis was none too pleased when he found out where his precious provisions were going. But, as the grandson had good cause to remember, Gethsemane's benevolence put the deacons under an obligation and they would not deny her a favour in return.
>
> So it came that every fortnight she would wrap up sets of Aristo's vests and pants in a parcel and would take them to church, where the deacons deposited them under the altar. The holy blessing upon them, Gethsemane would collect them a fortnight later to take them home in triumph. She put Aristo into the tub and scrubbed him ("as if I were the deck of a ship") until his skin was sore and he was very, very clean. Then she made him put on the blessed underclothes, and gave him a little homily: "Now I am sure that your sins of the past two weeks will be forgiven and that you will be a very good boy."
>
> It was a painful purgatory but it impressed Aristo, who tried hard to be good because he loved his grandmother and was loath to disappoint

5

her. This regular ritual, however, did not fill the cup of his suffering in the cause of religion. He became a choir-boy and, on the strength of Grandmother's "influence," joined the chosen few who were robed in short, gold-braided cassocks and surplices ("I looked like a miniature priest").

Aristo never did manage to emulate his grandmother's piety, though the experience in the choir helped him develop a fine singing voice which he never lost. The sense of his own worth, which was Gethsemane's chief gift to him, was provided by her love rather than her religion. He developed into an ebullient and aggressive little boy whose sense of privation at home had made him precociously adept at dealing with the rest of the world. When he was eight there was a brief craze in the neighborhood for making toy windmills which consisted of a paper sail affixed by a pin to a stick of wood. One of Aristo's little friends was so pleased with his efforts that he decided to go into production. His first prospect was Aristo.

"How much?" Aristo demanded.

"Um, er . . . one pin?" the friend replied.

"Nitwit," stormed Aristo. "You give me a pin, plus the paper, plus a piece of wood, plus your labor when you give me that windmill. You're crazy asking for just a pin in exchange. You make a loss."

"And so," concluded the childhood friend, Michael Anastasiades, who grew up to be a professor of electronic physics in Athens, "I had my first lesson in the meaning of profit."

Life at home, however, was increasingly remote from the ideal depicted in Gethsemane's lithographs. There were now two girls from the second marriage: Merope, born within a year, and Callirhoe, who completed Socrates' family. There is no reason to believe that Aristo did not love and accept his stepsisters as if they were his own mother's children, but it was always Artemis, his full sister, to whom he was closest. With stepmother Helen he remained in a state of open warfare. It was not what she did to him, it was who she had become. He always answered back, always gave lip, and never obeyed her. Socrates responded with the strap but with little success. At one point, when Aristo was about thirteen, things got so bad that he was sent or went to live next door with the Calogeropoulos family. This exile lasted several months.

Aristo's education began in September 1913 at the primary school attached to the local church. Yanni Voulgarides, Aristo's closest childhood friend, remembers practically nothing about him at the school, perhaps because Aristo was most conspicuous by his absence—he was a

6

hardened truant. Onassis himself had one vivid memory from the school which would stay with him the rest of his life. He was playing with other children in the schoolyard next to the church between classes. An old priest, watching from the church, beckoned him over and offered him some sweets. As he reached out to take them the priest slapped his hand away. "Now why should he have done that?" Onassis would ask. "I have never been able to understand."

Aristo and Yanni began their secondary education in Smyrna at the same time four years later. Yanni went to the Sophia School, Aristo to the private Aroni School. George Katramopoulos, now a jeweler in Athens, remembers Aristo as a popular boy at Aroni, one who never sneaked on other boys and who stood up for the smaller ones against the resident bullies.

His teachers were less sanguine about Aristo's virtues. One of them, Mr. Karaplias, would hesitate at the end of the morning roll call, for Onassis begins with an omega, the final letter in the Greek alphabet. "Ah," he would observe studiedly, "bottom of the alphabet and bottom of the form: Onassis?"

As the scion of one of the most prosperous and influential families in the community, Aristo could get away with behavior which would have resulted in instant expulsion for sons of lesser fathers—after all, the school depended upon patrons such as Socrates and his brothers for its continued existence. The most memorable outrage was when Aristo pinched the bottom of an attractive English lady teacher. Apparently Aristo had been working up to this "coup" for some time, but on this occasion he was considered to have gone too far. The English lady had something akin to hysterics and threw him out of the classroom. Aristo was reprimanded by Mr. Aroni in person and suspended for several days.

Socrates was desperate about his son's education. He turned for advice to another leading citizen, Michael Avramides, then supervisor of the Evangheliki School, the foremost school in Smyrna if not in the entire Greek-speaking world. In 1961, shortly before he died, Avramides made a statement for the archives of the Center for Asia Minor Studies, a government-sponsored institution in Athens dedicated to the recording and unraveling of the history of the Greek peoples in Ottoman Anatolia. The tone of the statement is pompous and self-important, but it offers some intriguing insights into Onassis's upbringing.

I knew the Onassis family even before Aristotle came to the Evang-heliki School. I lived in the Karatassi quarter and used to chant in the Ayia Paraskevi church. I was considered as a chanter with a good voice, so I

7

was always placed on the left side of the church during mass. Socrates, Aristotle's father, was the treasurer of the church; he was from Moutalaski, and had settled in Smyrna. His [second] wife was from Aksari.

Socrates was a very good-looking man, like a sultan. And what a kind person he was. Open-hearted, he was a merchant, and used to deal with tobacco and raisins. I used to go to his house regularly. One day he said to me: "Michael, I am really worried about this child of mine, Aristotle. I feel like committing suicide because of him. Whatever private school I send him to he gets kicked out. What do you think about sending him to the Evangheliki School, since you are also there, and you could also look after him a little? What do you think about that?"

Socrates must have known he was asking a lot. Competition for the fifty places available each year was fierce. Only nepotism or influence could secure Aristo's entry into such an establishment. The school had been founded in 1733 under the protection of the British consulate, and the Red Ensign—the flag of the British Merchant Navy—graced the school photograph each year. Its headmaster, Mr. Lithoxöos, was an austere disciplinarian with high pedagogic standards.

Avramides' memorandum for the archives continues:

> One day [Socrates] brought his son to the school. "I'm giving him to you, so please keep an eye on him," he said. I used to speak Turkish with Socrates, he preferred it this way, because he found it easier than Greek.
>
> The son was as terrible as the father was nice. He was a really naughty person, a disorderly child, shocking all around him, and bothered all the other students in the school. He wouldn't listen to anybody. During the whole time I spent at the school I never had such a child. He was the most difficult one there. I used to scold him quite often, saying in Turkish, *"Utanmiorsun?"* ["Aren't you ashamed?"], and he would ask me not to tell his father.
>
> He used to upset the teachers also, particularly the English and German ones. One day, instead of going home for lunch, he said he wanted to stay behind in school. The doorkeeper refused to let him do so unless he got permission to stay. So Aristotle came up to me and started complaining about the fact that he, being quite small, had a desk that was too big, whereas his good friend Christos Christou was very tall and his desk was too small. So, could they stay during lunch time and change these two desks around? I gave them permission, and they stayed in the classroom. But it all had nothing to do with the desks. He managed to build up a complete electrical installation involving wires and batteries between his desk and his friend's.
>
> That afternoon they had a German or English class—I can't remember

which—and when the teacher walked in Aristotle switched on, and all the electric bells started ringing. Then everybody started running into the classroom to see what was happening and there was complete chaos in the school for a while until we discovered what it really was. Aristotle was suspended from school for 15 days. Of course, when he came back, nothing had changed in his behavior. He was also mean with money. His father used to give him some to tip the doorkeeper and messengers but he used to spend it himself. But he was a good student and shrewd, capable of learning what he was being taught. Even when he was young you could see that he was one of those people who would either destroy themselves or succeed brilliantly.

The dour pedantry with which Lithoxöos ran the school could hardly be expected to spark off any academic interest in a child as rebellious as Aristo. The only lesson he ever enjoyed was history. All those who knew Onassis paint a similar picture: that of a quick-witted, personable, and rebellious child, popular with his peers and the despair of his parents and teachers.

Once school was out Aristo had little time for his egghead classmates, who often used to converse in ancient Greek. His gang consisted of Yorgo Mavroyannis, the boy who worked for Socrates, Yanni Voulgarides, whom Aristo called Yanko, and Yanko's brother Manolis. At recess time in their respective schools they would often converge on Socrates' office for a chat and a surreptitious smoke. After school they would rendezvous there again before returning, as they had come, on the boat together to Karatassi. Just beside the ferry dock was the Pelops Club, which was devoted to sailing, rowing, water polo, and swimming. Uncle Homer was president of the club, and it became the focal point of Aristo's leisure activities.

One of his favorite pranks when swimming was to pull himself up on to the stern of the boat just as it was getting ready to pull out from the jetty. This rear section was reserved for the *hanumises*, the veiled Turkish women, and no men, least of all infidel men, were allowed to defile them with their presence. Having raised a chorus of shrieks by his dramatic appearance, practically naked and dripping from the sea, Aristo would leap, convulsed with laughter, back into the water as the ferry pulled away. The whole performance gained an added piquancy and bravado from the fact that he was risking serious injury, if not death, from the pounding screws of the departing boat.

Aristo, with his broad shoulders, was as keen a racing rower as he was a swimmer. He would persuade Yanko to accompany him as coxswain

9

in his marathon training sessions along the coast. Leaving the Pelops Club at five in the morning, he would row solidly until two in the afternoon, timing his return to coincide with the departure of the ferry from Smyrna and racing it back to Karatassi. One of his pleasures when rowing was to hug the Karatassi shoreline, showing off his bronzed muscles and chatting with the women who bathed there. The high spot of these expeditions was passing the house where a pasha lived. Like all good pashas he had a harem, and the harem would besport itself in the waters during the late afternoon. As soon as the guardian eunuch saw Aristo heaving into view, he would hustle the ladies back indoors like a beefy mother hen. Aristo thought this performance was hilarious and provoked it whenever possible.

When they weren't at the Pelops Club, Aristo and his friends could usually be found across the road in the barber shop by the trolley stop. It was a good vantage point from which to watch Karatassi's comings and goings. The shop belonged to Yorgo Makronides, another Pelops man who, although older than they, enjoyed the company of the gang. The boys were intent on becoming men's men, and a barber shop was pleasantly masculine.

Aristo's first love was one of the Spanish Jewish girls who lived by the sea and whom everyone called Luna-e-Kinze—Latino for "moon-and-fifteen." Luna was her real name, and fifteen her age. Aristo would persuade the others to come and sing *cantadas*—old-fashioned Italianate love songs—beneath her window. Invariably the quartet would soon tire of this activity and end up lying on the beach, their drunken songs and laughter echoing through the empty midnight. But Aristo was not alone in his admiration for Luna-e-Kinze. There was also Spartalis, a rich Armenian boy who was threatening to gain the ascendancy in Luna-e-Kinze's affections. One night Aristo and his friends, deciding to put Spartalis in his place, marched over to his house and instructed him to turn his attentions elsewhere. Spartalis, who had his own friends with him, demurred, and a brawl resulted. In the end both boys were the losers—Luna-e-Kinze and her family emigrated to South America.

In those days, in Smyrna as elsewhere, there were good girls you married and bad girls you rehearsed with. Luna-e-Kinze was a good girl, and Aristo's passion for her was of a high romantic order. The same could not be said of his other erotic adventures. He was determined to lose his virginity. He later told Ingeborg Dedichen, a woman who was for many years his lover, that he would have accomplished this feat at the age of twelve with the assistance of the young and beautiful family washer-

10

woman if only his stepmother had returned home a minute or two later and had not decided to inspect the cellar. Aristo got the usual hiding from Socrates, and the washerwoman was replaced by "an old witch, skinny, with a magnificent mustache, a sour voice and a sour smell."

The next occasion arose when his father marched him off to private French lessons during the summer holidays. Aristo had resolved to behave so appallingly that his tutor would refuse to give a second lesson, which would allow him to return to the pleasures of the Pelops Club. All that changed when he saw the teacher. She was twenty-five, beautiful, insubstantially clad in the heat of high summer, and she "excited my imagination on the spot." After that he could barely wait for his daily French lessons. One day he overcame his timidity.

> The teacher sat down, as she always did, opposite me. She was dressed very lightly in a dressing gown that was nearly transparent, and barely hid her curves, exposing her ample bosom. My heart beating, my mouth dry with emotion, I tried to speak in Greek (not in French!): "Mademoiselle, you are indecently dressed. You are arousing me against my will. If you continue to dress in such a fashion nothing can stop me from violating you!"
>
> Not at all taken aback at my frankness she burst out laughing. I urged her on to the sofa and without hesitation showed her my admiration. She was my first mistress.

Smyrna had a spectacular red light district called Demir Yolu. Three men who were at the Evangheliki School with Aristo have, as their most vivid memory of him, the events of December 4, 1921—they are sure of the date because it was Saint Barbara's Day. On that day Aristo amazed classmates and masters alike by asking if he and any other interested parties could take a couple of hours away from school that morning in order to attend Communion in honor of the saint. The masters were too taken aback to refuse, but, once outside the school gates, Aristo halted the bemused group of about a dozen who were heading for the church. Instead he dragged them off to Demir Yolu. Although they at first indicated to us that the expedition came to an obvious and satisfactory conclusion, they decided—they are now elderly and respectable Athenians and were talking to us in their club—that, on second thought, they were prepared to divulge no more details than the fact that they went to Demir Yolu. But, they indicated, Aristo "did seem to know his way around."

Opinions vary on the degree to which Aristo exhibited a precocious

11

entrepreneurial streak. Onassis's rowing companion, Yanko Voulgarides, is of the opinion that Aristo was no more or less ambitious than any teenage boy of independent spirit in the mercantile atmosphere of Smyrna, where trading was a way of life, its rewards tangible, and poverty a painfully recent memory for most. The boys from the Evangheliki School, who came from more sheltered professional, academic, or clerical backgrounds, formed a rather different view of the incipient business abilities of their classmate.

One day there was a fire at the shop from which they obtained most of their school materials. It was called Kagit Hane and belonged to the Athanasoula brothers. Recollections are vague as to whether Aristo "salvaged" or purchased for a nominal sum a number of charred pencils which could no longer be offered for sale. But all agree that his next step was to invest in a couple of newfangled pencil sharpeners. He then persuaded a friend to arm himself with the second sharpener, and the two boys sat down with their pile of pencils and proceeded to cut them down until there was no more charred wood visible. Aristo then sold them to his fellow pupils at knockdown prices and made a handsome profit.

The Great Burnt Pencil Coup established Aristo's primacy at the school in a field where he had few competitors. The significant thing about it was that Aristo did not need the money. Socrates' wealth was proverbial—one of the school jokes was that he was so rich and so generous to Aristo that he had his son's initials inscribed on the walls of every Greek Orthodox church in Christendom. This was a reference to "I am the Alpha and the Omega"—the designation of God, the first and last letters of the Greek alphabet, and the initials of Aristotle Onassis.

The good fortune enjoyed by Aristo, Socrates, and the Smyrna Greek community did not endure the effects of World War I. It is customary for historians to inquire how and why the citizens of other European nations failed to anticipate that conflict, and it is worth asking the same question about the Smyrna Greeks. They could not conceive that their community might be totally destroyed, and when it was, they were consequently unable to offer resistance.

Part of the reason for this failure was that their situation deteriorated so gradually. Turkey's withdrawal from the Balkans was nothing new, nor was the propensity of previously subject races to assert themselves in the wake of this development. Previously, the Western powers had filled the vacuum left by the Turks, and there seemed no reason why they should

12

not continue to do so. When Greece, Serbia, Montenegro, and Bulgaria joined forces in 1912 to expel the Turks from Europe, the Smyrna Greeks quietly rejoiced. But they wanted things both ways—it never occurred to them that their strong desire to remain a privileged part of the Ottoman Empire and their no less strong wish to be considered Greeks would shortly become incompatible.

When Turkey joined Germany against the Allies in World War I, Smyrna was occupied by a force of Turkish and German soldiers. The German general Otto Liman von Sanders, who led the Turks in the Gallipoli campaign, was billeted in Karatassi only a few houses away from the Onassis family. At school, Aristo and his classmates had been obliged to furl the Red Ensign and exchange their English-style caps for Turkish fezzes and satin arm bands embossed with the star and crescent. Yet the Smyrna Greeks continued to offer covert support to Greece. Their church services (in Greek, of course, and consequently happily incomprehensible to the occupying force) ended with an invocation for a blessing upon Greece, her king, queen, and army. Aristo expressed astonishment at this inconsistency. "But I thought we were on the side of the Germans," he asked his father. "Why are we praying for the enemy?" He was told to be quiet or he would endanger his family and his friends.

There were, nonetheless, a number of portents of the disaster that was to engulf the Anatolian Greeks. Isolated Greek communities inland were summarily told that their safety "could no longer be guaranteed" by the Ottoman authorities. Their Greek inhabitants left and were replaced by European Muslim refugees from the Balkan Wars. But such casual shifts of population were not considered unusual. They did not affect Smyrna, and the Smyrna Greeks did not allow themselves to be affected by them. Nor was the fate of the Armenians in the Ottoman Empire, who were massacred throughout Asia Minor and Armenia itself in 1915, considered relevant. Such atavism seemed remote from a community that took pride in its cosmopolitan outlook.

In 1919, the Allied troops "liberated" Smyrna to rapturous displays of pro-Allied sentiment. The idea of *enosis*—unity with Greece—which the Smyrna Greeks had never really desired or sought, suddenly became a real possibility. Eleutherios Venizelos, the prime minister of Greece, was a proponent of Greek Anatolia. The Western powers—particularly Great Britain, whose prime minister, David Lloyd George, was a romantic philhellene—seemed disposed to support him.

On August 10, 1920, the Treaty of Sèvres was signed, awarding Smyrna and a generous portion of the Anatolian hinterland to Greece.

13

Meanwhile there had been another coup d'état in Turkey. The sultan was overthrown by Kemal Atatürk, who had the intention of resisting by force any imposed treaty, particularly one which involved the dismemberment of Turkey. Greece, exhausted by ten years of continuous war, its army hopelessly overextended in the alien hinterland, was quite incapable of imposing its terms.

The summer of 1922 started badly for Aristo. He had not expected to graduate from his school, and he was therefore not surprised when he did not. He hoped to prove himself in the annual games of the Pelops Club. His uncle Homer was one of the four judges that year. He was a strong swimmer, rower, and water-polo player, and, besides, most of the older boys had been called up for military service. Aristo had a reasonable expectation of doing well enough to be the "Victor Ludorum," or champion of champions.

In any event, he was among the prize winners at the games, held on July 30, but not the champion of champions. It was not enough to assuage his sense of failure. A few days later, one of his school friends who had graduated with honors and was about to leave for a German university found him disconsolately hanging around the public gardens in front of the governor's palace.

"Cheer up," he told Aristo. "There is always next year. You'll get your diploma then."

"Idiot," raged Aristo, "do you think I am going to hang around this piddling town? For me, the whole world is small. I don't need any diploma. You will marvel one day at what I shall do."

It was an accurate prediction of the course his extraordinary life would take. What he did not and could not know was the horror of the circumstances that would dictate his abrupt departure from Smyrna.

2
"THE CATASTROPHE"

THE TURKISH NATIONALIST ARMY under the command of Kemal Atatürk attacked the center of the Greek army on the plateau of Dumlupinar, two hundred miles east of Smyrna, on the morning of August 26, 1922. Within twenty-four hours the Greek front had collapsed. The retreating Greek soldiers, unable to destroy their opponents, set the pattern for the following days by slaughtering the Turkish population in the path of their flight. The advancing Turks found the bodies of their compatriots in the ruins and enlisted the survivors' help in taking their vengeance. Soon there were mutilated Greek corpses among the Turkish dead.

By September 2 the Greek retreat had become a rout. First refugees and then, wrote George Horton, the US consul in Smyrna, "the defeated, dusty, ragged Greek soldiers began to arrive, looking straight ahead, like men walking in their sleep. . . . in a never-ending stream they poured towards the point on the coast to which the Greek fleet had withdrawn." Then the Greek fleet upped anchor and sailed away. Smyrna had been left to the Turks. On September 9 it was occupied without resistance.

For twenty-four hours the city was quiet as the Turks took stock of their prize. On the night of September 10, a party of Turkish troops entered the Armenian quarter with the aim of finding and killing a

15

number of prominent citizens hostile to Turkish rule. The Armenians resisted, and the subsequent massacre acted like a signal. In the following days, encouraged by their officers, Turkish troops swept through the other non-Turkish quarters of the city, killing and looting. Men, women, and children were dragged from their homes and killed in the streets. The city's churches, crammed with refugees, were sprayed with gasoline and ignited. The wooden walls took fire instantly. Those who attempted to escape were bayoneted on the church steps.

As the fires spread, a cordon of troops was thrown around the burning areas to fence the refugees in. Fugitives were either shot down in the streets or driven back into the flames. Some of them made for the harbor, where British, French, and other Allied warships swung at anchor. They had come to rescue their own nationals, but their crews were largely occupied in repelling the pleading, screaming Greeks. Some refugees who swam out to the ships were mangled by their propellers.

The Smyrna catastrophe was the first occasion on which the western media carried a running account of the revenge of a victorious army upon the defenseless citizens of another race. Ward Price described the fire in the London *Daily Mail* on September 16: "What I see as I stand on the deck of the 'Iron Duke' is an unbroken wall of fire, two miles long, in which twenty distinct volcanoes of raging flame are throwing up jagged, writhing tongues to a height of 100 feet. . . . The sea glows a deep copper-red. From the densely-packed mob of many thousands of refugees huddled on the narrow quay, between the advancing fiery death behind and the deep water in front, comes continuously such frantic screaming of sheer terror as can be heard miles away." By the time the flames died down, five days later, over 120,000 Greeks and Armenians had perished. Infidel Smyrna was almost completely destroyed.

On the day the Turks arrived in Smyrna, Socrates Onassis had gathered his family around him in his house at Karatassi and closed the shutters. His wife, Helen, was there, along with Grandmother Gethsemane, Aristo, Artemis, and the two younger girls, Merope and Callirhoe. They spent the next four days indoors, watching the destruction of the city across the bay through a chink in the shutters. They were in a state of fear verging on terror. It was clear that their main source of wealth, the warehouse, had been destroyed in the blaze. Socrates was no longer young and suffered from heart problems, but he had more immediate reasons for apprehension. Distance insulated the family from the fire, but it seemed probable that the Onassises would be singled out by the Turks in any reprisals that might follow the holocaust.

16

Like most of the Smyrna merchant class, the Onassis family had long suspected that mainland Greece's commitment to Anatolia might prove inadequate. They were prominent members of a separatist movement aiming for an autonomous Greek area under the nominal sovereignty of Turkey, with Smyrna itself as an international zone. This, they had hoped, might be palatable to the Turks, who had historically permitted minorities to act as intermediaries between themselves and the outside world. An added attraction, at least to the wealthier merchant class of Smyrna, was that such an arrangement held the promise of being more auspicious for trade. The movement's military arm was called *Mikrasiatiki Ethniki Amina*—the "Asia Minor Defense League." Fundraising committees were created in the Smyrna area to arm the projected force. Two of Aristo's uncles, Homer and Alexander Onassis, were the local treasurers. But the league was never much more than a paper organization, and when the Turkish army arrived, no defense was offered. Nonetheless, a register of the organization found its way into Turkish hands. Since the citizens of Smyrna had never legally ceased to be Turkish nationals, supporters of the Ethniki Amina were designated "traitors" destined for summary execution. The consequences for members of the Onassis family were serious and in some cases fatal.

Aristo's uncle Homer had presciently fled before the arrival of the Turkish troops. Alexander, however, was immediately arrested and interned at Kasaba, forty miles inland, where he was later executed. Uncles Basil and John were transported to a concentration camp in the interior. Aunt Maria, her husband, Chrysostomos Konialidis, and one of their children had sought sanctuary in a church in Ak-Kissar in the old Greek town of Theatira. With five hundred other refugees they were burned alive. Finally, Socrates Onassis was arrested and taken to prison, leaving Aristo, age sixteen, the only male in the Karatassi house. Although not on the list of "traitors" himself, Socrates was clearly endangered by the fact that two of his brothers were.

Our principal guide to what happened during the next four weeks is Onassis's own version of events. It is a story he told many times, sometimes with unverifiable embellishments. But the basic theme and characters remained the same as when he told it to his friend Yanko Voulgarides on arriving in Athens shortly after his escape from Smyrna. Our own research indicates that the story is substantially true, though at times Onassis was inclined to exaggerate his role in the events he described.

It began shortly after his father's arrest, when Aristo decided to find

17

out for himself what had happened in the ruined city. He saw men being dragged from their homes, being hanged or shot or carried away. Turkish patrols, vigilante groups, and armed gangs of looters roamed through the streets. The severed heads of Greek girls floated in the river, tied together by the hair like bunches of coconuts. In the harbor, fully clothed men and women were swimming toward any ship they saw weighing anchor, holding onto the anchor chains, and pleading to be taken aboard. The foreign sailors pelted them with buckets, brooms, and refuse until they sank back into the sea.

The Turks decided to use the Karatassi house as a billet for one of their generals. When the requisition order arrived, the women left. Grandmother Gethsemane moved in with another woman; stepmother Helen and the three girls were sent to an evacuation center to await transport to mainland Greece. Aristo, who had some previous experience of the military mind, decided to try to stay on. When General Liman von Sanders had been billeted near the Onassis house during the German occupation of Smyrna, he had attempted to ease the loneliness of foreign command by ingratiating himself with the local children, giving them candy and free rides in his chauffered limousine. It had been Aristo's first insight into the way authority could be influenced by charm and guile.

When the Turkish general and his entourage arrived, Aristo was standing in the doorway of his family's house. A Turkish lieutenant came up to him and introduced himself as the general's aide-de-camp. Aristo explained that he did not want to go with his sisters to the camp and that he might be of some service. When the aide began to question him about various aspects of the house, Aristo was a model of concern. He explained that it was all rather difficult and suggested he should stay on for a while to allow the general to settle in comfortably. The aide was agreeable. "You usually find that if you make things comfortable for people they like you," Onassis explained at a period of his life when his ability to make things work was no longer in doubt. What he learned in Smyrna was the ability to convince people he could do things that were mutually beneficial. It was a skill neither his stern father nor his teachers had much appreciated.

The conflagration had created a number of shortages in Smyrna. With the Allied fleet in the bay and the Turks in the city, the remaining stocks of liquor were rapidly exhausted. To avoid any additional outbreaks of violence, the Turkish commander-in-chief imposed a ban on the sale of liquor. The soldiers became thirsty. When the general complained about this deficiency in his presence, Aristo suggested he might be able to do

18

something. With his protector, the aide-de-camp, he made the rounds of his family's business acquaintances. The expedition was a failure—the old family friends displayed an understandable reluctance to speak to Aristo in the presence of a Turkish officer.

He was sitting dejectedly on the porch the next day when a man drove by in an old Ford. Aristo recognized him as the US vice-consul, James Loden Park. A graduate of Harvard Medical School, he had come to the Middle East as a young man in 1919, lured by a taste for the exotic and an idealistic wish to participate in the League of Nations' relief work in Syria. In 1921 he was hired by the State Department and transferred to Smyrna, where he wrote a report explaining why figs packed in Smyrna and exported to the United States often arrived in a rotten state. Otherwise his duties were menial, mainly the routine registration of US sailors arriving in the port. After the catastrophe, however, in which he lost his possessions and his own car, he found himself in a position of unusual responsibility. When Aristo saw him, he was collecting a teacher of English at Aristo's school to take her to safety.

Park responded to the same sense of latent ability in Aristo as had the Turkish lieutenant. While the teacher packed her bags, he asked the boy where he could get some liquor. Aristo outlined his failure the previous day but said he thought it might be worth trying again. After ferrying the teacher to the port, Park returned to collect Aristo, and together they made the rounds of the city. This time the expedition was more successful—Aristo and Park found three gallons of raki and several bottles of scotch. The scotch and most of the raki went to the US Navy. Aristo received a bottle of raki and an Allied laissez-passer which gave him access to the heavily guarded US Marine zone. He took the bottle of raki home to his Turkish friends, who were delighted and impressed by his resourcefulness. They gave him a new suit of clothes and another laissez-passer, this one for the city itself. His role of middleman was now assured. He had the freedom of the city, even after curfew, and he set out to locate his family and insure their safety.

The girls and his stepmother were safe in the evacuation center. With Park's help they were put on a boat and taken to the Greek island of Lesbos. Grandmother Gethsemane was nowhere to be found, but it seemed that she had managed to get away. Aristo then turned his attentions to helping his father. Armed with his Turkish laissez-passer, he succeeded in visiting him in prison. His father was ill and depressed. The Turks were "trying" and executing between ten and twenty men each night. The prisoners never knew who might be next. Aristo orga-

19

nized a "Turks for Socrates Onassis" demonstration. His father had many friends in the Turkish business community, and Aristo persuaded about fifty of them, some carrying placards, to demonstrate in front of the city prefecture. Socrates was not sentenced to death, but neither was he released.

Aristo was approached by a Turkish friend of his father's, Sadiq Topal, who had left some of his possessions—stocks, bonds, and a box of jewelry —in the Onassis office in Vezir Hane. As a Turk, Sadiq was able to get a permit to retrieve his goods. Accompanied by a Turkish army officer and two witnesses, Sadiq and Aristo went to the wreckage of Socrates' office. The safe was still intact. Aristo boldly asked the Turkish officer if he could take some of the money which belonged to his own father. Although this was against the emergency regulations, the officer was sufficiently impressed to allow Aristo to extract several thousand Turkish pounds—over $10,000—for his own use.

His acquisition of the money posed a problem. All Greek males over eighteen had to register with the Turkish authorities, after which they were either interned or sent off to mainland Greece. Aristo was still not seventeen, but his natural precociousness might easily excite official curiosity. If he were interrogated and searched, the money might be found on his person and confiscated. He was torn between the desire to help his father and the feeling that he should leave now and go to the women of his family, who were marooned on Lesbos without funds. His two protectors, Park and the Turkish aide-de-camp, advised him to go while he could. His father, too, felt that Aristo should join the family and take them to Greece. Socrates was now confident his Turkish friends in Smyrna would protect him. Aristo acceded to his father's wish and with Park's assistance secured a passage to Lesbos on board a US destroyer.

Before departing, he went to say good-bye to his father. He had with him all the family money and some lamb chops and cigarettes. They kissed farewell, and Aristo handed Socrates 500 Turkish pounds—about $2,000—and the provisions.

As he left the jail he was arrested. The commandant, it transpired, had seen him pass the 500 pounds to his father. He was taken to the commandant's office and asked where he had got the money and how much he had left. Aristo lied. He said he had had to spend a great deal and had none left. The commandant was interested in this assertion. It became apparent to Aristo that he was suspected of bribing the Turkish general who occupied the Onassis house.

By now he was terrified. Not only was he carrying the rest of the family money, he also bore incriminating documents and messages from other prisoners to their families in Greece. Fortunately the commandant was called away for an urgent meeting. His guards strolled up and down the corridor of the prison chatting, Aristo between them. Gradually Aristo dropped behind and walked, as calmly as his pounding heart would let him, out of the prison gates. The guards at the gate made no attempt to stop him. He was, after all, a regular visitor.

As soon as he dared, Aristo ran for his life to the port and sought refuge in the office of the US vice-consul in the Hotel Majestic. Park hid the boy in his rolltop desk. A Turkish patrol came to ask Park whether he had seen the fugitive, who, they added for good measure, had stolen a lot of money and had killed a girl. Aristo listened inside the desk as the vice-consul lied manfully. Once the Turks had gone, Park found some bell-bottoms and a top small enough for Aristo. He then took him to the harbor and hustled him aboard US destroyer 219, the *Edsall*. An hour later Aristo was on his way to Lesbos in the guise of an ordinary American seaman.

At Lesbos, small boats surrounded the incoming ships and crowds milled on the quayside for news from Smyrna. The island had become a clearinghouse for the million or so Anatolian Greeks on their way to the mainland. The refugees, including seventeen women and children of the Onassis family, were living in tents. Food was short, and conditions were unsanitary—there was an outbreak of typhus which later spread to the mainland. The Onassises got out as quickly as they could. Three weeks after Aristo's arrival, they disembarked in Piraeus, the port of Athens. Aristo was still wearing the sailor suit in which he had left Smyrna.

They took lodgings in Piraiki, a run-down quarter of Athens near the Piraeus docks. Uncle Homer was of some assistance, but for the most part Aristo was still acting as head of the family, paying its bills and worrying about the fate of its missing members. There was tragic news about Grandmother Gethsemane. She had survived the catastrophe, had escaped the Turks, and had reached Greece. But as the old lady had struggled to disembark with all her possessions at Piraeus, a gang of thieves had tried to snatch her purse. The spirited woman had put up a fight and had died in a fall from the gangway to the quayside.

It was a bitter blow for the family and one which could have done nothing to improve Aristo's liking for Greece—a country he had never set foot in before and where neither he nor any of the refugees from

21

Ottoman territory were particularly welcome. The population of Greece was only five million, and the country was war weary and ruined, with shortages of food and medical supplies. During the months before the League of Nations had voted 100,000 gold francs to the Nansen relief organization for use in Greece, the refugees had represented a formidable problem of assimilation. They were known as *Turkospori*—"Turk's sperm."

Aristo came through the Smyrna catastrophe with something more than a sense of loss. The fatalistic outlook induced by what he had seen never left him, but it was accompanied by an overwhelming confidence in his own ability to survive. He had tested his luck and been rewarded. The notion that good fortune came to those who risked themselves became central to the way he perceived the world. But it took him some time to find out how to apply the principle in conditions less abnormal than those which had prevailed in Smyrna. Soon after he arrived in Athens, he experienced the first real failure of his adult life.

Socrates Onassis was still in prison in Smyrna, and Aristo was determined to secure his release. He bought a new suit of clothes, a suitcase, and a ticket to Istanbul aboard the *Abbazia*, an Egyptian passenger ship of the Khedivia Line sailing under the British flag. On the passage he hovered around the first-class dining room, awestruck at the contrast between the atmosphere of elegance and the prospects he and his family now enjoyed. What he did in Istanbul is not altogether clear. His own story was that he found his father's British, Italian, and Turkish business friends and with them evolved a plan to secure his father's release. What is certain is that the plan involved a good deal of expense and that Aristo, without consulting his family, handed over the rest of the money in his possession.

Soon afterward, Socrates was released—he came to Athens, via Lesbos, as the family had done—but he was not convinced by Aristo's representation of cause and effect. Nor was Uncle Homer. There was a turbulent family meeting at which Aristo was asked to give a detailed account of the way he had acquired and spent the family money. Onassis later glossed over the confrontation, most likely to minimize the humiliation it had caused him. "People forget quickly," he said. "Only a few weeks earlier they may have been on the verge of death. Then comes safety and the grumbles and complaints begin—over all sorts of trivialities."

He had good cause to feel injured. Whether or not his Istanbul trip had been necessary, his family could hardly begrudge him the role he had played in shepherding them from Smyrna to Athens. It seemed his hard-won manhood was being questioned. Most probably that was what Socrates, consciously or not, was doing. The contrast between his austere temperament and Aristo's unruliness had long been a source of family friction. While Socrates had been in prison, Aristo had, rather effectively on the whole, taken his place as the family's male protector. Now Socrates seemed determined to reclaim his supremacy. The fact that he was obliged to live in straitened circumstances irked him; the fact that his son had contributed to this situation provided an additional justification for his harshness. Aristo, for his part, was resentful of what seemed like parental ingratitude. Socrates had shrewdly maintained bank accounts abroad before the catastrophe, and those were sufficient to meet the emergency in the family's fortunes. Though infinitely poorer, the Onassises were still far from being poverty stricken.

For the next ten months, Aristo suffered from what he later termed a "feeling of futility." Socrates, his health impaired by his spell in prison, was nonetheless able to start up in business again, dealing in tobacco. Aristo did not join him. He lived a solitary, rootless existence. His former friends saw little of him, but they too were all preoccupied with collecting the shattered remnants of their lives. For all of them, Athens seemed like a frustrating provincial backwater compared with Smyrna. The brighter boys from the Evangheliki School were intent on resuming their plans for further education. The loss of their school and all its records posed a bureaucratic problem: how to convince the universities to which they applied that they had properly graduated? Headmaster Lithoxöos was located and undertook to sign an affidavit. Michael Anastasiades, who had helped Aristo in the Great Burnt Pencil Coup, was assigned to draw up a list for the headmaster's signature. He felt that, under the circumstances, he might just get away with putting Onassis's name in, as always at the bottom. Lithoxöos, however, was in no mood for forgiveness. As he reached the bottom of his list his brow furrowed and he struck out the final name with three firm lines of red ink.

Yanko Voulgarides remembers Aristo then as "running around trying to get out." He was humiliated by the rebuke he had received and was anxious to make good. Like most refugees, his reminiscences of Smyrna acquired an obsessional character with the status of personal myth. In Aristo's case, the need to establish that he, rather than his father, was in the right led him to exaggerate both the scale of the horrors he had experienced and his role in saving his family. He had seen his uncles hang, he told his friends; he had rescued the funds of Ethniki Amina and had taken them to Greece. Sometimes he had even swum from the quayside to the USS *Edsall.* The lies, if that is the word for them, were personally necessary for him, a means of constructing a self he could rely on in the hard life he had decided on.

Alexis Minotis, now Greece's foremost actor and the director of the Greek National Theater, met Onassis for the first time in Athens in 1922. Like Onassis, he was impoverished and ambitious. Like Onassis, he became preeminent in his field. It was the beginning of a lifelong friendship. Minotis recalls that Onassis's original plan was to emigrate to the United States, but this idea had to be abandoned when Onassis discovered that, under the quota system which then applied to immigrants, it would be years before all the Greeks who wanted passports would be allowed in. Finally his fancy settled on Argentina. It was a country where Greeks were reputed to be able to make good, and there were also distant relatives there. Onassis tried to persuade Yanko and his brother to accompany him, but they were among the lucky ones who had already found good jobs.

Socrates would not advance Aristo the fare. He regarded his son's plans as more evidence of his reckless nature. There were many mouths to feed and few males capable of earning enough money for the family. Aristo, he believed, should get a job in Athens instead of leaving home. Aristo turned to his friends for assistance. Yanko and his brother, Manolis, pooled their resources and gave him $200. They did not expect to get it back. "We did not want to profit from his misfortune," they explained.

Later, when it became clear that his son's decision was irrevocable, Socrates gave him another $250. As a refugee from Smyrna, Aristo was not eligible for a Greek passport. The only travel document available to him was good for one trip only. With this and a booking for Buenos Aires, he left Piraeus harbor in August 1923 on the first lap of his voyage. He went first to Naples, where he had to wait three weeks for a passenger ship to the Argentine. Onassis later recalled with great enjoyment his first experience of lodging completely apart from his family. The cooking of his Neapolitan landlady far surpassed that in his own home, while the landlady's recently widowed daughter advanced his amorous education. When he left for South America, both women were in tears.

The 12,000-ton *Tomaso di Savoya* was crowded with Italian emigrants traveling steerage and packed into cargo holds converted into dormitories, three hundred men to each hold. Aristo "sweet-talked" the boatswain, gave him five dollars, and persuaded him to allow him to sleep in the aft of the ship in a round cage enclosing the ship's stern lines. As the ship steamed northward along the coast of Italy and beyond, the emigrants pressed against the rails, crying out when they recognized a place—San Remo, Monte Carlo, Nice, and Cannes.

On September 21, 1923, the ship slid up the shallow, muddy waters of the Río de la Plata to the docks of Buenos Aires. Aristotle Onassis, age seventeen, struggled down the gangplank, through the Latin exuberance of family reunions, to set foot on a new continent. He had a battered suitcase in one hand and a few hundred dollars in his pocket.

3
TOBACCO ROAD

YANNI CATAPODIS, a Greek fruit peddler, was on the quayside as the passengers disembarked from the *Tomaso di Savoya*. He had come to the docks in the hope of finding a relative from his own country among the new arrivals. Failing to recognize anyone among the passengers, he was preparing to leave when he noticed an adolescent boy struggling with a heavy suitcase. Catapodis offered him an apple. When the boy thanked him in Greek, they began a conversation. "I was immediately struck by the kid's personality," Catapodis recalled. "It was not that he was particularly brilliant, but I'd rarely come across anyone quite so sure of himself."

The peddler took Onassis home with him and offered him a job in the fruit and vegetable business and hospitality for as long as he wanted it. Onassis accepted a night's lodging and a few days' work before moving on to live in the house of a distant relative in the La Boca docks area. He shared a room with a man who had the habit of spitting on the floor around his bed during the night. Onassis fastidiously put old newspapers on the floor of their room to make cleaning up in the morning easier. He found more salubrious lodgings in a second-floor apartment on the Avenida de Corientes, just across the road from the Mercado de Abasto, Buenos Aires's vast central market. The rent was twenty-five dollars a month for bed and breakfast (butter and jam, one dollar extra).

Finding work was Onassis's most immediate preoccupation. Fruit peddling with Catapodis was certainly not what he had in mind, but regular jobs were hard to find. For a while he helped to row people across the Riachuelo River, a stinking stretch of water along the southern boundary of Buenos Aires. Other temporary jobs included bricklayer's hod carrier on a construction site and dishwasher at a popular bar-cum-restaurant on the corner of Talcahuano and Corientes in the heart of the city's entertainment district. Years later, from the security of great wealth, Onassis would reminisce about how proud he had been to wash up the glasses used by a regular patron, the celebrated tango singer Carlos Gardel—tango singers and soccer players were then the working-class folk heroes. At the time, though, it was deeply depressing—humping bricks, washing dirty dishes, always being tired and hard up. It was not the life Onassis had dreamed about on the voyage over. After a rough six months, his verve and energy were flagging. Furthermore, the seasons in South America are the reverse of those in Europe: winter would begin in June, and he knew it would be colder and wetter than anything he had known in Smyrna.

Despairing of getting a job that matched his own high opinion of his talents, Onassis had decided to take the traditional Greek way out—going to sea. Wandering through the great port, he tried ship after ship, many flying the Greek flag, without success. At last, one master, an elderly Scot, promised to take him on. The ship, the *Socrates*, was owned by the British firm of Lamport & Holt. He arranged to go aboard in a couple of days and caught the trolley home, when he overheard two young men chatting in Greek.

With nothing to lose, Onassis introduced himself. He learned that they were both in steady work, converting the old manual telephone exchange to an automatic system. His new friends were sure they could get him taken on, though they told him he should remember to say that he came from Salonika since the boss of the company, a Colonel Smith, had fond memories of living there. He should also lie about his age. In this situation youth was not on his side, but the authorities would probably swallow a story about documents being lost during those terrible days in Smyrna.

On March 12, 1924, Onassis applied for a job with the British United River Plate Telephone Company, one of the many big Argentinian corporations controlled by British capital (Argentina was often called Britain's fifth dominion, so extensive was this financial influence). The application form still survives. Under "place of birth," Onassis naturally wrote "Salonika." He had no intention of being lumped in with the

hordes of Middle Eastern refugees—Syrians, Turks, and Armenians—
who had fled from the Turks to Argentina and were contemptuously
dismissed by Argentinians as "Turcos." For the purposes of the record,
he added a couple of years to his age, making himself almost twenty years
old (he was, in fact, just two months past his eighteenth birthday).
Onassis asked to be taken on as an electrician, claiming that he spoke
English, French, Turkish, and Spanish and that he could use a typewriter
but had no shorthand. He gave an address on Triunvirato, a street in the
northern part of the city. At this stage, Onassis changed lodgings with
what must have been distressing frequency. Even so, his story about once
being so poor that he was obliged to sublet his bed to another Greek
immigrant during his working hours appears to have been an unromantic
fiction.

By the winter of 1924, Onassis was settled in at United Telephone's
exchange in Avenida, one of Buenos Aires's smartest districts. He was
officially employed as an electrician, a rather grand way to describe a job
consisting of gathering up clumps of wires and welding them together
for the new automatic switchboard. Fortunately for Onassis, the work,
though grindingly repetitive, had its fringe benefits. The old manual
exchange was kept working during the conversion, staffed exclusively by
some two hundred girl operators. Onassis worked squatting on the floor
behind the switchboard where the girls sat. Wherever he looked, his eyes
fell upon a row of female legs. It was some compensation for those first
joyless months in Buenos Aires.

Onassis was popular with the girls. He had physical charm. A contemporary photograph shows a heavy-shouldered, solemn young man with
jet black hair, thick eyebrows, and full, expressive mouth—a face just
beginning to hint at the heaviness that would come a few years later but
pleasant enough. A distant cousin of his, Paul Kamatropoulos, was
friendly with him at the time and a slightly jealous observer of his
prowess: "Aristotle liked the girls a lot, as all boys do of that age, and
I must admit that he did have the gift of attracting them more than any
of the rest of us. He spoke Spanish with ease and I suppose they must
have found his conversation full of charm. But he lost his head over none
of them, and still less his time." Another acquaintance, Egidio Amadeo
Comité—a retired accountant who still lives in Buenos Aires—remembers Onassis, whom he admired greatly for his drive and ambition, in
vivid detail: "Cordial, with a frank look about him, lively, questioning,
lascivious eyes, red, thick lips."

Not everyone found Onassis so appealing. Enrique Gómez worked alongside him at United Telephone and is still bitter about the man he now calls "that cur": "I introduced him to a girl and I told him that she was serious and not to be a smarty. But like a good Greek he tried to make her and left me looking like an asshole to her family. Later I lent him a few *mangos* [Argentinian slang for pesos] and he told me he would pay me . . . and nothing happened. When I got on my high horse the guy put on the dumb act and I was left holding the bag." Such remembrances, however, appear to be the exception to the rule. Most of those who got to know him in his early life liked him.

After a few weeks at the telephone company, Onassis asked if he could work the night shift. He had "other things to do" during the day, he explained. He arranged to "retrain" as an operator and began to work from 11 P.M. to 7 A.M. at the Retiro Exchange, opposite the Buenos Aires branch of Harrods. The night shift was an easy number, mainly checking equipment from time to time, and Onassis could catch up on his sleep between teaching himself better Spanish.

It was a curious time for Onassis, the first months after joining the phone company demonstrating even then his ability to cram at least two separate lives into one day. By working overtime he managed to earn about twenty-five dollars a week, fair money at the time for a single man. The social climber began to emerge. Onassis joined l'Aviron—the Oar —a rowing and yacht club catering to the young middle class, and often sculled for miles on his own or with the girl friend of the moment. There were jolly picnics with boat parties on the islands in the Tigre River. And there were his "other things," including peddling neckties on the street and a business venture called Surprise. This involved dragging a cart loaded with sand through the city and charging kids a few centavos for the privilege of dipping their hands into the sand for hidden trinkets. Such enterprises were soon submerged by his attempts to break into the tobacco business, where he was to make his first serious money. Looking back on this period in his later life, Onassis often said that "the first five thousand dollars is always the hardest to make."

He began writing to his father again, and a reasonably cordial correspondence developed. A cousin who had left Smyrna for Athens with the Onassis family still remembers how Socrates would call everyone around when he got one of Aristotle's letters home and say, "Look what my son has written. He has sense, this one." Onassis's letters were full of news about the terrific business opportunities in Argentina. He was particularly interested in the possibilities of selling oriental tobacco to local cigarette manufacturers. Argentina imported vast quantities of Cuban

29

and Brazilian leaf but only a handful of oriental brands (at that time turkish tobacco came mainly from Greece). He eventually convinced his father to send out a few samples of the best leaf, the delicately flavored tobacco of Nafplion in the Peloponnese. When the shipment arrived, he made the rounds of Buenos Aires's cigarette manufacturers, a depressing experience which got him no further than leaving samples in the faint hope of one day hearing from buyers. The one day never came.

Despairing of any response, Onassis deliberately "selected" the managing director of one of the country's biggest firms, a Juan Gaona, as his target. Each day he would stand outside Gaona's office when he arrived at work, gazing silently, a little reproachfully, at him. Every other day he repeated the treatment outside Gaona's home, wistful, silent. Gaona stuck it out for fourteen days, then, understandably irked, asked his secretary who the hell Onassis was and why he was haunting him. "A little Greek boy," the secretary said. When Gaona asked him in, Onassis explained he wanted to sell first-class oriental tobacco to his firm. Amused and mildly relieved, Gaona sent him to the firm's buying office, where judicious use of the boss's name achieved Onassis's goal—serious examination of his leaf samples.

Since the quality really was excellent, Gaona's buyers promptly ordered $10,000 worth. Onassis charged his father the standard trade commission of 5 percent. The $500 he received, he often said, was the foundation of his fortune. With his foot firmly in one of the trade's most important doors, he soon received another order, this time for $50,000. As word got around, orders from other companies arrived, and Onassis cut down even more on his sleep to keep up with business. He opened a bank account for his commissions and was soon into five figures, but that was cash earmarked for the future. In the meantime, he stayed on the night shift at the Retiro Exchange, living on his pay.

The daughter of the manager of one factory which took his oriental leaf remembers Onassis well. Her father had told her he was "very intelligent and daring," destined for great things. One day a superb carpet from Smyrna was delivered to their house, a gift from Onassis in gratitude for some business advice her father had offered. It was an early example of Onassis's ability to transform a business relationship into a personal one.

Onassis took occasional small loans from the First National City Bank to tide him over until he was paid by his customers. He never borrowed more than $3,000 and always paid promptly, but during this time he did not receive a penny from his father in starting capital. Once Onassis had carved out the first openings, he effectively became his father's agent, taking orders and chasing deliveries. But the initial breakthrough was due to him alone, and he was soon pushing ahead with another enterprise of his own.

In May 1925, after about a year with United Telephone, Onassis decided to move on. The company's records state that he was dismissed "because his services were no longer required" (he is described as an engineer on temporary attachment to the engineering department). But the parting appears to have been amicable. His immediate boss had asked Onassis why he was leaving—wasn't he happy with the firm? Well, Onassis said, he had enjoyed working with the phone company, "but now I have an idea."

The idea was to branch out into producing cigarettes on his own, to become a manufacturer. He rented a pokey little shop on Calle Viamonte and hired a sign writer to inscribe on the window "Aristotle Onassis—importer of Oriental tobacco." He was assisted in this enterprise by his two cousins, Nicos and Costa Konialidis, who had been orphaned in the Smyrna massacre and had followed Onassis to Buenos Aires. The business was financed by the $25,000 Onassis had saved and a loan of $25,000.

Cigarette manufacturing is a traditional Greek skill. Instead of buying cigarettes and therefore paying the considerable excise tax, villagers blend and roll their own. Onassis knew about the blending from his father's business in Smyrna. He made a minimal capital investment in some hand-cranked rolling machines, barely larger than the variety favored today, and rounded up a number of Greek immigrants, paying them by the piece. There were two brands, Primeros and Osman, and Onassis inspected each pack with care before dispatching them to Quanta Tre, the large-scale cigarette manufacturer which distributed them on his behalf. Both were aimed at the luxury market, particularly at the daring young daughters of the rich who took to the delicate flavor of Onassis's oriental tobacco and chic innovations like rose-leaf tips and multicolored tins.

Onassis was not above doing some hand rolling himself. Zalman Fondebirder, now an optician in Buenos Aires, was then an observant and inquisitive schoolboy. He provided us with this touching memoir:

> The Greek, as Onassis was called then, rented a little furnished room in the house of my Aunt Fanny. The house still exists, it's at Sarmiento 2210. Onassis lived in a servant's room which was reachable only by a spiral

wooden staircase. In the room there was only a small clothes closet, a rickety bed, and a table where he rolled his cigarettes. I was a kid and I helped him make the Havana-type cigars and cigarettes which had pretty gold tips.

I remember that the Greek would spend a lot of time on the cigarettes. He stuck the cigarette together with a special glue and then put aluminum foil the color of gold on the tips. "Wrap the cigars up in cellophane," he would tell me in a Hellenized Spanish which frankly was very complicated.

Fanny had a relative, also called Fanny (Fanny la Negra to distinguish her), who was a great cook.

Onassis noticed this and began going [to her house] frequently. He "sucked his fingers"—*chupaba los dedos,* a Spanish expression for digging into one's food—with stuffed fish aromatized with herbs and with a big meat ball which included potato, the likes of which only Fanny la Negra could bake.

He was what you might call sober, a man of few words. In his room there was neither radio nor phonograph. He hardly said hello to the other lodgers. He was a man who didn't like to take part in a conversation circle, but he was much respected in the house. In spite of his apparent sullenness, I assure you that he was very affectionate and tender.

The business ethics of the tobacco trade were not particularly fragrant. Years later Onassis described to a friend a certain "sordid action" which some businessmen began to use against their competition.

A man would go into a tobacconist, buy a pack of cigarettes, and once out of the shop inject a chemical into the pack with a hypodermic syringe. He would then return and explain, "I made a mistake, this is not the brand I wanted. Can I please change it." The hole would be very small, invisible to the human eye. The chemical gave the tobacco an abominable taste. It would spread through the whole pack. There were very few brands of cigarettes in Buenos Aires, so it was quite easy to disgust the buyers of these well-respected products and they would turn to you, who sold superior tobacco with that incomparable taste."

Onassis thought this story uproarious, and the friend to whom he related it was left with a distinct impression that the tactic had been one favored by Onassis himself.

He also decided to market a new line under the brand name Bis, which happened to be one of Argentina's best-selling cigarettes at the time. Onassis priced his version below the real thing and was doing very nicely when the owner of the Bis factory, discovering this unorthodox competition, sued and forced Onassis to settle out of court for a few thousand pesos—the first and surely the cheapest of the lawsuits that his business methods were to attract.

Onassis's tobacco was sent via Genoa, where it was transshipped, and he apparently hit upon the idea of spraying the bales of tobacco with salt water during their stay in Genoa. His subsequent collections from insurance underwriters for "sea damage" formed a welcome addition to his trading profits. Insurance company employees were involved in the fraud, and when one of them eventually gave the game away, one of Onassis's agents in Genoa was arrested and served a term in prison.

It was Onassis's good fortune to have arrived at a time when an affluent, educated middle class was taking root in Argentina. Neutrality in World War I had done wonders for Argentina's economy: traditional exports like meat, grain, and hides had gone up enormously, while imports of manufactured goods had fallen off dramatically. The substantial trade balance that resulted had enabled the Argentinian peso to be quoted consistently higher than every other major foreign currency in the world between 1916 and 1919. The boom continued after the war, particularly for the new local manufacturing businesses which had sprung up to replace the loss of imported goods.

Many were owned or run by men who had been born in Europe or were the sons of immigrants. They were more cosmopolitan, more flexible and tolerant than native Argentinians. Relative newcomers themselves, they never developed the social prejudices of the *estancieros*, the great conservative families with their old money from cattle and land. Buenos Aires, the financial, commercial, and social center of Argentina, was full of thrusting young men making new money in new lines— communications, import-export, construction, transportation. Onassis may have found the city hard and intimidating at first—it had a population of some two million in 1923, six times as great as that of Smyrna when he had lived there—but it offered a society which was becoming increasingly accessible through hard work, ambition, and a decent store of chutzpah.

As the tobacco business improved, Onassis began to take more interest in his social life. He launched himself with some enthusiasm on the city's fleshpots. There were plenty to choose from. Buenos Aires in the mid-1920s was a very fast city indeed, with a nightlife as good—or bad, according to taste—as anything in Europe, Paris included, and infinitely better than the tawdry clip joints flourishing in the United States under

33

prohibition. Prostitution was officially illegal—outlawed by Hipólito Irigoyen's reform government in 1917, when Buenos Aires was generally reckoned to be one of the centers of the white slave trade—but the diversions offered in the La Boca area were spoken of with reverence by seamen the world over. In the Africa Room at the Alvear Palace Hotel —where Donald Dean's American Orchestra was togged up like Hollywood white hunters in pith helmets and safari suits against a decor of straw huts and tom-toms—in the Gong Club at the Calle Cordoba, and above all at Tabaris, which could only be described as a superior pickup joint, Onassis drank his evenings away in the company of other high-spirited young men-about-town.

One of his regular companions on these evenings was his cousin Nicos. Both liked the company of young women, but Nicos was much the more dedicated in pursuit. "In these matters," Onassis would recall, "he was insatiable."

Early in 1926, Onassis moved out of his lodgings and took an apartment in a hotel on Florida, one of the city's smarter streets. He started dressing better, although by the age of twenty he had already acquired the knack of making a good suit look like a Salvation Army handout after a few wearings. He employed private tutors to improve his French and English. He also bought a secondhand car and began scouting around outside Buenos Aires for new business opportunities. Juan Glicas, then a street peddler, came across Onassis and three other young men in the town of Berisso, thirty-five miles south of Buenos Aires, early in 1926. They were looking for somewhere to open a small shop and shoeshine stand. Glicas showed them around what there was to see of Berisso, very much a one-horse town. "When they left in the afternoon Onassis looked at me with his big eyes and said, 'Paisano amigo, I don't like small-town life.' "

In the late 1920s Onassis met and befriended the man who was to be his closest companion and confidant for the rest of his life. Costa Gratsos was a burly, gregarious young seaman working as an apprentice on one of his family's ships. His travels often brought him to Buenos Aires, where he and Onassis would go out on the town together. Born in Ithaca into a traditional shipowning family, Gratsos had been educated at the London School of Economics, where he had been taught by Harold Laski, the leading theoretician of British socialism. His socialist phase ended, however, when he went to sea and "entered the arena of life."

Gratsos was fascinated by Onassis's drive and energy. The mainspring of his personality, he felt, was the relationship with his father: "Onassis felt rejected by him. He developed this passion for money and power. He wanted to be better than his father. All his time in Argentina he wanted to be a success. So there was this desperate quality to his youth. He would be trying ten things at a time in the hope that at least one of them would make him into the success he wanted to be."

At the same time, Onassis rarely neglected the pleasures of life. "Money was never an end to him," Gratsos recalled. "However obscure and desperate those early years had been, he never confused accumulation with enjoyment. His money gave him a sense of power, and he used it for his own pleasure, even when he was a young man."

Onassis was just twenty-two years old when he allowed himself the luxury of his first serious love affair. The girl was a ballet dancer in Anna Pavlova's world-famous troupe, which was spending the winter in South America. Some of the dancers stayed at Onassis's hotel when the troupe arrived in Buenos Aires. According to Onassis, they met, went out together, and fell in love. When the season ended the girl refused to leave him. Pavlova herself arrived at the hotel to ask Onassis to persuade the girl not to jeopardize her career, but it was no use. She stayed in Buenos Aires and joined the local ballet company. The affair lasted a year. Another affair ended when Onassis suspected that he had contracted a venereal infection. It took several visits to the doctor before his fears were allayed.

He suffered a painful reversal in another area. Although the volume of business at the "factory" had grown so much that at one time Onassis had thirty men hand-rolling furiously in the back room, he began to lose money. He sadly decided to call it a day. A little cash was retrieved by the sale of the Osman and Primeros brand names, but he had to face the fact that his first wholly independent venture had folded.

Onassis was now almost totally dependent on the trading links established with his father in Athens. Although the demand for imported tobacco leaf remained buoyant, it was a narrow base for commercial success. In the summer of 1929 this base was suddenly and seriously threatened. The Greek government, involved in some testy and unproductive trade negotiations with Bulgaria, suddenly announced that the import duty on goods from countries with which Greece had no trade agreement would immediately be increased by 1,000 percent. The decree was aimed specifically at forcing recalcitrant Bulgars to conclude a trading pact, but it had considerable side effects elsewhere—in Argentina, for example, which also had no trade agreement with Greece. In Onassis's view, it was certain that the Argentinians—traditionally

35

touchy about their international standing—would retaliate with identical tariffs on Greek goods. His business could not stand the increase in costs. The only solution was to persuade the Greek government to exclude Argentina from the new regulations. His lever was to be the fact that in 1929 a large portion of the Greek merchant marine was engaged in carrying goods from Europe to Argentina. Huge increases in port duties would virtually wipe out this very profitable business for the Greek economy. Armed with a lengthy memo to the Greek prime minister, Eleutherios Venizelos, Onassis left for home for the first time in six years.

To Onassis's surprise, the memo for Venizelos actually found its way to the prime minister's desk, and he was summoned for a meeting with the great man. Venizelos, evidently impressed, arranged for him to see the minister of foreign affairs, Andreas Michalokopoulos, whose department had drafted the controversial trade decree. The story of his encounter with the minister was one of Onassis's favorites in later life.

When Onassis was shown into the minister's office, he found Michalokopoulos—a tall, imposing man—standing by a superb Louis Quinze desk. They sat down, and Onassis was curtly instructed to explain. Michalokopoulos seemed to resent having Onassis dumped upon him by the prime minister. As Onassis launched into his analysis, he noticed that Michalokopoulos was cleaning his fingernails with a letter opener, devoting exaggerated attention to the job. "I had not finished all my arguments when the minister suddenly looked at me over the top of his glasses and stopped me in midsentence, brandishing his letter opener. He closed the conversation: 'I appreciate your point of view, young man. Would you leave your name and address with my secretary. I'll think about it and keep in touch, Mr. . . . uh . . . Mr. . . . Anisos.' "

It was too much to endure. "Thank you very much," Onassis replied. "I hope that if I have to see you again you will be kind enough to pay more attention to my proposition. I thought you were a busy man, but I now see that you are busy only with cleaning your fingernails. You are more concerned with your hands that with the export trade of your country!"

Onassis turned on his heel and strode from the room, leaving Michalokopoulos sputtering, "Stop, come back here." Onassis allowed himself to be detained by two aides and led back. The air cleared, and he and the minister talked at length. The very next day Michalokopoulos ordered the opening of negotiations with Argentina.

Back at the family house in Athens, Onassis modestly accepted the family's adulation. "Michalokopoulos treated him very badly at first," a cousin recalls, still glowing at the memory, "but he soon realized how clever Aristotle was." Onassis's family reunion had a triumphal quality. Socrates, mellowed by age, was happy to defer to his successful son. Onassis had been sending money to the widows in the family for their children's education. He was acknowledged as "chief of the tribe" and gratified by his eminence. It seemed a vindication not just of the decision he had made to emigrate but also of his previously disputed handling of the money he had saved from the wreckage of Smyrna. The reconciliation with his father seemed complete. Socrates died two years later, in 1931, of a heart attack at the age of fifty-eight.

Despite the tenderness of the family reunion, Onassis never considered staying on in Greece. He was eager to get back to making money in Buenos Aires, and not just from tobacco. Shipping had been on his mind for some time. Buenos Aires was the sole Argentinian port handling the country's massive exports of beef and grain to Europe. Even during the Great Depression, nine thousand ships passed through it each year. If most of the ships were British, a high percentage of the captains and the sailors were Greek. Gratsos recalls walking around the docks with Onassis. "He was not in shipping when we met, but he thought all day about it and he was fascinated by ships. He wasn't particularly attracted to the idea of being a captain, but ships were cheap and people were making money. Greeks were making money, and he got the microbe, the virus. 'I must get into this business,' he told me."

Paul Kamatropoulos, his cousin, was around when Onassis got involved in his first shipping venture. During a visit to Montevideo, just across the Río de la Plata, Onassis noticed the rusting old hulk of a shipwrecked boat on the banks of the river. "I happened to be with him when he conceived the idea of putting the boat back into shape," Kamatropoulos recalled, "We all tried to dissuade him and convince him that he was going to ruin himself, but we could do nothing. In the company of my mother he set out to look for Greek salvagers who he employed to make the boat as good as new." The work dragged on for several months, but at the end of it Onassis had his first ship and had paid cash for it. The *Maria Protopapas*, as she was called, was a twenty-five-year-old 7,000-tonner. "She was supposed to be a trans-Atlantic ship," recalls Gratsos, "though I don't know whether she really deserved the name." Soon after Onassis had refloated her, she sank at anchor in Montevideo harbor during a cyclone.

The setback did not diminish Onassis's enthusiasm for ships, but he became more cautious. He was still making a great deal of money, extending his trade in tobacco leaf to Cuba and Brazil to supplement his Greek supplies. In 1932, at the age of twenty-six, his eminence as a trader was recognized by the Greek authorities, and he was appointed extraordinary deputy consul in Buenos Aires. The position brought him into even closer contact with the shipping activities of the great port. It also enhanced his capacity to make money. Onassis was able to use his official position to obtain substantial sums of currency at official rates, which he then resold on a flourishing black market.

He also took the opportunity to regularize his position with the Argentinian authorities by applying for and obtaining an Argentinian passport. Ever since his employment by the telephone company Onassis had come to appreciate the advantages of being thought older than he was. Older people in business felt less threatened. His passport, therefore, though valid, was a model of misinformation about its bearer. Onassis stuck to Salonika as his adopted birthplace, but devised a wholly new birthdate —January 7, 1900—making him, for official purposes, six years older than his real age.

He was ready for another, more calculated assault on the shipping business. In the fall of 1932 Onassis assembled his savings—amounting to $600,000—and sailed to London, the capital of the maritime world.

4
LOVE AND TANKERS

WHEN ONASSIS FIRST CONSIDERED seriously going into the shipping business, the Greek merchant fleet was the fastest growing and most antiquated in the world. Tramp steaming was dominated by the Greeks, and the business still bore the marks of its rough-hewn origins. Many owners could still remember the time when a number of families—sometimes an entire village—would band together to buy an old vessel and proceed to run it on a shoestring, with friends and relatives working all hours in deplorable, often unsafe, conditions.

With a handful of exceptions, the Greek shipowners had an unsavory reputation. Because their ships were so old and unsafe, Greeks found it hard, sometimes impossible, to raise money for buying more modern vessels. When European owners—Dutch, Norwegian, British—bought a brand-new ship, they put 10 percent down in cash and had ten years to pay off the balance. But a Greek customarily had to find 50 percent of the purchase price for a venerable tramp steamer and was expected to repay the rest in three or four years. In Lloyd's of London, the world's most important insurance market, there was a deep-rooted suspicion of Greek shipowners. Although the story about a sign on the door of the underwriting room declaring NO GREEKS appears to be apocryphal, a prejudice did exist based on commercial rather than national considera-

39

tions. In the early 1920s Lloyd's had taken the unprecedented step of issuing a statement about "the unusual number of shipwrecks in the Greek merchant navy." The clear implication was that many of the losses were insurance frauds. The position improved over the years but only gradually. Writing recently about the Greek shipping industry during the Great Depression, Andreas Lemos, Greece's foremost naval historian, delicately conceded that "under the pressure of circumstances some shipowners resorted to activities suggestive of fraud."

London, then the marine capital of the world, was the magnet for those Greeks who sought to rise above—or simply to bypass—the stereotype of the Greek shipowner. The Greek community, established there since the early days of sail, enjoyed a generally high reputation. There was, in fact, a lively envy of the success of the London Greeks and their ability to squeeze a pound or two out of the most unpromising circumstances. They did not care to be too prominent or obtrusive in the country where they had settled, but the names Livanos, Kulukundis, Embiricos, Goulandris, and Vergottis already meant a great deal in terms of world shipping.

Basil Mavroleon, now a millionaire shipowner, was an executive with the firm of Rethymnis and Kulukundis when Onassis first came to London in the fall of 1932. His first impression of the young Greek was pleasant enough but undramatic. "He called on us one day to make our acquaintance. He expressed total ignorance about shipping and made it clear that he had come to learn. There was a great humility about the guy, but personally I was too busy to worry about one of many newcomers." Onassis, he recalled, was already discussing a ship deal with a much smaller agency belonging to Pericles Dracoulis, an uncle of his friend Costa Gratsos. "I believe Onassis picked on Dracoulis because it was a smallish outfit, because he wanted to be an important customer, a big fish in a small pool if you like."

Onassis came back again later, in December 1932, to call on the young and dynamic boss of the firm, Manuel Kulukundis, who was known among London Greeks as *O Aitos*—"the Eagle." Kulukundis immediately sensed that Onassis had more grandiose aspirations. He was celebrating the purchase of the *Bampton Castle*, a liner from the old Union Castle Line, when Onassis was ushered into his office. He remembers Onassis "telling his life story, how the first three years in Argentina were terrible, a struggle to keep alive, down and out with no money." Onassis said he had come to London to buy ships and that Dracoulis had told him about the *Bampton Castle*. "I said, 'You can't have that ship, I've

got it. You are in too much of a hurry, there are plenty of ships around.' "
On another occasion, Kulukundis recalls, he sat up all night with Onassis
in the Café Royal in London talking business. "It was the only night I
spent away from my wife and family." The reproach is implicit. The
more staid London Greeks did not altogether care for young Onassis's
energetic nightclubbing and high living.

"Ships were cheap, you can't imagine how cheap," Costa Gratsos
recalls. "In those days you could pick up old, but still seaworthy, vessels
of 9,000 tons for the price of a new Rolls-Royce, around $20,000."
Despite, or perhaps because of, the depressed condition of world trade,
it soon became apparent to Onassis that the shipping business provided
a rare opportunity for expanding his fortune. He had come to London
to learn, and he learned fast.

The economics were simple and startling. A ten-year-old freighter
which had cost $1 million to build in 1920 was halfway through its
working life. In the early 1930s, as the depression worsened, such ships
were frequently up for sale at *less* than their scrap value, sometimes only
half the sum that could be recouped by breaking them up and selling
the metal. But the real opportunities went to those willing to gamble on
the demand for shipping recovering well within the vessel's remaining
ten years of useful life, in which case it could quite easily repay the
original investment within twelve months. If the gamble failed, it was
still possible to sell for scrap and take a modest profit. Lured by such
arithmetic, the more enterprising operators were snapping up aging
vessels around the world. Manuel Kulukundis bought and sold fifty-eight
ships in one year. Onassis did not intend to be left out. A quick visit to
Sweden and the great Gotaverken shipyard was enough to convince
Onassis that new ships were a waste of time—at least for the present.
There was the most graphic evidence of the depression: brand-new
vessels leaving the yard to be laid up by owners who could not find work
for them. Onassis was back in London, using Dracoulis's pokey office as
his base, when he heard of something that sounded good.

The Canadian National Steamship Company had ten vessels for sale,
none of them more than fifteen years old, some built in the early 1920s.
All were between 8,500 and 10,000 tons, and the asking price of $30,000
each was certainly no more than their scrap value. Onassis, even then,
was not interested in ships much smaller than this, estimating correctly
that the economics of shipping made the running costs of a single
10,000-tonner lower than those of a pair of 5,000-tonners and the profits
conversely greater. The Canadian ships had been laid up in the Saint

Lawrence River for two years when Onassis arrived with an engineer lent by Dracoulis to advise him. It was winter, Canadian winter, and the decks of the ships were covered with deep snow. Poking around with his engineer, Onassis suddenly let out a yell and disappeared from sight. He had stepped from upper to lower deck into a deep snowdrift.

Several of the vessels had been built by Canadian Vickers, then a famous name in shipping. Others were "standards," the British World War I version of Liberty ships. The engineer felt that they were still sound. Huddled on the windblown deck, Onassis offered to buy six vessels for $20,000 apiece. According to Onassis, the Canadians dickered at first, offering only two, which he promptly purchased. Later, having failed to call his bluff, they sold him the other four vessels.

Onassis paid cash for the ships. He had to as nobody in London, not even Dracoulis, could get him a loan for the deal, but he could claim to be a real shipowner at last. He was finally launched in a major venture and owed nothing to his father's influence or expertise. His career as an independent businessman of substance was about to begin. It scarcely mattered that his "fleet" remained at anchor for several months in the frozen Saint Lawrence until the moment was right to start operating. Onassis renamed them immediately: the first two, the *Canadian Miller* and the *Canadian Spinner,* became the *Onassis Socrates* and the *Onassis Penelope* after his father and mother. He opened an office in Buenos Aires, a modest place on Calle Santa Maria, but it said Aristotle Onassis, Shipping Agent, on the door. His cousin Nicos Konialidis was installed as manager.

Onassis had picked up enough about the tramp-steaming business— especially after he became consul in Buenos Aires with responsibility for a port clearing scores of Greek ships every month—to understand that it could be risky even in the fat years. Making money depended on being consistently right in finely judged decisions about the way that freight rates were going to move. They could fluctuate so sharply in a few days that an owner shipping grain from Argentina to Europe at what seemed like a very decent rate could end up with a thumping loss on the round trip if the rate for coal on the return voyage had slipped in the meantime. A ninety-day Buenos Aires–London–Buenos Aires voyage that went badly wrong could cost an owner a good deal more than he had paid for the ship. To stay ahead of the game, which could be immensely profitable, an owner needed considerable mental agility—juggling the complicated freight tables for half a dozen ports thousands of miles from each other—and a store of cold courage. Onassis possessed both qualities in abundance.

42

Onassis had come into the business with a powerful psychological advantage. He was an optimist. His readiness to take chances and make his own luck was something that set him apart from the majority of Greek shipowners. For them, the worst of the depression years—from 1929 to about 1932—had been a traumatic experience. Emerging from the nightmare shaken and poorer, their instinct was to keep a vicelike grip on what was left, hoard their assets, avoid credit, and never take unnecessary risks. For Onassis and a few other young Greeks getting into shipping for the first time in the early 1930s, no such inhibitions existed. They had never lost most of their cash, never found themselves enmeshed in a web of mortgages which had to be repaid while profits had virtually dried up. They were undaunted by "paper empires" of mortgaged fleets and long-term credit. Consequently, they were also more flexible and responsive to the opportunities that appeared as international trade began to recover.

In the summer of 1934 Onassis met and fell in love with Ingeborg Dedichen, a beautiful Norwegian socialite who was to be a key influence in his career as well as his character. She was among a party of Norwegians on the Italian passenger liner *Augustus*, bound from Buenos Aires to Genoa. Her second marriage was breaking up, and she turned instinctively to old family friends. Her late father, Ingevald Bryde, had been one of Norway's leading shipowners. The Norwegian party aboard the *Augustus* included Lars Christensen, the owner of a whaling fleet, and Gustav Bull, another prominent shipowner. Onassis was a fellow passenger, traveling first class.

By Ingse Dedichen's account, Onassis's interest in her became a source of amusement to her group of friends. The physical contrast was striking. Dedichen was tall, blond, and slim. She was also some years older than her admirer. Her friends were the first to notice that Onassis was following her around the ship, gazing intently at her. "Why does this little black man pursue you with such persistence?" they inquired. "He looks as if he wants to devour you." Dedichen began watching Onassis in return and observed "that gentle air of a woeful dog. . . . We thought he must be mute or incapable of expressing himself in any of the fifteen languages which we knew between us."

After several days of silent pursuit Onassis contrived a casual encounter in the swimming pool. He surfaced beside Dedichen to advise her that the Spaniard teaching her the crawl had it all wrong. To Dedichen's amazement, he spoke in broken Swedish, picked up, he explained later, from an acquaintance in Buenos Aires.

That afternoon, Onassis introduced himself formally—"Aristotle Socrates Onassis, a Greek shipowner." Dedichen replied with a fine torrent of abuse about Greek shipping practices, remarking on the antiquity of their ships and the underpayment of their crews. Onassis was taken aback, possibly because what she said was true. But the swimming pool kept them together. Onassis taught her the crawl. Dedichen continued her surveillance: "Signs already of a belly! A very muscular body with rather short arms. He was physically unusual, too squat, his heavy head emerged from shoulders as broad as any docker's. Black haired and olive skinned, he looked like a simple Asiatic workman, as if he labored on the quays of Istanbul or Trebizond."

Less equivocally, Dedichen found Onassis's dark eyes compelling, his voice warm and caressing, and his smile broad and winning. She was not, however, entirely unsuspicious about the reasons for his interest in her. She introduced Onassis to her friends, who also found him most agreeable. He would sit for hours talking about ships to the Christensens and Gustav Bull. Onassis seemed, in Dedichen's phrase, "a perfect chameleon," effortlessly adjusting to the company he kept and highly receptive to mood and atmosphere. Dedichen's underlying mood was bleak. Her father had recently died, and she was still upset by the failure of her second marriage. Onassis seemed to sense that the moment was not right for an adventure. Throughout the voyage he was tender and attentive but made no overt sexual advances.

When the *Augustus* docked at Genoa, Onassis suggested that Dedichen might like to drive with him to Marseilles, where he had some business, and catch the Paris express from there. It did not surprise her when, as they left Genoa, he confessed there was no immediate business in Marseilles. Why didn't they go to Venice instead—he had never been there. She could phone her family and explain that she was detouring to visit the wife of a sick friend. They became lovers that night in the elegant surroundings of the Hotel Danieli in Venice. "In his arms I took joy in his brown skin that seemed to complement mine. I had never before felt such a sensual pleasure. We fell asleep at dawn, alternating confidences with renewed embraces." They gave each other Italian pet names—Mamita (little mother) for her, Mamico (little daddy) for him. It was to Dedichen that Onassis confided the reasons for the end of his last serious affair in Buenos Aires. The experience had left an emotional scar, making him wary of all women. Dedichen recorded: "If the prescriptions and remedies of the doctors healed him physically, I helped to heal him psychologically."

They led a curiously rootless life at first, drifting from one city to another in Onassis's beloved Cadillac, doing some business in Trieste, then motoring to Monte Carlo, where they learned the fashionable new American sport of waterskiing. Dedichen tried it first and did very well, obliging Onassis to show her he was even better, "but he had the utmost difficulty staying upright." On a whim, they would bundle their cases into the car and drive for hours, sometimes days, to another five-star hotel in another country. Once, driving the eighteen hundred miles from Nice to Sweden in four days for a business appointment, they skidded into snow in the Brenner Pass, and Dedichen threw her best sealskin coat under the wheels for traction. In Livorno, Dedichen was bitten by a mosquito and caught a mild dose of malaria. There were epic rows, threatened walkouts, passionate reconciliations, more driving, more hotels, more frontiers.

He watched and learned from her all the time—"a sponge," she says, soaking up information and discovering how to be *comme il faut*. At Maxim's in Paris she barely prevented his summoning her old friend Albert, the owner, with a Greek "pssst" or a rattle of his knife on the wine glass. He was lost with the complex menu and grateful for her ordering the wine. Stumbling around the dance floor to the waltz of violins, he was quite unabashed. Dedichen shrewdly observed, "His indifference to others contributed to his prodigious success."

She was overwhelmed by his passion and force of character, yet she could also analyze their love affair with a detached and discerning eye. "Mamico would only meet people who were useful to his business, wherever we were, in Paris and later in Sweden and Norway as well." The others—Dedichen's many friends in the world of art, music, and literature—were brusquely removed from her life at Onassis's insistence. He was storming the Scandinavian shipping aristocracy, and culture was not going to come between him and his plans for the future.

For Onassis, tramp steaming was only a bridge, the means of acquiring capital to move into oil tankers. It was not just their profit potential that attracted him—it took no great genius to realize that oil would become steadily more essential for world industry and that ships were the best way to move oil from source to market. Equally important was the fact that there were virtually no Greeks in the tanker business. Greeks were by tradition "dry shippers." There was a modest tanker operators' pool run from London, but none of the established London Greeks took much interest in it. In bad years, when cargoes were scarce, the pool covered an owner's maintenance and mortgage charges. When business was good, the pool made very respectable profits. The British, Swedes, and Norwegians dominated the proceedings.

In the mid-1930s tankers were still a comparatively small business. Oil accounted for only 15 percent of the world's total energy requirements: coal was king, providing 75 percent of total fuel consumption. Onassis's plunge was a great departure, observed, as Basil Mavroleon recalls, with indifference by most of the other Greek shippers. "Nobody else was interested. It was a foreign business to most of us." They were, he implies, nervous about such new developments—the postdepression trauma was too strong.

Onassis was not the first Greek into tankers. Lazarus Kalliglas bought an aging 5,000-tonner, the *Irene,* in 1933, and, in the words of naval historian Andreas Lemos, "He did not regret it." One or two other small operators were active during the Spanish Civil War from 1936 onward, supplying both sides impartially. What Onassis perceived most clearly was that tankers could be much bigger than anyone then considered feasible. He envisaged heroic economies of scale in operating costs. Having done so, he had the courage to push his vision through.

Onassis had some knowledge of the Scandinavian shipbuilding industry before he met Dedichen. On a previous trip to Europe, he had befriended the Swedish shipowner Gustav Sandstrom and through him had made the acquaintance of Ernst Heden, the boss of the Gotaverken yard. He decided that his new Swedish company, A. S. Onassis, Goteborg, Ltd., would order its first tanker from Heden's builders.

His initial order to Gotaverken was for a 15,000-tonner, some 3,000 tons bigger than any tanker then afloat. The Swedes were startled and skeptical, but Onassis forced the deal through. Purchase price was $800,000, one quarter of which was to be paid during construction, the rest at 4.5 percent interest over the next ten years. There was no more "Greek" penalty rate: Onassis's credit rating was on the way up. Tanker tonnage was becoming clearly inadequate for the rising demand of a gradual economic recovery around the world, aided significantly by the first waves of rearmament in Europe. Onassis went to the United States for his first tanker charter, securing a nine-voyage contract—one year's work—to move oil which J. Paul Getty's Tidewater Oil fleet could not handle from San Francisco to Yokohama, Japan. In America, he also acquired the diminutive nickname that clung to him for the rest of his life—Ari.

Even before he ceased to be the deputy Greek consul in Buenos Aires in 1936, Onassis was spending less and less time in the Argentine. Much of his consular work and the South American end of his shipping and tobacco business was delegated to the Konialidis brothers. Their efforts

46

gave him the time and opportunity to explore the European shipping scene and to pursue his romance with Ingse Dedichen.

He was often in London, where his closest male companion was Panaghis Vergottis, a Greek shipowner who lived at the Ritz Hotel. Vergottis, a cultured bachelor, was one of the few established London Greeks who was immediately appreciative of Onassis's vivacity. He was sixteen years older than Onassis and sufficiently wealthy not to feel threatened by the newcomer. Onassis flattered him and treated him like a benign father figure.

Another London acquaintance dating from this period was Stavros Niarchos, who was to play an important part in his subsequent career. Like Onassis, Niarchos was a young Greek in a very great hurry. Unlike Onassis, he had by the age of twenty-seven already acquired a high degree of social polish. He dressed in Savile Row suits, favoring dark flannel cut to show his lissome figure to its best advantage. His hair was dark, his eyes yellow, and his manner feline. He spoke out of the corner of his mouth in the upper-class English style—at first meeting, some people were under the impression that he suffered from a speech defect. He drove a red Bugatti.

The Greek newspaper publisher Helen Vlachos, who knew Niarchos in those days, described him in glowing terms as "clever, quick, decisive and ambitious. He was also a snob: the best kind of snob. He was attracted towards quality, he wanted to enjoy the highest standard of living, and to meet the kind of people who knew all about it. Stavros Niarchos was untypical because his dream of power and riches progressed much farther than just ships and plush living and the obsequious smiles of head waiters in the exclusive night clubs of the world. He was clever enough to realize that he had a lot to learn about manners, food, art, sport and clothes."

He was also a parvenu in the shipping business. After his father had lost the family fortunes in a stock market speculation, Niarchos had started his working life as a clerk in his uncles' flour milling business in Piraeus. As a young man Niarchos was in the frustrating position of having access to wealth without himself possessing any money. His uncles helped him to join the Athens Yacht Club and lent him their yacht. He developed a taste for things which his clerk's salary could not satisfy. In 1930 he eloped with the daughter of Admiral Constantine Sporides. The admiral was furious and the marriage lasted less than a month.

Niarchos became interested in ships and persuaded his uncles to go into the business. The six 9,000-ton freighters he found in London were set to work transporting grain from Buenos Aires to Athens. As a reward for his initiative, Stavros was put in charge of the shipping department and traveled throughout Europe. When he met Onassis in London, he was considering breaking with his uncles' business and becoming an independent shipowner.

Onassis, meanwhile, watched over the construction of his first ship like an anxious parent. In 1937 he took a house in Sandefjord, Dedichen's hometown, and bombarded the Gotaverken yard with visits and phone calls.

Dedichen nervously introduced Onassis to her mother. She need not have worried—Onassis's touch was as sure as ever. "Mother, oh, Mother," he cried as she entered their reception room. There were tears in his eyes. Ingse thought the Rudolph Valentino style a shade excessive, but her mother had no reservations. By the end of dinner she had become a firm fan, convinced of the honor of Onassis's intentions.

Mrs. Bryde moved in with her daughter and Onassis, the ultimate seal of approval. Dedichen's Norwegian friends hastened to take him up. Onassis rose smoothly into Norway's high society as guest of honor at "Mother's" dinner parties, where he occasionally startled other guests by eating with his fingers, Greek style, and delighted them with impromptu performances of Greek and Argentinian folk songs sung in a pleasing, resonant voice. Mrs. Bryde could never quite understand why Ingse hesitated at the prospect of making Ari her third husband.

As his relationship with Ingse developed, Onassis revealed other aspects of his personality. Not all of them were as pleasant as those that beguiled Mrs. Bryde. There was a curious ambivalence about him. He needed to be liked and accepted but hated to feel under an obligation. The need for acceptance sometimes led to odd forms of affectation. Dedichen could, with some difficulty, trace a descent from the Scottish Earldom of Klerck. In Norway's democratic society such antecedents were not considered of great consequence. Onassis, however, seemed impressed and bought his new mistress a signet ring decorated with the Klerck crest. He liked to think of Dedichen as the Lady of Klerck and encouraged her to exhibit the ring at important receptions.

Onassis would sometimes consult Dedichen about business decisions, something he never seems to have done with any previous woman in his life. Dedichen did not always find the experience agreeable. On one occasion he asked her who could sort out a registration problem that arose on one of his vessels. She referred him to Anders Jahre, a lawyer

48

and an old family friend. Jahre promptly solved the problem but made it clear that he had done it more out of respect for Dedichen's dead father than out of concern for the living Onassis. It was a snub, but it was Dedichen who took the brunt of Onassis's resentment. He seemed, she said, to develop "a complex towards me which was like a vague sickness. He was too ambitious and too proud and could not admit that one of my friends had played a role in his climb to success." Onassis subsequently became friends with Jahre, but the episode made Dedichen reluctant to offer any further advice on business matters.

Another impediment to their relationship was Onassis's jealousy, which sometimes seemed to verge on the pathological. Dedichen, who had no other love interest at the time, inevitably found it wearing—an indication of mistrust rather than the strength of his affections. Yet despite these complications their physical attraction for each other remained constant. According to Dedichen, Onassis was not a great sexual athlete—"*un amoureux de classe, certainement pas*"—but he could communicate an extraordinary sensuality.

> We would undress and sleep in the nude—lying one next to the other. The scenario was always the same, even if we pretended to go to sleep.
>
> Ari would put two fingers on my shoulder and delicately stroke my back. Won over by his magnetism, I felt a tingling all over and pressed myself against him while he continued his caresses. This simple contact gave me the greatest pleasure, and he could make it last for ever. Finally we could no longer resist, our bodies expecting one another, and we let ourselves be carried away in the swirl of love that united us, incredibly attracted to one another. . . .
>
> Neither of my two husbands had skin that I liked to stroke as much as his. And neither of them provoked in me such an overwhelming emotion. Ari's skin had a smell, a warmth, a softness which fascinated me. Neither of us would have lived fully, if we had not met and loved each other, the one fulfilling the other, achieving an absolute fullness that relegated sexuality to a place below a more profound sensuality. . . .
>
> Often during the course of our amorous rites he would lick me between the toes, carefully, like a cat cleaning itself. He would embrace every part of my body and cover me with kisses before devoting himself to the feet he adored. He found them as soft as a baby's bottom and always complimented me on them. Even today I remember nostalgically the tenderness and gentleness of my adorable friend in these rare moments of abandon.

Ari's capacity for sexual intimacy had what some might consider less romantic aspects. His enjoyment of pantomime led him to dress up in

Ingse's clothes at times for their private amusement. He also liked anal humor. One evening in Oslo, walking back to his hotel after dinner, Onassis started to complain to Dedichen about some unspecified pain. Dedichen, all concern, inquired about its source. "Mamita," intoned Onassis, "I think I have got piles. I'll have to see a doctor first thing tomorrow." Back at the hotel Onassis undressed and hesitantly asked if she would be kind enough to inspect the relevant part of his anatomy. Ingse solicitously complied and was rewarded with a fart in the face. Dedichen recalls her lover finding the joke funnier than she did herself.

The first tanker had been christened long before it was off the slipway —the *Ariston*, a neat play on Onassis's first name and the Greek word for "the best." He had already ordered two more tankers from Gotaverken, the 15,000-ton *Aristophanes* (price, about $825,000) and the 17,500-ton *Buenos Aires*, which cost $870,000. All three ships were built to exacting specifications. The *Ariston* had a convertible swimming pool and two huge staterooms. The dour Swedes thought he was crazy, throwing away money on fripperies, until other prospective buyers began arriving to look over the *Ariston* and talk about ordering similar ships.

Flying the blue and yellow Swedish flag, she was launched by Gustav Sandstrom's wife in June 1938. Onassis took Dedichen and most of his own family on the *Ariston*'s maiden voyage to San Francisco, a twelve-day trip enlivened by playing practical jokes on Nicos Konialidis, who was honeymooning with his new bride, Merope, Onassis's half sister. Nicos took his sexual duties seriously. While he and Merope were sleeping in their cabin one afternoon, Onassis and Dedichen got hold of a syringe from the medical kit and began squirting the naked couple with a fine spray of cold water. Nicos's outrage at this rude awakening was apparently wondrous to behold. In San Francisco, the *Ariston* began her working life, shipping US oil for Japan's reserves while the Japanese army rolled through China.

Onassis's claim to be a pioneer in the independent oil tanker business is one that accords with the historical record. The other pioneering claim he made for his shipping activities in the 1930s is more suspect. By Onassis's own account, he was responsible for one of the major innovations of the postdepression years—the systematic exploitation of flags of convenience as a way of cutting red tape and, not so incidentally, avoiding tax. It was a story Onassis often told with relish in later life.

Late in 1932, according to Onassis, the *Onassis Penelope* was discharging part of her cargo in Rotterdam, bound for Copenhagen with the remaining freight. She was Greek-registered for sentimental reasons.

Onassis was enjoying himself in London when he heard that the Greek consul in Rotterdam had refused to clear the *Penelope* until a replacement was found for one crewman, an assistant cook who had been taken to the hospital. The consul had invoked Greek shipping regulations—the replacement had to be another Greek. Onassis dashed over to Holland to plead with the consul, a former schoolmate and good friend but a man devoted to the regulations. No Greek cook, no clearance. The delay threatened the *Penelope*'s carefully devised work schedule—it could mean lost cargoes, even, awful thought, late-delivery penalties. It was too much for Onassis. Come back tomorrow, he told the consul.

Cabling and telephoning throughout the night, Onassis managed to switch the *Penelope*'s registration to Panama. When the Greek consul returned the next day, Onassis greeted him with champagne and the Greek flag wrapped in brown paper. The punch line was always the same, gleefully remembered: "My friend, you are now aboard a Panamanian ship." The *Penelope* sailed away, leaving behind an impotent Greek consul suitably amazed at the resourcefulness of Aristotle Onassis.

Like some of Onassis's other favorite stories, this one does not appear to contain more than a grain of truth. Manuel Kulukundis has an oddly similar story which he, too, used to enjoy telling the London Greeks. In 1932 one of his ships was stuck in Rotterdam because it had an English radio operator. A Greek operator was waiting in Newcastle, but the consul refused to clear Kulukundis's ship without the Greek aboard. Kulukundis ordered his master to sail for Newcastle without papers and made up his mind to leave the Greek flag. Kulukundis is certain that he, not Onassis, was the first to switch to Panama. By 1938 he had almost twenty ships under that flag.

The historical records favor Kulukundis. The Canadian ship registration files show that the *Onassis Penelope* along with the *Onassis Socrates* were acquired by Onassis in 1933—one year *after* his alleged joust with the Rotterdam consul. They were both registered as Greek vessels owned by A. S. Onassis, Piraeus. The files at Lloyd's of London show that the *Onassis Penelope* did not switch from Greek to Panamanian registration until April 1938. The *Onassis Socrates* was registered in Panama six months later.

Onassis was not a consciously political animal. His adolescence provided a crash course in the evil consequences of racial animosity but did not encourage any fixed ideology. As a young businessman he evinced an almost Panglossian optimism about the way of the world. It was as if his

51

personal experience of the absurdity of war led him to believe that it must be obvious to others.

As the storm clouds gathered in the late 1930s, Onassis saw no necessity to choose sides. He reckoned they would go away. They could, he thought, only be bad for business. He was aware but uninvolved and, Gratsos thought, "naive in his attitude to world affairs, though he was basically pro-Allies." He displayed no interest, commercial or political, in the Spanish Civil War, which many perceived as a bloody curtain-raiser to a larger conflict. This was despite the fact that his business movements brought him into regular contact with partisans on either side of the European argument. In London and Oslo it was impossible not to be acquainted with the rising hostility to Nazi Germany. In Buenos Aires there was a strong current of sympathy for fascism.

The right-wing government of Argentina, which had returned to power after a military coup in September 1930, was leaning discernibly toward the Axis powers in its neutrality. The Argentine army was largely German trained and equipped, the big German community (some two hundred fifty thousand in 1938) was actively supporting the Nazi cause, orchestrated by the German embassy in Buenos Aires. Argentina's even larger Italian colony was, initially at least, ardently behind Mussolini. There were so many Axis spies around that the German ambassador had to ask Berlin for guidance on who was who.

When England and France declared war on Germany on September 3, 1939, Onassis could hardly have been in a worse position. He was in London at the Savoy. His Cadillac was stranded in Belgium. Ingse was in Paris. Two of his tankers, the *Ariston* and the *Buenos Aires* (still under construction), were in Sweden threatened by a government intent on demonstrating its neutrality. Only the *Aristophanes,* on charter at sea under the Norwegian flag, seemed safe. Onassis obtained permission to go to Sweden but got no satisfaction. The Swedes formally agreed with Germany that foreign-owned vessels under her flag and built in her ports would stay there for the duration of hostilities.

When Norway was invaded in April 1940, the government went into exile in London and promptly requisitioned the *Aristophanes.* Fifty thousand tons of the most modern tankers in the world were immobilized at the moment when they could have been most valuable to Onassis. For Onassis it meant concentrating on the ships he still controlled—the Canadian freighters and the "dry" business back in the Argentine. In June 1940, while the Battle of Britain was in progress, he sailed from London bound for New York.

52

5
A QUIET WAR

THE FIRST-CLASS CABINS on board the Cunard Line's SS *Samaria* were fully booked, and Onassis was put to the minor inconvenience of having to travel second class. It was, as it turned out, his first and only experience of wartime privations. But he was by now apprehensive about the war which he had so long ignored. According to the other London Greeks on the *Samaria*, Onassis spent the otherwise uneventful crossing in constant fear of enemy attack. His endemic insomnia became acute. Instead of using his cabin he preferred to doze in the empty saloons within striking distance of the life-jacket closets. During lifeboat drills he clutched the attaché case containing the deeds to his ships to his side. He apparently recovered only when the shining towers of neutral Manhattan came into view.

His behavior enlivened the tedium of shipboard life and later became the occasion for malicious remarks about his lack of physical courage. Most probably it reflected a sense of the danger that lay close to the surface of civilized life, which all his material success had never quite obliterated. He had first crossed the Atlantic to Buenos Aires in the shadow of the Smyrna massacre and had never lost his sense of himself as a refugee. Now, with his business in disarray and Europe in danger, he was on the move again, to a city and a business environment he hardly knew.

Unlike many less fortunate refugees, he passed rapidly through Ellis Island, the harsh sorting house for the tired and needy seeking entry to the United States.

He was thirty-four years old but still, for the purposes of the official record, carefully preserved the fiction about his age and place of birth. The transcript of his interview by the Ellis Island Board of Special Inquiry still survives in the US Immigration Department files. It begins,

Alien sworn in by Insp. Galvin, testified in English:
Q. What is your full and correct name?
A. Aristotle Socrates Onassis.
Q. Were you ever known by or have you ever used other names?
A. No.
Q. Of what country are you a citizen?
A. Argentina.
Q. What is your race?
A. Greek.
Q. Where and when were you born?
A. In Salonika, Greece, on September 21, 1900.

Onassis had come on a six-month visitor's visa, and the $500,000 he had on deposit at Barclay's Bank was more than adequate to insure he would not become a public charge. The nature of his business in the United States was left vague, probably deliberately—a ship of his had recently docked in Savannah; another was soon to arrive; there was the possibility of buying a vessel on the West Coast. Whether he wished at this stage to spend the rest of the war in New York is not clear, but for the next month he bombarded Dedichen with cables and letters. He had fallen ill and he was lonely. It was perhaps because of this that he appended another offer of marriage to his urgings that she exchange the hazards of Paris for the safety of New York.

By the time Ingse arrived, after traveling through Marseilles, Spain, and Portugal, he had found his feet, moving into a full-floor service apartment in the Ritz Towers, a luxury building on Park Avenue and Fifty-seventh Street. Their new life was celebrated with a burst of spending in the prewar style: for Ingse, a brand-new Cadillac to replace the beige one lost in Belgium; for himself, a tuxedo, the first he had ever possessed. In his haste to get at the good life, he made the mistake of buying off the rack, with the result that in smart New York restaurants he was sometimes mistaken for a waiter.

As he had elsewhere, Onassis began in New York by learning about

54

it from the street upward. To start with, his activity was modest and largely geared to his family's interests in Buenos Aires—imports of anise and olive oil, exports of American tobacco amounting to a turnover of only $150,000 in the last six months of 1940. But he went after business with characteristic intensity. Ingse noticed his ability to contain and harness the extraordinary nervous energy which he generated. He would return to his apartment from the temporary quarters he occupied in a downtown office, lie down fully dressed on the floor—never on his bed —and sleep for some hours. It was impossible to wake him while he slept. When he woke again he was relaxed. If he never kept regular hours, it was because his body had developed a personal clock that enabled him to ignore them.

The New York to which he became accustomed was the one he would return to for the rest of his life. A perennial, and later compulsive, refugee, he identified with a city that had given hope, refuge, and sometimes wealth to generations of immigrants. Its speed and transience matched his own rootless energies, and the elaborate pleasures it offered were in tune with his increasingly eclectic tastes. He and Ingse walked around the city a great deal, exploring the canyons of lower Manhattan and the city's huge docks. They spent an evening in a Harlem nightclub, where a knife fight broke out, causing them to leave in a hurry. Ingse's secondhand mink was going bald around the edges, and Onassis insisted she must have a new one. "Order the most beautiful and elegant one you can find," he told her. The coat cost $16,000, but he paid without flinching. It was, after all, a necessary expense, as much part of the ritual of New York life as walking down Fifth Avenue to celebrate the return of spring. Besides, the conspicuous admiration it aroused amounted to a recognition of his own wealth.

Onassis was probably not much richer than he had been in the late thirties. Indeed, since so large a portion of his fleet, and therefore his assets, was blocked in various Scandinavian harbors, his income was probably less than it had been. But he was more than comfortably well off. In 1945, applying for an extension on his visa, he told the US authorities he drew about $4,000 a month in living expenses from "a fund set up by his family." He also had $3 million worth of US war bonds invested in his name. The "fund" was a first strand of the tangled web that he subsequently constructed to disguise the size and nature of his assets. No doubt he preferred not to tell the US government how much he owned. But in those days $4,000 a month was more than enough to live the good life in New York.

For Onassis, the boundary between his business and social lives was never a clear one, and in New York he found both, not through the expatriate Greek shipping community but by means of an Argentinian acquaintance of his, Alberto Dodero. To the Greeks he was still not quite a serious shipowner. Dodero, however, saw the world much as Onassis did, and there was an instant rapport between the two men, cemented at weekend parties at the luxurious Dodero estate at Centre Island, a bare hour away from Manhattan on Long Island. Onassis's approach was very much the one he would use with equal success in later life with such patriarchs as J. Paul Getty and Winston Churchill—he was attentive, deferential, and charming. "He will go far," Dodero told one of Onassis's friends, "if only he learns to make up his mind." It was the classic Onassis role—the young, poor Greek gaining wisdom and experience at the feet of his elders.

In 1940, Dodero, a short, dynamic man, appeared to be at the high tide of his fortunes. Both his money and the sense of style with which he disposed of it had made him into the sort of creature of legend Onassis was to become. The youngest of five sons of an Italian immigrant who had made good in Uruguay, he was sent to a private school in Ireland. His father owned a small shipping business, but Dodero ran away and went to work for the Mihanovic Lines in Argentina. In the space of ten years he acquired a controlling interest in the business and merged it with his father's company. By World War II he had accumulated the largest private fleet in the world.

His expansion was financed largely by credit on the basis of the enormous profits he derived each year from the monopoly he retained on the six ferries that ran between Buenos Aires and Montevideo. For his second wife, the American starlet Betty Sunmark, he acquired an estate three miles outside Montevideo. Bet-Alba, as it was called, was entirely surrounded by a high, circular brick wall. Dodero's villa and a number of guest houses were built around the perimeter, against the wall. At the center of the estate was a huge marquee containing a forty-foot-long dining table and a movie theater where Betty could watch new Hollywood films.

It was at one of Alberto Dodero's famous Montevideo parties that Onassis met a remarkable Austrian tycoon, Fritz Mandl. A Viennese Jew, Mandl made his first millions in the manufacture of arms and munitions. He had already transferred most of his assets to the Argentine when Nazi troops rolled into Vienna in March 1938. When Onassis met him, Mandl was an Argentine citizen moving once again in the best circles and setting up new enterprises. Because of his small stature and the nature of his business, Mandl was known as the Pocket Zaharoff, after the famous World War I arms dealer, Sir Basil Zaharoff. He had married Hedy Kiesler, who appeared nude in the Czech film *Ecstasy*. She later moved to the United States and made great progress as a screen femme fatale under the name Hedy Lamarr. When her marriage to Mandl broke up, the *New York Daily News* headlined the story, "No Ecstasy for Pocket Zaharoff."

Mandl excited the interest of the American authorities for other reasons. His career had been closely observed by US intelligence, particularly after his contacts with the Hermann Goering steelworks in 1940. At the time Onassis became acquainted with him, Mandl was regarded with official hostility in the United States. He was subsequently put on the Anglo-American blacklist and refused entry to the country. Onassis's contact with Mandl and, possibly, with others out of favor with the US authorities (there were more Argentinians on the blacklist than any other nationality) may explain one of the most intriguing episodes of his early career—a recommendation by J. Edgar Hoover that Onassis should be spied on while he was in the United States. It came in a letter from Hoover to Admiral Emory S. Land, head of the War Shipping Administration, which controlled all civilian shipping operations during the hostilities. Dated July 16, 1942, and marked "Personal and Confidential by Special Messenger," it reads in full,

My Dear Admiral,

Information has been received from a confidential source that Mr. Aristotle Onassis, who is reportedly part owner of the tankers "Calliroy" and "Antiope," was scheduled to depart for the United States on Thursday June 18, 1942, by Pan American Clipper from Buenos Aires, Argentina. According to the informant, the purpose of Onassis' visit is to continue the negotiations for the sale of these two tankers to the War Shipping Administration.

The informant advised that there is no information available indicating Mr. Onassis has any other motive for making a trip to the United States, but it was reported that he has expressed sentiments inimical to the United States war effort, and that his activities and movements while in the United States should be carefully scrutinized.

Sincerely yours,
John Edgar Hoover

Onassis was indeed a part owner of the tanker *Callirhoe*—Hoover's agent got the spelling wrong—but there is no evidence that Onassis was ever "inimical" to the United States once the war began. However, apart from the Mandl acquaintance, there was something else which may have come to the attention of the FBI. Early in 1940, long before the Japanese attack on Pearl Harbor brought the United States into the war, Onassis had sold two of his former Canadian freighters to a shipping firm in Japan (his business contacts there had begun with the *Ariston*'s first contract running oil to Yokohama). The ships were pressed into war service by the Japanese and were later sunk by the Americans.

Costa Gratsos maintains that the "Hoover letter" was all a "misunderstanding." People traveling regularly between the Argentine and the United States naturally came under surveillance. "We could see we were being followed and that our phones were tapped. It was really just a routine occurrence." Three years later, Gratsos recalls, he met J. Edgar Hoover at a social function in Washington. "We joked about the whole thing."

Nevertheless, the confidential FBI records reveal that Onassis was the subject of investigation for almost two years. The FBI never did discover why Onassis allegedly expressed sentiments inimical to the American war effort, though one of the documents on file provides a plausible hypothesis. In 1941 Onassis was confronted with a demand by the US government to restore two of his Panamanian-registered ships to the US flag. Onassis initially tried to sell the ships, but the American authorities refused to allow the transaction. An FBI report concluded that the statements attributed to Onassis "may have been occasioned by annoyance over disruption of this undoubtedly profitable plan." Other reports in the Onassis file comment censoriously on the insurance and currency swindles that assisted his rise to riches in the Argentine, but none provides grounds for suspicion of specific anti-American activity. The last document on file, dated April 1, 1944, concludes, "Investigation to date has not reflected any activity of a subversive nature on the part of the subject [Onassis], no further investigation is deemed warranted and the case is hereby closed."

The relationship between Onassis and Dodero in New York was mutually supportive, but it had its limits. Despite appearances to the contrary, Dodero was in trouble. His business interests were too diffuse and he needed both cash and expertise. It was for this reason that he approached Ingse with the suggestion that she might persuade Onassis to take a share in his company. "Onassis can make money out of the most decrepit old tub," he told her. Ingse, who had made it a principle never to interfere in her lover's business dealings, suggested that Dodero should approach Onassis in person. Claims of friendship, unlike those of blood relations, were rarely allowed to affect Onassis's business interests, and in this particular case the fact that he liked Dodero did not influence his decision. He turned down Dodero's offer on the grounds that his personal share in the enterprise would not be sufficient to give him a controlling interest.

Dodero found the money—it came from the ubiquitous Fritz Mandl —but his subsequent career bore out the wisdom of Onassis's decision. Although Dodero became good friends with Juan Perón, the leading member of the military clique that took power in Argentina in 1943, it was not altogether to his advantage. In 1948, after Perón had become president, Dodero was forced to sell a controlling stake in his companies —including the precious ferries—to the government for the derisory sum of $3 million.

Although he rebuffed Dodero's offer of partnership, Onassis was shrewd enough to make use of his friendship. Then, as now, Centre Island, on the north shore of Long Island, was more than a suburban and weekend community. Its wealthy inhabitants mixed at the yacht club and called on each other with the informality peculiar to the American rich. One of the properties bordering on Dodero's estate belonged to Cecil Stewart, a member of an old New York shipping family with which Dodero had done business since 1912. Stewart was well connected and wealthy and on first-name terms with Franklin Roosevelt. According to his son, he had inherited a lot of money, lost it all, made it again, lost it in the depression—and made it once more.

It was perhaps this entrepreneurial streak in Stewart that attracted him to Onassis. In any event, Frank B. Hall & Co., the firm of which Stewart was chairman, became Onassis's insurance brokers soon after his arrival in the United States. In September 1940, Stewart's son, Jimmy, received a check for $2 million from Onassis's ship brokers, drawn on his account at First National City Bank, in payment for the *Santa Maria*, which Onassis had contracted to buy from the Union Oil Company of California. Jimmy Stewart had never met Onassis, and his father was away, so he contacted First National City and asked them to certify the check. When Stewart called with the check, he asked the First National City official who Onassis was and how a relatively young and obscure Greek could write checks for $2 million. After due reference to the proprieties of banking, the official said that he, too, had no idea how Onassis had so much money but that his arrangement with the bank was that it would certify checks on his behalf of up to $4 million.

Soon afterward, Cecil Stewart acquired a small share in one of Onassis's ventures. In the hope that freight rates would increase, Onassis and Stewart bought "an old rust tub" for $350,000 while she was steaming off the east coast of South America. The ship was to sail to New York for refitting. By the time it had reached the Caribbean it was worth $700,000, two days later $900,000. Onassis was delighted but uncertain whether he should sell or wait in the hope of selling later at a still higher price. Evidently, the dilemma became too much for him. Each time the tub increased in value, he called Stewart for advice. Should he sell, or shouldn't he? Stewart advised him to sell at once. Onassis, however, was unable to make up his mind. By the time the ship had reached Florida, it was worth $1.2 million, and Onassis's indecisiveness had reached fever pitch. Stewart was on vacation at his Palm Beach house, and Onassis flew to Florida especially to discuss his exquisite dilemma. "Every night I go to bed determined to sell," he told Stewart, "and every morning I wake up and say, 'No, I'll get more money for it tomorrow.' " Stewart stayed up with Onassis that night to insure his mood of determination lasted through the morning hours. Next day the ship was sold.

In the spring of 1941 Stewart's wife, Dorothy, called Ingse and casually invited her to Centre Island to keep her company while she opened up the estate for the summer. As she wandered around the property, Ingse noticed another, totally abandoned house on the beach a distance from the Stewarts' somewhat grander place. Dorothy explained that it was called Foster's House and that none of the family needed it. Stewart had acquired it toward the end of the depression as part of his efforts to prove to the town authorities that Centre Island property taxes were unjustly pegged to artificially high, preslump land values. After buying the house at a bargain price and thus proving his point, he had lost interest in Foster's House. When Ingse offered to rent the place and renovate it, Stewart said he would be delighted; she could have it rent free. Ingse, however, insisted on paying something for the house, and to Onassis's amusement set about scouring the local junk shops for furniture. As a result of her efforts, Onassis's first real home rapidly took shape. Its pièce de résistance was an enormous sofa that Ingse had spied on the back of a Salvation Army pickup truck and exchanged for the load of clutter left in the living room by the house's previous owner.

Ingse's efforts to create a home eventually aroused Onassis's interest. He employed a French couple as cook and butler, devised an appropriately maritime motif for the living-room bar, and bought Ingse a Chris-Craft cabin cruiser. The cottage was renamed Mamita in honor of Ingse, and for the first time in his life Onassis settled into a more or less domestic routine. Ingse and Onassis spent much of the summer on Long Island. Onassis commuted to New York when he felt like it, and, more often than not, conducted his business over the telephone from the cottage. There were barbecue parties where Onassis dressed up as a chef and all-night poker games at the boathouse near the cottage. Onassis's circle of friends widened. Many Greeks, including the Livanos and Embiricos families, had summer places on Long Island, and they would drop by to talk business. Onassis and Ingse also made the acquaintance of many of their American neighbors, including Jimmy Mooney, the chairman of the board of General Motors. Although Onassis spent most nights in her room, Ingse insisted on maintaining the fiction of a separate existence out of respect, as she put it, for the norms of American puritanism. When she showed friends around the house, she would pointedly draw attention to the fact that Ari and she had separate bedrooms. The formula fooled no one, she recalled, but "appearances were saved."

This arrangement, pleasant though it was, proved short-lived. The forties were a good time in New York, and the phrase "café society" came into use to describe the melange of rich exiles, restless old and new money, and Hollywood luminaries who congregated each night at the 21 Club or at El Morocco (Elmo's, for short) to see and be seen with each other.

Elmo's, in particular, became dear to Onassis's heart. Its founder, John Peróna, was Argentinian and so was its distinctive decor. In the forties it was known as glamour, but in these more discriminating days it would probably be called high kitsch. Beneath a sky-blue ceiling studded with discreetly twinkling lights were paper palm trees and zebra-striped banquettes. The food was substantial, if not elaborate—another plus with Onassis, who took a fancy to the giant hamburgers.

At that time, Elmo's was open to anyone who could convince the doorman he belonged there. Clients were effectively graded in importance, however, by the tables at which they were placed. For those whom Peróna wished to discourage there was always "Siberia," an area at the back of the club next to the kitchen where the view and the service were more or less equally deficient. Onassis was never consigned to Siberia. He used Elmo's as a convenient substitute office and one which had the advantage of keeping his hours, though he was discreet enough never to sign contracts on the premises.

Inevitably, these changes had their effect on his relationship with

Ingse. He had met her when he was still young and obscure, and their affair had survived as a result of his willing acceptance of her desire to initiate him into the ways of a world with which he was not yet familiar. She was his Mamita, he was her Mamico—the names they gave each other are by themselves indicative of the state of mutual dependence in which they held each other. Belatedly, perhaps, Onassis wished to assert his independence, and one day he came to Ingse with a request as startling as it was without precedent. "He had suddenly realized the years were passing," recalled Ingse, "that he was suffocating in his business and neglecting the life that was now within his reach. His friends lived a life he had never known, going out with the most ravishing women. He had begun to deceive me in order to imitate them, at first always asking my permission. He was now asking for some sort of amorous holiday. 'Mamita, we won't marry immediately,' he said. 'Let me have some freedom first.' "

Ingse assented to his request—she had no alternative, as she well realized, since he was likely to take his "amorous holiday" whether she agreed or not. But the degree to which she entered into the spirit of the new arrangement seems to have surprised even Onassis. They became, as she put it, "accomplices rather than lovers," although they still occasionally slept together. He had wished to be told to go and enjoy himself, but he was confused when Ingse participated in his playboy life, wanting to hear about his new liaisons so that she could pass judgment on his developing tastes.

His lotus life began on the West Coast. Two of his ships, the *Callirhoe* and the *Gulf Queen,* which he had bought from Gulf Oil, were carrying oil between San Pedro, California, and Vancouver, British Columbia. After Pearl Harbor the ships were chartered to the US government, but they still operated on substantially the same route. Onassis frequently flew from New York to Los Angeles to inspect the ships and talk to their captains. His friend Costa Gratsos was the Greek consul in San Francisco, and together they began to explore the possibilities of 1940s Hollywood. Gratsos always deferred to Onassis's superior luck, skill, and judgment in matters of the heart as well as business, but in this instance the field was so wide open that they were equally successful. "We sat in L.A., screwing the girls, a very pleasant occupation," Gratsos recalled. "There were starlets, semistars, and stars, an endless supply. . . . It was a very quiet war."

In his later years Onassis was cagey, even dismissive, about his palmy Hollywood days, expressing a puritanical distaste for the movie world and its hangers-on. In fact, he seems to have derived considerable enjoyment from the scene. His name was linked with a number of celebrities, including Paulette Goddard, Simone Simon ("the original pouty-lipped French sex kitten"), and Veronica Lake ("the girl with the peek-a-boo hairstyle"). Miss Lake subsequently claimed that Onassis had proposed to her but that she had turned him down because his piercing eyes unnerved her. "He was a very sweet gent," she told a reporter, "but, oh God, those black eyes! They look like they are going straight through the back of your head." She was, nonetheless, grateful to him for giving her items that were in short supply during the war—perfume, nylons, and fine wines. Costa Gratsos doubts the seriousness of Onassis's alleged proposal: "As far as marriage was concerned, Onassis was interested in heiresses rather than movie stars."

Onassis became friends with Spyros Skouras, the head of Twentieth-Century Fox, and made his way into Hollywood's café society as easily as he had New York's. He became a denizen of Romanoff's and a familiar of its owner, "Prince" Mike Romanoff, the first and most successful of the many Brooklyn Romanoffs. And he was also to be seen at the Mocambo on Sunset Strip, a nightclub perched on a high bluff overlooking Los Angeles which was much favored by South American millionaires for its Latin music, its tropical birds in glass cages, and its readily available supply of aspiring movie queens. There were other venues, too, with appealingly suggestive names—Perino's, the Villanova, A Bit of Sweden, and a restaurant called the Cock and Bull.

When he told Ingse about his adventures, there was no doubt a certain element of spite involved. He was, she rightly saw, "playing cat and mouse" and taunting her with his success. Nonetheless, he seems to have been as astonished as she by this sudden turn of events, and he would come to her for advice on delicate matters. He was neither by nature nor experience a collector of women, and he betrayed a touching ignorance of the sort of life-style he had chosen. One such incident involved a starlet whom he had seduced and whose subsequent importunities and sexual appetite he rapidly found distressing. Ingse ascertained that the lady was notoriously free with her affections and had acquired a reputation as a spreader of diseases among imprudent members of the smart set. Onassis, remembering his Argentinian misadventure, was appalled and hurriedly sought medical diagnosis. He was relieved to be told that nothing was amiss and was so grateful for Ingse's warning that they became closer for a while. He and the starlet became, in a much-abused phrase, "just good friends."

At least one of these West Coast liaisons was relatively serious. Onassis met and fell in love with Geraldine Spreckels, a San Francisco heiress. The whirlwind courtship that ensued introduced a note of cruelty into his relationship with Ingse. One Friday morning Onassis came to see her and announced his intention of flying to California to spend the weekend with Miss Spreckels. "I think I am rather in love with her," he said. "Who knows, maybe we'll marry." Ingse kept her cool, retaliating with a great show of concern for Onassis's health and dignity. He didn't have a lightweight coat. "You'll die of heat in that winter coat," she replied. "Anyway, you look like a peasant . . . who hasn't the money to buy a decent coat. . . . You will make me feel ashamed of you." When Onassis protested that he hadn't time to buy a new one, she went out and bought one for him. In any event, he never needed the coat. He was greeted in San Francisco by a message to the effect that Miss Spreckels was unable to meet him but would be grateful if he would join her for drinks at a specified address. Ari took the first plane back to New York and Ingse's powers of consolation.

Nonetheless, he persisted with his courtship. He once telephoned Ingse to tell her that he was going to marry Miss Spreckels. Two days later she received a check for $200,000 accompanied by a note explaining that it was "in compensation." Precisely what it was supposed to compensate was not made clear. Ingse kept the check to return it to him when he came back to New York. He was probably pleased to get it back. The announcement of his engagement to Miss Spreckels had been premature, and shortly afterward she married someone else.

Onassis had greater success with another sentimental interest developed on the West Coast. With Costa Gratsos he bought an old whaling station called Eureka, which dated from the great days of California whaling some fifty years earlier. Onassis had been fascinated by whaling since his days in Norway—Sandefjord, where he had lived with Ingse and her mother for a spell, was Norway's principal whaling port. The California venture was unambitious in scale but seemed viable as the war had inflated the price of sperm oil, needed for the lubrication of arms. Gratsos calculated that $15,000 was all the capital required to reopen the station and hire a pair of elderly tug boats. They found a Swedish gunner, somehow laid hands on an assistant for him—a fearful drunk, Gratsos remembers—and picked up a Greek merchant seaman stranded by the war to complete the crew. Operation Eureka was ready to roll.

The initial problem was finding the whales. According to Gratsos, some of the US Coast Guard came to the rescue, helpfully agreeing to act as spotters from their observation blimps high above the water. They would signal directions to the tug whenever they saw a school of sperm whales. The partners soon discovered that hacking the carcasses up for boiling was a time-consuming and cumbersome process. A much better bet, they realized, was selling the flesh as feed for California's many mink farms. Eventually they were approached by the Borden Company, which offered to buy all the whale livers they could provide. Whale livers, which can weigh several hundred pounds, contain vast quantities of vitamin A, one of Borden's main lines. The kills were unimpressive by Norwegian standards, but the two Greeks thoroughly enjoyed the business for the two years it lasted and made a modest profit.

When he returned from his forays in California, Onassis took up his life with Ingse where he had left it. She had moved out of his apartment to another in the Ritz Towers, two floors below, and began to live her own life, knitting bolero jackets for the Norwegian Relief Fund and selling them to society ladies in a Fifth Avenue shop. He still showered her with gifts, including a Steinway piano for her new apartment. Though he had never previously displayed much interest in music, he liked to listen to her play. She was learning Bach's Inventions, and he asked her if she would teach him to play one of the pieces. He couldn't read music but soon became surprisingly adept, even learning to use the pedals. His new skill served him in good stead the following winter in California. At a party given by a Greek actress, Katina Paxinou, he was introduced to Artur Rubinstein and embarked on a conversation about music. Rubinstein, intrigued by so evident an interest in music from such an unexpected quarter, asked if Onassis was a musician. Onassis, with becoming and no doubt contrived modesty, replied that he wasn't; he did, however, have a consuming passion for one of the Bach Inventions. Rubinstein insisted that he play it, and he did so successfully, to everyone's surprise. He afterward told Ingse that he had practiced the piece by himself for the past six months.

Onassis's California war was in striking contrast with the one fought by some of the more prominent Greek shipowners. By 1942 most of the London Greeks had moved to New York, where they occupied suites in such hotels as the Pierre, the St. Regis, and the Plaza. The ships they still had were operating on the hazardous Atlantic route. Losses of men and materiel were high. The Embiricos family, for instance, had lost three of its six ships by 1942. Nonetheless, they turned over their previous year's profits to the Greek War Relief Association. André Embiricos developed and patented a system for transporting material across the

Atlantic by means of a series of bargelike boats controlled by radio from a master ship in each convoy. At the slightest sign of enemy attack the barges could be dispersed. The family's yacht was adapted for war work and used to develop the system.

Stavros Niarchos had a distinguished war record. By 1939 he had made enough money to start his own fleet of tramp freighters operating from London. When the Allies took over his vessels for war service, Niarchos joined the Greek navy and served for a time on a destroyer on Atlantic convoys. He later served as an assistant to the Greek naval attaché in the Washington embassy. It was a position that allowed him to spend a great deal of time in New York. The war did not harm his business, despite losses at sea. In 1940 he bought the *Bayou,* a 7,000-ton Great Lakes ore carrier, and the *Olympic,* an old freighter converted into a tanker. Both ships were sunk by U-boats on the Atlantic run. The *Olympic* was lost with all hands.

The insurance money from these and other losses—estimated at $2 million—helped to propel Niarchos into the front rank of the younger generation of Greek shipowners. He rented a house in Lloyd Neck, Long Island, and began collecting art objects and frequenting the best New York nightclubs.

Onassis and Niarchos became more than mere acquaintances. Each man seems to have sniffed in the other a potential rival. As parvenus, neither was wholly acceptable to the established Greek community; as successful shipowners who wished to be admitted to that community, neither wished to be too closely associated with the other. They were already competing with each other—Onassis in waterskiing versus Niarchos in sailing—but as yet they were careful to limit the competition to spheres in which their separate interests were assured. The one exception to this tacitly understood rule was poker, where their skills were more or less evenly balanced.

Yet they were brought into somewhat closer proximity than either of them probably desired by the friendship that subsequently blossomed between Ingse and Niarchos's wife. In 1940 Melpomene Capparis Alexandropoulos—a twenty-year-old widow of a Greek diplomat and daughter of a bankrupt shipowner—had become Niarchos's second wife. Two years later the marriage was showing signs of strain. Niarchos spent most of his time in New York at an apartment he had rented from Harry Hopkins, President Roosevelt's adviser. Melpo, living in the suburbs, was taking drugs to cure her insomnia, and they had severely affected her ability to function during the daytime. She had drifted into an apathetic state, spending much of the day reclining on a couch in her housecoat and eating cookies.

Ingse decided she needed moral support and offered to help Melpo decorate her house. In effect this meant that Ingse became "gardener, odd-job man, and housekeeper" to the Niarchos household. One morning, when she was cleaning the front porch, Niarchos paid a surprise visit to his stricken wife. Ingse's hands were plastered with mud, her hair was streaked with leaves. Niarchos was astounded. "What's going on," he asked. "Are things so bad with Onassis that Melpo has hired you as our cleaning woman?"

Ingse remembers Niarchos calling one evening to tell her that he had quarreled with Melpo that afternoon. She had just phoned him to say she had locked herself in the apartment and taken a large dose of barbiturates. Niarchos had lost his key to the apartment and was panic-stricken. He had called Ingse because her apartment was managed by the same real estate company as his. To avoid any embarrassment, he wanted her to get a passkey from the janitor and let herself into his apartment as quickly as possible. Ingse found Melpo only marginally more comatose than her usual self. When Niarchos arrived with a doctor, however, she feigned insensibility. An ambulance was summoned, which took her to the hospital with Ingse at her side. Melpo winked at Ingse. "I'm just trying to frighten Stavros," she said.

It was after a dinner with the Niarchoses that Onassis, for the first time in their relationship, beat Ingse. There had been an argument on the Chris-Craft over her insistence on wearing a pair of green and yellow plaid pants that he found unbecoming. He was uncharacteristically silent throughout dinner and on the way back. When they were home again, his pent-up rage turned to uncontrolled violence, and he kicked and hit Ingse until he was finally exhausted and went to bed. The next day he had forgotten everything. "He had left no marks on my body," Ingse remarked. "He knew how to hit like an expert."

Onassis justified this behavior by reference to the traditional rights that Greek men possessed over their womenfolk. "Every Greek, and there are no exceptions, beats his wife," he told Ingse. "It is good for them. It keeps them in line." But this was bluster, as Ingse well knew. As his rages became more frequent, she discovered a pattern to them. He was, like Niarchos, resentful of any form of social humiliation. He could protect himself behind a mask of modesty and bonhomie—he was still "the modest young Greek." But her own outspokenness and social ease placed him on the defensive. And this could bring to the surface the aggression that was an integral part of his character. As Dedichen explained it,

> he was not only the charming young man he could play when he wanted to please. One could compare him to an electricity storage tank. He would work up energy during his many activities and when he could no longer contain it, he exploded. He needed some victim on whom he could release his nervous tension. It would not have suited his complicated character to discuss what was at issue between us and we never did. He was always trying to put me in the wrong, because he always needed to keep his victims within his power . . . he had to have them "in the palm of his hand." Oddly, these spasms of pointless violence seemed to satisfy him. . . . He would emerge from them as relaxed and happy as if he had just made love.

Alcohol exacerbated these violent moods, and by now Onassis had acquired the habit of heavy drinking. One attack left Ingse with a face "like a boxer who has just lost a fight" and torn ligaments. Onassis was so alarmed by the results of his handiwork that he bundled Ingse into the Cadillac next morning, drove her to Centre Island, sent the servants away, and left her behind to recuperate as best she could. She, in her turn, was so frightened at the prospect of any further "punishment" that it took all her courage to ask Onassis to take her back to her New York apartment. When she went to her doctor, she told him she had fallen down the staircase. The doctor refused to believe her and said he was prepared to see Onassis on her behalf. She declined the offer on the grounds that this would only put her in further jeopardy.

Only Onassis's possessiveness kept the relationship from ending. If he could not bring himself to leave Ingse, he also could not allow her to leave him. Ingse was by now in the process of recreating her own life, seeing old friends and having an affair with one of them. Onassis took to spying on her. He would stand in the street outside her apartment in hopes of catching a glimpse of the men she was going out with. It was after a rainy evening that he proposed to her again on the Park Avenue sidewalk. Ingse, to her own astonishment, accepted. They made plans for the imminent postwar future. Onassis promised Ingse a yacht, a tanker, and a Greek island. He bought her an antique Egyptian necklace to wear at the wedding. Ingse even ordered a wedding dress. Then Onassis put off the wedding date and disappeared to the West Coast once more. When she wrote to tell him she had had enough, he proposed once more. They would be married in the fall of 1944 in New York.

There remained one problem. Ingse required an operation to enable her to have children. She and Onassis had talked about that possibility before, but he had always been afraid for Ingse—his fear of doctors amounted to a form of superstition. Now his reluctance to let Ingse undergo the operation became a pretext for postponing their marriage once again. In the end, she arranged the operation without telling him. It was a failure, and Onassis responded not with sympathy but with another of his ferocious tantrums. Ingse, he maintained, had "disgraced" him, and all his Greek friends would be laughing behind his back. Ingse, exhausted by this "perpetual torture," plunged into a deep depression, and one evening, alone in her apartment, she took an overdose of Nembutal. Luckily, this was one of the occasions when Onassis decided to check up on her nightlife, and he arrived in time to bring her around by dipping her head in cold water. But her attempted suicide killed whatever feelings Ingse still held toward Onassis. She withdrew steadily from his life, seeing him less and less, and then only at his insistence.

6
AN UNCERTAIN PEACE

WHEN THE WAR ENDED, Onassis had as much cause to rejoice as anyone. Three of his ships were still chartered to the United States Maritime Commission, earning around $250,000 a year. His tankers were at last able to steam out of the Scandinavian harbors in which they had been blockaded since 1940. The *Ariston,* still one of the largest tankers in the world, sailed to New York, and Onassis threw a party on board for his New York Greek friends. Some of the guests must have been moved to contrast their own situation with Onassis's. Of the official total of 450 Greek ships that participated in the war, 360 had been lost. Onassis had not lost a single sailor or ship. Nor had all of the Greeks become "compensation kings." The windfalls that were made came early in the war, before the insurance companies experienced difficulties in meeting claims. Subsequently many shipowners had insured their fleets through the Greek Insurance Fund, which was poorly conceived and administered and by 1945 was running out of money.

Such money as the New York Greeks did possess, they were doubtful how to use. The war had left Europe's shipyards in ruins, with the exception of the Scandinavian ones, which were booked up several years ahead. There was spare capacity at most of the US yards, but a ship cost twice as much to build in the United States as it did in Europe. The older

70

and more conservative Greeks were in any case skeptical about the postwar future. Many of them had fathers or friends who had invested heavily in 1918 and gone bankrupt in the 1923 slump.

Onassis's view of the future was colored by no such evil memories. He was bullish by nature, and he felt that the wartime boom in America would soon be followed by a strong economic recovery in the rest of the world. If there were no ships immediately available, it was apparent that there shortly would be. The prodigious feats of the US war economy had made the federal government the largest single owner of merchant ships in the world. As the one-way flow of materiel and men from America to Europe slackened, much of the US fleet was laid up. By 1946 the East Coast ports and the Hudson and Delaware rivers were lined with rapidly deteriorating surplus ships.

The backbone of this growing mothball fleet was that triumph of American improvisation, the Liberty ship. In 1941 Roosevelt appealed for a crash shipbuilding program to replace the devastating losses suffered on the North Atlantic route. Henry Kaiser, a California cement contractor turned industrialist, saw that the enormous demand could not be met by orthodox methods. The East Coast yards still built their ships after the traditions of their craft—plate by plate, rivet by rivet. The technique had an element of loving care wholly inappropriate to wartime conditions. Many of these carefully designed ships would, after all, be sunk within months of going into use.

Like most successful business inventions, Kaiser's solution was as simple as it was effective. He began building ships as he had built the Grand Coulee Dam—in huge, prefabricated sections assembled in open lots where there was room for hundreds of welders and cutters to work without getting in one another's way. Later the process was refined, and the sections moved down an assembly line on trolleys the size of hockey rinks. But the principle remained the same, as did the entirely novel way in which the ships were ultimately put together. The separate elements —the deckhouse and the "front and rear ends," as Kaiser insisted on calling the bow and stern—were sewn together with a few passes of a welder's torch. The effect was spectacular. Only 194 days after he had entered the shipbuilding business Kaiser was turning out 10,500-ton Liberties in only 46 days, a quarter of the time it took to build a similar ship by conventional methods.

Because the United States lacked the crews to man them, many of the 2,700 Liberties were made available under lend-lease arrangements to US allies, including the Greek government. Between 1943 and 1945,

71

Costa Gratsos on behalf of the Greek government had operated a fleet of fourteen Liberties shuttling between New York and London, where many of his business conferences were held literally under the table because of V-1 and V-2 missile attacks. When Congress passed the Ship Sales Act in 1946—making Liberties available to private operators in allied countries as part of the US attempt to assist European recovery and thus avoid a world slump—Gratsos urged Onassis to act quickly. The terms were unbelievably good, enabling cash purchasers to acquire a ship for $550,000. Where the purchaser's government was prepared to guarantee the amount, a Liberty could be acquired for a down payment of only $125,000 with the balance to be repaid over a period of seven years at an interest rate of only 3 percent. Gratsos estimated that the market value of each ship was as much as $1.5 million.

Sophocles Venizelos, the Greek minister of finance, was in Washington negotiating a loan for the Greek government when the terms of the Ship Sales Act were made public. The US Maritime Commission required each country to stipulate how many ships it needed. Venizelos suggested the matter should be placed in the hands of the Union of Greek Shipowners, an organization set up by Manuel Kulukundis in the 1920s, which, like everything connected with the Greek shipping business, had moved to New York during the war. Onassis, who had never previously displayed any concern for this organization, now began to take a lively interest in its proceedings.

It was probably a strategic error. Manuel Kulukundis had canvassed the London and New York Greeks and had met with a disappointing response. The shipowners were dubious about the merits of prefabricated, welded ships. "At that time no Greek thought any ship was safe unless it was built in Britain," Kulukundis recalls. "They were wary about the Liberties. These ships will fall apart, they told me." Kulukundis determined that there were only enough purchasers for the Greek government to put in a request for sixty ships. Onassis went over Kulukundis's head to Venizelos with the suggestion that the bargain was too good to be passed over and that the Greek government should acquire "several hundred" ships. He also lobbied the Greek shipowners systematically at social gatherings and lunch dates, telling them forcibly that their excessive caution amounted to foolishness. His approach was anything but tactful. "Their quality is far superior to any of the ships you people ever possessed or ever dreamed of owning," he told them. The assertion, inevitably, was interpreted as a deliberate slight. The quality of Greek ships before the war had, it is true, often left much to be desired, but no Greek liked to be reminded of that fact, particularly by a relative newcomer to the business who had had the good fortune to survive the war with the bulk of his fleet in mint condition.

Nonetheless, Onassis's pitch was persuasive. A number of owners changed their minds. Stavros Livanos, for instance, put in a request for twelve Liberties. The feared world slump had failed to materialize, and the New York Greeks' previous mood of indifference gave way to a frantic scramble for new tonnage. Kulukundis increased the Greek quota to 100 ships. Even this was insufficient to meet the rising demand. A number of shipowners were disappointed, most notably Onassis, who was not allocated a single one of the thirteen ships he had requested. According to Kulukundis, Onassis's demand had never been seriously considered. "He was never concerned with Greek shipping. He wanted all his ships to fly the Panamanian flag. And, in any case, he had come through the war unscathed." The Liberties were being allocated to owners who had lost ships flying the Greek flag.

Onassis would not believe this simple explanation. He remembered that many of the upper-crust Greeks had originally responded to his campaign with derision—he was not a "real Greek," he was a Smyrnan, an Argentinian, a parvenu. Those slights had inflamed in him a sense of paranoia and resentment that was never far from the surface of his mind. Onassis became convinced that Kulukundis had personally dealt him out of his thirteen Liberties, and he decided to take revenge.

An opportunity arose the next year when the US government offered Greece seven 16,500-ton T-2 tankers. Onassis fired off a cable to the Greek government offering to take all seven ships. It was a direct challenge to both Kulukundis and to the established Greeks who were members of the shipowners union. Lest there could be any mistaking the intent of the message, Onassis tacked a preamble onto the cable in which he asserted that the expatriate Greeks had "never done anything for their government or their country."

Kulukundis retaliated with a tactfully worded cable to the Greek government. Onassis's request for the tankers should be considered on its own merits, but Kulukundis wished to lodge a formal protest about the "libelous implications" of Onassis's assertions. The Greek government got the point. When the T-2s were allocated, Onassis's name was omitted from the list of lucky recipients, although his experience in the tanker business should have made him a strong contender.

Once again, Onassis had been squeezed out. His frustration was compounded by a report from Costa Gratsos of a conversation with Kulukundis some days earlier. Gratsos had called to ask Kulukundis if he had received a copy of Onassis's cable, which was then making the rounds of New York Greek shipping offices. Indeed he had, Kulukundis had replied. "You should be ashamed of yourself," he had said. "It is terrible that you come from an old Greek shipping family and subscribe to slanders of this sort." Gratsos had protested somewhat disingenuously that the cable had nothing to do with him. "I can tell you wrote the cable," Kulukundis had replied. "Onassis would never draft anything in that style." Kulukundis later maintained that this remark was entirely innocent—he had merely wished to chide Gratsos, whom he had long regarded as a protégé. Onassis, however, interpreted it as another insult. He thought Kulukundis was implying that he was incapable of writing Greek.

In fact, Gratsos *had* written the offensive cable. He and Onassis had become more than close friends. Gratsos was still working for his uncle, Pericles Dracoulis, but he also received a yearly retainer from Onassis. He was the first person outside Onassis's immediate family to be drawn into the orbit of patronage that Onassis was in the process of creating. Gratsos, Onassis explained to an American friend, was "good with everybody's money except his own." But Onassis took care of that. Each Christmas he would sit down with Gratsos and pay off his outstanding debts. In later years Gratsos became Onassis's house intellectual, the only man in the Onassis entourage who could not only effectively execute the boss's orders but could also come up with new ideas. Much of the credit Onassis took for his innovations in fact belonged to Gratsos. Yet Gratsos did not mind. He enjoyed himself and was content to remain in his best friend's shadow.

Despite his family background, Gratsos was no more in awe of the Greek shipping establishment than was Onassis, and it was from a series of conversations related to Onassis's troubles with Kulukundis that the shape of their next joint project emerged. They had a lot of time on their hands, Gratsos recalls. "Ari would come around to my office and sit there for hours complaining about his failure to get ships. I don't know whose idea it was, but together we began to write a 'black book' of Greek shipowners. It was a wicked, muckraking book, frankly libelous, written more as a joke than anything else."

The joint effort reflected an attitude toward the written word, and particularly the journalistic written word, that they would retain in later life. "We twisted the facts when we felt like it. When we weren't sure of something we made it up." There were innuendos about harborside

74

sinkings of overinsured ships and jokes about the meanness of certain shipowners. Inevitably, the main butt of the "Onassiad" (as Gratsos, in punning reference to the *Iliad*, called it) was Kulukundis. Onassis claimed to detect a hereditary trait of stinginess in the Kulukundis family. Onassis cited in support of this theory the fact that Manuel's grandfather had been nicknamed "the Grabber, the man who got everything." The assertion was calculated to annoy Manuel since he himself had discussed the theory with Gratsos and Onassis, only to reject it. To the slur on the family name, always a potent form of insult among Greeks, was therefore added a second, no less offensive breach of the norms of polite behavior—the publication of a matter discussed in confidence.

To begin with, the black book was circulated in manuscript form to the New York Greeks, among whom it rapidly acquired a certain underground reputation. Kulukundis was not sent a copy. Gratsos and Onassis discussed the possibility of finding a publisher but perhaps wisely concluded that they would face some fairly considerable legal problems. They therefore took a blue pencil to the manuscript and planted the resulting twenty-five hundred words in *Atlantis*, a Greek-American newspaper published in New York, and in an Athens-based communist daily as an anonymous "Open Letter to Manuel Kulukundis." Kulukundis was distressed to see himself caricatured as an octopus enveloping the Greek shipping scene with his tentacles.

The bad feelings engendered by the open letter lasted until Onassis's death. Kulukundis routinely answered invitations to launchings of Onassis ships with the message, "If you wrote that letter, how do you expect me to come? If someone else did, just tell me and I will be delighted to accept your invitation." Onassis's silence on the question confirmed Kulukundis's low opinion of him; he was not, in all respects that mattered, a man of honor. Some years later, Kulukundis was dining at Le Pavillon in New York with Sophocles Venizelos when Onassis sent a note inviting them to his table. Kulukundis was reluctant to sit at the same table with Onassis, but he was persuaded to do so. "Onassis admitted to me that he had written the letter and that he had done wrong," Kulukundis recalled. "Still, in a way that was typical of him, he immediately took back the apology. He could not bear to be in the wrong."

The whole episode may have been petty, but it was not without significance. Up to the end of the war Onassis had seemed very much the modest and compliant new boy, eager to please his elders and be admitted to their informal club. After he had been cut out of the Liberty and T-2 deals, Onassis ceased to solicit, or even expect, favors from the New York Greeks. The virulence of his attack on Manuel Kulukundis is explained by the fact that, by common acknowledgment, Kulukundis was the leading light of that community; and Kulukundis was so deeply offended precisely because he was accustomed to deference. Onassis represented a newer, possibly harder generation of Greeks. He was, in Gratsos's phrase, a "new kid on the block," stridently asserting his individuality.

For Onassis's subsequent career, this assertion of individuality was of great importance. It renewed his sense of operating against odds, a factor which was at the root of all his entrepreneurial energy. More immediately, it drove him to finance his ventures without the protective assistance of the Greek government. Liberties were available to purchasers who did not have their government's backing—although the terms were inevitably less favorable—but Onassis was never particularly interested in them because they were dry cargo ships. According to Gratsos, he put in an application for thirteen Liberty ships merely to show that if the rest of the Greeks were going to have them, he would, too.

Onassis got his Liberties—and more important still, after some hesitation First National City Bank agreed to lend him 50 percent of the purchase price. The loan was by no means as generous as the ones the other New York Greeks had negotiated with the US government, but it was significant as a precedent since Onassis was the first Greek to buy ships with the money of an American bank. Though he was not aware of it at the time, he had his hand on the faucet from which his subsequent wealth would flow.

Onassis's life, public and private, was entering a new phase. He opened an office in New York at 80 Broad Street to handle his increasingly complex American interests. As managing director he selected Nicolas Cokkinis, a cousin of his friend André Embiricos. Cokkinis, though only just turned thirty, was already noted for his maturity and discretion. He provided the organization with a core of stability that freed Onassis and Gratsos from the drudgery of routine. The "family business" was now demonstrably too big for the social unit from which it had been created. Onassis's cousins, Nicos and Costa Konialidis, remained in charge in Buenos Aires and Montevideo.

Ingse Dedichen had long ago ceased to be important to him, and in 1946 she decided to go back to Norway. Onassis greeted her decision with an expansive gesture that appropriately closed their long and often painful affair—he placed the *Aristophanes* at her disposal. Ingse stocked up with all the delicacies that were still unavailable in Norway, becoming, as she put it, her own Marshall Plan. Not unnaturally, she felt bitter about the way things had worked out. "I had been the cement and the mortar of his fortune. I had been his companion, his confidante, his lover, his public relations agency and the person who taught him his manners. . . ." Now she had been phased out, like a ship for which he no longer had any use. Onassis took care of Ingse, as he did most of the women who crossed his path. She received an apartment in Paris, $35,000 in cash, and a monthly stipend of $500. She was advised by her New York friends to get a written agreement before she left, but she preferred not to.

Onassis was keenly interested in marriage when the war ended, but not with Dedichen. He had met the girl who was to become his wife three years before Ingse's departure from the scene—on Saturday, April 17, 1943, to be precise. On that day Onassis was first introduced to Athina Livanos, the younger daughter of Stavros Livanos, in the Plaza Hotel. Onassis was one of several Greek businessmen gathered in the Livanos suite. Some were talking ships, others were playing bridge. It was Livanos's favorite game, and he found no shortage of partners among those who sought his friendship and influence. At that time he was reputedly the wealthiest of the Greek shipowners living in New York.

Around 7 P.M. the dense masculinity of the occasion was interrupted by the entrance of Madame Livanos and her two daughters. The petite, blonde Athina, then fourteen, and the dark-haired Eugenie, sixteen, were solemnly introduced to each of the male guests in turn. There was no time for more than a few punctilious greetings before the ladies politely made their excuses and left. Tina hobbled through the social ceremony on crutches since she had recently broken her leg in a riding fall. This brief infusion of femininity had a profound effect on Onassis. He later immortalized the occasion by presenting Tina with a golden Alexander the Great coin inscribed with the legend: *Saturday 7 P.M. 17th April, 1943, T.I.L.Y.* The initials stood for Tina I Love You.

On Tina the effect of her first encounter with Ari was less devastating. She already had a quasi-romantic attachment to John Vatis, the son of a Greek shipowner, a boy close to her own age. But her most immediate ambition was to get off her crutches and back on a horse. In later life she told a reporter that she did remember the first meeting with Onassis but only vaguely. "To me he was just one of my father's friends, younger and better looking than most of them . . . nothing more." Pressed for

77

further recollections, she said, "My leg bothered me and I did not pay much attention to my father's visitors. But later Ari and I compared notes and it turned out that he was one of the two younger men—the other was called Stavros Niarchos—and he vividly recalled seeing me. It was, he said, the moment he fell in love with me."

Conoisseurs of the Niarchos-Onassis feud sometimes perceive its origins in that same evening. Niarchos, it appears, was also attracted to Tina and later, when he was divorcing Melpo, asked for an estimate of his prospects. He was told by Tina's father that she was "much too young to marry." Onassis, more presciently, bided his time and concentrated on wooing the girl before making any approaches to her parents. When ribbed by friends about his developing interest in the young schoolgirl, he would laugh off allegations of any serious intent—"Marry a daughter of Stavros Livanos and have him as a father-in-law? I'd rather jump out of the window."

Despite the difference in their ages the idea of such an alliance was by no means absurd. The attraction of a Livanos connection for Onassis is easily explained. It was not simply a question of wealth, though both Livanos daughters could expect the kind of dowry that would scarcely deter potential suitors. More important, particularly for men like Onassis and Niarchos, was the idea of ultimate acceptance by the Greek shipping community. The older members of its establishment described them patronizingly as "the Parachutists"—men who had dropped into their midst.

The Livanos pedigree was impeccable by even the most rarefied standards. The association with the sea stretched back to Stavros's grandfather, another Stavros and a simple sailor who plied a caique around the eastern Mediterranean in the early nineteenth century. The family was from the island of Chios, which had a special place in Greek history as the presumed birthplace of Homer.

The island was richer than most, and under the Turks the inhabitants enjoyed a status of qualified privilege. By tradition, Chios was the private property of the sultan's harem and was ruled by the sultana, his first wife. The wealthier inhabitants were allowed to send their children to school in Europe, and at one time most of the physicians with European training in the Ottoman Empire were Greeks from Chios. For poorer Greeks who wished to escape from oppressive reminders of Turkish domination there were only two ways out—through the sea or rebellion. During the Greek War of Independence seamen from Chios played an important part. The flagship of the Turkish fleet was burned by a raiding party operating from the island. Although mainland Greece achieved a form of independence in 1832 (under the protection of Britain, France, and Russia), Chios had remained under Turkish control. Its short-lived revolt had been put down with the utmost savagery, and thousands of its leading Greek citizens had been massacred.

Grandfather Stavros survived this perilous period, bequeathing to his own son, George, a love of the sea and a hatred of the Turks but little else. He died a poor man without ever achieving the dream of owning his own ship.

George Livanos was to realize it many times over. By the turn of the century he had become one of the first inhabitants of Chios to acquire a steamship—a 2,800-tonner originally built in Britain. Captain George sailed it with his eldest son, Michael, as co-captain and his second son, John, as mate. Soon his third son, Stavros, and fourth, Nicholas, were also initiated in the seagoing arts. It involved the family in the business, kept the wages bill down, and freed more money for the purchase of ships. By 1911 George Livanos had two steamships—one a 4,500-tonner —and several sailing ships. He finally handed over the seamanship to his sons and opened an office in Chios to direct operations of what had become a modest empire. The Balkan Wars of 1912–13 did nothing to impede its expansion. Chios was reunited with Greece, and Stavros returned from the wars ready to assume a more responsible role in the family enterprise. Shortly after the outbreak of World War I he was sent to London to open an office.

Stavros was a stocky, dark-haired young man of immense energy. In London his diligence and practical experience of ships made him an immediate success. Though his father insisted on a policy of cash acquisition, Stavros found ample opportunity to expand the fleet. In the early 1920s, when the postwar shipping boom collapsed, many Greeks who would not keep up their mortgage and loan interest payments went to the wall. The Livanos enterprise came through stronger than ever. Before Captain George died on Chios in 1926, he handed over the strategic direction of the business to Stavros.

Stavros Livanos married Arietta Zafirakis, the daughter of a wealthy Greek merchant. He was forty, Arietta fifteen. It proved to be a singularly happy marriage. He brought his young bride back to England, where all three of his children were born—Eugenie on August 11, 1926, Tina on March 19, 1929, and George on April 15, 1935. The Livanos life-style in London was comfortable without being in any way spectacular. Even among the hustling London Greeks, Stavros's dedication to work was regarded as a shade excessive. He was also notoriously close-fisted. The story is told of how a Greek sailor complained during the depression of the offered wage rate of one pound a month. Stavros is alleged to have reassured him with the thought that "maybe it's only a pound a month. But in a thousand months that would be a thousand pounds. If you saved your money, think of what you could do with a thousand pounds." But if Livanos was tight with his employees and acquaintances, he was not specially generous with himself. His tastes in food and clothes were simple to the point of mediocrity; his idea of gastronomic extravagance was sometimes to buy a few roast chestnuts; and he would walk miles to avoid taking a taxi. He rarely saw the necessity to think or talk about anything but ships though he did develop an enthusiasm for bridge and golf in middle age. Outside his working hours—which averaged a steady twelve hours a day—he was a family-centered man.

His daughters were strictly brought up. A chauffeur-driven limousine —Livanos's one concession to conspicuous consumption—took them to school every day from their home in Holland Park, West London. Family attendance at the Greek Orthodox church every Sunday was obligatory. After a while the girls were moved to Heathfield, a boarding school for young ladies in Ascot. They were taken to Chios on holidays and taught Greek and French, but they were most at home talking English with clipped, upper-class accents. At the age of ten, Eugenie launched one of her father's new freighters at West Hartlepool, but for the most part they were insulated from business concerns. Both were counseled to be thrifty and to have reverence for the value of money but without any real expectation that they would ever have to earn it. Neither learned to cook anything more demanding than a fried egg. Eugenie, to please her mother, displayed enthusiasm but little talent for playing the piano. Tina, who emerged as the more tomboyish of the two, was passionately fond of riding horses. They developed a closeness based on the singularity of their background that never deserted them in later life.

In 1940 Stavros Livanos moved his operation and his family to Montreal. The girls were sent to Villa Maria, a convent in the suburbs. Two years later they were again uprooted for the move to New York and the suite in the Plaza Hotel. Tina was sent to a school in Greenwich, Connecticut, to continue her studies; Eugenie went to Miss Hewitt's Classes, a fashionable New York establishment where the daughters of the rich were given their final coat of educational lacquer.

Both girls were attractive, and Tina showed signs of becoming a genuine beauty. Their upbringing, which the accident of war had rendered cosmopolitan, gave them an assurance beyond their years without destroying their childlike good spirits. Stavros Livanos can have had no worries about their being left on his hands even without the inducement of a dowry. On the other hand, he was not anxious to see them catapulted into unions that seemed unsuitable. His own experience of married life naturally inclined him to favor the attentions of older men— men who had established themselves—as candidates for his daughters' favors. Tina's schoolgirl crush on John Vatis was frowned on and declined in strength.

Onassis's courtship of Tina was a model of old world courtliness, flavored with élan. During the summer of 1945 they met frequently and informally in Oyster Bay, Long Island, where both Onassis and Livanos had seaside residences. Onassis favored the young girl with a bowdlerized version of his fascinating life story and yarned engagingly with her father. He cut a slightly paunchy but essentially dashing figure on his waterskiing trips around the bay. On one occasion he engaged Tina's interest by trailing a streamer behind his speedboat. It was emblazoned with the first mention of T.I.L.Y. "What does it mean?" asked Tina. Onassis told her.

Early in 1946 Onassis formally asked Stavros Livanos for Tina's hand in marriage. He was rebuffed, not because Livanos had anything against the suitor but because he thought that it was unseemly for his younger daughter to be married before her sister. Onassis said later, only half jokingly, "Livanos regarded his daughters like ships and wanted to dispose of the first of the line first." The rift, however, was short lived, and Tina's evident unhappiness at her father's decision led him to reverse it.

On December 29, 1946, *The New York Times* formally recorded the outcome among its reports of society weddings:

ATHINA LIVANOS BRIDE

Wed in Greek Cathedral Here to Aristo S. Onassis

Miss Athina Livanos, daughter of Mr. and Mrs. Stavros George Livanos of the Plaza, this city, and London, England, was married yesterday afternoon in the Greek Orthodox Cathedral to Aristo S. Onassis of this city and Oyster Bay, L.I., son of the late Socrates Onassis and the late Mrs. Penelope Onassis, of Athens, Greece. The ceremony was performed by Archbishop Athenagoros with the assistance of Father Euthimion.

The bride had a sister, Miss Eugenie Livanos, as maid of honor. Bridesmaids were Misses Nancy Harris, Andree Maitland, Janet Bethel and Joan Durand, all of this city. Beatrice Ammidown and Cornelia Embiricos were flower girls. Andre Embiricos was best man. A reception was given in the Terrace Room of the Plaza.

Tina was seventeen, Onassis was forty. Stavros Niarchos was notably absent as the guests assembled in the Terrace Room of the Plaza. Despite the fact that Onassis had been in intimate communication with Ingse Dedichen up to the date of the marriage, there seems no reason to doubt that he felt a powerful and genuine affection for his young bride. He and Dedichen had exhausted their reserves of passion. He was ready to start again and was keenly interested in establishing his own dynasty. He needed a son and heir. Tina naturally brought a less complex personality to the union, but it was totally engaged. "Greek marriages," she said, some years later, "are not infrequently arranged. It would have been the usual thing in my case, too. But my marriage to Ari was 'arranged' only by Eros, the god of love."

The honeymoon lasted two months. It started with a leisurely cruise down the inland waterways of America from New York to Florida, then proceeded to Argentina where the possible threat of the growing Perónist movement to Onassis's business interests worried him. All the same, it was an ostentatiously long honeymoon, a conscious statement of relaxed togetherness. Onassis, despite or perhaps because of the swiftness of his mental reactions, always succeeded in radiating an unhurried air. "My father never walks," said Tina, "my husband never runs." Spyros Skouras, who met them in Argentina, later recalled that "they made a splendid pair, so much in love!" When the honeymoon was over, they returned to New York and their first home.

Number 16 Sutton Square had been bought by Stavros Livanos for $460,000, cannily deeded to the specially created Tina Realty Corporation, and placed at the newlyweds' disposal. Onassis had reciprocated by spending as much again on decorating and remodeling the house. It was four stories high, overlooked the East River, and, unusual even for this most exclusive area of New York, had a garden. For a million dollars they had what was probably the most luxurious and desirable house in New York, but at the time Tina described it in quite matter-of-fact terms: "It is so tiny you can hardly get into the front door ... sometimes you think it is going to collapse any minute. When the cars go by [on East River Drive] all the candelabras rattle." In later years, in the mellowness of retrospect when it became clear that it had been the only home in the conventional sense they were ever to enjoy, she would see it as the lost love nest, recall that it was situated in a traffic-free cul-de-sac, and describe it as "a gem of a house . . . not very big, but I loved it."

One day in 1949 Onassis and Tina went to the Broadway production of *Bells Are Ringing*, which, like the later film version, starred Judy Holliday. When the curtain rose the couple caught their breath. "Do you see what I see?" exclaimed Ari. "Our house!" cried Tina. The set was an exact replica of their home: the same delicate French period furniture, the same patterns on the tapestries, the same expanses of marble, even the paintings were more or less the same as their own (Onassis had acquired a Renoir as the pièce de résistance). Upon their return to Sutton Square all was revealed when a servant "confessed" that, one day when the couple had been out, the set designer had dropped in. Explaining that he wanted to gain a firsthand impression of how New York's superrich lived, he asked whether he could look around. The servant, seeing no harm in it, had allowed him to do so. The designer had apparently decided that he need look no further and had reproduced the Onassis house's interior in toto.

He had not been the only person who had concluded that Onassis's life-style merited imitation. In November 1947, Stavros Niarchos, having wooed and won Tina's sister, Eugenie, took her as his third wife and moved in to 25 Sutton Place, just around the corner. It was a larger establishment, and Niarchos proceeded to decorate and furnish it in a manner calculated to outshine his in-laws.

Onassis soon had the heir he desired. On April 30, 1948, a son was born to the couple at the Harkness Pavilion, New York City. He was christened Alexander, after Onassis's uncle who had been martyred by the Turks and after Alexander the Great.

Shortly after the birth of Alexander, Onassis announced that he was thinking of moving his base of operations to Europe and suggested he and Tina go over to find a house or two. The brief interlude in which Tina had a house which was definitely a home—and a husband who regularly came back to it—was already over.

Soon—in addition to the house in Montevideo (which Tina had never seen), the permanent suite in the Plaza Hotel in Buenos Aires, and the Sutton Square house—Onassis had become the owner of a seaside villa on the outskirts of Athens and an apartment on the top floor of 88 avenue Foch in Paris and had rented the Château de la Croë at the tip of the Cap d'Antibes. The gleaming white château—with its private beaches, twenty-five acres of pines, tennis courts, swimming pool, and a drawing room roof which opened to let in the sun—numbered King Leopold of Belgium, King Umberto of Italy, and the Duke of Windsor among its previous occupants. Niarchos followed hard on Onassis's heels, taking the nearby Château de la Garoupe, which the Onassises had briefly rented but never really lived in. When the Château de la Croë had become vacant, they had decided to live there instead. A housekeeper, two cooks, two "maîtres d'hôtel," three maids, a washer-woman, a scullion, two chauffeurs, a butler, a valet, a lady's maid, assorted gardeners, and, later, two governesses for the children were needed to keep the palatial establishment ticking. Shortly after they had acquired it, Tina returned to New York and gave birth to their second child on December 11, 1950. It was a girl, and she was named Christina. Onassis, whose international commuting was now assuming a frenzied pattern, was there for the occasion. Then the family went to winter in Saint Moritz, but Onassis did not stay long. "When I went skiing," he recalled, "it was mainly on my backside." He did not like it. Besides, Niarchos, who for once had installed himself somewhere before the Onassises, was also there. And he was a rather good skier.

7
OTHER PEOPLE'S MONEY

IN THE SUMMER OF 1947, Eva Perón, the young and beautiful wife of the president of Argentina, left her country for a tour of Europe. The visit was designed to combine state business with pleasure. Among the people accompanying her on the journey was Onassis's old friend, Alberto Dodero. When the party arrived for a short stay at the Hôtel de Paris in Monte Carlo, old acquaintance was renewed—Onassis and Tina, who were holidaying in the south of France, were also among the luncheon guests at the hotel.

Onassis told Dodero of his admiration for Juan Perón's consort. Although they had never mixed socially, they had previously established one intriguing connection. During World War II, the Greek immigrant community in the Argentine had collected a large number of food parcels to send to Greece when the country was under Nazi occupation. But Argentine authorities had refused permission for the food to be sent on the grounds that the country was neutral and that such benevolence might be interpreted by the Germans as a hostile act. Onassis, who was visiting Buenos Aires at the time, was consulted about the problem by his fellow Greeks. His solution was to have Eva Perón's photograph displayed on all the parcels. He then went to see her and formally suggested that it would be a pity to deprive the Greeks of the pleasure of possessing her photograph. Permission to send the parcels was granted.

After their lunch at the Hôtel de Paris, Onassis asked Dodero to arrange for him to meet Eva in more intimate circumstances. The necessary introductions were made, and Onassis was invited to another lunch with the Argentinian leader's wife at her holiday villa at Santa Margherita on the Italian Riviera. Eva received Onassis privately with unfeigned enthusiasm. They made love, and she cooked him an omelet. Onassis showed his appreciation by writing out a check for $10,000 as a donation to one of her favorite charities. He later described the omelet as tasty but "the most expensive I have ever had."

Onassis's boldness as a suitor of eminent ladies was equaled by his audacity in the sphere of high finance. What initially distinguished him from the other Greek shipowners was his uninhibited use of long-term credit. He thrived by ignoring the conventional wisdom summed up by the phrase "cash and ships," preached most assiduously by his father-in-law, Stavros Livanos. Among certain Greeks, that "wisdom" had become more than a prescription for sound business—it amounted to a sort of obsession. For them, banks were malign institutions conspiring to lure the unfortunate into evil habits of living beyond their means. Livanos carried this attitude into later life, when bankers, in the words of his insurance broker, Jimmy Stewart, were "jumping out of the window in their eagerness to lend to him."

Onassis's key speculation was made in the fall of 1947 when he first made contact with the Metropolitan Life Insurance Company in New York and began a series of discussions that led to his borrowing a staggering $40 million for the construction of new ships. His basic conception was to circumvent the hazards of borrowing by getting the financial institutions to lend long against the security of a charter with an oil company that lasted as long as the term of the loan.

The implications of this idea were revolutionary. In effect, the institutions were lending not to Onassis but to the oil company. The charter fee paid by the oil company could be "assigned" to the bank without passing through Onassis's hands. There was little or no risk involved since the credit ratings and reputations of some of the largest and most profitable oil companies in the world were substituted for Onassis's word and ability to make payments. It was, Onassis later explained, like lending money to someone who proposed to rent a house to the Rockefellers. It did not matter whether the house "had holes in the roof or was gold-plated; if the Rockefellers had agreed to pay the rent, that was good enough for anyone lending money on the house."

86

Henry Hagerty, then the president of Metropolitan Life, and Walter Saunders, his legal adviser, were impressed by this exquisite formula. Hagerty liked Onassis's grasp of "conservative economics," while Saunders was dazzled by his salesmanship. "I got the feeling," says Saunders, recalling his first encounter with Onassis, "that here was a guy who could sell refrigerators to the Eskimos. But I also felt that he had everything totally worked out."

Onassis had been propelled in their direction by officials of the First National City Bank, from whom he had recently borrowed to acquire his Liberty ships. First National had explained to Onassis that it was not their practice to lend long against charters but that the insurance world might view his proposal differently. Insurance companies were constantly looking for viable long-term loans. Their experience during the depression had established the rule that, no matter how bad things became, people rarely canceled their insurance policies. There was no such thing as a run on an insurance company. And the companies were flush with money as a result of the wartime boom. In 1948, Metropolitan Life had $250 million in funds to dispose of on behalf of its clients. Hagerty and Saunders explored the reactions of the oil majors to Onassis's concept and found it almost entirely favorable.

There were hardheaded reasons why the oil companies desperately needed Onassis—and others like him—and were prepared to go to extraordinary lengths to facilitate the growth of independent tanker fleets. All the major companies had been taken by surprise by the scale of the postwar recovery and the increasing dependence of Europe on imported oil. Since they all had massive, long-term capital expansion plans in the areas of exploration and refining, they were looking for areas where expansion could be checked, or at least reduced, by bringing outsiders into the scope of their operations. Exploration, refining, and marketing were clearly not the kind of operations that could be offered to outsiders. Transport was another matter. It, too, required massive expansion that could not be engineered on the cheap—two supertankers, for instance, could cost as much as a sizable refinery. To solve their capital problems in the area of transport, the companies were prepared to pay what Onassis later described as "philanthropic" guaranteed charter rates to encourage the development of independent fleets. Onassis wittily likened the plight of the oil companies to that of "any Wall Street executive who throughout the pre-Christmas rainy and snowy days would be only too glad to play the philanthropist with the cab drivers. All he prays is to get the cab."

Onassis got his loan from Metropolitan Life and passed the formula on to his brother-in-law. Soon afterward Hagerty and Saunders were doing big business with Stavros Niarchos. Both Onassis and Niarchos had found the financial mechanism that would put them in the front rank of Greek shipowners. "The oil companies made the Greeks," says Hagerty. "We wouldn't have lent them a nickel without that connection."

Onassis pioneered that connection, but he did not, as he later claimed, invent the basic idea. The credit for that belongs to Daniel Ludwig, a Michigan-born businessman whose skill is only matched by his reticence. He never talks to reporters. In the 1930s, after many years spent operating unsuccessfully on the fringes of the American shipping world, Ludwig conceived of "creative borrowing," or OPM (other people's money) as it was subsequently called, almost by accident.

Ludwig wished to buy a dry cargo ship and convert it into a tanker. When the Chemical Bank refused to loan him any money for the purchase and conversion, he had the bright idea of offering another ship, which he owned outright, as collateral. His idea was simple and ingenious. His original tanker would be chartered to an oil company with the proceeds "assigned" to the bank. In five years' time Ludwig would own both ships. He could then recharter the vessels and use the income they provided as repayments on another, larger loan.

Ludwig then took the process a step further. Instead of borrowing to purchase old ships, he went to the banks and suggested they loan him money so that he could build new ones. The loans were to be of a deferred payment variety, under the terms of which the banks stood to retrieve little of their money until the ships had been built and chartered out. Ludwig was now in a position to offer better collateral. He had paid off the mortgages on his other ships, which were still chartered and therefore producing increased profits. This new loan was therefore backed by his own considerable reserves as well as by those of the oil companies to which he proposed to charter the vessels. In bankers' jargon, this refinement of OPM became known as "two-name paper" since a bank would possess double collateral on its loan, in each case from a company of some standing.

Ludwig continued to play the market, chartering his ships long and steadily increasing his fleet to satisfy the demands of the oil companies for long-term charters. The profits he made were reinvested outside the shipping business, which became a sort of cash machine servicing his other and increasingly diverse operations in real estate, mining, jungle reclamation in Brazil, and saltwater conversion in Mexico. By 1976 he

88

was in control of one of the world's largest private multinational corporations, second only to the one controlled by the late Howard Hughes. His fleet of 5.6 million tons was larger than the ones controlled by the Niarchos and Onassis organizations, but it occupied a less important role in his organization. Ludwig made his money in shipping, but he was not, as the Greeks interpreted the term, a real shipowner.

The distinction may seem pedantic, but the Greek definition of what constituted a shipowner was based on a real perception of the tanker market that had evolved after the war. Although the oil companies had gradually built up their fleets, they still carried only about 50 percent of their own crude oil, leaving the rest to operators like Onassis, Niarchos, and Ludwig. What distinguished the two Greeks from Ludwig was their use of the different types of charter arrangements they could make with the companies, particularly in what is known as the "spot market."

The spot market developed as a result of the oil companies' natural reluctance to charter more tonnage than they could use, but the dramatic increase in oil consumption meant that their calculations were usually highly conservative. Consequently, they often found themselves short of ships and were prepared to pay a premium for charters on short notice. Thus the spot market offered potentially higher rewards than the "time charter" market favored by Ludwig but with a certain element of risk. Rates were dependent on how much tonnage was available, and the oil companies went from one independent operator to another in search of the best bargain they could find. In a bad market, the oil companies would squeeze the operators with the full knowledge that they would in their turn be squeezed in a good market. However, there were limits to how far the oil companies would go since it was not in their interest to destroy those on whom they depended.

Playing the spot market demanded a high degree of nerve. A successful operator needed to know not just how many ships his competitors had and whether they were available, he also had to have a grasp of how the market was likely to move. It was no use, for instance, making a great deal of money from one "spot charter" if the ship was subsequently idle for six months.

Being gamblers, Onassis and Niarchos were instinctively drawn to the spot market. It was for this reason that, as soon as they had paid off their initial long-term, charter-linked mortgages, they devised a different method of borrowing money from the finance houses. Instead of financing ships on an individual basis, they negotiated "packages," borrowing whatever they could on the basis of the current cash situation of their whole fleet. It was, in the words of Walter Saunders, "altogether a more sophisticated operation." They could order their ships and decide how to play the market when they were completed.

Like most successful gamblers, Onassis and Niarchos were prudent. For the most part they kept 50 percent of their fleets on long-term charters, another 20 percent on three-year charters, and committed only the remaining 30 percent to the hazards of the spot market. But in the postwar years their mutual feelings of competitiveness pushed them into greater risks than they would otherwise have taken. Their rivalry was more significant in this respect than in their claims and counterclaims as to who had the larger fleet at any specific time. They judged themselves successful to the degree that they were able to keep up with each other. In the process, and with a certain degree of luck, they made each other's fortunes.

Both Onassis and Niarchos began their building programs in the United States at the Bethlehem Steel yards at Sparrows Point, Maryland, and Quincy, Massachusetts. Onassis built one 18,000-ton tanker and another five 28,000-tonners, while Niarchos built one 18,000- and one 28,000-tonner. Onassis's ships had bright green decks. He personally conceived of the distinctive sloped funnel design. A ship, he explained, had a personality, just like a woman, and its funnel could be compared to a hat or a nose; the most minute cosmetic adjustments imparted a sense of rightness to the ensemble. Niarchos was less fanciful, but his stubby red funnels contrasted effectively with his ships' sober black hulls. There was a contrast, too, in the symbolism evoked by the names given to each vessel. Onassis's generic "Olympic" suggested striving and recalled his increasingly tenuous links with the mother country. Niarchos's "World," as in *World Glory* and *World Enterprise,* was a hopeful evocation of global reach.

The press in those days was still excited by the sight of ships being launched, particularly large ones. Niarchos and Onassis already held differing views on the whole question of publicity. Niarchos's celebrations were quiet affairs, marked only by the presence of an important banker and a few members of the local business establishment. Onassis wanted and got something more. When the *Olympic Games* was launched and fitted, he sailed her up to New York and gave a party for the national press on the boat's fantail. He appeared in person, dressed in what looked to reporters like Army-surplus khaki trousers, and gave a brief and rousing account of his impoverished youth. "Look where I am now," he continued. "I am married to the daughter of the richest

90

shipowner in the world and I am going to build bigger and better tankers." It was the classic Horatio Alger story, and the reporters were happy with their copy.

The vessels sailed into a shipping boom of staggering proportions. The harsh 1948 winter boosted the price of oil in the United States from $1.50 to $4.00 a barrel, and tanker rates soared accordingly. The Marshall Plan was well under way, and the flow of oil, raw materials, and manufactured goods to Europe continued well into 1950. Tankers, as Onassis pointed out, had become "a sort of San Francisco gold rush."

It was in this auspicious climate that Onassis went back to Europe to negotiate the next phase of his business expansion. American shipyards were getting increasingly expensive as a result of high labor costs and full order books. Onassis's American backers, however, were happy to lend money for ships that would be built outside the United States, and he began looking around for yards capable of meeting his ambitious requirements. He found what he was looking for amid the ruins of postwar Germany, which he and Tina visited in February 1949.

The trip was his first experience of the destruction and suffering wrought by the war. He arrived by sleeping car in Bremen wearing a lightweight vicuna overcoat. Tina was swathed in mink and was trailing a set of Louis Vuitton luggage and several hatboxes with Paris labels. The Germans greeted the Onassis party like apparitions from another life, staring at them openmouthed, following them out of the station to the main square, where a battered car awaited them. During the drive to Hamburg, Onassis was uncharacteristically subdued. It was only later that he recovered his aplomb sufficiently to tell Kurt Reiter, the shipping executive accompanying them, that the Germans were not the only people to have suffered as a result of a war. "You got off lightly compared to the Smyrna Greeks," he said repeatedly. It was, as Reiter perceived, only partly the gesture of sympathy it seemed to be. Onassis was genuinely horrified by postwar Germany, and he was dealing with it in the only way he knew how—by relating it to the horrors of his own experience. But there was also an element of braggadocio about his sympathy —he never liked to be outdone in any respect.

The party was first exposed to the hazards of German rationing at the Kaiserkeller restaurant in Hamburg and then driven to the A. G. Weser shipyard, which was little more than open space, having first been leveled by Allied bombing and then been stripped of its remaining machinery by the Russian army. "How can you build ships here?" Onassis asked. "You haven't even got a damn crane." The yard should be totally rebuilt on an adjoining plot, he suggested. Although he had no experience as a shipbuilder, he was sufficiently impressed by the possibilities to consider doing the job himself. While snowflakes drifted through the holes in the office roof, Onassis scribbled on a piece of brown paper and came up with the sum required: $2 million. It was a grandiose idea, later scaled down in the hard light of convenience.

Some of the other yards—notably Bloehm and Voss and the Howaldt Werke—were in better condition. Onassis was introduced to Adolph Westphal of the Howaldt Werke at Kiel. Together they produced detailed plans for the conversion of a T-2 tanker into a whaling ship. The *Herman T. Witton* was dispatched to Kiel, the yard was put into operation, and some months and $4 million later she went to sea again, this time as the *Olympic Challenger.*

Onassis was impressed by the speed with which the conversion had been completed and the deferential treatment he had received in Germany. It was natural, therefore, that as he expanded his fleet he should increasingly turn to the German yards. He put Reiter on his payroll and sent Nicolas Cokkinis to Hamburg to learn about tanker construction. In 1950 negotiations began with the German yards, not without some difficulties. Reiter was startled to discover that Onassis knew next to nothing about the minutiae of ship construction and had a decidedly original approach to doing business, at least by German standards.

Meetings characteristically took place in two select Hamburg restaurants, Ehmke's and the Halali, to which the cream of German industry was summoned. Not only was Onassis vague about his plans to begin with, he was also exasperatingly inconsistent. He would pin the Germans down to a lower price than they had offered by the end of the evening and then call them next day to renegotiate the agreement. He was obsessed with fine print. Reiter once spent four hours with him debating a single word in a contract which he later jettisoned in the process of negotiations. It was part method and part compulsion. He was always suspicious. "When you have been through what I have been through in South America," he told Reiter, "you know that everyone is out to swindle you."

The compulsion was acted out in the solitary "midnight strolls" he took after every negotiating session, when he methodically went through every detail of the previous day's business. To the fury of everyone concerned, he would invariably decide that some clause or some word would have to be changed. The Germans, wisely bearing with Onassis's eccentricities, were rewarded with the biggest single order they had ever

92

received. From the New York banks $100 million was funneled into three yards for six 20,000-tonners from Weser-Hamburg, ten 21,000-tonners from Howaldt-Kiel, and two 45,000-tonners from Howaldt-Hamburg.

Onassis became a local hero. He was credited with giving the decisive shove to the German recovery and introducing the dry martini to Hamburg. In Hamburg his favorite haunt was the Tarantella, a rather sober nightclub where businessmen gathered for earnest conversation and innocuous entertainment. By this time Onassis was drinking heavily. Reiter recalls that the evenings would routinely end in shouting matches, usually between Onassis and one of his captains, George Coutsouvelis, who refused to defer to the boss on the question of who knew more about shipping. They would sit face to face abusing each other in vivid Greek, much to the consternation of the stolid German clientele. Onassis was never asked to leave. His importance already carried with it the prerogatives of princely immunity.

He developed what Reiter considered an eccentric interest in details, poring over the records of various ships for hour after hour. He once wished to know why one ship used twice as many light bulbs as another. He became furious with a captain for not having purchased enough eggs to last the whole voyage at one Middle Eastern port where they were cheap, instead of paying a few cents more per dozen later in the trip. On one of his midnight strolls he conceived of another grandiose scheme —he would buy the Howaldt-Hamburg shipyard. Reiter was opposed to the deal even before the German government imposed the daunting condition that the work force should not be reduced for ten years. Onassis commissioned dozens of feasibility studies, only to lose interest when they were accomplished. Sometimes it seemed like business was a game, entertaining for Onassis but exhausting for his underlings. Yet, unlike shipowners who had an enduring interest in ships for their own sake, Onassis spent little time in the yards while they were being built.

It was a different matter with the launchings. Hamburg, Bremen, and Kiel were cities with an old maritime tradition, and a launching was an occasion for celebration in which the entire population participated. In the early fifties it was also a means of expressing thanks for the fact that the community had been rebuilt from the ashes and rubble. Onassis was treated with near feudal respect, and he responded in kind. It was Reiter's job to organize the celebrations, but Onassis took over the selection of commemorative gifts and mementos—lighters, scarves, brooches, and lace handkerchiefs embroidered with the symbol that

93

graced his funnels and a rendering of the ship which was to be launched.

At the dock gates the crowds gaped at the celebrations—women in minks, men in long overcoats and wide-brimmed hats. There were diagrams describing the new ship's vital statistics and speeches by local worthies and national politicians. The dockworkers were, at Onassis's request, given two hours off to watch the ceremonies with their wives from specially built stands.

For the launching of the *Tina Onassis* at Hamburg on July 24, 1953, Onassis brought his wife and the children, Alexander and Christina. The 45,000-ton tanker, then the largest in the world, had cost over $6 million. Tina declined the honor of launching the ship named after her. Instead, Christina, only two and a half years old, managed to guide the champagne bottle in the direction of the ship's hull while Alexander, age five, pressed the button which sent her down the slipway into the water.

Onassis was forty-seven years old but showed no signs of slowing down. His corporations, according to the leading American business magazine, *Fortune*, had an asset value of around $100 million. Only Niarchos could keep pace with him, though many other Greeks had managed to enrich themselves by imitating his methods. Even Livanos made a belated discovery of the joys of credit by adopting the borrowing habits of his sons-in-law, though when acquaintances remarked on the fact, he responded with all the virulence of a man whose closest and guiltiest secrets have been made public. The wonder is that he managed to do without bankers for so long, and the explanation lies in the fact that he lived so long. His fleet, unlike those of Onassis and Niarchos, was built "brick by brick." He continued to express disbelief in the reality of "paper fortunes" until late in life. Shortly before his death in 1963, he was still traveling around the world, inspecting his ships while they were being built. When Jimmy Stewart asked him why he bothered to do so, he explained that he "liked to look at the whole thing." Shipowners, he went on—with his eye on his two charismatic sons-in-law—were now nothing but "speculators or intermediaries of banks."

It was difficult for the older Greeks to be generous about the success of newcomers to their ranks. But the resentment of Onassis and Niarchos had been replaced by a grudging respect. As a direct consequence of following their lead, Greek shipowners had acquired a new status in the shipping world. By 1953 they had more than replaced their war losses. They controlled the third largest fleet in the world, bettered only by such traditional seafaring powers as the United States and Britain. More important, perhaps, was the fact that they had finally succeeded

94

in effacing the stigma previously attached to Greek shipping. Much of the 13 million tons in their possession were, if not like new, at least in relatively good condition.

From being the pariahs of the international shipping community they had come to occupy a relatively privileged place. Their relationship with the banks, insurers, and charterers—whether oil companies or clients in the dry goods business—was transformed. Instead of being obliged to hustle for business, in unequal competition with more reputable fleets, Greek shipowners could enjoy the spectacle of others bidding for their favors.

Onassis's preeminence in this development was not much appreciated outside the shipping magazines and the business columns of newspapers. He was accessible to the press but only as a method of furthering his business interests. At this stage of his life the pursuit of fame for its own sake was not one of his passions. He did not employ a public relations officer, and the press, for its part, saw no particular reason to treat him as anything more than one successful businessman among a host of others.

All this changed in the summer of 1953 with the announcement that Onassis had acquired control of Monaco's Société des Bains de Mer et Cercle des Etrangers—literally, the Sea Bathing Society and Foreigners' Club. The Société (SBM, for short) owned or controlled a great deal of Monte Carlo, including the celebrated casino, the Hôtel de Paris, and the magnificent gardens. The event was irresistible to headline writers. Onassis was catapulted to celebrity status overnight as "The Man Who Bought the Bank at Monte Carlo." He was to claim that the publicity had come as a complete surprise, that he had never sought fame but had had it thrust upon him. There appears to be some truth in this assertion. What is also true is that once fame had arrived, he adored it.

It was Onassis's sentimental claim that he had set his heart on buying up Monte Carlo from the moment he first saw its beautiful skyline from the deck of the ship carrying him to a new life in Argentina. He visited there for the first time in the 1930s with Ingse Dedichen and was utterly captivated by its atmosphere. Nostalgia undoubtedly played its part, but there were sufficient hardheaded business reasons for the decision to buy into Monte Carlo twenty years later. Onassis urgently needed a base of operations where he could centralize the empire which now sprawled from Buenos Aires and Montevideo to New York and London. Paris was getting very expensive and was too far away from the Riviera, whose climate Onassis found very pleasing. It would be even more pleasing if

95

it could be combined with the benevolent fiscal climate of Monte Carlo. Monaco offered the convenience of minimal personal and corporate taxes, and those could be eliminated altogether with the agreement of the French government. It had strategic advantages, too. Situated between the great ports of Marseilles and Genoa, Monaco lay about halfway between the Middle Eastern oil fields and Onassis's biggest consumer markets.

The takeover of the SBM was effected with Onassis's customary blend of stealth and panache. It originated over lunch with the French banker, Charles Audibert, at the Café de l'Opéra in Paris. Onassis happened to mention that he was thinking of moving his headquarters down to Monte Carlo. Audibert pointed out that SBM shares were then quoted very cheaply on the Paris Bourse. Scribbling on his napkin, he worked out that Onassis could acquire control for some 800 million francs— about $3 million. That was roughly the value of each of his T-2 tankers, Onassis said. Monte Carlo was certainly worth the price of one of them. He asked Audibert to start buying on his behalf through various front men to avoid forcing up the price.

The strategy did not escape the notice of Monaco's monarch, Prince Rainier III, but it was not distasteful to his own designs. The SBM had become moribund, and Rainier welcomed the prospect of an infusion of new blood—and money—into the principality. Onassis had his blessing. By the beginning of 1953 Onassis owned about one-third of the issued capital, which was enough, with Rainier's personal holding, to move in. It took just forty-eight minutes for Onassis's representatives to take over at the SBM's annual meeting in the summer. Onassis put in his own man, Charles Simon, as administrator and agreed to appoint Rainier's confidant and mentor, Pierre Rey, as president. The Old Sporting Club on the avenue d'Ostende, overlooking Monte Carlo's lovely harbor, became the headquarters for Onassis's controlling company, Olympic Maritime.

Within a week of the Monte Carlo takeover, Onassis flew to Hamburg for the launching of a ship which was to become the emblem of his glamorous new life. The yacht *Christina* was the only ship for which Onassis ever felt a deep affection that transcended the balance sheet. Whenever Onassis sought confirmation of his status in international society, he could take comfort in the *Christina*. The guests who cruised on her gave Onassis an index of his own standing. If Monte Carlo had made him a public figure, the *Christina* invested Onassis with the ability to sustain the role.

She had started life as the *Stormont,* a 2,200-ton Canadian frigate. Onassis bought her from an American racetrack owner for $50,000, then spent over $4 million more converting her at the Howaldt-Kiel yard. He took an obsessive interest in every detail of the work. The Germans, who were accustomed to Onassis's comparative indifference to the construction of his tankers, occasionally found this trying.

Onassis had hired a distinguished German professor of architecture, Caesar Pinnau, to redesign the yacht. His elegant sketches presented a brilliant white vessel with lovely rakish lines flowing back from a high, slender bow. Howaldt's naval architects were delighted at the chance to build something infinitely more beautiful than oil tankers but were perturbed to learn that Onassis wanted deck space for two airplanes, several speedboats, a hydrofoil, and a sailboat in addition to the usual lifeboats. Some fine calculations were required to insure the *Christina*'s stability. The striking bow also presented problems. It had to be made in one piece and welded on to the original frame before it was smoothed and given a dozen coats of paint. The first time Onassis saw it, a few tiny ridges could just be made out on the metal skin. He ordered that it be scrapped.

The same attention to detail was applied to the *Christina*'s interior. Onassis insisted on being able to step *down* from the sunken bath in Siena marble in the master stateroom (an exact model of one in a palace in ancient Crete). The presence of main deck stanchions below the bath made that difficult, so the entire floor was raised to provide Onassis with a descent of a few inches.

The long-suffering Kurt Reiter was generally on the receiving end of Onassis's complaints. Inspecting the ship with him one day, Onassis noticed a few knots in the wooden screening that concealed the metal of the interior bulkheads. Reiter explained that this was just preliminary screening which would eventually be covered with oak paneling. Get rid of it, Onassis shouted, take it all down.

Onassis had insisted on so many gadgets that every corner of the ship was crammed with electronic equipment. A vast air conditioning plant was squeezed in between decks. A sophisticated alarm system, triggered off by open portholes or a sharp rise in temperature, was to be monitored from the wheelhouse. Another circuit maintained the sea water in the outdoor swimming pool a few degrees below air temperature so guests would feel pleasantly refreshed when they dived in. Onassis's desire to have somewhere to dance on the main deck considerably taxed the ingenuity of Howaldt's experts. In the end, they designed the bottom

97

of the pool—which was decorated with fine mosaic scenes from Greek mythology—so it could be lifted electronically to the level of the deck to provide a dance floor. With a forty-line radio-telephone system and all the latest radar gear, the *Christina*'s power requirements were so great that four diesel generators ran virtually nonstop just to keep her ticking. An insulation specialist had to be flown in from Berlin to soundproof them.

The rooms were decorated with immoderate luxury. The vast open fireplace in the smoking room was inlaid with lapis lazuli at a cost of four dollars a square inch. A pair of doors leading to the main deck were finished in antique Japanese lacquer. Quantities of marble and mosaic were used in the nine double guest cabins, each of which was named after a different Greek island. The French artist Marcel Vertès was personally commissioned by Onassis to do four large oil paintings on the panels of the dining room. Their theme was the four seasons, showing the Onassis family in a variety of allegorical poses: spring had Alexander and Christina frolicking on a grassy lawn; winter showed Tina as a pretty skater whirling on the ice. Among the more traditional works were El Greco's *Madonna and Angel* hanging behind Onassis's ornate desk, some exquisite Russian icons, and a scattering of other expensive objets d'art.

Onassis acknowledged to Kurt Reiter that the *Christina* was a rich man's toy, but he took it very seriously. He was infuriated by any suggestion that Niarchos's graceful three-mast schooner, the *Creole*, was somehow more of a real yacht (and, by extension, that Niarchos was the real sailor). A benevolent employer in other areas, Onassis was deeply unforgiving of sloppiness on the part of the *Christina*'s crew. He would fire men without hesitation where the skipper might have settled for a dressing down. "You could smash a $20,000 speedboat to pieces and not a word would be said," a former deckhand told us. "But spit on *Christina*'s deck and you were out of a job."

Shortly after the *Christina*'s launching, Onassis heard that the West German chancellor, Dr. Konrad Adenauer, was anxious to meet the man who had done so much to revive his country's shipping industry. Onassis met the chancellor at the Palais Schaumburg in Bonn and, with Reiter acting as interpreter, made a graceful impression. The conversation ranged over a variety of topics, including Onassis's interests in Monte Carlo. The chancellor recalled that it was almost fifty years since he had first visited Monte Carlo. The memory was fresh because it had been his honeymoon and because he had gambled a gold twenty-franc piece

98

and had lost it. Onassis retrospectively gilded the occasion by having his staff find a 1904 gold twenty-franc piece and a good jeweler. The coin was mounted on a letter opener which was inscribed with a capital *A* and was sent to Dr. Adenauer with Onassis's compliments. The chancellor was touched.

By now the basis of Onassis's wealth seemed so secure that he could indulge in risks that were beyond the conception of his peers. He came to view his business as a vehicle for his instinct for adventure rather than as a source of continuing security. Yet the basis of his fortune was more fragile than it appeared, and within the space of two frantic years Onassis managed to drive himself to the brink of bankruptcy.

January of 1954 found Onassis in Purfleet, England, to celebrate the return of the *Tina Onassis* from her maiden voyage to Kuwait. The guest list reflected his commercial potency, and the party from London included the chairmen of Lloyd's and Britain's Big Five banks. The captain's quarters were decorated with mimosa flown in from the south of France. It was a fragrant start to the year but not much of a portent. Before the year was out, Onassis would suffer his first serious public reverses in all his main areas of operation—shipping, oil, and whaling. In the process, he would become not just the most famous but also the most notorious Greek in the world.

8
UNDER ARREST

ON THE AFTERNOON of Friday, February 5, 1954, Onassis lunched at the Colony Club, a fashionable restaurant in midtown Manhattan. He was embarked on his first dry martini when his office called with the information that a federal marshal had arrived with a warrant for his arrest. The main charge against him was conspiracy to defraud the United States of America.

The occasion developed out of a side of Onassis's postwar activities that received rather less publicity than his grandiose shipbuilding ventures. The problem for him and a number of other Greek shipowners arose out of the 1946 Ship Sales Act, which governed the disposal of surplus tonnage after the war. Several of the more desirable classes of vessel were specifically unavailable to foreign buyers on the grounds that they were of strategic importance. The T-2 tankers, sturdy 16,500-ton welded ships, were in this category. Onassis applied for twenty such tankers in 1946, only to be turned down. As was usually the case, the setback made him more anxious to get his hands on the ships.

The story of how he went about circumventing the citizenship requirements can now be pieced together from documents recently made available by the US Department of Justice. His first move was to consult a number of eminent New York law firms which gave him the sort of advice he was looking for. The Ship Sales Act merely laid down a requirement for American ownership. Not only did it neglect to say in any great detail how the ownership should be exercised, it also did not specify whether the ships also had to be *operated* by American citizens. As Onassis was beginning to find out, this was a crucial distinction. As far as the question of profits was concerned, it was of very little importance who owned a ship. Onassis's entire fleet was mortgaged to the institutions which had financed his building program. All he really owned was the air over his smokestacks. And yet the tankers were making comfortable profits on his behalf.

The solution was to find a number of American citizens who would acquire a majority holding in the companies in which the T-2 tankers were registered without being excessively concerned about the nuts and bolts of ship chartering. Onassis characteristically went straight to the top to find his "quiet Americans," as they were subsequently called. Joseph F. Casey, a former Democratic congressman, put Onassis in touch with Edward Stettinius, former secretary of state under Roosevelt and Truman and first US delegate to the United Nations.

Posterity has not been kind to Edward Stettinius. He is remembered, if at all, for the manner in which he was summarily fired. He had been in the habit of calling President Roosevelt each morning to ask what he should do. When he adopted the same procedure with Truman, the new president responded somewhat differently. "If you don't know what to do, then I'd better find someone else who does." In 1947 Stettinius was out of work. He had made his career as a highly successful executive of United States Steel, and he had been brought to Washington, along with a number of other industrialists, to form part of the burgeoning military-industrial complex that dominated wartime Washington. Now he was anxious to combine some not too strenuous business enterprise with the honorific posts that habitually fall into the laps of elder statesmen.

Onassis met Stettinius at the latter's elegant country estate in Virginia. He admired Stettinius's mementos from Stalin and Molotov. Stettinius's white hair made a profound impression on him, as did the older man's courteous and deferential manner. As reported by Onassis, the after-lunch conversation had a touchingly delicate quality. "Ari, I consider you as a most enterprising man in international business. I want you to do some thinking and come along with some ideas enabling me to make an honest dollar." The "honest dollar," Stettinius added, was not primarily for himself. He had taken care of his family, but he had

101

a number of friends whose "total devotion to patriotism" had most regrettably led them to neglect their own interests. Stettinius also dwelt on another of his current hobbies. As a good, anti-imperialist Democrat, he had become concerned with the future of the tiny West African state of Liberia and had set up the Liberian Trust Company to promote American investments there. He sought Onassis's views on the possibility of making Liberia into a maritime country. "I feel I must do something for the Liberians," he concluded.

After "a few words of modesty and humbleness" Onassis left, promising to think the matter over. He undoubtedly already knew what conclusions he would arrive at. Stettinius and the Liberian ministers were subsequently feted at Sutton Square, where a suitable strategy was discussed. Shortly afterward the US oil companies and banks agreed to accept Liberia as a flag of convenience. The Liberian flag became the cornerstone of the business edifice Onassis created to insure that he operated with minimal interference from regulatory bodies while paying next to nothing in taxes.

But Stettinius was less certain about the merits of some of Onassis's other proposals. "Millions of honest dollars," Onassis assured him, would come his way if he would just "take his US citizen friends, form a Panamanian corporation, and apply for forty [T-2] tankers." Onassis was prepared to raise $20 million—25 percent of the purchase price. The rest would come from the US government. "You will end up with the ships paid for in five years . . . and anybody will be willing to buy the whole package from you," Onassis suggested. Stettinius seems to have been taken aback by the scale of Onassis's suggestions and the breezy, hustling style in which they were delivered. "He couldn't believe it," Onassis later explained. "Neither could his associates. It sounded almost crooked. I don't blame him."

Although Stettinius and his associates did eventually purchase five T-2 tankers, Onassis was not admitted to their syndicate. Stettinius informed Onassis that he was "obviously a man of great wealth and large fleets" and thus had no need for any additional dollars, honest as they might be.

Onassis was undeterred by this rebuff. If Stettinius was reluctant to be involved in a venture with him, there were undoubtedly a great number of American citizens, admittedly less eminent ones, who would be only too delighted. Accordingly, at Onassis's instigation, on September 27, 1947, United States Petroleum Carriers was duly incorporated in the state of Delaware with American nationals holding the majority of the stock. Over the next two years the company acquired, in its own name or in the names of various wholly owned subsidiaries, nineteen vessels—ten T-2s, seven Victory ships, and, for good measure, two Liberties.

Onassis's participation in the deals came to light in a circuitous fashion as a result of a Senate investigation into the corruption that surrounded the Truman administration in its last days. Senator William Fulbright was interested in the activities of the Reconstruction Finance Corporation (RFC), a body set up by Herbert Hoover to pump government money into ailing industries during the depression. Lately, the RFC had been notably free with the taxpayers' money, lending to a number of racetrack and casino operators. In the course of his attempts to throw light on the profligacy of the RFC, Fulbright summoned a number of lobbyists to his hearings, including Joseph F. Casey.

He was an amiable witness. Casey justified the $75,000 commission he had received from the Atlantic Basin Iron Works of Brooklyn by blithely remarking that it was a small sum of money compared with the $250,000 he had made on an investment of $20,000 in surplus tankers. Having whetted the committee's appetite, however, he refused to go into any details of the deals on the perfectly legitimate grounds that shipping did not fall within the jurisdiction of Fulbright's committee.

More than anything, it was the timing of Casey's revelation that was disastrous. Since June 1950 the United States had been at war in Korea. The Republican majority in Congress was looking for ways to embarrass the Truman Administration, and the issue of profiteering was an attractive one. There was also the question of the uses to which the recycled mothball fleet had recently been put. Onassis had anticipated that the issue might be raised. In August 1950, he fired off the following cable to the Department of the Navy: "As president of Olympic Oil Lines Panama SA owners of five newly built supertankers by Bethlehem Steel Company and administering disponent of various other tankers . . . I respectfully request the honor and privilege for the duration of present abnormal conditions and in case of need to dispose of our resources as if they were of United States ownership." He offered the United States "all courtesies and facilities free of charge" should the government wish to send a whaling party to the Atlantic. If there was anything he could do to help the war effort, he was ready for action "no matter how humble or risky or dangerous." He received a polite pro forma letter regretting the United States could find no use for his fleet or his person and thanking him for his interest in the US Navy.

103

Nonetheless, he persisted with his attempts to ingratiate himself with the US government, and in October of 1950 he once again offered to make his tankers available. "Please allow me to inform you that I am not soliciting any business," he informed Vice Admiral Cochrane. "As a matter of fact I find it very difficult to satisfy our daily customers." Onassis followed this up with a still more fulsome letter expressing his willingness to "enlist as a humble sailor" should the wartime emergency demand it. On the basis of his record in the previous war, it is safe to assume he had no such intention. Onassis rarely adopted a humble posture gratuitously. On this occasion his motives were transparent. Government investigators were unraveling the threads of the surplus tanker scheme that Casey had so carelessly alluded to the previous year. They had already got to Onassis. Thomas Stakem, a Department of Commerce official, had spent the past six months going through Onassis's books. Onassis was naturally apprehensive at this awkward turn of events. He reminded Vice Admiral Cochrane of "the words of one of your good friends who happens to be one of the most popular shipbuilders in America, 'I prevented the dismantling of the Bethlehem Sparrows Point shipyard.' . . . I hope and wish that if no encouragement is offered to foreigners like me, at least the peace of mind that the pioneering struggle requires will not be impaired."

His pious wish was not fulfilled. The whole question of the surplus ship sales was formally reopened in March 1952 by the Senate Subcommittee on Investigations, whose members included Senators Joseph McCarthy, Karl Mundt, and Richard Milhous Nixon. The senators were given a lengthy and confusing account of precisely how some of the ships had been disposed of. In the course of their inquiry they were intrigued to discover that a special investigator appointed by President Truman to sniff out government corruption had been instrumental in setting up a corporation to enable a group of Nationalist Chinese to acquire a couple of tankers. Light relief was provided by the testimony of a lady called Olga Konow, who described in halting English how she had become a tanker owner. "It was the greatest day of my life," she said. The press gave her a nickname—"Oilboat Olga."

But once again it was Casey who was the most useful witness. He was happy to acknowledge the $3 million profit his group had made as honest speculation. Risk, he asserted, was at the heart of the free-enterprise system. He was proud to be associated with Edward Stettinius and the other eminent men who had formed part of his syndicate. He switched to the attack, accusing the committee of chauvinism. "I would be less

104

than frank," he said, "if I did not catch somewhere in the room the atmosphere of a raised eyebrow at the mention of Chinese or Greeks or British citizens." Casey, along lines suggested by Onassis to Stettinius, had acquired his five tankers by means of an American corporation and chartered them to a Panamanian one. They had then been "rechartered" to an oil company. It was a simple tax-saving device.

In 1950 he had sold both companies, one to the Delaware Tanker Corporation, incorporated in the United States, the other to Greenwich Marine, a Panamanian company. A majority of the shareholders in the US company were, it is true, US citizens. But the Panamanian company, which did the chartering and hence acquired the bulk of the profits from the ships, was owned wholly by Stavros Niarchos.

Niarchos had also managed to buy nine T-2s through the US–based North American Shipping and Trading Corporation. His own holding in the company amounted to only 40 percent, but his sister, Mrs. Andrew Dracopoulos, who had been born in the United States, made up for this deficiency. Her share effectively gave Niarchos a majority holding in the company.

Not surprisingly, the senators were considerably confused by the spiderweb of organizational charts displayed before their eyes. Few of them had any familiarity with the elaborate fashion in which business is sometimes conducted by the shipping fraternity. But the implications of the investigations were relatively simple. A group of eminent US citizens, mostly Democrats, had made a great deal of money out of what had been government property. The money had come to them tax free. And it looked as if the ships had ended up in foreign hands at a time when the United States was at war and might well need them. Senator Mundt expressed the senators' gut reaction. "I am getting just a little bit weary of having to sit here day after day trying to protect the taxpayers' interests and getting smeared in the process by witnesses who try to engage in invective and scurrilous remarks. If you can stop it at the source," he said turning to Thomas Stakem, the official who had organized the investigation, "congratulations and orchids to you."

Initially, however, it was the rambunctious anticommunist senator from Wisconsin who made the running in the tanker investigations. Joe McCarthy's attendance at the hearings had been sporadic; he had no time for the intricacies of ship finance. He was only interested in whether the foreigners who had acquired the US vessels were using them to undermine national security by trading with the Reds. He was at the height of his power in 1952, and the Department of Defense moved quickly to ascertain whether his allegations had any foundation. The department discovered that twenty-eight of Livanos's ships had at one time or another visited communist ports. Kulukundis was also named as a lesser offender. There was nothing illegal about this—the ban on trading with communist countries applied only to US ships. Allies, including Britain, still traded behind the Iron Curtain. But the Greeks were based in the United States, and thus de facto dependent on US policy. Livanos valued his privacy next to his life. Joe McCarthy's interest in his business augured badly for the future.

Stakem's report on Onassis's role in the surplus ships affair was forwarded to the Justice Department, where it gathered dust for some months. The delay was easily explained. The country was in the midst of an election campaign, and the Democrats were not eager to proceed with a number of cases that had been drawn to their attention as a result of Republican investigations into corruption in the Truman Administration. Portions of the Stakem report were, however, leaked to the press by an impatient official. When a Republican president came to the White House in January 1953, the Justice Department stirred into action.

Stakem's findings concerned the circumstances in which United States Petroleum Carriers (USPC) had acquired a number of surplus vessels either in its own name or in those of wholly owned subsidiaries. In particular, the report dwelt on the elaborate way in which the company's shares had been traded and the mysterious personnel changes that had occurred during the first months of its existence. The combined effect of these changes was to draw the strings of the company's operation into the hands of Aristotle Onassis behind an ostensibly all-American front. USPC had gone on to acquire some eight other corporations controlling nineteen ships. Of the total of $35 million that had gone into USPC, $21 million had been provided by Onassis. Of the remainder, about $8 million came from US government mortgages.

Stakem uncovered a similar pattern when he examined the way in which the ships had been chartered. On February 20, 1948, the SS *Arickaree*, one of the original T-2s USPC had acquired, was chartered to the Socony-Vacuum Oil Company for five years at two dollars a ton. Subsequently USPC "rechartered" the ship to another Panamanian company of Onassis's for a period of ten years at one dollar a ton. The original Socony-Vacuum charter then reverted to a subcharter between Socony-Vacuum and the Panamanian company. The oil company got the same service for the same money as before but the arrangement had felicitous consequences for Onassis. The purpose of this move became apparent when the investigators developed a hypothetical balance sheet for the *Arickaree* under the original corporate setup and compared it with the actual one. On an annual revenue of $396,000 the device had saved $80,000 in US taxes. USPC, of course, received a charter fee from Onassis's company, but it was barely enough to meet its mortgage payments—its net profit under the new arrangement was $8,680, of which only $4,400 went to Onassis's partners. Under the old order, they would have received $69,000. Onassis, of course, received the lion's share of the profits tax free through his Panamanian corporation—a total of $198,000.

To begin with, the Justice Department was dubious about its chances of success if it proceeded against Onassis. There was the problem of the time which had already elapsed since USPC (or Onassis) had acquired the ships. If the transactions outlined in Stakem's report were indeed illegal, it seemed Onassis was safe since the statute of limitations had already expired. Then, too, there was the inherent difficulty of defining in legal terms what constituted "control" of a corporation. The Ship Sales Act of 1946, on the basis of which the sales had been made, was deceptively simple. It stated that a controlling interest in the companies must be owned by US citizens. Onassis had clearly been careful to comply with this stipulation—that was the explanation of the complex series of sales of USPC stock. But the act went on to define the ways in which it might be considered to have been violated. Among them was the eventuality that control of the company was "conferred upon or permitted to be exercised by any non-citizen." That, it seemed, was what had happened in the case of USPC.

There was another, still more vexing factor affecting the cases. The Maritime Administration had unloaded many of its surplus ships in the most trying circumstances. At the height of the demand for ships it was difficult to process the many requests. In this bazaar atmosphere, some officials skimped on the question of the legality of what they were doing. But one maritime commissioner forcefully resisted this impulse. In response the Justice Department's general counsel had produced a memo approving in general terms the notion of selling to corporations of which a substantial minority of stock was foreign controlled. It was because of this that the department's attorney to whom Onassis's case was first passed reluctantly recommended dropping proceedings, although he made it clear that he did not agree with the original opinion.

A further complication was provided by the appointment as attorney general of Herbert Brownell, Jr., a close personal friend of the new Republican president, Dwight Eisenhower. As a New York attorney, Brownell had previously given advice to clients about the Ship Sales Act. One of them had been Manuel Kulukundis, who had acquired a number of surplus ships in a manner that was currently under investigation by the Justice Department.

Another team of investigators thumbed through Onassis's books in search of additional irregularities that would strengthen the existing case. They soon found them. In 1950 Onassis had played fast and loose with the rules of accounting in his last application for ships through Victory Carriers, a wholly owned subsidiary of USPC. The company's cash position had been bolstered by a four-day infusion of funds from his brokers to meet the US government's criteria for applicants. The investigators decided that that was a fraudulent practice designed to conceal the dummy status of Victory Carriers. It conveniently fell within the statute of limitations and, grafted onto the earlier findings, could form a basis for a conspiracy case against Onassis, his syndicate, and his companies. A grand jury was impaneled in March 1953 to assess the evidence.

Its proceedings took place against a lively backdrop of public interest in the Greek fraternity. Senator McCarthy moved to the offensive again with the announcement that his committee would shortly investigate the whole question of trade between the Eastern and Western blocs. As usual he gave demagogic warning of his findings before the committee heard the evidence. At least ninety-six ships which the United States had sold to foreigners were engaged in a "blood trade," carrying strategic materiel to the Iron Curtain, where it was being used to "kill Yanks in Korea." Like most of McCarthy's actions, the style in which the charges were delivered was more important than their substance. The US government had already taken a number of measures that made it improbably difficult for the Greeks to trade with the communist bloc. But in the cold war atmosphere, whipped up by McCarthyism, a presumption of guilt could be as damaging as a conviction.

None of the Greeks was eager to appear in the spotlight of the McCarthy committee—not even Onassis, who had had no dealings with the communist bloc. Once again he sent a plaintive telegram to the Justice Department. "I am proud to claim," he said, "that I am the only owner . . . who spontaneously volunteered his ships to the American government having no other obligations of duty than those to my Christian faith and principles whose trustees on earth I consider to be the US of America." He went further than pious expressions of loyalty, offering his services as an honest broker with "sound ideas" as to how the Greeks could satisfactorily be brought into line.

His assistance was not required. Kulukundis and Livanos both traveled down to Washington to meet with a young and hawkish Robert Kennedy, then working as a McCarthy staffer. Kennedy was brief and to the point. The committee knew some Greeks had been trading with China; besides, they had some "other dirt" on the shipowners. It was a naked threat. Kulukundis and Livanos were happy to fall in line with the committee's suggestions. The result was a "secret pact" in which Kulukundis and Livanos agreed to stop trading with the Reds. In return, McCarthy implied that those Greeks who assented to the "pact" would not be examined in the hearings he planned to hold on the question of foreign sales in general.

McCarthy then proceeded to upset the Eisenhower Administration by announcing to journalists that his diplomatic foray would have "some of the effect of a naval blockage . . . and should hasten the day of a victorious and honorable conclusion of the Korean War." It was one thing for McCarthy to be harassing the Democrats with his witch hunts, another thing for him to be meddling with foreign policy when a Republican occupied the office of president.

The State Department dismissed the deal as "phony." Harold Stassen, head of the Mutual Security Administration, accused McCarthy of blackmail. The situation became so tense that Vice President Nixon moved in as mediator, arranging a "working lunch" between McCarthy and Secretary of State Dulles. Between the tomato juice and ice cream a communiqué was drawn up, lacking only the formality of red ribbon and sealing wax. Both parties conceded that foreign relations were "in the jurisdiction of the chief executive." Both, however, felt that McCarthy's initiative had been "in the national interest." The breach in the Republican ranks was temporarily healed.

McCarthy's move, however, like many of his other feats of public "exposure," prompted a craven government response in private. The Justice Department files reveal that one of its most senior officials was visited by two officials from the CIA and the Defense Department within a week of McCarthy's announcement of the "secret pact" with the Greeks. At this meeting the status of the surplus ships cases against Onassis and Niarchos were discussed in terms that had little to do with the simple requirements of the law. The visiting officials suggested that the government might seize the US ships they had acquired and threaten

109

"to tie them up." This would, they argued, "force all the Greek owners to comply with US policy." Pressure, in other words, might well be placed on Niarchos and Onassis, and their cries of pain would be more effective than the senator's diplomatic initiative.

Both Onassis and Niarchos, oddly, suffered from the delusion that they were in some way cat's-paws of their father-in-law, Stavros Livanos, whose ships had traded fairly extensively with Iron Curtain countries before the US government began to take umbrage. After hearing the CIA case, the Justice Department official expressed his conviction that, on the current evidence, any move to seize ships would be improper unless it could be ascertained that Niarchos and Onassis had in fact traded with the Reds.

Yet another investigation was set in motion. Onassis came out clean, Niarchos only marginally less so. The FBI found that a decrepit tanker of his had, indeed, passed into the hands of the Polish government and had been used to move kerosene to Korea, but Niarchos denied any personal knowledge of the transaction. The CIA plan had to be abandoned.

By the fall of 1953 Onassis was in the curious situation of knowing that the US government had instituted some form of legal proceedings against him but being uncertain of their precise nature. The grand jury had worked its way through the entire series of transactions by which foreigners had acquired ships, but the indictments it had returned remained sealed. This was because many of the people named—Niarchos and Onassis included—were out of the country. At the same time, ships were now being "seized" on a lawful basis. Each time an Onassis ship docked in the United States, a customs official would inform its master by letter that the ship was "under seizure." A few hours later a federal marshal would appear on the scene to post a "letter of attachment" on the ship's bridge—a time-honored means of representing a litigant's claim on a vessel. The captain was sworn in as a deputy marshal and allowed to continue with his duties. The US government paid the crew at the previously established rate and retained the ship's profits in the hands of a specially designated "shoreside custodian" pending the resolution of the dispute. In effect, the government was operating Onassis's fleet on his behalf.

Inevitably, the existence of a number of indictments did not remain a secret. An enterprising newspaperman was present when Allen Krouse, the government attorney dealing with the case, called to register the indictments in the clerk of the court's book. The news trickled back along the shipping intelligence network, eventually reaching Onassis and Niarchos. Both men were initially advised to do nothing and stay out of the United States. Livanos, out of concern for the family name, persuaded Spyros Skouras, head of Twentieth-Century Fox, to go to Washington to make some inquiries. The Justice Department was not communicative. It was only after Niarchos had dispatched an English lawyer, L. E. P. Taylor, on his behalf to Washington that the situation was clarified. The Justice Department was not prepared to discuss the future of the impounded ships until Niarchos had "submitted himself to US justice." The implication was clear—there was a criminal case as well as a civil one.

It was at this point that Onassis decided to move. For him the whole affair remained very simple, in spite of the cartloads of evidence which had accumulated in the Justice Department. He was never concerned with legal niceties. The thrust of the whole investigation—a matter of ascertaining whether he "controlled" the ships—seemed too obvious to quibble over. It was an uncontested fact that the companies were owned 51 percent by Americans. Beyond that, there lay the question of what constituted personal honor. A cardinal point of the moral code to which Onassis claimed to subscribe was that a bargain, once made, was always kept. It was a matter of self-preservation as much as self-respect. Onassis frequently modified verbal agreements so much that it could be said he had actually broken them, but he rarely broke signed contracts. And yet the US government appeared to be doing precisely that. It had sold surplus ships to USPC and now seemed to want them back on the grounds that the terms of the contract had been unfavorable. The fact that vessels in private hands had yielded revenues of over $50 million and an operating profit of $20 million was no business of the US government. Onassis, in short, felt victimized.

His response showed commendable moral courage. On Monday, February 1, 1954, he flew into New York, expecting the worst. To begin with, he was pleasantly surprised. He passed through customs unchallenged, installed himself in his office, and held a meeting with his lawyers. After three days the sense of anticlimax had exhausted his patience, and he sent the following telegram: "Honorable Herbert Brownell, Jr., Attorney General of US Department of Justice. I wish to inform you that having arrived from Europe on Monday night I place myself at your disposal during my visit for any information you or your department might care to have."

Next day, the federal marshal arrived at his office to take him into

111

custody. On receiving the news at the Colony Club, Onassis promptly phoned his lawyer, Edward J. Ross. Ross complained to the marshal, contacted the local sheriff's office, and promised to deliver his client to the district court in Washington.

The following Monday, Onassis flew to Washington accompanied by his legal entourage. Scores of reporters saw Onassis stride into the office of Leo Rover, US district attorney, with a serious expression on his face. He was asked for his particulars, photographed from all angles, finger-printed, and committed to jail in the company of a group of Puerto Ricans who had allegedly tried to bomb Congress the previous day. It was only a formality; ten minutes later, after he had pleaded not guilty and bail had been fixed at $10,000, he left the courtroom.

At least as far as the law was concerned he was no longer a free man. Onassis felt personally insulted. He had come with the intention of resolving the dispute as one power dealing with another on personal terms, and he had been rebuffed. He returned to New York, where, with Costa Gratsos's assistance, he composed an angry defense of his role in the surplus ships affair. He represented his interest in the US mothball fleet as the result of his personal indebtedness to the United States and his response to Stettinius's request. "We rarely think of psychological effects though our whole existence is based and depends on them," he said. He contrasted his fate with that of a number of Americans who had made huge profits out of tankers, yet only he—the outsider, the client, the "young Greek"—was being prosecuted. It seemed as if he was being made into a scapegoat. "Whose fault is it? Who is responsible for creating such an artificial demand by hoarding said tankers?" he con-cluded. "Who else but the Administration? When such artificial de-mand is created . . . could favoritism, influence, or otherwise be avoided? Better late than never, thank God, that someone broke the ice and this huge pipeline began moving for the good of America and her dependent friends. Indictment or not, I remain proud of what I have done."

He did not forward the document to his accusers. Perhaps its composi-tion had been an end in itself, a way of letting off steam. More likely, his lawyers advised against it on the grounds that it might prejudice his case. But his anger spilled over into a series of telephone calls and cables to Washington. His desire to "talk things over" was complicated by the Justice Department's insistence that the two proceedings against him were being handled separately. The criminal one was nonnegotiable. However, Warren Burger, the assistant attorney general in charge of civil proceedings, who had carried out the tortuous and time-consuming program of ship seizures, was ready to start talking. Onassis was de-

112

lighted and launched into a long self-justification on the telephone, but Burger interrupted him. "I'm sure you have good reason to be proud of it," he said, "because $20 million profit in two and a half years is a great earnings record."

When they met face to face in Washington, Onassis immediately set the tone of the subsequent negotiations. "Mr. Burger, what is the ransom?" he inquired. It was a move designed to secure Burger's agreement on the basic principle that the criminal and civil cases were interdependent and that a speedy resolution of the one would lead to a more sympathetic attitude toward the other. "Ransom," Onassis later explained, meant "recapture of your freedom. Release out of a certain position that circumstances put you in. It used to happen to the best people. Kings used to take kings and pay ransoms." Burger laughed and suggested the figure of $20 million might be appropriate.

Then, in Onassis's words, "the horse-trading began." Burger's position was weakened by the fact that Onassis now had no more use for the ships than the government itself. They had already served their main purpose, producing a 250 percent profit in their seven years of service. Now they were almost ready for the scrap heap. But Onassis was still meeting the mortgage payments on $800,000 of the original purchase price, an income which compared favorably with the one the US government would receive were it to resell the vessels. And Onassis was employing US seamen, always a sensitive point at a time of some difficulty in the US Merchant Marine. Onassis made the most of the leverage he possessed. "Mr. Burger," he said, "if I had done all this in England or some other country, I would have been knighted. Here I am indicted."

Burger relented somewhat, conceding that the "ransom" should be determined not by the size of Onassis's profits but by the current market value of his twenty ships, then around $12 million. The solution bore even less relation to the merits of the government's case than his original suggestion, a measure of how far Onassis's extralegal approach had prevailed. But Burger had not reckoned with the dizzying fluctuations of the shipping market. Soon after his original undertaking, the market slumped twice, bringing the fleet's worth down dramatically. After another round of negotiations, both parties finally agreed on the sum of $7 million. Niarchos, meanwhile, negotiating in absentia through his lawyers, settled at a cost of a little under $5 million. Several of the corporations in which he had an interest entered guilty pleas to technical infringements and were modestly fined. The charges against him personally were dropped.

The criminal case against Onassis was looking distinctly the worse for

113

wear. An internal Justice Department memo, dated August 8, 1955, indicated the government's pessimism about its chance of success. Most of it dealt with what were termed the "weak spots" in the case. A case against members of the Casey group had already been dropped. The central problem in many instances was that the US maritime authorities often seemed to emerge with less credit than the potential defendants. Although the investigators contended the case against Onassis was "much stronger," they also had in mind a recent verdict acquitting Manuel Kulukundis in a similar case.

The end came on December 21, 1955, in a flurry of legal activity and a decorous press release from Warren Burger. "It was all dressed up to look like a government victory," recalled Edward J. Ross, Onassis's lawyer, "but even they knew we had won." Onassis was not only allowed to keep his American ships, he was also permitted to transfer them to a flag of convenience in return for a commitment to build more ships in America and operate them under the US flag. The $7 million fine was not as onerous as it appeared to be since Onassis was allowed to spread the payment over several years. The "reorganization" of his American interests prescribed by the settlement was little more than a confirmation of the status quo, with the qualification that the Justice Department, rather than Onassis, would choose "the quiet Americans" who sat on the boards of his American companies.

As far as Onassis was concerned, the Justice Department's decision to drop the criminal charges against him in return for a series of technical guilty pleas on the part of his corporations merely confirmed his original low view of the government's motives. He was a free man again, and to celebrate his release he switched to an obscure brand of whisky called King's Ransom.

9
WHALES TO THE
SLAUGHTER

THE MAIN-DECK BAR of the *Christina* was a popular meeting place for guests at the end of a leisurely day's cruising in the Mediterranean. Perched on high stools covered with a soft, snowy white material—the skin of the scrotum of a mature whale—the beautiful and the famous could steady themselves on a handrail made of the purest whale-tooth ivory, delicately engraved with scenes from the *Iliad* and the *Odyssey*. Their feet might conveniently encounter footrests made from the teeth of a sperm whale.

It did not require an especially alert guest to perceive that whales and whaling meant something special to his host, something apparently more vivid and romantic than the routine transportation of oil around the world. Those prompted by an instinct to please would ask him about it and be rewarded by a rich vein of reminiscence.

Whaling, Onassis would observe, was real gambling for the highest stakes. A fleet owner could make or lose as much as $5 million in a single season. Storms, icebergs, fog, sudden changes in commodity prices— almost anything could ruin the gamble. There was, he implied, something elemental about whaling: man against nature's leviathans was a raw, bloody business. It also involved competition with men operating one of the toughest commercial cartels in the world. Onassis knew because he had taken them on, beaten them at their own game, and survived to tell the tale. The fact that Onassis's postwar whaling enterprise produced the best-documented cases of illegal slaughter on record was never part of his edited reminiscences. As far as it went, Onassis's story was true—it was just not the whole truth.

It was certainly an exceptionally rugged business. Whaling had traditionally been dominated by one or two nations for long periods with a few eager competitors surviving on the fringes. Norway had seized the lead from the United States at the beginning of the twentieth century by developing the grenade gun to replace hand-thrown harpoons, and she had stayed in first place despite a strong challenge from Nazi Germany. Hitler had ordered high priority for building a whaling fleet in an attempt to make Germany self-sufficient in the supply of animal fats. The Norwegians maintained their lead largely because of the unrivaled quality of their native gunners, the quirky prima donnas who could make or break an expedition. Furthermore, a law passed in 1934 forbade Norwegians to work for foreign whaling companies; those gunners who did were deprived of their citizenship.

In the immediate postwar years, Norway held onto her dominating position. All the other big fleets—British, German, Russian, Japanese— had suffered badly in the war, losing most of their floating factories, the heart of any expedition. Norwegian losses had also been serious, but several factory ships had survived, four in good working order. The Norwegian fleet was back at sea in 1945 and doing better than ever. The huge demand for animal fats from the shattered economies of Europe helped push the price of whale oil up to record levels. The average price per ton was running at more than $360 compared with about $130 before the war, and some catches were selling for as much as $480 a ton.

Even when the Russian and British fleets returned to the hunting grounds, using factory ships taken as war reparations from the Germans, the demand for whale oil remained well above their combined catching capacity. The Unilever Group, far and away the biggest single customer on the market, could take everything that was offered, primarily for use in the manufacture of margarine. Unilever effectively determined the world price of whale oil—along with trends in the market for vegetable oils which were also used in margarine production—and was happy to deal with new fleet owners since it increased competitive pressures on the Norwegians. Onassis observed that, despite bitter protests, Norway had been unable to prevent the return of Japan to the whaling business. The Japanese venture was sponsored by the United States in an attempt to reduce the costs of postwar occupation.

116

Father and mother. Socrates Onassis was a successful merchant, a pillar of the Smyrna Greek community, and a strict disciplinarian. Penelope Onassis died when Aristotle was six. From Onassis's own collection.

The destruction of Smyrna, September 13, 1922. When the Turks captured the city, the Greek quarter was set on fire and its population massacred. The Onassis family lost most of their money and all their property. Those who survived fled to mainland Greece. Aristotle emigrated to Argentina the following year.

The consul. Onassis made his first fortune dealing in tobacco. At the age of twenty-six, he was appointed deputy Greek consul in Buenos Aires. According to an FBI report, he used his position to obtain substantial sums of money at official rates, which he then resold on the black market.

Onassis and Ingse Dedichen on the Ariston, *his first tanker. He originally met Dedichen, the daughter of a leading Scandinavian shipowner, on a cruise from Argentina to Europe.*

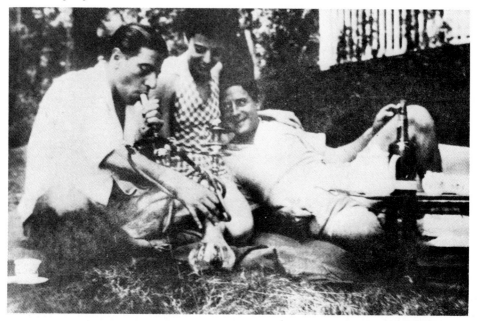

Onassis, Stavros Niarchos, and Melpomene, Niarchos's second wife, Long Island, 1944.

Stavros Livanos, patriarch of Greek shipping.

Athina (standing) and Eugenie, Livanos's daughters. Onassis married Athina in 1946; Niarchos, after obtaining a divorce from Melpomene, married Eugenie in 1947.

Go-betweens. Spyridon Catapodis (left), who helped arrange and later undermine Onassis's Saudi Arabian deal; Robert A. Maheu (right), the former FBI man who assured its failure.

The witness. Onassis was indicted on charges of fraud in connection with the US surplus ships he had acquired. The charges were dropped, but in 1958 he appeared before a Congressional committee to justify his style of doing business. The congressmen were charmed and baffled.

Money talks. J. Paul Getty and Onassis in afterdinner conversation. Onassis persuaded Getty to pose for the benefit of an aspiring photographer.

Moby Aristotle. Slicing up a sperm whale for processing aboard the Olympic Challenger. Onassis's fleet was attacked by the Peruvian navy and hounded out of business by its Norwegian competitors. But while it lasted, his whaling career was lucrative.

The chatelain. Onassis and Tina in the grounds of the Château de la Croë, near the Cap d'Antibes in the south of France. The château contained fish-shaped, gold-plated bath taps. Onassis rented it from 1950 until 1954, when Niarchos bought it.

Family man. Tina, Alexander, and Christina with Onassis at the top of the Christina's gangway. In the background is the port of Monte Carlo, where Onassis acquired a majority share of the company controlling the casino. For thirteen years the principality was the center of his business operations and the focal point of his social life.

The Christina *was moored in the prime berth in Monte Carlo harbor. Onassis bought the former Canadian frigate for $50,000 and spent over $4 million making her into the most luxurious yacht in the world. The ship was his home. Below, the* Christina's *library, with a portrait of his daughter, after whom the yacht was named, above the wood-burning fireplace.*

A section of the Christina's dining room, with a seating capacity of twenty-two. Below is the yacht's swimming pool. Onassis's desire to have somewhere to dance on the main deck was ingeniously resolved. The pool—which was decorated with a fine mosaic scene depicting the Bull of Minos—could be drained and its bottom raised to deck level to provide a dance floor.

Tina and Onassis take the floor at a gala in the Casino de Monte Carlo.

Alexander Onassis and Sir Winston Churchill aboard the Christina. Sir Winston was a regular guest. "I enjoy living on your yacht," he told Onassis, whom he once described as "a man of mark."

Onassis in the Salle Empire of the Hôtel de Paris in Monte Carlo. "He was in heaven every time he came in," an aide recalled. "It was like a diamond that belonged to him."

The 1960 Rose Ball. Seated around the table, from left: Princess Grace, Onassis, movie director Michael Audley, Roger Crovetto (friend of Rainier and sometime Minister of State of Monaco), Ava Gardner, and Prince Rainier. In Monaco, Onassis achieved his distinctive social mix of business, show business, and society.

Onassis at work in Monte Carlo. His offices were located in the Old Sporting Club on the avenue d'Ostende. After his feud with Rainier in 1966, he returned only once to Monaco. His 180 employees stayed on.

Onassis gave a supper party at the Dorchester Hotel when Maria Callas sang Medea *at Covent Garden in June 1959. It was London's most glittering social event of the year. The evening ended with the diva being jointly embraced, Onassis on one side, her husband, Giovanni Meneghini, on the other.*

La Callas, Tina, and Lady Churchill admiring the temple of Apollo at Delphi, July 1959. When the cruise reached Venice, Onassis left his wife and children on board the Christina. "It is all over," the diva told her husband. "I love Ari."

Jeanne Rhinelander, the "Mrs. J.R." named in Tina's divorce suit. She and Onassis were alleged to have had an affair "by land and by sea."

The diva at sea. Callas off the Christina, *1965.*

Christina and Alexander, ages ten and thirteen. After their parents' divorce they were shuttled between Onassis's various pieds-à-terre and Tina's home in England, where she married the Marquess of Blandford.

Maria Callas and Onassis in Monaco.

In 1949 Onassis quietly got in touch with Finn Bryde, the brother of his former lover, Inge Dedichen. Bryde was then an experienced commander with Lars Christensen's whaling fleet in Sandefjord. Onassis beguiled the solid, seafaring Norwegian and his wife with the sights of Paris. They dined at Maxim's and made chauffeur-driven trips to Versailles and the castles of the Loire. Onassis never counted the pennies on important brain-picking operations. After the Brydes returned to Norway, Onassis incorporated a new business in Panama—the Olympic Whaling Company.

The elements of a large whaling fleet were rapidly brought together. The Howaldt yards at Kiel produced the factory ship, the *Olympic Challenger*—a refitted and "stretched" T-2 tanker—and worked at breakneck speed on the conversion of seventeen corvettes, Canadian and British vessels which had done Atlantic convoy duty, into hunter-killer catching ships. Acquiring gunners was a problem until Onassis came across Lars Andersen.

Andersen, alias Fa'an or Old Nick, was a larger-than-life figure generally reckoned to be the best harpoonist alive—a man who could smell out whales instinctively and would follow them anywhere without fear. A huge, muscular fellow with an uncertain temper, still quick with his fists at the age of sixty, and foulmouthed by even the impressive standards of whaling men, Andersen was in disgrace in Norway when Onassis first approached him. In 1936 he had "deserted" to Germany's new whaling fleet, impressed by Teutonic efficiency and determination and the money. After the Nazi invasion of Norway in 1940 Andersen had become a collaborator, a quisling working with the German occupiers. He was put on trial after the war and fined one million kroner ($150,000). A pariah in his own country, he had taken Swedish citizenship and had moved to Buenos Aires to advise Juan Perón on Argentina's whaling plans, when Onassis made him a better offer. With Andersen's help, Onassis rounded up another fourteen exiled Norwegian gunners and signed on three experienced Germans.

The Norwegian Whaling Association was not amused. Onassis's lavishly financed operation was a direct threat to the Norwegian share of the annual catching quotas fixed by the International Whaling Commission (IWC). In addition to the quotas, the IWC established the opening and closing dates for catching seasons, the minimum catching sizes for different species, and the rules banning the killing of certain types of whales in an attempt to preserve stocks.

Even if Onassis operated within the international conventions, the projected cost to the Norwegians looked daunting. They estimated that

—as a result of Onassis's joining the eighteen other expeditions which would share the 16,000 "units" (that is, whales) allocated by the IWC for the coming season—their own intake of whale oil would be reduced by some 10,800 tons. At the going price, then about $320 per ton, their anticipated loss would be on the order of $3 million. If, as seemed inevitable, Onassis intended to participate in the next four or five whaling seasons, Norway's revenue might well go down by more than $14 million. The Norwegian whaling authorities decided to try to head off the threat before Onassis's flotilla could steam out of Kiel harbor.

They moved at several levels. The first and most ironical was an attempt to appeal to Lars Andersen's patriotism. He was intercepted in Sweden en route to Kiel and urged not to betray his country by joining Onassis. Andersen, inflated by the prospect of leading a new fleet, was deeply unmoved. The Norwegians' next tactic was a clumsy attempt to intimidate Howaldt. An emissary from Sandefjord was sent to Kiel to point out that another big operator would seriously cramp the market. Howaldt should be "cautious," he advised: nobody would like to see them lose the valuable repair and maintenance work they did for the Norwegian fleet. It was an ill-conceived threat, as Norway did not have the capacity to do all her own repairs.

The third and most promising tactic was bribery. Onassis was known to be fond of the proposition that anyone could be bought, provided the price was right. The Norwegian Whaling Association was concerned to find out what Onassis's price would be to stay out of whaling. Anders Jahre, who had known Onassis since before the war, was sent to Paris to find out.

Jahre returned in time for the association's meeting in January 1950, where he produced a telegram several feet long—Onassis's reply. Canceling the expedition, Onassis stated, would cost him directly some $650,000 plus perhaps $100,000 in compensation payments to Howaldt for halting conversion work. The Norwegians could not legitimately oppose his entry into whaling since he had prudently made Olympic Whaling of Panama a subsidiary of one of his US-registered companies, and as an original signatory to the International Whaling Convention, the United States had the right to send out expeditions. It would not look good for Norway to shut the door on America. Almost as an afterthought, Onassis warned that if Norway did persist in trying to freeze him out, he was quite prepared to lay his fleet up for a couple of seasons, regardless of cost, while he trained non-Norwegian gunners, which would "break up the long-established Norwegian gunners ring."

118

Behind the apparent obduracy of Onassis's reply the Norwegians sensed there might be some room to maneuver. Jahre was told to keep talking while various formulas were explored. Eventually, the association came up with an intriguing "package." With the British owners, then the second biggest whaling nation, they offered to *give* Onassis 4,000 tons of whale oil a year for the next four years if he quit the industry for good. It was an adroit proposal, reflecting the immense value Norway attached to her domination of the whaling business. At projected prices between 1950 and 1954, sixteen thousand tons of oil would have been worth about $4.2 million, offering Onassis a clear profit of some $2 million after all expenses for doing nothing.

Onassis was seriously tempted, but it was too late. His natural pugnacity overrode his instinct for a quick profit. Besides, his fleet was almost ready, and whale oil prices were still rising. On October 28, 1950, *Olympic Challenger* and twelve catcher ships sailed out of Kiel harbor for the antarctic whaling grounds with a crew of six hundred Germans under the command of Captain Wilhelm Reichert, late of the German navy. On December 6, 1950—sixteen days before the official IWC opening day of the blue whale season—Lars Andersen harpooned the expedition's first whale, an event duly celebrated back at the head office. As Andersen and his fellow gunners continued the preseason killing, *Olympic Challenger*'s German crewmen became alarmed, protesting formally to Captain Reichert that it was jeopardizing Germany's prospects of being reaccepted into the whaling business. Reichert talked to Andersen, then tried to reassure his crew. The *Olympic Challenger*, as they knew, was registered in Panama. Since Panama had not signed the International Whaling Convention, it was perfectly in order to ignore the official seasons.

When the season started, Olympic Whaling, like every other whaling company, was supposed to report its catch each week to the authorities in Sandefjord. Figures of a kind were normally routed from the *Olympic Challenger* through Onassis's New York office. Walter Saunders of Metropolitan Life, which had put up money for the whaling enterprise, remembers Cokkinis calling him one Monday and lamenting the fact that the weekly catch report had not come through. He called again more cheerfully two hours later to say that the report still had not arrived but that he had received a cable from Lars Andersen asking him to order a Cadillac with whitewall tires. "I think," said Cokkinis, "it must have been a great week."

When the IWC declared the season over on March 9, 1951—the full

119

quota of whales having been caught—Onassis was still not entirely satisfied with his catch. Hunting continued. A round-the-clock radio silence was observed. When other ships were sighted, the *Olympic Challenger*'s name and funnel markings were hastily covered over. On one occasion she was obliged to hide behind a convenient iceberg to avoid detection. Illicit catching continued until March 19. The misgivings of the German crew were allayed by the fact that every whale hauled aboard the factory ship meant a better signing-off bonus.

The expedition's original plan had been to sail home after the antarctic season, but early in April Captain Reichert informed all crews that Onassis had ordered the fleet to offload its oil into the tanker *Ariston*, then go sperm whaling off Peru. The outraged Germans downed tools, demanding extra payment. Reichert was sympathetic, but Andersen, in overall charge of the expedition, flatly refused to radio the head office. The *Olympic Challenger* was not a happy ship.

At this point, to general amazement, Onassis himself suddenly appeared with Tina, Kurt Reiter, Nicolas Cokkinis, and a party of American businessmen and their wives in tow. They boarded the factory ship from a catcher ship that had picked them up in Chile. Onassis was determined to show his guests a fine time. Walter Saunders still recalls "an incredible first day." The guests went aboard one of the hunter-killers, which covered hundreds of square miles in search of schools of sperm whales. It was marred by only one thing. The sum total of marine life they saw was a single flying fish. Onassis seemed to take the conspicuous absence of whales as a personal affront. His guests had come to see some sport, and they must have it. Back on the *Olympic Challenger* he complained to Lars Andersen. The big Norwegian disappeared for a moment, then returned carrying the ship's cat. "I have this special method of finding whales," Andersen announced. "I swing the cat three times round my head."

Naturally it worked. Next day the Saunderses, the Pratts (Socony Oil), and the Dodges (marine brokerage) saw whale after whale hit and killed. They were invited to take a shot with the harpoon gun. Marshall Dodge and Frederic Pratt both made hits. As the whales were pulled alongside, mortally wounded by shrapnel from the harpoons' grenade warheads, the crew jabbed at them with long poles with knives attached. Compressed air was simultaneously forced into them so they would not sink. It usually took twenty minutes before the crew was satisfied that no life was left. "It was one of the most extraordinary things I have ever seen," Saunders recalled. "The water was red with blood. My wife liked it, too, although she felt rather weak in the stomach. It was all a bit gory for her."

120

The guests found the stench aboard the *Olympic Challenger* rather strong at times, particularly on the flensing deck, where half-naked crewmen hacked the carcasses to pieces, cutting up the huge bones with a power saw and stewing the blubber in vast cooking pots. The VIP quarters, in contrast, were air conditioned, the wardroom food was excellent—the chef had been lured away from the German passenger liner *Bremen*—and the wine could not be faulted. There was even a cabaret of sorts, a penguin which would jump and lurch around to music from a record player.

Between these diversions Onassis was frantically trying to soothe the angry German crewmen. The hunt would definitely be over by June, he promised, and everyone would get a 50 percent increase in wages. After animated bargaining, the crew agreed, "as a present to the owner," to carry on until May 10. Onassis promised each of them an extra three bottles of beer and two shots of schnapps a week, shook a few hands, then departed with his guests as abruptly as he had first appeared. Kurt Reiter was left to sort out the details.

A few days later a message arrived from Onassis. It was imperative that the fleet work on until late in June. Everyone would go on double time at once, and he would fly most of the crew back to Germany after that. It was well worth the money. At the beginning of his first season Onassis had turned down Unilever's advance offer of $282–$294 per ton that had been accepted by most of the Norwegians. Onassis had gambled on the fact that the Korean War, which began in June 1950, would increase industrial demand and the price for whale oil. When the *Ariston* arrived with its oil the price was up to $448 a ton and still rising. With almost half the capital cost of his investment already written off, Onassis was determined to prolong his winning streak. But there were limits. The German crews, by now close to mutiny, refused to work past May 10. After six and a half months at sea, the expedition set course for home.

It was still a resounding financial success for Onassis. By the time the *Olympic Challenger* got back, the price of whale oil had risen to almost $490 a ton. His net profit on the expedition, he delightedly told anyone who asked, was in the region of $4.2 million. Not bad for a beginner.

For the Norwegians, it was purgatory. They were convinced from the start that Onassis was breaking every rule in the IWC's book. What they learned from trade gossip and deduced from comparing the official catch returns submitted by Olympic Whaling with those of other expeditions left them in no doubt that Onassis's fleet had been hunting out of season. They also suspected that Onassis's fleet had killed virtually every whale to swim across the gunners' sights without observing the rules that exempted certain species from the slaughter.

Proving it, if it could be done, would bring immense pressure on Onassis from the established whaling nations, even though Panama was then outside the IWC. The Norwegian Whaling Association set about doing so, accumulating leads, tip-offs, and scraps of information for its master file. Meantime, Onassis's fleet continued to make money for him. There were antarctic expeditions in the 1951–52 and 1952–53 seasons. In the 1953–54 season Onassis switched the *Olympic Challenger* to carrying fuel oil as whale oil prices dropped sharply. He had, however, held back 40,000 tons of whale oil from previous catches for just such an eventuality. Few owners had enough capital to sit tight like this and most relied on advances from Unilever to equip their next expedition. With the only sizable quantity of "free" oil, Onassis set about playing the market with some skill, waiting for the price rise he believed was coming before selling his stocks. Prospects for the 1954–55 season looked excellent, and Onassis, with a most satisfactory contract from Unilever, prepared to send his fleet out again for both the South American and antarctic seasons.

This was depressing news for the delegates assembled at the IWC's annual meeting in Tokyo in July 1954. The Norwegian campaign against Onassis's methods was already beginning to influence the other whaling nations, though as yet no hard evidence against him had been produced. Some took comfort from the fact that Panama was now a member of the IWC and obliged to send two qualified inspectors to the *Olympic Challenger* to monitor all catching. But the main topic of conversation at the convention cocktail parties was whether Onassis would manage to circumnavigate the regulations once again.

By an ironic quirk of fate, Onassis suddenly found himself cast in the role of defender of the freedom of the seas, the Sir Galahad of the whalers. In late August 1954, the *Olympic Challenger* and fifteen catchers arrived off the coast of Peru, where they intended to hunt until the antarctic season began. It is no exaggeration to say that the eyes of the marine world were on Onassis's fleet. It would be the first flotilla to test a decree drawn up in Santiago in 1952 by the governments of Peru, Ecuador, and Chile to create "a protection, control and economic exploitation area at a distance of 200 nautical miles from the relevant country's coast . . . within which area they can exercise military administration and fiscal jurisdiction." In other words, no foreigners could fish or hunt whales there without their permission.

122

The legality of the Santiago decree had been vehemently challenged by the major maritime nations, including Great Britain, Norway, and the United States, but no government had cared to bring the issue to a head by encouraging its shipowners to test the resolve of the three signatories (one Norwegian expedition had, in fact, canceled plans for catching off Peru). Peru was the real problem, more bellicose and outspoken than its minor partners, and it was off her coast that the vast majority of sperm whales were caught. As Onassis's fleet approached, the Peruvian press and public opinion, encouraged by the government, prepared for a showdown.

"The whaling pirate Onassis insists on disregarding our national sovereignty," Peru's leading newspaper, *La Nación,* declared. "This will not be tolerated. . . . His ships must be seized by our navy." An unflattering photograph of the Greek shipowner was captioned, "Aristotle Socrates Onassis—in spite of his pompous names his behavior is not precisely that of a philosopher."

Onassis seemed unconcerned as the hysteria mounted in Peru and the agitated families of the six hundred German seamen on the expedition pestered Kurt Reiter in Olympic Whaling's Hamburg office. He told the press that the Panamanian government, whose flag the fleet still flew, had interceded with Peru at his request. Meantime, he had ordered Captain Reichert to stay outside the 200-mile limit. Diplomacy, he was sure, would find a way. But he was coming under increasing pressure. Every day the fleet stood off the best hunting grounds it was costing him money. He had business problems in the Middle East, and the surplus ships affair in the United States was not going well. Onassis was a natural attacker when his interests were threatened. In October he discarded his statesmanlike role and publicly denounced the Peruvian government's behavior and its "illegal" claims. He was reserving the right to arm his ships for self-defense.

Peru sent out two destroyers, the *Aguirre* and the *Rodriguez,* to establish a threatening presence at sea. It was clear that the slightest aggravation would cause a crisis. It duly arrived on November 15, when Ferdinand Kreugel, a contractor for the German seamen with the fleet, boasted to the press in Hamburg that the Peruvian bluff had been called. The fleet was already catching well within the 200-mile limit and it would continue to do so. Herr Kreugel was not impressed by Peru's naval might and traditions. Within a few hours, a Lima evening newspaper had reprinted the German's observations. The president of Peru, Manuel Odría, and most of his cabinet were at a cocktail party when an aide

123

dashed in with the paper. Orders to seize Onassis's fleet were issued on the spot.

The major engagements in what was dubbed the War of the Whales were brief. That same day two catchers, *Olympic Victory* and *Olympic Lightning,* were boarded and sailed by prize crews back to Paita, a small port north of Lima. *Olympic Conqueror,* another catcher, was escorted into Paita a few hours later. On the following day Peruvian planes spotted the *Olympic Challenger* and ordered her by radio to steam directly for the coast. *Olympic Challenger* responded by heading away from the coast at top speed. The first and last shots of the whaling war were fired—a machine gun burst close to the ship followed by a stick of small bombs which exploded in the water around her.

"We are being attacked and strafed by Peruvian planes," Captain Reichert radioed to Olympic Whaling's office in Panama. There were no more messages, but that was alarming enough for the crew's frantic relatives to besiege Kurt Reiter back in Hamburg. Reichert's run for the open sea was short lived, although the *Olympic Challenger* was a few knots faster than its venerable Peruvian pursuers. He surrendered when the *Aguirre* warned him by radio to turn for the coast immediately "or the Peruvian air force will destroy you." Arriving in Paita to an ecstatic reception by the locals, the *Olympic Challenger* was followed in by the *Olympic Fighter.* The rest of Onassis's fleet, ordered to scatter and aided by some foul weather, straggled back to Panama. A Peruvian official communiqué, redolent with redeemed pride, marked the end of hostilities. Four hundred German sailors and five ships were in captivity.

It soon became clear that the exact position of Onassis's ships when they were seized was to be of comparatively minor importance in the diplomatic skirmishing that followed. There is evidence that some of the catchers had been sent inside the 200-mile limit. The *Olympic Challenger* was probably captured outside it, but since Captain Reichert had chucked the log book overboard in a weighted bag, no one could be sure. Germany and Panama went through a minuet of protest and dismay on behalf of their subjects and flag flyers respectively. The Peruvians took no notice. They became marginally more accommodating when the British government unexpectedly intervened in the dispute.

The British ambassador to Peru, William Montagu-Pollock, was instructed by the Foreign Office to reserve Britain's right "to support any claims for compensation for damage done to British interests." The reason for this cryptic message soon emerged. All the insurance covering Onassis's fleet had been placed with Lloyd's of London. Only 10 percent of the risk had been reinsured in the US market, and estimates of the potential liability of Lloyd's to Onassis ran as high as $14 million.

As more details of this emerged, there was considerable interest among professionals in London about the precise nature of the coverage which Onassis had taken out. His annual hull insurance, covering risks to the vessels, had been extended to take in an optional war risks clause, which in certain circumstances increased the protection to include seizure and capture. Onassis also had the normal coverage for trading risks, an anticipated profits policy based on estimates of the value of the catch. It would cover him for oil "lost" as a result of the Peruvian action. But it was Onassis's third policy that the experts found most intriguing. It presciently insured him against the risk of his vessels being detained between October 7 and November 20, which meant that it had less than one week to run when the Peruvians made their move. Under the terms, Onassis could claim payments of $30,000 for every day that the fleet was held in port up to a ceiling of $900,000 for thirty days. It was, London insurance cautiously observed, an "unusual" policy.

The United States also had an interest in the affair but seemed oddly lethargic. The US government was strongly opposed to the idea of 200-mile territorial waters and touchy about the status of Panama. She was a favored protégé not to be treated lightly by lesser powers, particularly in Latin America, which the United States considered one of its zones of influence. These considerations had influenced Lloyd's underwriters when they agreed to insure Onassis against seizure just before the crisis began, in spite of the obvious risk. Onassis, however, was in uniquely bad graces with official Washington over the surplus ships deals and had incurred the hostility of the immensely influential US oil cartel over his activities in the Middle East. Washington's studied neutrality during the clash with Peru seems to have been governed by a desire to see Onassis humiliated. In any event, Onassis had calculated the odds rather better than the underwriters of Lloyd's and the US government.

While the diplomatic exchanges continued, Onassis flew to London on November 26 and held a press conference in his suite at Claridge's, in which he underlined how much the dispute was costing British underwriters. The Peruvian action, he said, was a case of "tropical madness." The idea of claiming 200 miles of territorial water was a pipe dream. If 200 miles, why not 2,000? Vancouver might become a Soviet possession overnight; before the Australians knew what was happening, they might become Incas. Applying the claim specifically to whaling was not the issue—"whaling, waterskiing, what's the difference?"

The reporter from the London *Times,* evidently impressed by Onassis's combative style, wrote an engaging portrait of him in the next morning's issue:

> Mr. Onassis is rather a small man to be a satisfactory legend. He wore dark glasses for most of the time last night, and complained a little when the photographers were too insistent. "What are you going to do with all those pictures? I'm not Marilyn Monroe." A Greek born in Asia Minor who settled in Argentina, his complexion is swarthy, his hair greying, his accent indeterminate.
>
> He denies the rumour that his third name is Homer ("my ambition did not take me that far"): but his talk, none the less, has a vaguely epic quality about it. He was not sure last night where he would be going next: perhaps to Paris, perhaps to visit his casino at Monte Carlo, perhaps to Arabia, whose merchant navy he plans soon to institute. His home was wherever he happened to be. He had forgotten how many different flags his ships sailed under—four or five, he supposed. Yes, some tankers were being built for him in Germany: two or three, he thought, but he could not be sure.
>
> Certainly, though he makes no claims for statehood, he does not disguise his international influence. His talk ranged from continent to continent, flaying a Government here and there, expressing willingness to comply with all the "rules and regulations" of the international whaling conference, gently ridiculing Peruvian power, testily rejecting the American Government's recent legal charges against him.
>
> He bestrides this narrow world, an unlikely Colossus, and when asked what he planned to do about his whaling fleet, replied with a smile that was barely perceptible: "Why, build another one, of course."

At the end of November a Peruvian naval court announced that Onassis's fleet had killed an astonishing total of 2,500–3,000 whales during the three weeks it had been operating off Peru before the seizures. The court fined Olympic Whaling 57 million Peruvian soles—about $2.8 million—and ruled that if the cash was not produced within five days, the captured ships would be confiscated and auctioned off. The British government quietly asked for and received two extensions in the time limit while Lloyd's thrashed out a settlement at a series of gloomy underwriters' meetings. The Peruvian fine seemed to offer Lloyd's a cheaper way out than other distasteful possibilities. If the ships were sold off, Onassis would have a valid claim for their total value. But the problem was that Britain and the United States were anxious to avoid any implied recognition of Peru's right to levy a fine. It did not prove insurmountable.

126

On December 13, 1954, a check for 57 million soles was handed to the Peruvian finance minister by Roberto Arias, Onassis's Panamanian lawyer, watched by two unsmiling representatives of Lloyd's. The check was signed by Aristotle Onassis and drawn on his account at First National City Bank in New York, but the money had come from Lloyd's. Officially, it was a "loan" to be repaid if the money was recovered "elsewhere." The pretense was sustained to the end. Arias received permission to appeal against the fine. The men from Lloyd's formally reserved all rights to recover the money from either side. The Panamanian government recorded its opinion that the fine did not imply recognition of Peru's 200-mile claim. There was a stilted exchange of courtesies, and the War of the Whales was over.

When the ships were released, Onassis directed the whole fleet to the antarctic for the January 1955 season. The catch was excellent, and whale oil prices were buoyant. The fleet's return to Kiel was an emotional occasion with Captain Reichert saluting the quayside crowds from the bridge of the *Olympic Challenger*. Onassis's status in the whaling community seemed assured. During the War of the Whales, Norway had joined with the other maritime nations in condemnation of Peru. Onassis believed that his action, which helped defend the interests of other whalers as much as his own, had taken the edge off the hostility of his Norwegian competitors. He was mistaken. At the IWC's annual meeting in Moscow in July 1955, the Norwegian Whaling Association moved in for the kill.

It was neatly managed. First, the Japanese delegation produced a short report with photos purporting to show that Onassis whalers had killed humpback whales out of season. It was not a particularly impressive document, but it helped create a receptive atmosphere. The Norwegian delegates then circulated something far more damaging—a formal protest by the Norwegian government to Panama about the activities of Onassis's fleet, alleging with a wealth of precise detail which could only have come from an insider that Olympic Whaling had systematically breached IWC regulations on a massive scale on every expedition it had undertaken since 1950. Onassis's whalers, it alleged, had killed out of season; had caught thousands of whales which were too young, too small, pregnant, or otherwise protected; had, in fact, harpooned everything that crossed their bows and then cooked the records to camouflage the illegal slaughter. It also questioned the competence of the Panamanian inspectors, whose job it was to insure that Onassis complied with the IWC regulations.

There was a counterattack of sorts published in the January 1956 issue

127

of the *Norwegian Whaling Journal*. The two Panamanian inspectors, Adolfo Quelquejeu and Antonio Isaza, rejected the allegations against them as "the products of fantasy to serve commercial interests." In an accompanying letter, Onassis, wearing his Olympic Whaling hat, laid into the Norwegians with gusto, setting out at length their earlier efforts to prevent his challenging their lucrative monopoly and the "ridiculous" offers to buy him out once he was established. He alleged that the Norwegian Whaling Association had tried to subvert his Norwegian gunners by offering free pardons in exchange for phony declarations about the breaking of IWC regulations. It was noticeable, however, that neither Onassis nor the Panamanians attempted to demolish the mass of damning statistics in the association's original report. The association responded coolly by releasing extracts from the confidential files of Olympic Whaling. Reports by the chief chemist and first engineer on *Olympic Challenger* appeared to confirm the most serious allegations.

They followed this up in April 1956 by publishing the testimony of seven German crewmen on the *Olympic Challenger* who between them had sailed on every expedition Onassis had mounted. There were long, detailed statements, a daily diary of a complete expedition, photostats of catch records, photographs showing whales aboard the factory ship clear enough for identification and approximate measuring. Everything was legally witnessed in Hamburg before the royal Norwegian consul general. The seamen's declarations—"given of our own free will"—were thoughtfully translated into English.

The diarist was Bruno Schlaghecke, who was employed as a factory worker on the *Olympic Challenger* during the autumn season of 1954. On September 7, 1954, before the opening of the season, he noted: "Killed almost only blue whales today. Woe if that leaks out." A few days later, on September 11: "Killed only small sperm whales today. The sight of these small animals, which had not even grown teeth, makes me inwardly dumb and empty." The entry for October 22 reads, "Shreds of meat from the 124 whales killed yesterday are still lying on the deck. Scarcely one of them was full grown. Unaffected and in cold blood everything is killed that comes before the gun." As the tempo of catching increased, Schlaghecke observed, "Today, October 31, production surpassed 60,000 barrels, an output never before recorded. More whales are continually coming in, sperm whales, blue whales, fin, humpback. This time nothing will stop them."

Schlaghecke took many photographs aboard the *Olympic Challenger*, frequently to the displeasure of the gunners. They showed undersized and protected whales being butchered on the flensing deck and others

128

being towed behind the ship until they could be handled. He also captured a moment when the *Olympic Challenger,* towing three illegally shot humpback whales, cut its catch adrift and slipped behind an iceberg to avoid being seen by a Japanese catcher.

Four other crewmen on the *Olympic Challenger,* veterans whose combined experience embraced all but one of the Onassis expeditions, made equally damning declarations. The four men had kept notes on whales illegally shot until the final season, when they stated, "Since the reckless exploitation of the whale stocks was so frightful, we have declined to take part in this year's expedition, although we were invited to join." In 1952–53, the *Olympic Challenger* had shot a gigantic North Cape whale. "As far as we knew, this species is preserved and must not be killed under any circumstances. It was on this occasion strictly forbidden by the captain to take photographs or to remove whalebones." Of the Peruvian operation they declared, "It was mostly undersized sperm whales that were killed. In processing sperm whales of the permitted size, up to 30 whales can be dealt with in a 12-hour shift. We, however, processed as many as 90 sperm whales in one shift. Many sucklings were killed from which only the harpoons and entrails were removed, whereupon they were put into the cooker without having to be cut into pieces."

The 1954–55 expedition, which followed the clash with Peru—when Onassis ordered an all-out effort to make up for lost time—was the most thoroughly and damagingly documented of all. Friedrich-Wilhelm Lehnert, a clerical assistant, was employed in logging the full details of every whale caught by the fleet for the company's catch record. "As a matter of personal interest," Lehnert declared, "I made daily copies of the catch log showing the results of all operations." Lehnert's photostats filled seven pages of the *Norwegian Whaling Journal,* a neatly handwritten record which established beyond any doubt the extent of the illegal slaughter that had taken place. Lehnert had personally measured many of the undersize whales for his log. The witnesses all agreed on one thing: the Panamanian inspectors had *never* been on the factory deck when whales were being measured or processed. They were, therefore, never in a position to cross-check the records.

In its summary of the evidence against Onassis's fleet, the association came to the following conclusions:

(1) The "Olympic Challenger" has not observed the opening and closing dates for the whaling seasons during the years 1954/55. On the contrary the expedition has repeatedly started the catch in advance of the

date agreed upon for the opening of the season and has continued operations up to 13 days beyond the established closing date. By thus violating the internationally recognized seasonal time limits, the expedition has been able to produce substantial quantities of whale oil during periods when the killing of whales has been expressly forbidden. More particularly this is the case for the season 1952/53 when about 44,000 barrels of oil were illegally produced.

(2) Blue whales and humpback whales have been killed out of season in extraordinarily great numbers. Thus during January 1955, 450 humpback whales were killed, although the killing of whales of this species was limited by the International Whaling Commission to the period from 1st February to 4th February. After 4th February 1955 a further 389 humpback whales were killed, bringing the total number up to 839 whales of this species illegally caught.

(3) Whales of all species have been killed in violation of the size limits for the particular species established by the International Whaling Commission. This applies with regard to every season mentioned above and particularly regarding the catch of sperm whales off Peru during the autumn of 1954, when the greater part of the whales killed were under 38 feet.

All in all, the Norwegians concluded, at least half of the whales killed by Onassis's fleet since 1951 were either caught out of season, were below minimum size, or were specifically protected. From these illegal catches, it was calculated, Onassis had acquired a revenue of at least $8.6 million. The damage his expeditions had done to the whale population as a whole was incalculable.

Even the partisan West German press could not overlook the strength of the Norwegian case. "Norway harpoons the Onassis whaling fleet," was the headline in *Bild-Zeitung*. There was never an official riposte from Olympic Whaling to the final barrage of evidence, though Onassis muttered darkly about "commercial envy" and the protection of monopolies. He knew it was time to quit.

Hounding Onassis out of whaling, it transpired, was not enough for the Norwegian owners. They were determined to hit him in the pocket, too, claiming some $700,000 as "compensation" for the damage done to the industry. As their last disclosures were being published, they obtained a court order in Hamburg to seize a $2.1 million cargo of whale oil in one of Onassis's tankers. A month later, when the *Olympic Challenger* docked in Rotterdam for overhaul, she too was arrested at the request of the Norwegians. Onassis retaliated the same day by securing the arrest of the whaler *Kosmos III* in the same port. The *Kosmos* belonged to Anders Jahre. Onassis hated doing this to an old friend, but he felt he had no other choice.

The negotiations which followed were complicated by the fact that Onassis claimed to have sold his entire whaling fleet, including the *Olympic Challenger*, to a Japanese concern at the end of March 1956. Costa Gratsos had been hunting a buyer for months. According to Onassis, he got an excellent price: $8.5 million, far more than they had hoped for. The compromise which was eventually hammered out in May 1956 left neither side with more than moderate flesh wounds. The seized ships were released, all current lawsuits called off, and something called the Pelagic Fund was set up into which Onassis paid the lion's share of 4 million kroner ($570,000) and the association the rest. Under the terms of the settlement, the Norwegian Whaling Association agreed to take no further legal action against Onassis's companies "in cases deriving from their whaling operations or activities connected thereto until this day." Onassis described his contribution to the Pelagic Fund as "an expression of goodwill and an appreciation of the experience one has gained from the Norwegian whaling industry."

His whaling career was over.

10
AN ARABIAN NIGHTMARE

Tɪɴᴀ Oɴᴀssɪs once said of her husband, "If Ari had been an artist instead of a businessman, he would paint nothing but immense murals." It was a remarkably astute perception of what distinguished him from most of his business rivals—the capacity for the grand design. He instinctively felt that if an idea was sufficiently bold, all the elements that made it possible would fall naturally into place.

At the same time, he felt restricted by the main source of his increasing wealth. When talking of his tanker empire he would sometimes say, only half joking, that he was "but the porter of the oil companies." The sense of dependence on the favors of the oil majors became more pressing when he met and befriended the fabulously wealthy J. Paul Getty, who also summered in the south of France. "Mr. Getty is in a rich man's business. He produces oil and carries it," Onassis remarked to an English journalist. "I am in a poor man's business. All I do is carry it."

In this context his whaling escapade can be seen not simply as an interesting adventure but as an attempt to break out of what he felt was a pattern of dependence. Onassis was never much interested in diversification for its own sake. What he wanted more than anything else was control, and he became increasingly interested in how Getty had achieved his enviable independence.

132

Getty had made his fortune by ignoring the threats of the great American oil companies. In 1934 he had bought Tidewater Oil, a medium-size company previously controlled by the Rockefellers. His greatest success, however, had been in the Middle East. In 1948 he became the first independent to break the monopoly held by ARAMCO over the extraction, refining, and shipping of Saudi Arabian oil. ARAMCO actually comprised four major American oil companies. Standard Oil of New Jersey, Standard Oil of California, and the Texas Company each owned 30 percent of ARAMCO; the remaining 10 percent was held by the Socony-Vacuum Oil Company. Getty managed to negotiate a side contract with King Ibn Saud of Saudi Arabia which was considerably more generous than the one the king had with ARAMCO. "I think it proved to the Arabs that up till now they weren't getting the best terms," Getty remarked after closing the deal.

Nowadays it is difficult to recall how thoroughly the Arab world was dominated by the policies of the great oil companies. There were no oil embargoes by developing countries in the fifties and sixties. The great Western powers, in particular America and Britain, effectively controlled the Middle East through the oil companies to such a degree that it was often hard to perceive the distinction between commercial and diplomatic interests. In an era of cold war geopolitics it was a form of control that Western governments were anxious to preserve. Several of the Arab oil nations were exhibiting symptoms of irritation at this state of affairs, although their dependence on foreign know-how and capital tended to muffle the more extreme forms of resentment. But the resentment was there, waiting for a chance of expression.

Onassis had neither the capital nor the expertise to follow Getty's tracks in the prospecting business, but the principle of qualified independence from the major oil companies was one that intrigued him. If he, like Getty, could offer the Saudis something they were not getting from ARAMCO, they might reciprocate by agreeing to make full use of his ships. The "something" Onassis had was the basis of a Saudi Arabian merchant fleet, calculated to appeal to nascent Arab nationalistic sentiment. Gratsos thought the idea had "the elements of genius." It certainly offered a creative direction for the Arabs' feelings of frustration. They, like Onassis, were deeply interested in exercising greater control over their destiny.

Like many new ideas, it was one that came to arouse extraordinary hostility. Onassis's epic lament at the end of his Arabian adventure— "never before in the history of business was so much power combined to fight and destroy an individual"—did not, for once, seem excessively farfetched.

The man who set the whole deal in motion was Spyridon Catapodis. In the early 1950s Catapodis was the quintessence of the Riviera demi-monde. Though not nautical in manner, he described himself as having been "in the shipping business" all his life. He owned a villa in Cannes and, more important, a yacht—a necessary possession for anyone with pretensions to the good life on the coast. His circle of acquaintances was wide; barmen and croupiers in Monte Carlo, Nice, and Cannes remember him with pleasure and affection. His bulky, flannel-clad form had graced the *salles privées* for many years. His histrionic gestures belonged between the chandeliers and thick pile carpeting of five-star hotels. Raconteur, gambler, and inveterate middleman, he lived by an abundant supply of wits.

Born in Ithaca, he was a school friend of Costa Gratsos and had crossed the path of Onassis in London during the thirties. In London he had prospered in a limited way. His handful of tramp steamers had plied the eastern Mediterranean between the Russian Black Sea ports and Alexandria. The Spanish Civil War increased the prosperity of his fleet. In 1940 he moved to France, where he spent a quiet war. When the Americans landed in the south of France in 1944 he offered them his services, becoming an all-purpose fixer to the Sixth Army, in which capacity he earned the commendation of General Arthur Wilson.

In 1948 he rendered Onassis some small services on his first trip to Europe. He found him the best suite in the Hôtel Prince de Galles. Later he became a frequent guest at the Château de la Croë. They naturally found that their interests overlapped in some areas. Catapodis had resumed his business contacts in the Middle East after World War II. He was in contact with a number of Arab governments and was deeply aware of their desire to maximize their stake in the oil business and minimize their dependence on American and European know-how.

On one trip in which he unsuccessfully attempted to sell a batch of rusting Liberty ships to the Iraqi government, Catapodis encountered a suggestion that aroused his interest. The government was keen on the idea of forming a fleet of tankers to operate under the Iraqi flag to transport Iraqi oil. Catapodis offered his services and as middleman sped back to Cannes. Was his good friend Onassis interested in providing the ships? he inquired. Onassis was interested, and for the next year the project was under consideration, but it ran into snags. There was a coup

134

d'état in Iraq as a result of which Onassis's contacts summarily lost their jobs.

Saudi Arabia seemed a much better proposition. For one thing, its autocratic regime seemed much more stable. For another, it had a lot more oil. In August 1953 Catapodis and Onassis met at the Carlton Hotel in Cannes and decided there was a great deal of money to be made in Saudi Arabia.

There was, later, to be much argument over the precise nature of the agreement made between them. Catapodis maintained that Onassis had made him plenipotentiary ambassador to the Arab world and that he had been promised a share of profits amounting to a million dollars a year tax free if a suitable contract was concluded. Onassis maintained that Catapodis was essentially representing the Saudi cause to him—how Catapodis profited by it was his own affair. The distinction later became crucial, but at the outset it did not seem so very important. What is certain is that the two men formed what is known in the south of France as *une combine:* an association for their mutual enrichment. If all went well, there would be more than enough money to keep all the interested parties happy.

Catapodis made the initial connection with the Saudi regime. Two eminent Saudis were then staying at the luxurious Hôtel Martinez in Cannes. Mohammed Alireza and his brother, Ali, were members of the Saudi class of merchants who operated in a close relationship with the feudal government of their country. They were essentially entrepreneurs, holding the Lincoln automobile franchise in Saudi Arabia, controlling the port of Jidda, and owning a substantial portion of Saudi-registered shipping. But they were also periodically involved in running the country, depending on whether they were in or out of favor with the ruling clique of the royal family. Mohammed Alireza was president of the Saudi Arabian chamber of commerce, and Ali Alireza was minister of state. In their role as links to the outside world, they were accompanying the finance minister, Sheikh Abdu Abdullah Al Suleiman Al Hamdan (Suleiman, for short), on a mission to Europe which combined public and private business in somewhat elusive proportions.

After a preliminary meeting at the Cannes Yacht Club, the Alireza brothers expressed cautious enthusiasm for the idea. The shape of a practicable deal began to emerge after further meetings in Paris and London. All the parties were aware of the need for a solid agreement before news of it leaked out to ARAMCO, whose agreement with the Saudi Arabian government, dating back to 1933, included rights to

135

transportation as well as prospecting and production. Secrecy in negotiating the new deal was imperative. Sometimes, however, it appeared that Onassis's obsession on this point would threaten the whole operation.

At one stage the German banker Dr. Hjalmar Schacht, Hitler's former finance minister, was drawn into the orbit of the negotiations. At a meeting in Geneva he discussed the outlines of the proposed deal with Finance Minister Suleiman. The meeting prompted a near-paranoid response from Catapodis, who suspected that Onassis might be exploring the possibility of cutting him out of the deal. The breach was healed when Onassis explained that Schacht's interest was peripheral, governed by the fact that the Germans were interested in building ships to be assigned to the Saudi Arabian flag. It was, nonetheless, an indication of the low level of trust between the parties involved. Another poorly defined area between them was the level of "commission" receivable by those who were acting as agents. It was an area that naturally obsessed Catapodis, but it did not, at that stage, much impede the process of discussion.

By December 1953 a draft agreement was in existence. Onassis, for his part, promised to assign a tanker fleet of 500,000 tons to the Saudi Arabian flag and pay royalties for the initial privilege of carrying a guaranteed 10 percent—about 4 million tons—of the country's annual oil output. In exchange for the modest royalty Onassis enjoyed the right to fix his rates well above the market level. The agreement also provided mechanisms that would enable Onassis to increase his tonnage rapidly at the expense of other carriers. Within ten years he would enjoy a monopoly position. The fleet was to be operated by a new enterprise, the Saudi Arabian Maritime Company, registered in Jidda. Onassis also promised to build a marine training school for young Saudis; its graduates would find employment on his tankers. There was a clause exempting the new company from payment of income tax.

In January 1954 Onassis, Tina, Nicolas Cokkinis, his wife, and Catapodis flew from Nice to Cairo. Cokkinis and Catapodis then flew directly to Jidda while the rest of the party boarded Onassis's newest tanker, the *Tina Onassis,* and steamed down the Red Sea. On the day after they docked in Jidda the agreement was signed without fanfare in Suleiman's villa. Onassis and his party were feted by the Saudis. There were picnics by the Red Sea and official banquets in the presence of members of the royal family. While Onassis, Catapodis, and Cokkinis posed uncomfortably for official photographs in their Western flannel

136

suits, Tina was taken to tea at the palace of the king's four queens. Onassis was granted an audience with King Saud, who presented him with a series of traditional gifts—two gold sheathed swords and two Arab ponies.

The actual terms of the agreement still remained a closely guarded secret. Neither Onassis nor the Saudi government had yet seen fit to inform ARAMCO of its contents. It was a salient omission as ARAMCO would necessarily be producing most of the oil which the new fleet was supposed to transport. The need for delicacy in dealing with the oil companies scarcely needed underlining. Under the terms of its concession, signed by the king in 1933, ARAMCO enjoyed production rights to Saudi oil until the year 2000. The agreement also stipulated that ARAMCO enjoyed the exclusive right to arrange transport of the oil. This was normally done through long-term contracts with various independent carriers. They, as well as ARAMCO, were threatened by the new deal.

Onassis wished to conduct this next stage of the operation personally. It was one that required his deepest reserves of charm and persuasion. Unfortunately these were suddenly and seriously engaged on another project. The surplus ships affair had just reached a critical point, and in February 1954, after his arrest in Washington, the problem of ingratiating himself with the US oil companies became less pressing than the problem of talking his way out of a US jail. Meanwhile, news of the Saudi agreement began leaking out in a way that could hardly have been more prejudicial to Onassis's interests.

Catapodis returned to the gaming tables and the bars of the Côte d'Azur, where he told anyone who would listen to him that he and his great friend, Aristotle Onassis, had negotiated a contract with the Saudis that would make them fabulously rich. The terms of Catapodis's payment have never been satisfactorily explained. Catapodis later maintained that he was to be paid a share of the profits amounting to $2.8 million a year and a lump sum of $350,000 the day the first vessel left a Saudi port. Onassis denied this but conceded that he had lent Catapodis $25,000 in February to cover his gambling debts.

Garbled versions of the Saudi agreement inevitably leaked in the European and American press. ARAMCO was outraged and lodged a strong protest with the Saudi government. They rapidly grasped that the agreement was the thin end of a much larger economic wedge—Onassis would start with 10 percent but his long-term objective was to transport 100 percent of Saudi oil. ARAMCO's concern was shared by the other

137

independent carriers, all of whom stood to lose from the development of Arab national fleets. Under the terms of the agreement, the existing carriers could not expand their tonnage or renew their charters with new vessels when their ships became too old. All the new business created by increased production and the expired charters would go to Onassis's Saudi flotilla.

Stavros Niarchos was more than outraged; he decided to do something about Onassis. Although under indictment himself for his role in the surplus ships deals, he had a shrewd grasp of what moved official Washington. A dispute between commercial interests would not necessarily excite the US authorities, but if Onassis's Saudi deal could be established in a context of hostility to America's long-term foreign policy objectives, it would be a different matter.

Niarchos's New York office was given the assignment of finding someone who "knew his way around Washington." They came up with Robert Maheu, a burly, former FBI man who ran an industrial consultancy business in the capital. Maheu, who later became the boss of Howard Hughes's Las Vegas gambling empire, was an exceptionally able operator with abundant connections in the US security services. Part of the expenses of his Washington office were even paid for by the CIA. Maheu also had a world view that enabled him to perceive almost any conflict with America's economic interest as being the result of an encroaching communist menace. After a briefing in the New York office, Maheu gladly accepted the assignment of mobilizing opposition to Onassis's deal in Washington.

Since money was no object to Niarchos, Maheu began by engaging several former FBI men, who helped to produce an analysis of the Onassis-Arab contract. This was then delivered to the National Security Council. Maheu's "presentation" contained estimates of the amount of money Onassis stood to make over a long period of time. More significantly, it represented Onassis's agreement as a wedge that could be driven between the US government and the Saudis, thus leading to a serious erosion of American influence in the Middle East. Maheu indicated that the only reason Prime Minister Moussadek's attempt to nationalize BP Oil's holdings in Iran had failed was that the Iranians had been unable to transport their oil as a result of the oil companies' efficient boycott. Onassis, he asserted, was placing just such a capability in the Saudis' hands. The presentation was successful. The State Department instructed its Saudi ambassador to contact ARAMCO's director in Saudi Arabia and to express its concern at the situation.

In March 1954 another Niarchos emissary arrived in Washington

138

with an immodest proposal. Robert L. McCormick met with a number of State Department officials to pass on Niarchos's thoughts on the Saudi deal. According to State Department files, McCormick explained that, although Onassis and Niarchos were related, "they were violent competitors." Niarchos regarded the deal as "unfortunate" for American interests and "had been interested in discovering some form of solution to this difficult problem in the light of his own experience." Niarchos's prescription was seductively simple. Onassis had borrowed money from American banks and insurance companies to construct the fleet destined to carry Saudi oil. Initially, as Niarchos well knew, American lenders had required US registration for any ships they financed. Next they had allowed flags of convenience from such countries as Panama and Liberia. Now Onassis wished to fly the Saudi flag. "It was Mr. Niarchos's proposal," reported the confidential State Department document, "that the Department approach the above loaning agencies and suggest to them that it would not displease the Department if they were to refuse to change their present registry requirements and that it would be preferable if they were to cancel their agreement with Onassis."

John Jernegan, the State Department official in charge of the Onassis case, thanked McCormick for the thoughtful suggestion but turned it down. The scheme had the disadvantage of involving the State Department rather too directly. It would have the appearance of an ultimatum, precisely what the State Department wished to avoid. Nonetheless, Jernegan was sufficiently appreciative of Niarchos's suggestion to agree to McCormick's parting request. The account of his conversation was passed on to the Justice Department as evidence of Niarchos's friendliness to the US government, an attitude in stark contrast to his brother-in-law's apparent hostility.

The US government was by now thoroughly embroiled in the affair but less than confident about how to proceed. Important questions of "face" were involved. ARAMCO's initial aggressive response had inflamed Arab pride and periodic sense of resentment against the overwhelming American presence in Saudi Arabia. Edward Wadsworth, the American ambassador, noted with alarm the Saudis' increasing "self-complacency." The louder the noises the American oil companies made, the happier they became. "High Saudi circles," cabled Wadsworth, "obviously lack background experience to really appreciate questions of principle involved and to their shrewdly trader mind it follows that if the foreigner cries he must be hurt financially and they gain in corresponding measure."

Wadsworth gained an audience with King Saud on April 30. The

139

ambassador had delivered a written communication, drawing attention to the potential threat the Onassis agreement posed to American interests. This communication was read to the king by Prince Faisal because, noted Wadsworth, the "king's weak eyesight does not permit him to read ordinary type." The king's response was ambivalent: while he was prepared to discuss the contract, the matter was in all respects closed, and the Saudis would act as they thought fit. "He spoke with some heat and, I thought, irritation," reported Wadsworth, "not with me but rather, I surmise, because the whole matter was distasteful to him."

There ensued a curious hiatus in the affair. Not only the shipping world but also the chancelleries of the West were aware that Onassis had negotiated an agreement with the Saudis, but they knew next to nothing about its contents. The Saudi government further confused matters by denying that the contract had been signed. Onassis himself was unusually silent, most likely because he realized that the adverse publicity generated by his arrest had made it inevitable that any further announcements would be greeted with hostility. But there were other problems. The king had not yet formally ratified the agreement—his hand seems to have been stilled by the vehement protests from ARAMCO and the US government. And his council was divided—while Prince Faisal, Finance Minister Suleiman, and, of course, Alireza supported the agreement, three other royal ministers opposed it.

Onassis flew to Jidda to give events another shove in the desired direction. He made a series of concessions calculated to go some way toward meeting ARAMCO's demands that the discriminatory and monopolistic features of the agreement be eliminated. First, he had agreed to abandon the artificially high rates incorporated into the original contract. Second, he eliminated the provision whereby ARAMCO's existing carriers would be able to use only those ships that were in service prior to the date of the agreement. They would now be able to replace their old ships as they decayed. They would not, however, be able to increase their tonnage—every additional ton of oil over the level carried in December 1953 would have to go to Onassis's Saudi fleet. On May 18, 1954, the agreement was formally ratified by King Saud.

Onassis was by now thoroughly aware of the fact that the US government was involved and represented an infinitely more formidable opponent than ARAMCO. If the government could be convinced of his good intentions, the oil companies would naturally fall into line. Through his friend Spyros Skouras he arranged a meeting with the Middle East desk of the State Department. Onassis was at his most emollient and reason-

140

able. He told the officials that states emerging as new members of the world diplomatic community "felt the nationalistic urge to have vessels operating under their own flags." Onassis had recognized this development and warned the oil companies of its existence. They could not "expect to enjoy their monopoly indefinitely." He went on, somewhat disingenuously, to represent himself as a reluctant participant in the agreement.

The State Department officials heard his case with polite skepticism. When Onassis had finished they asked him whether he had been aware of the hostility which his own prospective monopoly would arouse. Onassis's answer was a model of inconsistency. He had attempted, he said, to limit his participation to a small share. But the Saudis had rejected this suggestion, and he had been obliged to sign on their terms in order not to lose the contract. In any case, the agreement was not monopolistic since its terms should not be taken too literally. He was, he added, prepared to renegotiate the agreement to make it acceptable to the US government and the oil companies. The problem was that he could not "double-cross" the Saudi government. Onassis, commented Parker T. Hart, one of the State Department officials present, "gave the impression of being a man who is in a tight spot."

The next day Onassis met with the ARAMCO brass and was told what he must already have guessed. The American oil companies refused to recognize the validity of his contract on the grounds that it violated their own concession. They were not prepared to negotiate, even though they realized that such a move might jeopardize their position in Saudi Arabia. Onassis was told that when his ships arrived at the ARAMCO terminal at Ras Tanura to take on their first loads of Saudi oil they would be turned away.

Onassis reacted to this crisis with a mixture of bluff and guile. *Baunummer 883*, the latest 46,000-ton addition to his fleet, was nearly ready for launching in Hamburg. Onassis resolved to name her after King Saudi I and put on a ceremony at the Howaldt-Hamburg yard. A delegation from Riyadh arrived bearing holy water from the fountain of Zem Zem near Mecca. One hundred thousand Germans, including the cream of German industry and society, turned out to watch and applaud. But the launching, like the venture itself, began ominously. The Saudis refused to supply a woman to smash the holy water against the ship's side. Only under considerable duress would they accept Onassis's candidate, Princess Anne Marie von Bismarck. The princess hurled the holy water against the hull, but the bottle would not break since water, unlike

141

champagne, does not exert sufficient pressure. She tried again, but the bottle lodged in the elaborate floral decorations surrounding the ship's prow. The Arabs frowned, regretting perhaps that they had ever agreed to allow a woman to launch the ship. On the third attempt the bottle broke, and the *Al Malik Saud Al-Awal* slid down the slipway.

Returning to Paris, Onassis moved to circumvent ARAMCO's flat refusal to do business in the only remaining way open to him. If ARAMCO would not recognize his contract, there was someone else who might—J. Paul Getty. Onassis contacted him, explained the situation, and offered to place his ships at Getty's disposal. Getty was tentatively interested. He instructed John Pochna, his general manager, to begin negotiations with Onassis, and the two men met at the Château de la Croë. The result was a draft agreement that went some way to shoring up Onassis's precarious position. Getty was willing to charter the *Al Malik* for three voyages, though he offered and got a price considerably lower than the one Onassis had written into his Saudi contract. On Pochna's advice, however, Getty contacted the State Department to make sure the US government had no objection to this move. The State Department replied that they could not stop Getty from entering into an agreement with Onassis. However, it would be grateful if he would "hold off finalizing the deal" until the delicate situation was clarified.

Within the State Department the debate pivoted around two options. Either ARAMCO should be encouraged to resort to legal action under the provisions for arbitration established in its original concession agreement with Saudi Arabia in 1933, or it should rely on a sustained diplomatic offensive on the part of the US government. ARAMCO was naturally apprehensive about the effect on their relations with Saudi Arabia of an elaborate process of litigation. Clearly, the Saudis were reluctant to go to arbitration; equally clearly, there were a number of ways in which they could make life difficult for the oil companies while arbitration was taking place. The State Department legal staff, moreover, was not entirely confident about a favorable outcome from arbitration. In a confidential memo addressed to the Middle East desk, Bob Metzger, State Department legal adviser, drew attention to certain ambiguities in the original ARAMCO concession document in which the Saudis granted ARAMCO the right to "explore, prospect, drill for, extract, treat, manufacture, transport, deal with, carry away and export petroleum." The list seemed as comprehensive a definition of ARAMCO's activities as one might wish. Metzger's lawyerly mind, however, discerned a loophole through which Onassis might legally sail his Saudi fleet.

142

"What, then, does 'export' mean?" asked Metzger. Webster's dictionary, he pointed out, defined it as meaning "to carry or send abroad." But which? "If it means to carry abroad, the right might encompass the exclusive right to carry by whatever means the company chooses. If, on the other hand, it means 'to send abroad,' this right does not necessarily carry with it the exclusive determination by which the oil is to be physically carried." The distinction might seem overnice, but it is from such pedantries that successful lawyers' careers are made. "I should note here that I am by no means certain the company would lose in arbitration," concluded Metzger. "On the other hand, I am not confident that they would win."

The opinion weighted the argument in favor of a diplomatic offensive, and John Foster Dulles, Eisenhower's austere secretary of state, was anxious to insure that there should be no confusion about US policy. Meantime, he was in receipt of a stream of advice on, and evaluation of, Onassis's Saudi deal from the CIA—all of it hostile. A CIA information report, dated July 1, 1954, discussed the process that led to the contract in almost racist terms: "We believe it was a case of 'a smart Greek' selling the SAG [Saudi Arabian Government] a bill of goods and the prestige-hungry Arabs jumping at the deal. Onassis apparently has some mighty plans to monopolize the tanker industry by playing the same theme to Kuwait, Iran and Iraq. . . . Though the SAG is becoming more cantankerous and difficult we do not believe they dreamt up this arrangement." A report from a CIA agent in the Middle East noted: "I was told by a source I consider reliable that Suleiman pocketed approximately U.S. 100 thousand in return for his signature." Another agent, reporting on the maiden voyage of the *Al Malik* from Hamburg to Ras Tanura, declared a belief that the voyage was "to satisfy the ego of the Saudi Arabian Government and King Saud and to possibly influence other Near East countries to sign similar agreements with Onassis."

On July 16, 1954, Secretary of State Dulles personally cabled a long series of recommendations for action by Ambassador Wadsworth. Dulles began by reaffirming ARAMCO's determination: "Present position is that parent companies will refuse cargo . . . although realize shutdown and eventual nationalization could result. Officials fully realize seriousness of step but agree must stand ground and have sought assurances that U.S. government agrees and will support them." The cable continued crisply, "Agreed USG should back companies."

Wadsworth's marching orders came later in the cable. If the Saudis still felt they had concluded a satisfactory business deal, they should be speedily disabused:

From practical business viewpoint U.S. believes Saudi Government would run grave danger substantial loss by implementation Onassis agreement. Financial benefits to Saudi government bound to be infinitesimal compared potential loss oil royalties. Loss of markets for only one million barrels of oil would roughly cancel contemplated annual financial benefits. If contract implemented resentment and resistance on part many oil buyers likely impair ARAMCO production, income and hence Saudi royalties to much greater extent. There is increasing evidence that resistance will be tremendous. From dollars and cents viewpoint Saudi government appears to have been seriously misled.

Dulles's "dollars-and-cents" argument unsubtly masked what was in fact a naked threat. The resentful "oil buyers" were none other than the American oil companies themselves, who in effect were ARAMCO. What Dulles was in fact saying was that if the Saudis persisted in their scheme, the companies would cut back their Saudi production, thus leading to a catastrophic decline in Saudi revenues. This Dulles made clear in a confidential section appended to his recommendations:

FYI. It looks to us from here as if this issue may produce critical point in our relations with Saudi Arabia and might lead to situation similar to that in Iran in 1950 and 1951. Judging by tone of Saudi communications to ARAMCO it would seem quite possible that King would declare ARAMCO concession nationalized on being confronted with clear-cut, flat refusal of company to deal with Onassis.

King's decision to take such drastic step might be based on mistaken impression that he could find others to exploit and sell oil for him and that by dispensing with American collaboration he can make himself hero of the Arab world.

On the other hand, it seems possible King is engaged in a species of bluff, encouraged by past successes in wringing concessions from ARAMCO and past acquiescence by USG in such concessions.

If King has decided to dispense with American companies we should of course utilize every means to make him and his advisers realize disastrous effect this would have on his position, his government, and country.

Dulles went on to draw attention to the catastrophes which had befallen Iran after Moussadek's government had attempted to nationalize BP's interests there in 1950. Iran had been without oil revenues for three years and had "barely survived." (He refrained from mentioning the fact that Moussadek's removal from office had resulted from a coup engineered by the CIA.) Unlike Iran, Saudi Arabia depended entirely on oil for its crucial foreign exchange. "King and advisers," Dulles said,

144

"should ask themselves where they would stand after three years or even one year without the oil revenues." Wadsworth's approach to the king should stress the international storm of protest that had greeted the Onassis agreement and the fact that it clearly violated the original ARAMCO concession. However, not too much should be made of this last point since "resolution Onassis matter may not repeat not depend primarily on legalities involved."

At the same time, Dulles was concerned with avoiding any unnecessary blows to the Saudis' pride in the form of gratuitous humiliations. The United States was "especially anxious," he explained, to avoid any "public showdown" between ARAMCO and the Saudis, particularly since the State Department judged that Saud's somewhat prickly character "would make him doubly reluctant to lose face" by giving way after having taken a strong public position. It would be a different matter for Onassis. He had already agreed to modify the terms of his agreement; he could surely, one way or another, be induced to make some further concessions. Dulles ended the cable: "He probably anxious squirm out."

In Jidda, Wadsworth set about the task of bringing the stern Dulles doctrine home to the Saudis. His cables back to the State Department indicated that he was more hopeful than before but that the operation was not without its hazards. On August 6, recording a meeting with Prime Minister Mohammed Ali and another senior official, Wadsworth confided, "I entered 15 minutes late having been directed first to Minister Finance's harem."

The ambassador's representations were at least partly successful. The king agreed to meet with ARAMCO, and by August he told Wadsworth that he wished "to get out from under" the Onassis agreement, convinced, no doubt, by Wadsworth's dollars-and-cents arguments. There remained, however, the question of amour propre. The king had to be given a satisfactory pretext for breaking the Onassis agreement.

Robert Maheu had been working on that very problem for some months. His original brief from the Niarchos organization had been to explore the reaction of the US government to Onassis's activities in Saudi Arabia. Thereafter his mission was, as he told us, "to scuttle that contract." But, to begin with at least, Maheu's employers had no precise idea how this might be accomplished and left it to Maheu's initiative. He began by contacting his friends in the CIA to secure their cooperation. Onassis's offices were bugged for a week with disappointing results. Maheu then adopted a more methodical approach. Since his knowledge of the Middle East was restricted to memories of Rudolph Valentino

145

movies, he sat down to some serious homework beneath the vast dome of the Library of Congress in Washington.

The volume which ultimately caught his attention was *Saudi Arabia* by Karl Twitchell, a sober-minded factual account of the mineral wealth of Saudi Arabia and its subsequent exploitation by the American oil companies. But Maheu was interested in the book's author as much as its content. Twitchell, an American geologist, had first come to Saudi Arabia as a result of an afternoon King Ibn Saud spent motoring through the desert with Harry St. John Philby, a renegade British Foreign Office man and Arabist whose son, Kim Philby, later acquired his own share of notoriety as the master spy who betrayed Britain's intelligence service to the Soviet Union. King Saud was, as usual, in desperate need of money, and Harry Philby, who had embraced Islam and become one of the king's most trusted advisers, suggested that he might find it by exploiting his country's resources. When the king reacted favorably to this suggestion, Philby arranged a meeting with an American philanthropist, Charles Crane, who in turn arranged for Twitchell to prospect for minerals. Twitchell was impressed by what he saw. In August 1933, after a year of negotiations with the American oil companies, he arranged the historic agreement between them and the king.

Maheu was intrigued to discover that Karl Twitchell was alive and well and living in retirement in Greenwich, Connecticut. He checked out Twitchell's credentials with the State Department—the geologist, he discovered to his satisfaction, was "extremely pro-American." Maheu visited Twitchell and persuaded him to go back to Saudi Arabia to undertake what was in effect a private mission to the Saudi court to convince the king that it would not be in his interest to implement the agreement with Onassis. Maheu's line of argument was identical to the one he had employed earlier at the State Department. The motives of his client were left deliberately hazy, as was his identity.

In August Maheu was abruptly summoned to Niarchos's suite at Claridge's in London. Maheu had met the shipowner briefly in New York before, but this was his first opportunity for an extended discussion with Niarchos. The former FBI man was impressed—"Niarchos had a lot of class." The meeting started at breakfast time and went on throughout the day as Niarchos and two of his senior aides rehearsed the various options open to them. At 1 A.M. the following morning, Niarchos opened a bottle of brandy and took the company out on to the terrace with the invitation, "Let's start again." The meeting finally ended at 5 A.M.

146

Niarchos dominated the proceedings from start to finish. He spoke of the dangerous precedent that Onassis's agreement set and its potentially dire effect on the balance of power in the Middle East. He explained that if the contract went through, Onassis would be able to eliminate his own interests in Saudi Arabia. He could then take his profits, estimated to be $17 million in the first full year, and increase his tonnage, thus enabling him to repeat the scheme in other oil producing countries. There would be no way to stop him from extending himself indefinitely. Onassis's one serious weakness, however, was his current cash position, which Niarchos estimated to be a mere $5 million. If it was possible to block the Saudi deal, Niarchos concluded, the situation would be entirely different. Onassis would be in considerable trouble, with excessive tonnage, high debt repayments, and the implacable hostility of his clients, the oil companies.

The discussion over strategy centered around the question of whether the Niarchos forces should content themselves with feeding suggestions to Washington, along the lines of the messages back in March, or whether they should strike out on their own.

The principal subject of their discussions was Spyridon Catapodis. It was common knowledge on the Côte d'Azur that Catapodis's previously friendly relationship with Onassis had gone sour. The delay in implementing the deal worried Catapodis since his chances of being paid clearly now depended on the outcome of the increasingly complicated negotiations between Onassis, the United States, and the oil companies. By all accounts, he felt cheated. There had been reports of an ugly encounter between Onassis and Catapodis in the departure lounge at Nice Airport some weeks earlier. After a noisy and confused discussion Catapodis had wrestled Onassis to his knees and delivered the ultimate rebuke. "You are not even a Greek," shouted Catapodis, "but a goddam Turk, that's what you are."

Shortly after the Claridge's meeting, there was a natural fusion of interests. On September 24, 1954, in the presence of the British consul in Nice, Catapodis signed a lengthy affidavit accompanied by thirty-four exhibits—cables, letters, and photographs. It was a remarkable document and, if true, highly damaging to Onassis's cause.

The affidavit was Catapodis's version of the Saudi deal portraying Onassis as a compulsive schemer and containing "revelations" calculated to cause dissension within the Saudi camp. The documents alleged that Onassis had set up the deal and obtained exemption from Saudi Arabian income tax by a system of payoffs. They purported to show that $1.25

million had been paid in bribes to various Saudi ministers and palace officials. The documentation was imposing but less than conclusive. One crucial document outlining Catapodis's contract with Onassis was conspicuous by its absence. Catapodis alleged that it had been signed with disappearing ink. When he had asked Onassis to freshen up the signature, it had been taken back and not returned. Even so, the evidence of payoffs—which, given the scale of the deal, did not seem so excessive —was less damaging than the affidavit's general tone. Onassis, Catapodis maintained, was no particular friend of the Americans or the Arabs.

In one passage, Catapodis recalled Onassis's alleged reason for preserving secrecy *after* the agreement had been signed:

> I asked Onassis why he did this, and he said that the reason was that he expected to enter into an agreement with ARAMCO, whereby he would get either a large amount of money or some other valuable concessions in return for canceling his agreement with the Saudi Arabian government. . . . I vigorously objected to this scheme, and informed Onassis that it amounted almost to blackmail. Onassis then pointed out to me that he did not care very much to do business with the Arabs anyway, and that was the reason why he insisted that no penalty clause for nonperformance of the agreement be incorporated in his agreement with the Saudi Arabian government.

The affidavit ended with the somewhat contradictory but equally damaging allegation:

> Onassis repeatedly boasted to me that with the aid of Mohammed Alireza he was going to break up the influence which ARAMCO has been exercising in Saudi Arabia for many years. I cautioned Onassis not to embark himself in such intrigues which may lead to political repercussions and strongly advised him not to antagonise ARAMCO. Onassis told me that he knew exactly what he was doing, and that he felt confident that, in the end, he would play an important part in the development of the natural resources in Saudi Arabia, which ultimately would make him the richest and most powerful man in the world.

When the Catapodis affidavit was presented to Bob Maheu by one of Niarchos's aides, he realized that he was about to earn his money. His job was to acquaint King Saud with the allegations it contained. He had the Niarchos organization and the CIA on his side but only at a remove. "I had to go in," Maheu recalled, "as a potential fall guy." Before going in, he had one more face-to-face meeting with Niarchos on the shipowner's yacht, the *Creole,* anchored off Voulgameni near Athens. A speedboat service was provided to and from the *Creole*, where Maheu briefly acquainted Niarchos with his mission.

In the fifties, the Saudi government would grant a visitor only an entry visa, and anyone who wished to leave the country had to wait until his request for an exit visa was processed by the government in Jidda. Maheu was understandably alarmed by the prospect of having to wait around in Saudi Arabia after he had delivered his message at the king's court. He reckoned that Onassis had made payments to some of the cabinet, but he had no idea how many people were effectively in Onassis's pocket. As soon as he arrived in Jidda he contacted the US ambassador. The embassy was friendly but not reassuring. "The government," said Maheu, "would take no position as regards my operation. If I got into trouble, I was on my own." He was, however, granted one privilege— he was allowed to send messages to Niarchos through the CIA network by means of a prearranged code. Twitchell, meanwhile, had secured an interview with the king and had arranged for Maheu to meet with the king's confidential adviser. The drawback was that the king had insisted that Finance Minister Suleiman—who was, of course, deeply implicated by the material in Maheu's possession—should also be present to hear whatever charges Maheu wished to press.

Maheu spent the next few days with an "empty feeling in the gut." On the day he was due to make his "presentation," the king drove through the streets of Jidda on his way to his winter palace at Riyadh. Maheu watched the parade from the balcony of his hotel room and was alarmed to see Sheikh Alireza riding in an open Cadillac at the king's side. At eight o'clock in the evening, Twitchell and Maheu went to Suleiman's villa. Twitchell argued the "official" US line while Maheu went through the evidence of payoffs contained in Catapodis's affidavit. The Saudis were polite but undemonstrative. Twitchell had briefed Maheu on various matters of Saudi etiquette but had omitted to describe the niceties of Saudi sign language. Every time Maheu put his hand over his empty coffee cup, a servant came to fill it up. Maheu became increasingly jumpy. After four hours of one-sided conversation, the king's adviser thanked Maheu and Twitchell and said they would receive the king's answer at noon the following day.

Maheu met the king's adviser in his hotel lobby the next day. The adviser thanked Maheu for drawing the details of the payoffs to his attention and said that the king was personally grateful for the information. The king had decided to "have done with Onassis." However, he had signed the contract, and there were delicate questions of personal

149

pride involved. Evidence of the payoffs would in fact provide a satisfactory pretext for backing out, and the adviser informed Maheu that the king desired maximum publicity to be given to the charges, with one important proviso—Maheu should leak the documents to any and every European or Middle Eastern paper that would touch them, but he should not make them available to the American press. The king's adviser explained that negotiations between Saudi Arabia and the United States were at a rather sensitive stage and that, while the king acknowledged that the revelations would in any case be damaging, he was concerned about limiting the damage by avoiding publicity in America. The stipulation betrayed a touching ignorance of the way in which information is disseminated by the Western press, but Maheu was not disposed to point this out. He thankfully accepted his exit visa and left the same day.

Maheu's visit finally broke the deadlock. Suleiman was made the scapegoat for the affair and compelled to resign "for reasons of health." In October 1954 Onassis was summoned to Riyadh by the king to answer the charges Maheu had delivered. Onassis gave a good account of himself, representing himself as the victim of a conspiracy, but King Saud's patience with the deal was nearly exhausted. He privately informed ARAMCO and the US embassy that if Onassis could be shown to refuse a reasonable renegotiation of the agreement, he would gladly let it go to arbitration. This was exactly what they wanted to hear. There was to the diplomatic mind all the difference in the world between taking the Saudis to court and their volunteering arbitration as a way out of their mutual difficulties.

The process of renegotiation was rapidly completed over tea in Jidda. Fred Davies, the chairman of the board of ARAMCO, was confident of failure though Onassis began by designating two areas of the contract where mutual agreement might be found. He was prepared to drop the monopolistic clauses of the contract in return for a guarantee on ARAMCO's part that a fixed percentage of Saudi oil would be carried by his ships. He was also prepared to settle for less than the artificially high rates he had demanded previously. Davies saw his chance. If he stipulated that Onassis should only receive the standard market rate, Onassis would be bound to refuse. If the market fell, Onassis would find himself in the position of having to tie up his fleet at rates which would mean that he would certainly operate at a loss. The ploy was successful. Onassis conceded that his rates could not be competitive at *all* times.

ARAMCO offered this to the Saudis as proof that Onassis was not

150

seriously prepared to make concessions. The Saudis agreed. If no settlement were achieved within thirty days—a foregone conclusion—the case should go to arbitration. Wadsworth ebulliently summed up the result in a cable to the State Department: "ARAMCO has yielded nothing in substance or in principle and has gained valuable Royal assurance that, whatever be result arbitration, Saudi-ARAMCO relations will continue on basis full cooperation; and Onassis, when finally pinned down on rates issue, has weaseled and outsmarted himself."

Onassis returned to Europe to discover that he had, as he put it, been "stabbed in the back." As the Saudis had suggested, Maheu had circulated the Catapodis allegations throughout Europe. Editors, oil company executives, and shipowners received copies through the mail without any explanatory material to determine their provenance. But the story was not seriously picked up until November 19, when Catapodis filed suit against Onassis in Paris after summoning a press conference at the Hôtel George V to announce his intention of punishing Onassis for having ill-treated him. "If I get a judgment in the case," he said, "I intend to give most of the money to charities in France and in Greece." Onassis promptly denounced Catapodis's action as "part of the propaganda that has been going on ever since the agreement was published, with the sole purpose of jeopardizing it."

As ARAMCO and the Saudi government quietly submitted their cases to arbitration, the newspapers found the Catapodis allegations a continuing source of good copy. The legal battle shifted across the Atlantic when Catapodis filed suits against Onassis in Washington and New York. Onassis replied with a countersuit for damages on the no doubt reasonable grounds that Catapodis's allegations had harmed his reputation and his business. The story of the contract was reenacted over the next two years in Paris and New York. In Paris, Getty was one of the witnesses summoned to Judge Gojon's chambers. He was treated with due respect, though the judge told him his testimony was irrelevant. Gojon said he was concerned with one question, and one alone—namely, whether Catapodis possessed a copy of the famous contract with Onassis on which the ink had allegedly vanished. It was, the judge remarked with some asperity, the only document relating to the case that Catapodis had omitted to copy. Catapodis apologized for the unfortunate omission, but the judge was adamant. The case was dismissed.

In New York it dragged on interminably. Onassis's lawyers maintained that New York was not the place to try the case, since the contract had been signed in France and neither Catapodis nor Onassis were

American residents. It was not until December 1955 that pretrial hearings were finally held.

The proceedings were enlivened by the attempts of Onassis's lawyers to probe the Niarchos-Maheu-Catapodis connection. Catapodis blithely described Niarchos as a "friend and neighbor." Niarchos haughtily begged to differ. The south of France, he said, was "a village. . . . You see people a lot. You may see Catapodis in the casino. If I used to go to the casino every other night he may have been there. On the other hand, we never had any serious discussion. Nowadays a lot of people say he's my friend and that depends on what you call a friend. In my theory the definition of friendship is entirely different and his frame of mind may be different. By being only your compatriot, being of the same race, he may have called me a friend. As far as I was concerned, he was not my friend. I want to put it that way."

Niarchos did, however, concede that his organization had employed Maheu in connection with the Saudi deal and that Maheu had shown him the Catapodis affidavit before going to Saudi Arabia. Then, to the astonishment of the court, he announced he could reveal no more about his part in the affair because there were questions of security involved. "We are going to waste our time, because the whole thing is coming down to a wall and I would like to be clarified by Washington whether I am going to answer these questions or not."

The hearing was adjourned to give the CIA and the State Department a chance to consider whether Niarchos should, indeed, be further questioned. The government considered the matter and came to the conclusion that it would not oppose further questioning. Four days later Catapodis dropped the action. Charles Tuttle, Onassis's chief lawyer, drily observed that this effectively prevented further inquiries into "the whole vicious scheme of the Nice affidavit."

Niarchos had evidently not enjoyed his days in court, but he had every reason to be satisfied with the overall operation. Onassis had not been humiliated, but he had experienced the worst two years of his business life. While the arbitration was in progress Onassis was in no position to extend the idea of Arab tanker fleets (the court at The Hague finally passed judgment in favor of ARAMCO in 1958).

Bob Maheu was both rewarded and given a lesson. He and Niarchos privately celebrated the success of the operation at the Mayflower Hotel in Washington. According to Maheu, Niarchos complimented him on his "gutsy and imaginative" style of work, but he also scolded him. "You're a lousy businessman," he said. Maheu had been entitled to draw expenses on an account of Niarchos's, and they had been pitifully small. Maheu replied that Niarchos might well make up for that omission. "It's not too late," he said. "Yes, it is," replied Niarchos. "If I gave you the money now, you'd never learn the lesson." Niarchos said he felt that Maheu's life-style left something to be desired. "I don't like the house you live in, I don't like the car you drive. If you promise you'll get a new car and a new house, I'll send you $1,500 a month until you have $50,000." Maheu remembers absorbing the lesson and being paid in full.

Onassis continued to believe that his idea made general economic and political sense for the West and that most of the opposition to it was misguided. The passage of time provides some support for this view. It is hard to escape the conclusion that Arab intransigence over oil supplies and prices in recent times is partly the consequence of decades of frustration. "My mistake," said Onassis, looking back on the Saudi misadventure, "was that I woke up too early and disturbed those who were still asleep, and as a result I got into the biggest mess of my life."

11
FORTUNE OF WAR

TOWARD THE END of 1955 a small tanker of Monacan registration docked at Rotterdam loaded with oil for Esso. The port was not particularly busy. Bigger tankers were being briskly unloaded, but the Monacan-registered ship's turn never seemed to arrive. After five days of waiting, the owner hurried to Rotterdam to protest. He discovered that Esso was under the mistaken impression that the ship was owned by Aristotle Onassis.

The major oil companies had decided that Onassis had to be taught a lesson regardless of any agreement that might be reached with him over the Saudi venture. Keeping his ships hanging around in port up to the very last moment permitted under the charter contract was one way of punishing him. Time is money in the tanker business, and owners generally reckoned to have their ships back at sea and earning again within the load and discharge periods set out in their agreements. A delay of twenty-four hours in port could ruin Onassis's chance of securing another charter when one of his tankers was coming on the market.

These skirmishes had a cumulatively damaging effect on Onassis's business, but it was nothing compared with the impact of the oil companies' main weapon—a worldwide boycott on new charters for the Onassis fleet. There was nothing on paper, no formal boardroom

154

motions that might upset the lawyers at ARAMCO. The word was just allowed to go around that the great oil companies wanted Onassis frozen out of charters. Few small concerns could afford to ignore the hint.

From New York, Costa Gratsos reported that traditional sources of business were drying up at an alarming rate. Every time a charter expired, Gratsos would make the routine call to Onassis's brokers to offer to renew it. The answer from the oil companies was always the same—nothing doing. A day or two later Gratsos would learn that the charter had gone to a competitor—Lemos or Goulandris or, worst of all, Niarchos. Onassis became convinced that the companies were deliberately giving Niarchos "his" business to rub his nose in the dirt. That was not so, but the general pattern was depressing enough.

On one occasion a clerk at Texaco got his papers mixed up and canceled a charter on Onassis ships *before* it had actually expired. Since the ships in question had been financed with money from the Metropolitan Life Insurance Company, Gratsos appealed to Metropolitan's board chairman, Harry Hagerty, for help. Texaco admitted the error and agreed to stand by the charter agreement, but Hagerty was left in no doubt about the existence of a concerted boycott operation. It naturally worried him since Metropolitan had a lot of money tied up in Onassis's fleet. He told Texaco that he thought the punishment outweighed the crime. Onassis had just been a bad boy. "What the hell," Hagerty declared. "You oil companies don't smell like roses anyhow."

The loss of momentum after almost a decade of uninterrupted growth could have been disastrous to Onassis. Many of his ships were on two- and three-year charters signed in the early 1950s, which were beginning to expire. Their future earnings had already been projected for the purpose of meeting mortgage payments on Onassis's more recent acquisitions. Every owner with heavily mortgaged ships dreaded the thought of falling behind on repayments to the point where a ship might actually be repossessed. His revenue would then drop even further, making it impossible to maintain repayments on another vessel, which itself would be repossessed.

By the end of 1955 the boycott had cost Onassis over $20 million. Almost half his fleet was idle. To some fascinated observers it looked as if the oil companies were determined to drive Onassis out of business completely. There seemed a distinct possibility that he would be celebrating his fiftieth birthday in bankruptcy. Gratsos had certainly come to the conclusion that "they probably want to wipe us out." Brokers and businessmen working with Onassis at the time remember how profoundly disturbing the crisis was to him. George Moore, who handled Onassis's main account at First National City Bank in New York, remembers Onassis coming to him with a suggestion that the bank take over management of his assets. A Shell executive recalls how Onassis would alternate between fury and self-pity when he came through London. "You are really hurting me, you know," he said at the end of one tirade. "You guys are giving me the worst time of my life." Onassis was forced to acknowledge how much of a final say over his operations the great oil companies possessed, and it was a severe blow to his sense of independence.

At one point he considered selling his entire tanker fleet, at another he considered filing an antitrust suit against ARAMCO in the United States. The sale of his whaling fleet to the Japanese in the spring of 1956 helped ease his precarious cash position, but it was no more than a palliative. The tanker market began to improve but not enough to alter materially Onassis's prospects. His highly mortgaged fleet needed more than a few grudging charters to survive. The very scale of his operation made it imperative that he should be close to the head of the queue when the oil companies were dispensing favors.

By the summer of 1956 the chances of this happening seemed more remote than the Second Coming. Onassis needed a miracle, and it was provided by President Nasser of Egypt. The conflict with Britain, France, and Israel prompted by Nasser's nationalization of the Suez Canal was a godsend to the tanker market in general and to Aristotle Onassis in particular. With the outbreak of hostilities in October 1956 and the consequent closure of the canal, the terms of the market were turned upside down. Almost alone among the major independent owners, Onassis had the bulk of his fleet free when the stampede for the extra tonnage to carry oil around the Cape of Good Hope began. The oil companies, whose boycott had forced him to lay up so many of his tankers, were now elbowing each other aside for the privilege of securing a single-voyage spot charter at astronomical rates.

Suez made a fortune for Onassis. By his own account, he made between $60 and $70 million on the spot market in the hectic six months during which the canal—blocked with wrecked ships—remained closed. Carrying oil to Europe around the cape involved a journey of 11,300 miles, almost twice as long as the trip through the canal. The world's tanker fleets had been carrying about 95 million tons of oil a year through Suez, but they could only handle a maximum of 50 million tons on the route around Africa. Twice as many ships were required merely to maintain Europe's supply of crude oil. The Worldscale Index—a complex formula designed to equalize prospective revenue per ton per day on any voyage between two ports—moved to a record level of 460 within a few days. For most of the year it had hovered around 220.

A profit of more than $2 million from a single Persian Gulf–Europe voyage was by no means unusual at the peak of this market. That was often enough, Onassis would recall, to wipe out a big chunk of the outstanding debts on the ship concerned. Another shipowner, who had taken delivery of a brand-new tanker from Japan and sent it straight to the gulf before the Suez war began, was able to pay off more than a third of his ship's capital cost with its maiden voyage. "It was very touching," Onassis's insurance broker, Jimmy Stewart, recalled. "The oil companies had set out to screw Ari and in the process they made him one of the richest men in the business." A New York shipbroker suggested a more vivid simile. "Until then Onassis had been like the most beautiful babe on a Saturday night. She had everything but nobody would touch her because she was a hooker. After they'd had five drinks, there was money all over the place."

The initial advantage Onassis enjoyed over rivals who had their fleets tied up on long-term charters did not endure for long. A wave of contract-busting began as other shipowners endeavored to free more ships for the spot market. Breaking a contract was not that difficult. The drafting tended to be deliberately loose, both sides leaving loopholes in case they suddenly wanted out. The favorite escape clause for owners specified the exact dates on which the chartering company made its payments. Since oil companies are large and bureaucratic organizations their checks often arrived a day or two late, providing adequate grounds for cancelation.

The equanimity with which the major companies accepted charter-busting was rooted in what an experienced shipbroker described as the "controlled Darwinism" of the market. There are no fixed rules, no surefire system for playing the charter market. It is understood that the oil companies normally call the tune. If they can squeeze owners in a bad market, they will. But if the tables are turned—as they were at Suez—and the owners start squeezing them, "they will take it, they'll even respect you for doing it." When the scramble for Onassis's ships began, the hostilities of the previous two years were forgotten on both sides. Grudges were not allowed to stand in the way of business.

As Onassis's profits mounted, he displayed a marked aversion to discussing plans for operations after the boom had subsided. His faith in perpetual prosperity had never been more apparent. The spot market was still strong—Worldscale was about 420 at the end of 1956. There was gasoline rationing in Britain and France, and the US government, having secured the withdrawal of Anglo-French forces from the canal zone, was increasing the supply of American oil to Europe. Even with every seaworthy ship withdrawn from mothballs, Onassis argued, tanker tonnage would remain scarce. The boom, nonetheless, depended on the Suez Canal's remaining closed. Onassis's New York office decided that it was psychologically impossible for him to contemplate the thought of the canal's reopening. He seemed more concerned about getting back to Monte Carlo, where he set about planning a spectacular New Year's Eve gala to celebrate his restored fortune.

While Onassis enjoyed himself in Europe, Gratsos and Captain Granville Conway, head of Onassis's main US shipping company, Victory Carriers, were getting worried. They both believed that the canal would reopen much sooner than Onassis anticipated. It was time, they agreed, to get out of the spot market and grab the attractive time charters which some oil companies—hard hit by the huge rise in spot rates—were now offering. Onassis brusquely rejected Gratsos's suggestion, but Conway, whose interest in charter rate movements verged on the scholastic, stood firm. Under the agreement with the US government that settled the surplus ships affair, Conway was formally in charge of Victory Carriers independently of Onassis. It did not always work out like that, but on this occasion Conway acted unilaterally. Early in 1957 he reported that he had chartered Victory's twelve tankers to Esso on a thirty-nine-month contract.

Onassis was livid, abusing Conway for throwing away good money. A few weeks later, he burst into Conway's office and kissed him resoundingly on both cheeks. The canal was to reopen well ahead of schedule and the tanker boom had collapsed almost overnight. Worldscale plunged to 100 by March and continued to fall. The Persian Gulf–Europe run around the cape scarcely brought in enough revenue to meet operating costs. "Suddenly they found there was more oil, enough oil coming out in enough tankers that they did not know what to do with them," Onassis reflected a year later. The advantage had swung back to the oil companies, and tanker owners began cutting each other's throats for break-even charters in approved "Darwinian" fashion.

Onassis was not immune to the recession which hit the tanker business, but he and a few other owners—including Niarchos and Daniel

158

Ludwig—had made enough money out of Suez to cushion the blow. They had been plowing their profits back into shipping at a time when money and new ships were relatively cheap. Onassis had ordered the world's first 100,000-ton tanker from Bethlehem Steel. Niarchos soon topped him by ordering a 106,000-tonner, and Ludwig outdid them both with an order for *four* 100,000-tonners. Onassis was still no Livanos— unencumbered by mortgages and laying up idle ships for no more than maintenance costs—but he was in a strong enough financial position to withstand a serious slump. "When you own something worth $300 million," he informed journalists who asked whether his life-style was suffering, "you don't begin selling your cars and sacking your servants for economies of a few thousand dollars. It is meaningless. The crisis is all part of the game."

Another aspect of the game was his continued rivalry with Niarchos, which surfaced again in Paris early in 1957. The issues were tiny in comparison with those raised by the Saudi venture but no less strenuously fought. Niarchos claimed that he had advanced money to his brother-in-law to invest on his behalf in Monte Carlo. Onassis counterclaimed that it was simply a loan. There was also a disagreement over money owing after an exchange of private airplanes. The dispute was arbitrated by René Thorp, a Paris lawyer who ruled that Onassis owed Niarchos 130 million old francs (about $280,000). Niarchos was quoted as saying that the judgment had given him "the happiest day of my life." Onassis informed the press that "100,000 or 100 million francs, it's all the same to me."

Onassis's "quotability" was a boon to newsmen, and he liked to be quoted, though he affected unconcern for his "image." Fame, he grumbled, was like having a wonderful laugh that left you with a sore throat. Even so, he took particular delight in being recognized in public. He was invariably courteous to gawkers and autograph hunters and, for the most part, civil to the journalists who began to dog his tracks. It had its drawbacks, of course. Onassis began to receive crank mail and begging letters. Tina was cornered in bed one morning in Claridge's by an overenterprising lady reporter who wanted to know how it felt to be rich. Tina, naturally irritated by the intrusion, replied with irritation. Mrs. Onassis, the reporter later divulged, found it "boring" to be rich.

Onassis began to feel the need for help in coping with press inquiries. Nigel Neilson, a young New Zealander, was hired in London as a public relations consultant. Neilson's deft touch was soon detectable in the

159

flattering articles in the better class of newspaper, though he could scarcely have wished to claim the credit for one profile of Onassis which began, "Like a poem in a desert of arid prose, his poetic Greek name blossomed forth into topical news."

A more solid piece of work was a series on Onassis's life which appeared in *The News of the World,* Britain's most popular Sunday newspaper, in the summer of 1957. Arranged by Neilson and based on exclusive interviews with Onassis, it contained the best account to date of his life and state of mind. It was a highly sanitized version—there was, for example, no mention of Ingse Dedichen—but it made good reading. Onassis clearly perceived himself as a member of a human species that was rapidly becoming extinct. Asked what advice he would give a modern boy, Onassis replied,

> Our system of life outlaws individualism today. Everything is done through public corporations, associations, groups of people.
> If an individual is mediocre today, he can get away with it. If he's outstandingly successful, he becomes suspect.
> Outstanding individualism aggravates and disturbs the rest of society. A pity, perhaps, but it is so.
> For those reasons it is harder for a boy to succeed today than when I first started. The social system has changed so much.

Asked to nominate the quality he most disliked, Onassis replied, "Ingratitude and meanness. I've seen some people whose greatest satisfaction is to hurt needlessly. Others like to be nice. . . . Sometimes without realizing it at the time I know I've been ungrateful. That makes me suffer most. Because there is no excuse."

Yet Onassis's own account of his early life seemed less than generous to those who had helped him. The omission of Dedichen may have been due to discretion, but the same consideration did not apply to others who had been on his side during the early years of struggle. The impression Onassis strove to create on this and many other occasions was of a rugged individualist triumphing over the odds stacked against him. There was no margin for self-doubt. It was as if it was his manifest destiny to find a place in the sun.

The personality of Aristotle Onassis fascinated his intimates until the end of his life. It seemed impossible to reconcile the poles of extreme egotism and extreme vulnerability that were both central to his character. In public he always seemed the most ebullient of men, yet the bouts of melancholy which afflicted him at times became more intense as he

160

got older. The source of this melancholy is hard to define, though the early loss of his mother and the trauma of the "catastrophe" in Smyrna were clearly contributing factors. Onassis would speak readily about his early life—indeed he paid almost as much attention to the construction of his personal myth as to the making of his millions—but in a curious way. It was almost as if he needed to feel self-made psychologically as well as economically. There must have been times when he doubted the validity of his creation.

"He wanted history to start with him," one of his closest friends told us. "You have a definite impression of B.C. and A.D. in Ari's life. When he spoke about his youth he never mentioned friends by name. His adventures were never joint ones whereas most people's recollections of their youth involve stories in the first person plural. A.D. begins at about the point he made his first million. After the advent of Jesus Christ there are very vivid recollections of joint ventures."

Nigel Neilson became a fixture on the Onassis payroll, but Onassis needed few lessons in the art of self-promotion, or, where necessary, self-effacement. He had to draw on both skills in the summer of 1958 when the US Congress once again took an interest in his business activities.

The wretched business of the surplus ships had returned to plague him just when everything seemed to be improving. The "final" settlement reached in 1955 was turning out to be anything but that. As part of the settlement Onassis had promised to operate his main American interests through a trust operated by Grace National Bank of New York. Under its terms, 75 percent of the stock in Onassis's main US corporations—United States Petroleum Carriers, Victory Carriers, Western Tankers, and Trafalgar Steamship Company—was assigned to his two American-born children, Christina and Alexander, whose interest would be represented by the American trustees until they were twenty-one. Onassis himself retained a 25 percent interest through Ariona, a Panamanian corporation. Shortly after the trust was established it entered what was known as a "trade-out and build" agreement with the US Maritime Administration. The trust was allowed to transfer fourteen of its American-registered ships—twelve of them tankers—to the Liberian flag. In return for this privilege, the trust undertook to build three new tankers, totaling almost 200,000 tons, in American shipyards. The orders were placed with Bethlehem Steel.

The benevolent tax laws of Liberia and the absence of union-scale

161

wages did wonders for the profitability of Onassis's aging fleet. By the summer of 1958 they had earned the trust some $20 million. The "build" part of the program, however, had been less impressive. In March 1958, the trust, after consultations with Onassis, informed the maritime authorities that it intended to default on the construction contracts. The tanker market had shrunk, and the trust calculated that it was more sensible to pay the $8 million penalty for cancelation rather than proceed with the contracts.

In June 1958, Onassis was summoned to appear as a witness before a House subcommittee on the merchant marine. Although it was essentially a fact-finding operation, it was regarded in the maritime community as a public "trial" of Onassis's shipping record in the United States.

It took Onassis a little while to gauge the mood of the committee. He began badly by interrupting an earlier witness to ask for "just ten minutes" to save wasting precious time. The committee's chairman, Herbert C. Bonner, was furious, crashing his gavel down so hard that he accidentally smashed a glass of water on his desk. "We'll run this hearing," he bellowed, to the delight of the massive press corps.

Onassis's main adversary on the committee was Herbert Zelenko, a liberal Democrat from New York City. Zelenko was a formidable opponent, a tough lawyer with an encyclopedic knowledge of US shipping and a rooted dislike of foreign shipowners operating under flags of convenience. "I am a little sentimental about jobs for Americans," he warned, before Onassis took the stand. Onassis began his evidence with an expression of gratitude to the committee for giving him the chance to defend his good name. "You are here under subpoena," Zelenko observed sharply.

Zelenko's main concern was to demonstrate that Onassis had weaseled on his obligations to the US government and shipbuilding industry by manipulating the independent trust. His efforts to demonstrate this hypothesis led to some of the hearing's liveliest exchanges. Onassis shrewdly declared a passionate interest in the trust's operation, ordained not by law but by the Almighty. He was, he told the committee, bound by "the God-made interest and there is no law or constitution by man-made law that can interfere or change in any way whatsoever that God-made interest. By that I mean, Mr. Zelenko, the fact that I happen to be the father of those two children [Christina and Alexander]. No matter what laws you can put, that is made by God. I belong to those children and they belong to me. Therefore, I have a great, great, great interest."

Onassis was, nonetheless, careful to preserve a distinction between an

162

interest and control. He had a say in the trust's affairs, but it was not, as Zelenko wished to imply, his creature. Zelenko then tried to argue that Onassis's financial stake did give him effective control whatever the fine print of the trust document.

"Let me ask you this," Zelenko said. "You have been in business all your life?"

> ONASSIS: I think so.
> ZELENKO: I believe you are quite familiar with it. Would you say that the man who controls the purse . . . controls the business?
> ONASSIS: In other words, money talks. That is what you mean.
> ZELENKO: You know what I mean. I guess you can take it in a number of languages.

Onassis stood his ground. Money did not always talk, he maintained; on occasions it was completely mute. Zelenko was curious to know when that might be.

> ONASSIS: I will give you 30,000 examples in any business, Mr. Zelenko. Take a bank for instance. Do you want anybody more than a bank to apply the proverb, "Money talks"? If a bank gives me $50 million tomorrow, payable over a period of 10 or 15 years, what say does that bank have with me? Nothing, as long as I am not in default. They have $50 million of their money in my hands. However, as long as I am not in default, what saying that bank can have? Their money doesn't talk at all. It talks as much as a fish. I can give you examples like that until tomorrow morning.
> ZELENKO: I see.

Zelenko was not easily deflected. When Onassis, hands spread wide, observed that he might be cutting his own throat by giving straightforward answers, Zelenko said sourly, "You haven't done that up to now and I don't think there is a possibility." Onassis responded, "There is always time for that to happen, Mr. Zelenko, so one has to be a little careful also."

Onassis was proving a difficult witness to discomfort, though Zelenko did achieve this feat when questioning him about Ariona, the company through which Onassis held 25 percent of the stock in the US corporations. It emerged that the corporate structure of the Onassis empire had become so complex that Onassis himself could not remember how it all fitted together.

> ZELENKO: Give us your exact interest in Ariona, how much stock you own, what company it is.
> ONASSIS: I can't tell you exact, sir, but very close to exact. Ariona is a

163

Panamanian corporation, and I think at the moment I own about 85 percent of the stock.

ZELENKO: In your own name?

ONASSIS: No. Name of another corporation which will end up with me.

ZELENKO: In what corporation's name do you have your interest in Ariona?

ONASSIS: You are asking quite technical things. There are 70-some corporations. I can't remember exactly. You say to me if it is in my own name. If it isn't I said no, but it might be in the name of another corporation whose stock is in my name. I don't remember those things. If you like, I will find them out and let you know.

ZELENKO: Let me get back to the proposition. . . . Now I ask you, sir, do you have an interest, in your own name, in Ariona?

ONASSIS: I don't remember.

ZELENKO: Do you know where the books of Ariona are?

ONASSIS: I have to look into records.

ZELENKO: Where are the records?

ONASSIS: Down in South America, sir.

ZELENKO: In whose custody?

ONASSIS: In the office we have there.

ZELENKO: Can you get us those records?

ONASSIS: I can. They are here, the records. Aren't they? They are in the Maritime Commission. They are in the Justice Department, except that it is not specified who the stockholder—there is nothing new about Ariona.

ZELENKO: I want to know, Mr. Onassis, whether you have any stock or interest in Ariona in your own name. . . .

ONASSIS: I have more than the majority stock. I said almost 85 or 90 percent.

ZELENKO: In your own name?

ONASSIS: Whether it is in my own name or through another corporation whose stock is in my own name, that is a detail which I cannot answer because I don't know.

ZELENKO: You say you don't know whether or not you have an interest in your own name in Ariona? Is that your answer?

ONASSIS: That's right; in my own name.

ZELENKO: In your own name.

ONASSIS: I don't know. It might be in the certificate. The certificate might be to the bearer. I don't know.

The chairman, Herbert Bonner, attempted to clarify matters but only succeeded in compounding the confusion.

CHAIRMAN: You made the statement that you own 85 percent of Ariona.

ONASSIS: I do, sir. I haven't changed that. That remains as I said it.

CHAIRMAN: How would you own it if it were not in your own name?

ONASSIS: I am saying, Mr. Chairman, that beneficially I own it. In other words, it might be to the bearer, the certificates; it might be in the hands of my custody; it might belong to another corporation, which corporation I own myself and whose stock is in my name. I don't know.

Eventually, an exasperated Onassis told the committee that it was possible that the shares were in the name of someone else, but "I am telling you if it is someone else, I own that someone else." When the Ariona documents were located, Onassis's claim to an 85 percent holding was confirmed.

The most acrimonious exchange took place after Zelenko—a Jew—asked Onassis why, when he professed devoted loyalty to the United States, he had been discussing a Suez Canal pipeline project with President Nasser at a time when relations between the United States and Egypt were exceedingly bad. In less exalted company this would have been called a smear. Onassis, genuinely angered, counterattacked. Was Zelenko not aware, he asked, that at the very same moment he was talking to Nasser some very senior US officials were also in Cairo negotiating with the president to get the canal open as soon as possible? Chairman Bonner took Onassis's side; he could see no profit in this line of questioning and Zelenko was obliged to abandon it.

Onassis even made the committee laugh. Taxed about his right to own and operate US ships, he told Chairman Bonner that no man had been more thoroughly investigated by the authorities—"I even had to state whether my grandmother knew how to swim." Asked to describe the function of a service company in shipping, he replied, "They service. From painting the vessel and dry docking it to providing the lipstick of the captain's wife."

But it was not so much his humor as his evident conviction of his own probity that impressed the committee. His affairs might sometimes become tangled, but Onassis in the eyes of Onassis could do no wrong. On several occasions he volunteered evidence that Chairman Bonner and his own lawyer, Edward J. Ross, said he was not required to give. Onassis insisted that he had nothing to hide and would answer any question.

By the end of his four-hour grilling even Zelenko conceded that Onassis had been an unusually "cooperative" witness. Most of the committee were inclined to accept Onassis's claim that the trust was essentially independent and that the cancelation of the shipbuilding program had been caused by a combination of the post-Suez recession, the glut

165

of tanker tonnage, and the US government policy of restricting oil imports. On the evening after the hearing, Ross received a call at his hotel from the committee counsel. "Let me tell you," he said, "Onassis was the best goddam witness we've ever had before this committee."

The US maritime authorities insisted that Onassis continue his building program with Bethlehem Steel but sweetened the pill by contributing a loan of $14 million toward the cost of construction. Onassis was bemused by the absurdity of the settlement but happy enough to comply. "I am," he said, "building the largest ship in the world although at this moment I cannot see the slightest chance of employing it. I try to think what sense there is in the American government refusing an indemnity of $8 million while insisting on making a loan of $14 million of the taxpayers' money. It seems a hard way of learning that logic and politics do not go together."

Onassis was by now not only a celebrity but a collector of celebrities. The list of guests for parties aboard the *Christina* for her regular summer cruises had come to resemble a guide to the international beau monde. There was invariably a clutch of famous names from Hollywood. The cast, in strictly alphabetical order, included Marlene Dietrich, Douglas Fairbanks, Greta Garbo, Ava Gardner, Cary Grant, Jack Warner, and Darryl Zanuck. Those who owed their eminence to birth included ex-King Peter of Yugoslavia and his wife, ex-King Farouk of Egypt and his latest companion, the Begum Aga Khan, and the Maharani of Baroda. Onassis usually leavened the mixture with a few contacts from the oil and shipping business, who were suitably dazzled. It amused Onassis to throw groups of very different people together. He would hover on the sidelines, endlessly painstaking, as charming to the showgirl mistress of a Greek industrialist as he was to the wife of an American banker.

Everything on the *Christina* had to be the best. The finest wines were purchased and served by a sommelier who traveled on the yacht. There were usually two chefs on board, one for French cuisine, the other for Greek. Onassis had the habit of slipping down to the crew's mess and sampling what they were eating before dinner was served to his guests. He would reappear, exclaiming in delight at the taste of this dish, the delicacy of that. Dinner frequently consisted of Greek and French courses served simultaneously, with most of the guests eating Greek as a compliment to their host.

Onassis's personal tastes and habits were by now deeply ingrained. He drank heavily but more sensibly than he had in the period during and

166

immediately after World War II. He would drink champagne, always Dom Pérignon, with lunch and dinner, and follow the meal with cognac, usually Courvoisier. At the cocktail hour on board ship, his preferred drinks were ouzo and mezes rather than the more elaborate concoctions. The irregularity of his life made him prone to indigestion. Sometimes he omitted breakfast altogether, and when he took the meal it was invariably light—French coffee, scrambled or poached eggs, and fresh figs. His two favorite dishes at other times were stuffed tomatoes and *papatsakia*—eggplant cut lengthwise and baked with a covering, usually of onions, cheese, celery, tomatoes, and peppers. He did not like heavy or greasy food and preferred fish and game to the heavier meats. If he ate meat, all the fat had to be trimmed. He was not a big eater.

He smoked very heavily—cigarettes during the day and good cigars after dinner. His favorite cigars were Monte Christos. He sweated profusely. The large handkerchief he always affected in the breast pocket of his blue or gray flannel business suit was functional as well as decorative. He changed his clothing frequently and was fastidious about personal cleanliness. He preferred showers to baths. He rarely took exercise for its own sake but would make a point of going for a long swim in the sea twice a day if the weather was suitable. He used to say it gave him a chance to be alone and think his own thoughts.

He called regularly at the headquarters of Olympic Maritime in Monte Carlo, which now had a staff of over a hundred to monitor the movements of his ships worldwide. For the most part, however, he was content to leave the day-to-day running of his business to his two trusted lieutenants, Costa Konialidis and Nicolas Cokkinis, who specialized in shipping and finance respectively. The lawyer for his Panamanian corporations was Roberto Arias, the husband of the British ballerina Margot Fonteyn. When possible Onassis preferred to deal with Arias on a relaxed basis. In her autobiography, Margot Fonteyn wrote,

> Onassis had extraordinary charm and was a perfect host, always relaxed and unhurried. I thought he lived in a very intelligent and civilized manner. His preferred hour for discussing business was about two in the morning in a night club, so Tito [Arias] sometimes slept for a couple of hours after dinner in order to have a fresh mind later on. As Onassis never went to the theatre or ballet, I was surprised to find he knew a bit about entrechats-six. He said he had greatly admired Anna Pavlova when he was a very young man in Buenos Aires, and his eye had been caught by one of the dancers in her company.

Among others who sampled the hospitality was Randolph Churchill, the son of Sir Winston. The young Churchill was deeply impressed by Onassis's appearance—"like the black knight on a chessboard"—and his wit. One day the conversation on board turned to the role of Jews in the shipping business. "What Jew," asked Onassis, "has ever run a shipping line successfully?" "Ellerman—the British shipping magnate," came the reply. Onassis, still unimpressed, said, "He was only half a Jew. He was really a German." "And Noah?" Onassis surrendered happily. "You've got something there. But that damn fellow had a monopoly!"

An able journalist and historian, Randolph Churchill wrote what is still the best description of Onassis's conversational style in an article for the London *Evening Standard:*

> His most characteristic stance is with shoulders slightly hunched, arms spread out, and swaying a little on the balls of his feet like a bantamweight watching which way his opponent is going to move.
>
> As well as Greek, he speaks fluent Spanish, French and English. Though his choice of words in English is sometimes slightly off-center, his sense of the balance of a spoken sentence is uncannily acute. He is a born orator with a poetic sense and can build up a list of adjectives in an ascending order of emphasis and weight which are as perfect as a phrase of music.
>
> Just as his listener is caught by the spell, he will suddenly bring the whole edifice tumbling down by a deliberate piece of comic bathos. He will burst into laughter at the very moment when almost any other man would be exploding into passion. Sometimes he changes from a gentle whisper to a deafening bellow between two words.

In the summer of 1958, Randolph effected an introduction between his famous father and Onassis. Sir Winston and his wife, Clementine, were holidaying on the Riviera and accepted an invitation to lunch with Onassis in Monte Carlo. There was an instant rapport between the two men. "We talked all through lunch, discussing politics, history, human affairs, and human nature," Onassis said afterwards. A few days later, Sir Winston came to lunch on the *Christina*. It was the beginning of a remarkable friendship from which Churchill derived considerable pleasure during the final seven years of his long life.

There was on Onassis's side a certain element of celebrity hunting. He basked in the exalted company which generally surrounded the Churchills. They were people of *real* class, Onassis told a friend, very different from the international socialites who were then flocking to Monte Carlo. With Churchill aboard, the *Christina* would be met in foreign ports by ambassadors, governors, prime ministers, even royalty.

A constant flow of distinguished visitors passed through to pay their respects. On a cruise to New York, Onassis met the future American president, John F. Kennedy, then a senator from Massachusetts. He invited some of his Wall Street acquaintances along to dine on the yacht. In Barbados the former British prime minister Sir Anthony Eden came aboard. The social pinnacle for Onassis was an invitation to spend a weekend with the Churchills at Chartwell, their famous country house in Kent. He and Tina played croquet on the lawn.

There was no doubt that the sincerity of Onassis's affection for Churchill extended beyond the simple thrill of being acknowledged by the great man. Costa Gratsos believed that the key to the relationship was Onassis's rooted belief in the hegemony of the Anglo-Saxon races. "He thought the system created by the British and the Americans at the end of the war would last for ever—and he revered Winston as the embodiment of that system." Churchill's personal physician, Lord Moran, who accompanied his patient on several cruises, testified to the delicacy of Onassis's concern. His diaries, which later furnished material for his book, *Churchill*, provide intriguing glimpses of the two men together on board the *Christina*. "Ari, as Winston calls him, hardly takes his eyes off his guest: one moment he will fetch him a glass of whisky and the next, when Winston finds it cool on deck, he will tuck him in a blanket. Once, noticing hairs on the collar of his coat, he hurried away to find a clothes brush."

One night in the Caribbean, Moran recorded a remarkable scene. "When we were in the games room, waiting for dinner, Ari pulled his chair nearer and held a teaspoon of caviar to Winston's lips, as one feeds a baby. Three times he repeated this little ritual." Onassis saw nothing demeaning in their relationship. He was perfectly happy to learn to play bezique for the sole purpose of giving Churchill the pleasure of winning a few pounds from him across the card table. To test the cruising speed at which there was least vibration in Churchill's cabin—he always had the Chios suite—Onassis and the *Christina*'s chief engineer lay on the bed while the engines were speeded up and slowed down. When Churchill felt like a sing-along, Onassis would sit unself-consciously at his feet, deftly improvising what must have been, to him, the profoundly incomprehensible choruses of "Tipperary," "Tarara Boom-de-ay," and "Take a Pair of Sparkling Eyes." When Churchill's pet canary, Toby, escaped from the Hôtel de Paris in Monte Carlo, Onassis mobilized half the principality for the search and did not go to bed until Toby turned up again twenty-four hours later, alive and well in Nice.

Such devotion did not always save Onassis from flashes of Churchill's well-known testiness. On one occasion Onassis strove to interest Churchill in his theory of historical "necessity." It was one of his favorite topics, based on his observation that where nature provided an idyllic climate and plentiful food, people were not disposed to be very energetic. Some degree of adversity was required as a spur to any great effort. On finding that Churchill was showing little interest, Onassis tried to engage it with a personal observation. "You told me, Sir Winston, your father died very young, if he had lived to your age you might not have had to struggle so hard. Your life would have been easier, and you might not have done what you did."

"We were very different people," Churchill replied.

Onassis plunged on: "Yes, of course, you were different, but you would not have been driven on by necessity. My mother died when I was six. If she had lived, I might not have worked as hard as I have done."

Churchill, still deeply unmoved, responded with a question: "Would you like to play a little cards instead of talking philosophy?"

"Not philosophy but history," Onassis protested.

"They are not very different," replied Churchill. "I enjoy living on your yacht."

On an occasion when they did talk history, both agreed that President Eisenhower had acted limply in the scandal that led to the resignation of his adviser, Sherman Adams. Lord Moran recorded an illuminating exchange between them.

"You must either wallop a man or vindicate him," said Sir Winston.

"Yes," replied Onassis, "Eisenhower just allowed him to resign. You must let your nearest and dearest go to hell when they are no longer any use to you."

It was an odd remark. In economic terms at least, Onassis's nearest and dearest had few causes for complaint. On the other hand, it appears to have been something more than a remark designed to satisfy the prejudices of a friend. Onassis's regard for others was essentially an extension of his own self-regard. His kindness, though considerable, was reserved for those who were useful to him or whose acquaintance reflected his own glory.

Churchill's fondness for Onassis remained undimmed despite the disapproval of one of his closest wartime cronies, the Canadian-born press magnate Lord Beaverbrook, who owned the *Express* Group in Britain. Another critic of their friendship was Churchill's own wife, Clementine. "She thought he was keeping bad company," Churchill's grandson, Winston, told us. "She disapproved of rather a lot of his

170

friends." He thought his grandfather and Onassis shared the same broad view of the world even if from very different vantage points. "There was a very considerable empathy between them." Sir Winston described Onassis simply as "a man of mark."

Lord Moran, an able doctor and diarist but a somewhat unimaginative man, could never really understand the fascination Onassis had for his patient. One diary entry records his bafflement: "Onassis seems a very ordinary man to be set apart. What does Winston make of him? Is it the man or the yacht that attracts him? Ari's face is dark, his long greying hair grows wild and seems naturally to form a coif above an inch of forehead. Below is a beak of a nose. When amused Ari bears his white teeth like a dog, to the accompaniment of a harsh laugh. He is a little fellow, not as tall as Winston when they stand side by side. He wears an old blue-black sweater, and nondescript faded grey trousers, and his small bare feet are generally thrust into canvas tennis shoes."

What Lord Moran missed, perhaps because he never experienced it personally, was Onassis's intense quality of attention. All those who achieved any kind of close relationship with him were struck by it. While in his company, they felt that Onassis considered them of unique importance.

It was a quality that made him especially attractive to women.

12
ENTER MARIA CALLAS

THE RIVIERA SET had dubbed the marriage of Tina and Aristotle Onassis "the happiest between Cannes and West Palm Beach." No irony seems to have been intended, though both the Cap d'Antibes and Monte Carlo, which then had the best claims to being their homes, were to the east of Cannes. Their relationship appeared to combine intimacy with adventure—Tina and Ari hunting whales off the coast of Peru; Tina and Ari flying to Cuba on a sudden whim; Tina and Ari in Saudi Arabia; Tina and Ari going to Kiel in Germany to collect the *Christina*. They made a handsome and glamorous couple, and wherever they went photographers followed. It was all "tremendous," Tina later revealed. "He loved it, and so did I. Ari was a wonderful man to be with then."

Yet their paths and lives had begun to diverge. Ari never acquired, and Tina never lost, the passion for wintering in the Alps. Tina adored parties and gatherings of the star-studded Riviera set, but her appetite was limited while Ari's was insatiable. Ari's preferred way of rounding out an evening was talking ships with men. Business bored Tina stiff. His restlessness, his compulsive peripatetics, meant that they saw less and less of each other even when they spent the night under the same roof. Ari's idea of home was cafés, restaurants, clubs, or wherever there was a telephone and he could unpack a suitcase. Home was something he could take with him. Tina's idea of home was closer to the conventional image: evenings at the fireside, family portraits on the wall, the children playing (though whisked off by a nanny if they became too tiresome), and her husband doing something husbandly. Home was not necessarily somewhere she wanted to stay all the time—far from it—but it was somewhere she wanted to be able to go back to. By the mid-1950s Ari was away for weeks, then months, on end, although he invariably made a point of calling Tina at 6 P.M. her time wherever in the world he might be.

The Château de la Croë had been dispensed with after an unhappy contretemps. One day, when Tina had been sunning herself beside the pool of the nearby Hôtel Eden Roc, she had heard a voice calling, "Hello, Tina!" It was an old school friend, Jeanne Rhinelander, who was now living nearby in Grasse. Tina invited her to visit them at the château, and their friendship was renewed, though Tina often found herself wishing that Ari would not lavish quite so much attention on their glamorous guest. On an afternoon when Ari's increasingly distant manner was making her particularly unhappy, Tina drove over to Jeanne's house on an impulse. Arriving there, she found Ari in circumstances which appeared compromising.

When, a few months later in the spring of 1954, the Château de la Croë came up for sale, Tina announced that if Ari bought it she would absolutely refuse to live there. It was no longer "divine" (Tina's adjective of approval), it had too many unhappy memories. Onassis was ready to move to Monte Carlo, now his business base anyway, and a luxurious apartment was acquired there. The château was bought by Stavros Niarchos after it had been vacated by his brother-in-law. Besides, the *Christina* was often at anchor in Monaco harbor. "I suppose," said Tina a little uncertainly when Willi Frischauer interviewed her in 1956, "that *Christina* is my real home." Nevertheless, it was to the avenue Foch apartment that Tina returned most frequently once the children had begun their education in Paris. Ari, who had few business interests in Paris, was there less often.

The facade of a happy marriage was preserved, but by the late 1950s it had lost its emotional core. Occasionally with intimates even the facade slipped. A high-ranking employee of Onassis's remembers an embarrassing dinner party on the *Christina* at which Tina paid unusually close attention to one of the male guests. After the meal, the *Christina* weighed anchor for a cruise while Onassis and the employee took a speedboat for Monte Carlo.

173

Onassis's first question on the boat was, "What do you think of him?"

"What do I think of who?"

"Don't pretend you don't know what is going on."

The employee, who had originally thought they had left the party to discuss business, suddenly found himself involved in a six-hour drinking bout, with his boss exhibiting all the self-doubt of male menopause. Onassis, then just past fifty, rambled on about his potency and his wife's infidelity, oscillating between the roles of male chauvinist and complaisant husband. Of one thing the employee was convinced: Onassis's regard for his marriage had deteriorated to the extent that he allowed his wife to go on a cruise with a man he assumed was her lover.

Jimmy Stewart, the American who handled Onassis's insurance, remembers a typical evening in Monte Carlo. Onassis had thrown a party for eighty guests at the casino. Stewart was seated next to Tina at the banquet, and she confided that he was one of only four people she knew there. After the banquet, he danced with Tina and then went upstairs for a while to gamble. When he came back, Tina asked if he would take her home. But, he protested, the apartment was only fifty yards away. No, said Tina, she was living on the *Christina,* and when she got there she didn't want to be left alone with all her jewelry. They decided on a last attempt to pry Ari away from the bar, where he was seated with three cronies talking business in Greek. "I want to go home," pleaded Tina. "Well, go home, then!" snapped Ari. Driving to the yacht, Stewart confessed that he had found the whole incident quite embarrassing and that lately Ari seemed unpleasant. "No," said Tina loyally, "he is a wonderful person, but I am a very simple one. I don't like dining with something between twenty and eighty people every night. This life is killing me." Later she was to tell the William Hickey column in the London *Daily Express* that success and Monte Carlo had ruined Ari, implying that about 1957 he had become less fun and more interested in vulgar ostentation. "All that Monte Carlo stuff! Buying up the place! I can't tell you how much I dislike Monte Carlo. . . . He had his friends and I started to find mine." Among them was the Venezuelan oilman Renaldito Herrera, who was frequently photographed in her company. In 1958 Ari and Tina spent their first Christmas apart—Tina had gone to New York where her sister was having a baby.

In the early summer of 1959 Ari and Tina were reunited aboard the *Christina* after one of his increasingly protracted business absences. The yacht swung majestically at anchor at the mouth of Venice's Grand Canal, and the season was getting under way. Many members of what had come to be known as the jet set were arriving in the city. On the day after Onassis's own arrival, the couple received an invitation from the Countess Castelbarco, whose annual ball at her magnificent palace was the high spot of the season.

The return of her husband, the gathering of her friends, and now the countess's ball were all happy occasions for Tina. Clad in a gown by Jean Dessès—a longtime friend of Ari's who had dressed his women since the Dedichen days and who was now Tina's own preferred couturier—and wearing a spectacular headdress, Tina accompanied Ari to the ball. Around her neck she wore a diamond and emerald necklace with matching earrings. On her wrist was her favorite piece of jewelry, which Ari had found in an antique shop—a Russian bracelet in the form of a glittering, flexible snake studded with diamonds and rubies, winding in three coils up her forearm. By any standards she was stunning, eclipsed only by the guest of honor at the ball, the operatic superstar Madame Maria Callas.

Tina was acutely aware of her husband's glance tracking the diva around the crowded ballroom. Finally he edged away from Tina, and, after a diversionary feint in the opposite direction, intercepted Callas and settled down to chat with her in a corner. As if by common instinct, both Tina and Callas's husband, the elderly Italian industrialist Giovanni Meneghini, arrived simultaneously in hot pursuit, and the gathering became a foursome. Ari, as was his custom when he met interesting people, invited the Meneghini-Callases to join them for a cruise on the *Christina* some day. Tina dutifully echoed the invitation: "Yes, do join us!" Maria said they would love to come someday, but she had a crowded engagement diary and was due to open in *Medea* at Covent Garden in June, the first time the opera had been performed in London since 1870. Tina could hardly believe her ears when Ari, whose opinion of opera had hitherto been unprintable, responded, "We shall be there!"

Tina Onassis was not a jealous wife. "Other women" were nothing new for her, not because Ari was overly amorous—he was not—but because he was simply a target at which seductive females frequently launched themselves. On one memorable occasion an attractive guest aboard the *Christina* had been discovered reclining hopefully in Ari's bed and had been promptly airlifted ashore at dawn. Being married to Aristotle Onassis bred a certain stoicism in these matters. Even so, Tina was instinctively alarmed at the first encounter between Ari and La Callas.

175

Maria Callas and Aristotle Onassis had much in common. Each was Greek yet not Greek—neither had been born in Greece but each had lived there during a brief time of youthful crisis. Both had passports which were neither Greek nor bore their correct date of birth, and both their childhoods had been scarred by war, sudden privation, and family quarrels. She, like him, had felt it necessary to break away from the strong Greek sense of family in her single-minded quest for success, deliberately distancing herself from her parents. Both could lay claim to having come up the hard way in the face of heavy odds, and both had become maverick superstars in their chosen fields, where they owed their success as much to their gladiatorial temperaments as to their talents. Quite simply, he was the most famous Greek man in the world and she the most famous Greek woman.

La Callas's reputation for tantrums, sulks, and general "prima donna-ishness" was unrivaled. It sometimes obscured the fact that she was the most remarkable female singer of the twentieth century. Her voice was never beautiful in the classical sense, and music critics often detected in it what they called a "touch of metal." The American critic Claudia Cassidy, describing Callas's voice as "part oboe, part clarinet," noted the instability of her top notes and the bottled-up feeling of her lower register. Nevertheless, as *Time* observed in 1956 when she appeared on the magazine's cover, Callas could "sing anything written for the female voice . . . ignoring the conventional boundaries of soprano, mezzo-soprano and contralto as if they had never been created." It had been a long time, probably at least a century, since anyone had been able to do that. And whatever Callas's voice may have lacked in conventional prettiness, it more than compensated for in the emotional and dramatic effects of its delivery.

Callas was not only a great singer but also a superb actress, particularly adept at expressing hatred, snarling contempt, and venom. "Operagoers, long reconciled to the classic, three-gesture range of other prima donnas, are astounded and delighted," reported *Time*. In later years—when her ability for vocal gymnastics deteriorated and she was evidently losing what she herself termed "the battle of the [high] C," seemingly doomed to become a mere mezzo-soprano like the rest—some critics seriously urged her to abandon opera and take up acting. John Ardoin, former New York music critic for *The Times* of London, writes in his biography of Callas that "she has perplexed and infuriated as many as she has excited and inspired. One thing is certain—no-one is indifferent to her. . . . Callas alone in our time has had sufficient dimension to make the

176

influence of a singer again felt beyond the boundaries of the musical world."

It had not been easy. Maria Callas was born in New York City of recently arrived Greek immigrants in December 1923. Her passport and the hospital register give her date of birth as December 2, the Manhattan civil registry gives December 3, and both Callas and her mother have always been adamant that it was December 4. Part of the attraction of the latter date for Callas is that it is Saint Barbara's Day, and she has always pleaded a special and self-mocking devotion for the patron saint of artillery, whose feast day had been celebrated a couple of years before her birth by the young Onassis and his friends in the red-light district of Smyrna.

Much of the confusion about Maria's birthdate, and her subsequent unhappiness, is attributable to the fact that she was an unwanted child. Her parents had lost a son named Basil in a typhoid epidemic in Greece earlier that year. The loss was the culmination of several misfortunes which had prompted their emigration, and another son had been fervently hoped for. When a daughter arrived instead, the parents at first refused to see the baby.

Her parents, George and Evangelia Calogeropoulos, never had another son, and Maria grew up with only her elder sister, Jackie, for company. George Calogeropoulos was a hardworking pharmacist who soon had his own store in Manhattan, and he painted the more manageable name Callas on his sign. In 1929 he lost his business as a result of the stock market crash. He was forced to move his family to a more modest apartment and take a job as a traveling salesman. Evangelia, a domineering and voluble woman, took their straitened circumstances badly and refused to economize on the girls' piano lessons. Maria remembered her infancy as being an endless family quarrel.

At the age of six she was badly injured in a car crash and, after her recovery, began to put on weight. The dumpy girl was also myopic and wore glasses with very thick lenses. Soon she was not merely plump but obese, caught in a vicious circle of taunts about her physical appearance and the search for solace in compulsive overeating. Even her mother called her an ugly duckling. There were signs of the swan beneath, however, and as soon as her mother realized that her daughter had a remarkable voice, she vented her frustrated social ambitions by compelling her to sing in public at every opportunity. This new turn of events only compounded Maria's misery, for as often as not the audience would howl with laughter as soon as she walked on stage. On one occasion the hypersensitive girl rolled on the floor in the wings, shrieking that she would not compete in an amateur talent contest. She did anyway, and she won. In 1934 in Chicago she competed for the first time on a nationwide radio contest hosted by Jack Benny. An accordionist beat her, but Maria came in second and won a wristwatch.

Evangelia also had hopes for her daughter Jackie, who was a promising pianist. In 1937 she gathered together her brood and her pet canaries and departed for Athens. Husband George was left behind. It was, for all intents and purposes, the end of the marriage.

There were two immediate problems. First, at thirteen years old Maria was too young for enrollment at the music academies; and second, her Greek was poor. The first problem was solved by lying about her age, the second by a crash course in the Greek language. Potential teachers were impressed, and she was given scholarships, first to the Odeon Athenon and then, in December 1939, to the premier school of Athens, the Ethnikon Athenon. Her teacher was Elvira de Hidalgo, the famous coloratura soprano, who later became a close friend. Under her tutelage Maria worked maniacally, arriving early, leaving late, and learning in one week librettos which took most singers two months. In 1940 she gave her first professional performance, as Beatrice in von Suppé's opera *Boccaccio*.

Her voice was stunning, if undisciplined, but nobody yet appreciated its range. Hidalgo had spotted her dramatic abilities and was working hard to develop them, but Callas, weighing 200 pounds, was still hampered by her appearance. In 1942 she got her first major role when the lead in an Athens National Opera Company production of *Tosca* fell ill, and Callas took over at twenty-four hours' notice. Just as she was about to go on, she heard someone backstage exclaim, "That elephant can never be Tosca!" She leaped on the offending man with a shriek of rage, tore his shirt off, bloodied his nose, and stormed on stage with an embryonic black eye. Fortified by rage, she sang magnificently and earned rave reviews.

Greece, then occupied by the Axis powers, was starving. When the company gave performances for opera-loving Italian officers, it requested payment not in money but in food. When Maria gave performances on her own at the officers' social gatherings she made the same request. She was now the family breadwinner, returning home with bags of sugar, flour, and macaroni. Stories that she actually roamed the countryside in search of food seem improbable if only because a 200-pound girl would hardly have been an obvious candidate for charity, but she certainly walked miles to give performances.

178

Like World War I, World War II did not end for Greece when the principal antagonists made peace. This time the country drifted into a civil war between the communists and the monarchists. The Callas apartment was machine-gunned, and the canaries were killed. Now a pharmacist working in a prison, George Callas wrote to Maria in 1946, "You are American, come back; the ticket is enclosed." She caught the first boat.

Maria spent nearly two more years in America but never once had an offer to sing in public. She was convinced that her weight was to blame, though Edward Johnson, director of New York's Metropolitan Opera Company, when later asked why he had passed her by, implied that weight was not the problem: "All the young ones are too fat." In the end there was but one remaining chance, and Maria took it by sailing to Italy, the home of opera. She flunked an audition at Milan's La Scala before she lowered her sights and was hired to sing *La Gioconda* in Verona at sixty-three dollars for each performance. "I knew I had failed," she later said. "All that work and all those years for nothing. I understood why people kill themselves. One thing I learned—don't ask anybody for favors. You won't get anything anyway." The show opened on August 3, 1947, and then the embittered singer met her improbable Svengali.

Giovanni Meneghini, the man who filled her dressing room with flowers, was a millionaire building-materials manufacturer more than twice her age. A stocky, balding man with rapid-fire speech and a reputation for ruthlessness in business, he began to woo the singer in courtly fashion. In April 1949 they were married. Not only had Maria found love and affection for the first time in her life, she had also found a patron, manager, and father. Her relationship with her mother had cooled. Maria had come to resent her domineering ways in which she detected not affection but the instincts of an impresario. Soon she completely broke with her mother in a celebrated letter in which Maria said, "If you are not capable of feeding yourself you ought to jump out of the window." Communication between mother and daughter ceased, but Evangelia never missed an opportunity to paint the "true" picture of Maria for any journalist who cared to listen: "She has treated me very badly. An egotistical monster!" Maria responded: "I'll never forgive her for taking my childhood away. During all the years I should have been playing and growing up, I was singing or making money."

Meneghini sold his business in order to devote his entire time to Maria's career. He gave her an environment of love, protection, and freedom from financial pressures, which was responsible for fully developing her talents. It was he who persuaded the conductor Tullio Serafin to coach her, and it was Serafin who first suspected that what he had on his hands was not, as Maria and all her previous teachers had believed, a dramatic soprano but the long-lost unlimited soprano. When the scheduled singer fell ill five days before the opening of Bellini's *I Puritani* at Venice's Teatro de la Fenice in January 1949, Serafin persuaded her to step into the role of Elvira and coached her night and day for the part. The performance was the turning point of her career. Soon other Bellini operas, including *Norma,* and Rossini's *Armida,* which had not been heard for 116 years, were being revived as fast as the prodigy could rehearse them.

The rest was a succession of well-publicized triumphs and tantrums. She was carried through the streets of Genoa on the shoulders of cheering fans and went on to conquer Latin America, the United States, and finally La Scala in Milan. She grabbed solo curtain calls and conducted an enthusiastic feud with rival La Scala soprano Renata Tebaldi (Maria would sit alternately cheering ostentatiously and glowering at her from a prominent box, whereas Tebaldi pointedly stayed away from Maria's performances). Maria walked out after the first act of a performance for the Italian president, and the Rome police banned her next performance on the grounds that she was a threat to public order. She even broke with Serafin after he recorded *Tosca* with another soprano. She thrived on these fights. "As long as I hear them stirring and hissing like snakes out there, I know I am on top," she said. "If I heard nothing from my enemies I'd know I was slipping."

She even lost weight dramatically. Maria had weighed 230 pounds on the day she married but only 140 when she reigned as Queen of La Scala in 1954; for a brief period she was down to 120. There were said to be two great European postwar miracles: Germany's economy and Callas's waistline. Although Callas herself always insisted that the secret was nothing more mysterious than love and happiness, the skeptics were not so sure. A rumor that she had swallowed a tapeworm went the rounds, while the enterprising Prince Marcantonio Pacelli, a nephew of the Pope, contended that she had gone on a diet of the "physiological macaroni" produced by his pasta company. Callas sued the prince and won, witnesses testifying that she had cut pasta out of her diet altogether.

Callas initially gave most of the credit for her success to Meneghini. She was billed as Maria Meneghini Callas and was extravagant in her public displays of affection. She reacted savagely to any innuendoes. "I know what is being said. But I also know that women married to younger men are not as happy as I am. . . . My career would not exist were it not for my husband." She once pounced into the crowd outside La Scala and slapped a man who insulted Meneghini.

Nonetheless, the goddess Meneghini had created was leaving him behind. Successful, confident, wealthy in her own right, and a supreme artist, Maria was drifting into an elegant society in which he felt ill at ease. Once shy, she now wanted to see, and be seen in, all the most exclusive places. Meneghini, a bourgeois at heart, was happier in their palatial home on the shores of Lake Garda. At first he was not too concerned—after all, he seemed indispensable to her career. Or was he? Maria was growing increasingly resentful of his management of her affairs. She was inclined to believe that a great diva simply stated her price, and opera houses could either pay or go without. Later she was to blame Meneghini for most of the arguments with opera house managements. She felt he was trying to monopolize her affairs, just as her mother had once done. When Onassis met the Meneghini-Callases, he met a very jealous and worried husband.

Onassis kept his promise to be in London for the opening of Callas's *Medea* in June 1959. One hundred sixty people received invitations reading, "Mr. and Mrs. Aristotle Onassis request the pleasure of your company at a Supper Party to be held at the Dorchester at 11:15 P.M. on Wednesday 17 June," immediately after the first performance. La Callas was to be the guest of honor at London's most glittering social event of the year. Forty friends of Onassis's were promised tickets for the performance itself—they were like gold dust, and most had been acquired on the black market. Onassis took up his position in the bar forty-five minutes before the curtain went up and dispensed tickets and champagne to his guests as they arrived. The Churchills, though not Sir Winston, were there in force, as well as several members of the royal family, sundry tycoons, and film stars.

Afterward at the Dorchester, Onassis's excitement overflowed. When Callas expressed a passing desire to hear a tango, Onassis summoned the conductor of the orchestra, thrust £50 ($140) into his hands—then double the weekly earnings of the average Briton—and ordered tangos. Tina did not appear to be impressed by Ari's protestations that he was doing it all as a gesture of Anglo-Greek friendship, which had been sorely strained by the independence struggle in Cyprus. Friends noticed that she was unusually subdued. The evening ended with a memorable photo-

181

graph of Callas being jointly embraced, Onassis on one side, Meneghini on the other. Their view of each other blocked by her great height, the two small men ended up by clasping each other's hands around her.

Worse was to come. The Meneghini-Callases accepted the invitation to join the Onassises for a cruise. In the last week of July the *Christina* sailed from Monte Carlo. With the Meneghini-Callases were Sir Winston and Lady Churchill; their daughter, Diana; their doctor, Lord Moran; their canary, Toby; Winston's secretary, Anthony Montague-Brown, and his wife; and Fiat boss Umberto Agnelli and his wife, Antonella.

The illustrious boatload made an ostensibly dignified three-week cruise through the Gulf of Corinth—pausing for Onassis to drive the Churchills on a sight-seeing tour of Delphi—then on to Izmir, the Turkish name for Onassis's birthplace, up the Dardanelles, where Churchill's proposed visit to Gallipoli was canceled on Lord Moran's orders, to Istanbul, and then home again. The only immediate item of news to emerge when the *Christina* docked in Monte Carlo was that Onassis had hurt his back diving into the swimming pool. Most of those on board preferred to draw a discreet veil over the real significance of the voyage.

In fact, the yacht had run into heavy weather shortly after leaving Monte Carlo, and Meneghini had succumbed to chronic seasickness. Only Callas and Onassis seemed unaffected, and when all the watchdogs were in bed, they chatted into the early morning hours in the deserted saloon. "I have always had a great admiration for Madame Callas," Onassis later explained. "More than her artistic talent, even more than her success as a great singer, what always impressed me was the story of her early struggles as a poor girl in her teens when she sailed through unusually rough and merciless waters."

The rest of the voyage consisted of the Meneghini-Callases squabbling as quietly as possible and radiating tension. For once not mesmerized by Churchill, Onassis fussed over the angst-ridden diva and spent hours closeted with her discussing her business affairs. Prince Rainier had mentioned the possibility of a Monte Carlo opera house reigned over by Callas when he had seen them off. Onassis and Callas had "disappeared" for several hours in Istanbul, and Callas told her husband, "It is all over. I love Ari."

When the cruise ended in Monaco, nobody was quite sure what was supposed to happen next. The Meneghini-Callases made their excuses and left. The other relieved guests followed hard on their heels. The

182

Christina, with only Tina and the children on board, weighed anchor and started a leisurely cruise toward Venice. Onassis stayed behind, apparently returning to the cares of business. Twice he flew to Milan and dined discreetly with Callas. Then, on August 31, he had her brought to the Riviera in his private plane, a Piaggio. On September 2 the couple flew to Milan, and Onassis went on to Venice alone. His Piaggio touched down on the sea beside the *Christina* as it approached the harbor.

Tina was apparently unaware of how often her husband and Callas had been meeting. The next day they met again, when Onassis returned to Milan. He dined out with Callas that evening, and the paparazzi were there in force to record the occasion. From then on even the flimsiest report of an Onassis-Callas sighting was enough to send the press scurrying from one end of Europe to the other. On Friday, September 5, Callas was reported dining *à deux* with Onassis in his hotel suite. Afterward she returned home with her lawyer, and Onassis again flew back to Venice and Tina.

The next morning Onassis flew out, picked up Callas in Turin (the press had been waiting in Milan), and turned up in Nice that evening. "The plane has never flown so much since Mr. Onassis bought it," pilot Angelo Pirotti exclaimed. On Monday the couple flew back to Milan, where Callas was due to start work on a recording of *La Gioconda* (which, the press noted, was set in Venice and involved lots of sailors). On Tuesday both Callas and Meneghini ("she has repaid my love by stabbing me in the back") publicly declared that all was over between them and that Meneghini had also ceased to handle Callas's business affairs. Onassis, cornered by reporters in his Milan hotel, cryptically announced, "I am a sailor, and these are things which may happen to a sailor." He pronounced the press conference over and prepared to return to Venice and the *Christina*. When he arrived, the ship was deserted—Tina had taken the children and gone. Tina later said that she and Ari had not had time to discuss the "unhappy situation" and that she was inclined to believe that, handled calmly, it would all have blown over. But this seems like wisdom in hindsight. At the time Tina herself was not in an accommodating frame of mind.

Onassis traced Tina and the children to the Livanos family home, also on the avenue Foch in Paris. The weary Pirotti flew him in hot pursuit. Old Stavros Livanos could merely mutter, "I knew it, I knew it," and Tina was in no mood for a reconciliation. She, too, had her *philotimo*, and Onassis's public flaunting of his relationship with Callas had been the last straw. She did not believe his protestations that Callas was merely a very good friend whose business affairs he had been discussing, and it would probably have made no difference if she had.

On September 11 Onassis was back in Venice and ordered the *Christina*'s crew to prepare for another cruise to the Aegean. This time there was to be only one guest on board—Maria Callas. They arrived back in Monte Carlo two weeks later to find that their respective spouses had not been inactive. Meneghini had talked freely to several Italian newspapers. According to one account, Meneghini first learned that his wife was going to leave him on August 7. Meneghini was quoted as saying, "At first, Maria sounded nebulous. She hinted that she had arrived at a turning point in her life. She acknowledged loving another man, but would not say who he was, although I urged her to be frank. Then, an hour later—to me it seemed eternity—she admitted that the man she loved was Onassis." Meneghini said he thought Onassis wanted to marry Callas, but his view of Onassis's motives was highly uncomplimentary —"Onassis wants to glamorize his grimy tankers with the name of a great diva." Tina Onassis had said nothing to the press, but her actions spoke eloquently enough: she had decamped with the children to New York.

Onassis was outraged. He told friends, "She has kidnapped the children and is demanding $20 million ransom." Onassis henchmen were instructed to telephone the press with the same unprintable allegation. Friends were subjected to tirades of recriminations and self-justification. Onassis reacted sharply to the suggestion that he was ill advised to treat the daughter of Stavros Livanos in this way. He belligerently told a reporter that his father-in-law "has not even enough money to buy Niarchos's art collection or my hobby enterprises."

Basil Mavroleon, a close friend of Tina and Ari, was alarmed by Onassis's mood when he met him in Monte Carlo. Onassis, who rarely opened his heart to anybody, insisted on driving Mavroleon around for hours and talking about Tina. "It was disgusting, and I don't want to talk about it, but I had the impression that he was trying to justify himself, accusing her of carrying on with other men." Mavroleon, a leading figure in the Greek shipping community, was shocked by the blatancy of Onassis's behavior. "I am sorry to say it," says Mavroleon, "but I suspect his real motive was publicity. He had had all the publicity he wanted from Tina. She was a good-looking girl and was photographed wherever she went. But her usefulness had come to an end. When Callas's usefulness came to an end, he did the same thing and married Jackie. Onassis never admitted that he craved publicity, but he did."

184

Again, this seems like wisdom in hindsight. Onassis undoubtedly enjoyed public attention but not, it seems, at the expense of his marriage. He consistently denied having any intention of divorcing his wife.

Events, however, were no longer within his control. Meneghini was the first to resort to the courts, filing suit for a legal separation from his wife in Brescia, Italy. In his writ of application, Meneghini spoke of years of happy marriage with his "loyal and grateful wife" and went on, "All of a sudden, this great happiness was shattered. After a cruise in which we both took part alongside of persons who are reckoned the most powerful of our time, the attitude of Signora Callas changed abruptly in an altogether unexpected and unforeseen manner." After the cruise, Meneghini related, Callas had told him of her intention of leaving him because of her love for another man. The writ did not mention Onassis by name but spoke of Callas's adopting an attitude "incompatible with elementary decency," going to night clubs and other places with a man "whom she described as her lover." The Brescia court went through the motions of reconciliation but to no avail. On November 14 it pronounced the separation legal and devised a financial settlement between the parties.

Eleven days later, Tina Onassis filed suit in the New York State Supreme Court for a divorce from her husband and custody of the children. Reporters were summoned to her Sutton Square home, where Tina read a prepared statement. There was no mistaking its elegiac quality.

> It is almost thirteen years since Mr. Onassis and I were married in New York City. Since then he has become one of the world's richest men, but his great wealth has not brought me happiness with him nor, as the world knows, has it brought him happiness with me. After we parted this summer in Venice, I had hoped that Mr. Onassis loved our children enough and respected our privacy sufficiently to meet with me—or, through lawyers, with my lawyer—to straighten out our problems. But that was not to be.
>
> Mr. Onassis knows positively that I want none of his wealth and that I am solely concerned with the welfare of our children.
>
> I deeply regret that Mr. Onassis leaves me no alternative other than a New York suit for divorce.
>
> For my part I will always wish Mr. Onassis well, and I expect that after this action is concluded he will continue to enjoy the kind of life which he apparently desires to live, but in which I have played no real part. I

shall have nothing more to say and I hope I shall be left with my children in peace.

It was a dignified statement, but there was an unexpected sting in the action. The grounds on which Tina sought a divorce were the only ones valid in New York: adultery. But the alleged adulteress was not, as everyone had expected, La Callas, but a "Mrs. J. R.," with whom her husband was alleged to have had an affair "by land and sea." It was commonly assumed that Tina had declined to give Callas the satisfaction of being named as the woman who stole Ari from her. The identity of Mrs. J. R. was soon revealed by the gossip columnists as Jeanne Rhinelander.

The Grasse home of the unfortunate Mrs. Rhinelander was promptly besieged by reporters asking for clarification. They were rewarded with another prepared statement.

"I am," she said, "an old friend of Mr. and Mrs. Onassis. I am astonished that after so many years of friendship of which everybody knew, here and in the United States, Mrs. Onassis should try to use it as an excuse to obtain her freedom.

"I am astonished that my name should be brought before the public in connection with a scandal in which I have played no part. I repeat that I know Mr. Onassis and that I remain a devoted friend."

Mrs. Rhinelander denied allegations of misconduct with Onassis and threatened to sue Tina Onassis for slander.

The divorce seemed to have had all the makings of an ugly society scandal. Mutual friends offered themselves as intermediaries. Princess Grace of Monaco phoned Ari; Elsa Maxwell, the society hostess, phoned Tina. Even Winston Churchill, to Onassis's fury, was asked to use his good offices. Onassis himself began to plead with his wife, blaming most of their difficulties on the attentions of the press. Spyros Skouras recalled how Onassis had asked to use the telephone in his London hotel room, making a tearful, hour-long call to Tina in New York, begging her to drop the divorce.

In April 1960 Onassis told a British journalist, "A reconciliation with my wife, Tina, would please Sir Winston a good deal. After all, he's a friend of both of us." Soon afterward Onassis and Tina met in Paris, and it seemed possible that the marriage would survive, though by this time Tina was pointedly referring to herself as "Tina Livanos" and her husband as "Mr. Onassis." The meeting was amicable enough, but appearances of marital bliss were long past preservation. All that remained was

186

to reach an agreement about custody of the children. Alexander was then age twelve, Christina nine. It was agreed that they should continue to live with their mother, though Onassis would have generous visiting rights. Financial provision for them was assured through the American trust, which then controlled 25 percent of the Onassis fleet. Tina did not claim any alimony for herself.

She made one other important concession by dropping her New York divorce suit and with it her allegation of adultery. In June 1960, Tina went to Alabama and was granted a "quickie" divorce on grounds of mental cruelty. Her petition was not contested. Six weeks later, the William Hickey column in the London *Daily Express* reported another Onassis-Callas sighting at the Maona night club in Monte Carlo. The reporter observed, "It is impossible for them to dance cheek-to-cheek as Miss Callas is slightly taller than Mr. Onassis. But as they danced she has lowered her head to nibble his ear and he has smiled rapturously."

Did Onassis love Callas? Some acute observers were inclined to think not, and these may have included Callas herself. "I only wish it *were* a romance," she later told the press when denying it. It may be significant that not once in the next nine years during which Onassis and Callas were regular companions did either publicly proclaim that they were in love or intended marriage. Meneghini had said that Onassis would marry Callas, but in the understandable heat of the moment he had failed to appreciate the Greek distinctions between a wife, a legendary business property, and a kindred spirit. Onassis certainly felt a deep affinity with Callas, but there is no evidence that he considered her a potential wife.

Onassis always maintained they were "just good friends," and it is possible that, for once, this hackneyed phrase conveyed the essence of a relationship. This does not mean that their friendship was not more passionate than most marriages or love affairs. It was. They recognized each other as worthy allies and evidently drew strength from their mutual attachment.

In any event, Tina was the first to remarry, little more than a year after the divorce. Her second husband was an English aristocrat, the thirty-five-year-old Marquess of Blandford. For their honeymoon they went on a cruise in the Aegean Sea.

Onassis's emotional energy was engaged by other concerns, the most important of which, after Callas, was Monte Carlo. His long love affair with the principality was coming to an end that was to prove both painful and expensive.

13
A PRINCELY REVENGE

Native Monacans are forbidden by law to gamble. Nonetheless, they have great faith in the guiding principle of chance. It is, in a sense, the only credible explanation for Monaco's curious history. There is nothing inherently valuable in its rocky acres—as a natural site it is less promising than the other towns along the Riviera. Its dimunitive size—six-tenths of a square mile—would not seem to be an asset in a world of intensely competitive nation-states. Yet, in defiance of historical laws, it has not only survived but prospered. Its real estate values are as high as those of Paris, London, or New York. There is no income tax and none of the more obvious and disturbing varieties of crime.

Ever since 1297, when Monaco was captured by the Grimaldi family retainers disguised as Franciscan monks, the principality has made its way in the world with low cunning and sleight of hand. It is not in the conjuror's interest to divulge his methods while the crowds still line up to see him perform—Monaco survives and prospers because the world still believes in its mystique. In the cafés beneath the palm trees and in the ornate *belle époque* hotel bars, the Monacan phenomenon remains an object of lively controversy. Perhaps illusion has triumphed over reality, but the Monacans prefer to say that the illusion, for all intents and purposes, *is* reality. An eminently practical, if not exactly sober-

188

minded, people, they are prepared to live with such contradictions. There have been bad times, but chance has always tended to restore their affluence. The chance that brought Aristotle Onassis to Monaco was a case in point. For ten years, from 1953 until 1963, Monaco was not only what he described as "my headquarters of convenience" but also the closest thing he had to a real home. Both in business and personal terms, it was a period of transition for him.

At the precise moment of Onassis's arrival, the principality was in the throes of what might be called an identity crisis, the result of its failure to come to terms with some of the harsher realities of the twentieth century. It still depended for its livelihood on the sort of people whose own chances of survival seemed doubtful. Most of the White Russian fortunes had long ago passed beneath the croupier's rake. England was on its way toward socialism, and currency controls already made it difficult for any but the most ingenious to risk their money at the tables. One failure led to another. The neglect evident in the deteriorating hotels and empty gambling halls only made it harder to attract a new clientele, a problem compounded by the fact that the principality still lacked what most twentieth-century vacationers would consider the prerequisite of any successful resort—a decent beach.

Even more disturbing were the unprincely attitudes of young Rainier III, who in 1949 succeeded his own grandfather after his father, Prince Pierre, had been excluded from the succession and banished from the principality. As a child, Rainier had unwillingly experienced the rigors of a private school education in England and a number of unhappy years during which he was shuttled back and forth between the divided royal family. After his accession, much of the young prince's behavior seemed largely self-destructive. He entered a motor race under an assumed name and nearly killed himself. He also seemed in no hurry to marry and produce an heir, a condition of the principality's survival as a result of a treaty between France and Monaco. His primary amorous interest was Gisèle Pascale, a film star and divorcée a few years older than he whose parents, he was frequently reminded, had once owned a vegetable and fruit stall in nearby Nice.

It is no exaggeration to say that Onassis's presence alone reversed the principality's decline. From the beginning, he was perceived as a legendary figure possessing magical powers. Even before it became known precisely what he had come to do, it was assumed that he wished to be the man who created "a new Monte Carlo." There is no evidence that he had this intention at first.

189

In Monte Carlo Onassis created a more organized version of the vagrant life he had led in New York, Paris, and London. His office was halfway down the hill between the casino and the harbor, where the *Christina* occupied the prime berth at the edge of the breakwater, a position conspicuous by its distance from the lesser yachts that lined the shore. He made a pied-à-terre over his office and installed an elaborate communications system in the Salle Empire of the Hôtel de Paris so that he could take calls while he entertained. He had always loved the great dining room with its huge mural of *belle époque* cuties. Its unabashed opulence was like his own, an elaborate display of hedonism that transcended conventional notions of good or bad taste. "He was in heaven every time he came into the Salle Empire," recalls Charles Audibert, one of the SBM directors. "It was like a diamond that belonged to him."

People both richer and more famous than Onassis had made Monte Carlo their temporary home or dabbled in its affairs, but they had been content to enjoy it as a convenient backdrop for their social ambitions. Onassis was an interloper of a different sort, one with whom the Monacans could identify. Like them, he was of Mediterranean origin and thus shared their addiction to intrigue as a legitimate and pleasurable feature of business life. And unlike a number of Anglo-Saxons with whom Onassis had business dealings, the Monacans were never offended by the autocratic way in which Onassis sometimes treated his employees and associates. The conviction that a real *patron* should occasionally behave like one is a distinctively meridional trait.

Onassis's first direct attempt to revive Monte Carlo involved a degree of discreet social promotion. He was acutely conscious of the principality's need to attract tourists who could spend large quantities of money, and in the early 1950s that could only mean Americans. Onassis entrusted George Schlee, an American friend of Greta Garbo's who had spent some time on the *Christina,* with the task of bringing American money to the gaming tables. Schlee, whose wife was a dress designer, made the rounds of New York society offering rent-free villas to socially prominent figures who would agree to spend the winter in Monte Carlo. He was not immediately successful.

Schlee took his problems to Gardner Cowles, the publisher of *Look* magazine, who immediately suggested that, since Americans were infatuated with royalty, the key to Monte Carlo's success lay in an astute promotion of its royal family. Why didn't Schlee and Onassis marry Rainier off to "an American celebrity"? Schlee displayed a cautious interest. Rainier was "a plump young man but attractive enough," and there would be no problem finding someone willing to marry him. But who would do the trick? "Well, what about a movie star?" Cowles suggested. "Why not start at the top—Marilyn Monroe."

A rendezvous with the actress was accordingly fixed for the following Saturday at Cowles's farm in Connecticut. This is Cowles's account of the meeting.

> George and I managed to get Marilyn to walk with us round the pool so that we could talk alone. We put the idea to her. She listened very carefully and said, "Is he rich? Is he handsome?" Those were the only questions she asked. I don't think she even knew where Monaco was. But she agreed that we should go ahead and arrange a meeting.
>
> As an afterthought I said to her, "Do you think that the Prince will want to marry you?"
>
> Her eyes were full of light. "Give me two days alone with him and of course he'll want to marry me."

Marilyn's charms were never put to the test. Before the plan could be put into operation, Prince Rainier had fallen in love with a somewhat more regal movie queen. In January 1956 he announced his engagement to Grace Kelly. They were married three months later.

The Monroe incident reflected something of Onassis's attitude toward Prince Rainier. His charm was laced with a measure of condescension. The deference accorded to Monacan royalty did not come easily to Onassis, the more so because his holding in the SBM gave him the sense that he, rather than the prince, was the most powerful man in Monte Carlo. When Onassis was asked to comment on the prince's match with Grace Kelly, he made a point of stressing its benefits as a cure for Rainier's isolation—"It must be very lonely for him to be stuck up in that palace surrounded by all those old courtiers." Asked his opinion of Onassis by an editor of Look, Rainier's reported reply was, "That man! I won't have anything to do with him. He'd like to turn Monte Carlo into Monte Greco. Last time Onassis came to the palace I told him: 'Mr. Onassis, your money has brought you everything except an education. You were badly brought up.' "

When these remarks were conveyed to Onassis, he was indignant— "Did that kid have the nerve to say something nasty about me? I thought that when we got him that boat he wouldn't talk so much." The boat in question was the Deo Juvante, a 135-foot yacht that Onassis had been able to procure for Rainier for $200,000. The fact that Rainier had paid in full for the yacht himself was obscured by Onassis's ambiguous style

191

of expression. Amends were made, and the row was blamed on inaccurate reporting, but the evident touchiness of both parties augured ill for any lasting collaboration.

Even the least mean-spirited of Onassis's gestures could provide grounds for another falling-out. Such was the case with his "wedding gift" to Princess Grace. A small but regular source of income for the SBM was the *tir aux pigeons* located in the rocky promontory that formed the base of the casino. Interest in the pastime of shooting pigeons was declining, but, like much else in Monaco, it was useful since its very rarity attracted practitioners from all over Europe, most of them rich and elderly. A special breed of pigeon was imported from Spain. The birds' wings were clipped to make sure they flew neither too far nor in a straight line. They were then released from a number of whitewashed boxes outside the casino a short distance from the marksmen. Such skill as the sport required involved guessing from which box the next bird would emerge. On a lively day the carnage was considerable. The dead birds fell into the sea, while wounded ones (of which there were many) were retrieved from the casino terraces and delivered to the hotel kitchens.

When Onassis received a gracious letter in which the prince mentioned that his bride-to-be found the sport distasteful and would be grateful if it could be stopped, he gladly assented. He also showed the letter to an American reporter, with the result that the prince's deferential request and his own response received wide attention. Onassis was complimented on his delicacy—the local consensus was that this was "the gesture of a Grand Seigneur." But the episode had unfortunate results for the royal family. The following spring there were fewer visitors, no pigeons on the table d'hôte, and the local papers tartly referred to the "Grace Kelly recession." Onassis escaped the consequences of his gesture; as far as most Monacans were concerned he could do no wrong.

Later it was asserted that Onassis fell out of favor with the Rainiers after his marriage broke up and that, as practicing Catholics, they disapproved of the possibility that Onassis might marry Maria Callas. It is true that the relationship between Onassis and the prince was strained around the time of Onassis's divorce, but this explanation is too simple. If Rainier, *père de famille* and bourgeois monarch, did disapprove of the goings-on across the bay from his palace, he kept it to himself. Grace and Rainier continued to mix socially with Onassis until 1964, even attending some of Maria Callas's entertainments in the *Christina*'s lounge.

192

The yacht was periodically placed at the prince's disposal. Onassis encouraged him to make up a guest list and entertained Rainier's friends in person. The atmosphere on these cruises was certainly convivial. Rainier's children came on board and used to pull Onassis out of the deck chair in which he took his siesta. "They would tease him, tweak his ears, and pull him into the pool," Rainier recalls. "He wasn't young then and we used to get rather worried. But he loved it and although he did not appear to be the typical playmate for the children, they adored him."

The reasons for the hostility that developed between Onassis and Rainier were more complex than most contemporary observers appreciated. Marriage wrought changes in Rainier and his concept of monarchy. What had passed for moodiness now appeared to be an intense seriousness about his own person and a concern that the world should appreciate that he was exercising in full the prerogatives of divine right over the affairs of his princedom. To begin with, the question was how Onassis could best be fitted into this new scheme of things. Later, as the prince gained in confidence, it became a question of whether Onassis's presence in the principality could be reconciled with Rainier's authority.

There was no single dramatic break between them. Despite his aloofness, Rainier was always susceptible to Onassis's charm. "One day they would be going for one another," one of Rainier's ministers recalls, "next day they would be kissing each other on the cheek." But the accumulation of disputes over what sometimes appeared petty issues inevitably eroded their capacity to make up. Eventually, the kissing had to stop.

The root of the problem lay in the distinctive character of the SBM. Founded in 1862, the company reflected the peculiar circumstances of its origins and the business acumen of its first operator, François Blanc. On hearing of the parlous state of the Grimaldi family fortunes, Blanc secured the privilege of operating a gambling monopoly in the principality on conspicuously favorable terms. In return for 10 percent of the casino's proceeds, to be paid annually to the prince's treasury, Blanc acquired most of the best sites in Monte Carlo. He also undertook the responsibility for bringing water and electricity to the principality. This was no altruistic gesture—it was evident to Blanc that no one would wish to visit Monaco in its then unsanitary condition.

Blanc's agreement established the SBM as a diminutive but powerful entity within the barely larger principality surrounding it. For many years the arrangement proved entirely satisfactory. The Grimaldi family had the privilege of receiving a large yearly income without having to concern itself in any significant way with the affairs of its princedom. Its wealth accumulated steadily with each spin of the roulette wheel, each pull of the croupier's rake. Some adjustments had to be made in the 1930s when the SBM experienced a number of lean years and the Monacan state agreed to take over its services as a public utility. It was, however, the decline of postwar Monaco that made the SBM's management a serious concern of the state.

As an institution it was showing a serious inability to adapt to changed circumstances. Monte Carlo's hotels (of which the SBM controlled a substantial portion) had always been run in a spirit of virtual indifference to their profitability. This strategy had its rationale: guests who lost all their francs at the tables were more likely to return if the question of their hotel bill was discreetly waived. Less economically justifiable was the practice of allowing those who had ruined themselves in Monte Carlo to live out their days in some of the less prepossessing rooms of the Hôtel de Paris at the company's expense. Among those enjoying this privilege was a former captain of the czar's yacht, whose roulette system had not brought him success at the tables.

Such largesse may have been of minor importance, but it reflected the general spirit in which the SBM was conceived by its shareholders, its managers, and its employees. There was the added problem that the SBM alone among Monacan institutions was responsive to public opinion. Its annual shareholders' meetings, held in the splendor of the opera house, reflected an intense conservatism. The shares, despite their low yield, were a patriotic investment. Many of the SBM's three thousand employees owned shares in the company. They viewed any attempts at modernization with some suspicion, particularly when these involved proposals to limit some of the notorious featherbedding which had been considered one of the functions of the SBM as a means of insuring high employment in the principality.

Beyond these considerations lay the company's inescapably central role in any series of measures designed to modernize Monaco. The casino had so declined in importance that it contributed only 5 percent of the principality's revenues, but it was still the hub around which the rest of Monte Carlo turned. Discussion about Monte Carlo's future began and ended with the gaming tables.

Onassis did not much like gambling. He ventured into the casino only when his guests insisted he should accompany them. He would escort Sir Winston Churchill to the roulette wheel, place his chips for him, and

194

double whatever bet the old man made with his own money. He was delighted when Sir Winston won and appropriately lugubrious when he did not. Aside from this, he retained a puritan attitude to games of chance. He did not mind if rich people risked their money at the tables, but his attitude toward gamblers of more modest means was different. "He was not setting himself up as a sort of moral authority," recalls Rainier, "but he believed that less rich people were corrupted by gambling. He knew the odds against winning and he thought they shouldn't be allowed to take those sorts of risks. It probably had to do with his poor origins. For all his wealth and generosity he was always very careful with his money."

Onassis's reservations about gambling would not have bothered Rainier but for the fact that they colored his perception of Monaco's future. The only development projects Onassis would consider were those designed to restore Monte Carlo to its former glory without effecting any substantial change in its appearance, for example, a new wing with a rooftop restaurant for the Hôtel de Paris and an indoor swimming pool connected to the hotel by a tunnel. Onassis seriously expressed an interest in turning Monte Carlo into a dietary center. There would be a "rest cure" for tired businessmen and intensive beauty care programs for their flagging wives. Rainier was astounded by the improbable nature of this project. "I said, 'Mr. Onassis, that's all very well,' " he recalls, " 'but are there enough tired businessmen willing to come here and resist temptation?' "

The situation was rich in paradox. Rainier, the heir to many centuries of tradition, was determined to "modernize" Monte Carlo. The annual visits he made to the United States with Princess Grace gave him a taste for American business methods. He wanted to "democratize" Monte Carlo by attracting a package-tour clientele, building medium-class hotels, and establishing a convention center. Onassis, on the other hand, whose fortune had been made in the contemporary business arena, wished to preserve the principality's anachronistic nature. Its function, in his view, was to be *the* place where the rich and famous could enjoy each other's company. His argument was that plans to "popularize" Monte Carlo would probably fail to attract new clientele and almost certainly drive out the old.

For the rich had returned. By the late 1950s the principality was enjoying another era of prosperity. There were Greek shipowners, American movie producers, and émigré royalty at the tables. Their losses were not on the scale of the great prewar profligates, but the casino was

195

showing a handsome profit. Princess Grace's presence added a certain luster to the social scene, but most of the publicity had been the direct result of Onassis's efforts. The results of publicity are hard to evaluate in cash terms, but there could be no doubt of the usefulness of Winston Churchill's presence in Monaco, even if his contribution to its social life was limited.

Onassis's very casualness made him popular with the personnel of the SBM. Monaco, he admitted, was his hobby. He interfered little with its workings and then only when some detail of its facilities displeased him. His pride in what he considered his demesne was so great that it was easy to manipulate him. Jacques Reymond, then the prince's minister of finance, recalled meeting him in the square outside the casino one evening. Onassis asked him what he thought of the gardens. Reymond, who had been instructed by Rainier to find ways of inducing Onassis to spend more money on Monte Carlo, saw his chance. He had seen better, he averred. Onassis was furious and asked where. Reymond said that he personally preferred the Tivoli gardens, near Rome. Onassis replied that he had never been there. Next week Reymond learned that he had surreptitiously sent one of his employees to Rome to take pictures of the gardens and was busy working with plans to reorganize the space around the casino.

This attitude extended to issues where a spirit of largesse ran counter to his own interests. A tradition of the SBM was the Christmas bonus, paid out of the casino's earnings in December. On the occasions when the casino had a bad month and was consequently unable to pay its bonus, Onassis would insist that the funds be found by some other means.

Onassis's seigneurial view of his role in the principality was increasingly at odds with Rainier's vision of a "new Monaco." Each had the power to frustrate the other's designs. As the largest shareholder, Onassis could appoint his men to the SBM board. Rainier not only had the right to appoint two directors of his choice, he also had veto power over Onassis's appointments and did not hesitate to use this prerogative. There were frequent shifts of personnel in the company as each set of administrators failed to live up to Rainier's rising expectations. At Onassis's suggestion, the company acquired a special negotiator who shuttled between the palace and Onassis's headquarters in the hope of finding common ground between the two parties. This device was a failure. By nature conspiratorial, both Onassis and Rainier attempted to secure the exclusive services of the unfortunate mediator with the result that one of them was invariably disappointed.

Onassis eventually agreed to one of the prince's pet schemes. He was prepared to build an artificial beach, a heliport, and a new luxury hotel, but he made these undertakings contingent on the prince's willingness to abandon his veto power and allow the SBM to be run without outside interference. Rainier flatly rejected the idea. "The prince had always believed in divine right," one of his advisers recalled, "and he now wished to apply it to corporate practices. If Monaco was to become a modern business, there should be no doubt about who was in charge."

Onassis tried another stratagem. In 1959 there was some unexpected activity on the Paris Bourse. SBM shares, which had stood at around 1,700 francs, jumped in one month to 4,200 francs. A number of reasons for the heavy trading were put forward, among them the possibility that Stavros Livanos was furious with his wayward son-in-law and determined to wrest control of Monte Carlo away from him. Like many things written about the old man, this was the purest fantasy. Whatever his feelings about Onassis, he would no more have invested in a casino than put his daughters on the streets. The identity of the real buyer was shortly made public when Onassis announced that a company in which he "was interested" now possessed more than 500,000 shares. He was now the majority shareholder, regardless of Rainier's holding. "I am the boss here now," he remarked to Louis Vuidet, the maître d' of the Hôtel de Paris.

Rainier appeared to be in trouble on other fronts. The centerpiece of his ambitious plans, the long tunnel designed to hide all physical evidence of the trains that made their way through the heart of Monte Carlo, was badly behind schedule. And the normally docile national assembly took offense at one of the extravagant schemes dear to Rainier's heart—the construction of a "marinarium" and a "floating laboratory" where the prince's friend, Professor Jacques Cousteau, might pursue his underwater research in peace. Rainier promptly dismissed the assembly and determined to rule Monaco without any assistance. "I cannot tolerate any pressure whatsoever which might undermine my complete rights," he explained to his subjects.

To begin with, Rainier's experiment in autocracy met with some success. In the absence of any commitment on Onassis's part, Rainier set up the Monaco Development Corporation to attract foreign capital and businesses. The principality's climate and tax-free status were energetically touted. Hundreds of businessmen—American, German, and British—together with refugee colonists from Algeria, Morocco, and Indochina, established their corporate headquarters in Monaco. Many could hardly be said to have come to Monaco, having simply acquired

197

expensive office suites and tastefully engraved brass nameplates and letter boxes. But the resulting boom meant good business for Monaco and popularity for the prince. There followed a number of good years. Not only were the tunnel and the marinarium completed, the Monaco soccer team brought the principality attention by winning the French League and Cup championships.

Rainier's brand of enlightened despotism might have continued had it not been for the hostility of another ruler with rather similar notions of good government. Charles de Gaulle accepted Monaco's success on the soccer field, however injurious to Gallic pride; but he could not overlook the fact that French citizens could avoid paying French taxes by living in Monaco. This primarily benefited certain French-Algerians, for whom, as a group, de Gaulle had little sympathy. In 1962, he gave Rainier six months' notice of his intention to abrogate the convention guaranteeing friendly relations between the two countries. The crisis came to a head that autumn with the installation of temporary customs barriers at Monaco's frontier and a threat to cut off its gas and electricity supplies if no agreement was reached.

Rainier had no alternative but to sue for peace. A convention was signed which made it difficult for French citizens to live in Monaco and evade French taxes. Its effects were spectacular, if not precisely those which de Gaulle expected. Two-thirds of the estimated 16 billion francs held by Frenchmen in Monte Carlo found their way to Switzerland. Overnight Monaco's prosperity evaporated as its escaping Frenchmen either canceled their orders for new apartments and offices or sold them at rock-bottom rates.

Onassis played a minor but mischievous role in the crisis. In September 1962, he offered to sell Rainier his entire holding in the SBM, ostensibly to help him in his difficulties with de Gaulle. The gesture, like many of Onassis's actions in Monte Carlo, was made largely for public effect. The principality did not have the funds to take advantage of Onassis's offer, particularly since he had been careful to attach an artificially high price tag to his holding. When the option was not taken up, Onassis confessed to heaving "a big sigh of relief."

As it turned out, his relief was premature. A side effect of the brush with de Gaulle was Rainier's need to rally Monacan opinion behind his regime. Rule by divine right was abolished in favor of constitutional monarchy with regular elections and a supreme court. With Rainier's encouragement, Monaco's new political consciousness was directed toward another examination of Onassis and the SBM. Aside from its obvious use as a means of diverting criticism from Rainier's own performance, the strategy made sense. De Gaulle had drastically limited Monaco's future as a business center; the alternative of developing its recreational facilities now seemed more pressing.

Rainier's encounter with de Gaulle had taught him some of the techniques of the French president's grand manner. These were now deployed against Onassis. Rainier's offensive began with an obscure reference, in his 1964 New Year's address, to the shortcomings of the SBM. "It is necessary," said the prince, "that it should reexamine its duties and, in a true conception of its proper role, play its part without reticence in the future of the principality." Onassis took umbrage: "The Prince wants to institute a ten-year plan for Monaco. Fine. But the SBM has not yet been given details of this plan—so how can it approve or disapprove?"

Charles Audibert was dispatched to the palace to discover precisely what the prince wanted. Rainier insisted that Onassis should first unveil his own vision of Monaco. Onassis, wary of any definitive commitment, demurred, whereupon Roger Crovetto, minister to the prince, was dispatched to the Onassis camp to repeat Rainier's request. Crovetto found Onassis drinking in the Salle Empire. He took a dislike to Crovetto, who announced he had been insulted and left in a fit of pique. Onassis mellowed to the extent of following Crovetto in his white Rolls-Royce on a mission of apology. Crovetto, already intimidated by Onassis's threatening manner, was anxious to avoid another confrontation. Onassis managed to catch up with him in the square outside the palace by taking the traffic circle in the wrong direction and plowing into the fender of the minister's car. Apologies were made, the minister was promised a new car and departed shaken but to some degree mollified.

Only after his verbal presentations had been rejected as "too imprecise" was Onassis induced to deliver a formal written offer of cooperation to Rainier. "We cannot really turn the place into a second Brighton because there is not enough beach—the place is too small," he remarked to a British journalist. He was prepared to build one hotel—no more. In return, he asked Rainier not only to abandon his veto powers over the SBM but also to take over much of the unprofitable "cultural expenses" of the organization, such as the maintenance of the Monte Carlo National Orchestra. These requests might have been deemed reasonable had the SBM been a conventional business operation. But this, as Onassis well knew, was not the case.

Rainier brought the confrontation into the open by securing Audi-

199

bert's resignation from the board of the SBM. Audibert's principal role had been as a liaison between the prince and Onassis. If the grounds for his leaving were not specified, they were widely understood. Rainier considered him an Onassis man. Audibert called Onassis in the middle of the night. "Don't you understand he'll get rid of you, too?" he said. Onassis was skeptical. Gildo Pastor, Audibert's replacement, a genial Italian immigrant who had made his fortune and had entered the prince's favor during the recent office construction boom, seemed like a man after Onassis's own heart. He began discussions with Pastor, threatening to cut back some of the SBM's less profitable activities, including the regattas, operas, and rallies it organized each year. For Rainier, it was a none too tactful reminder that Onassis could ruin as well as help Monte Carlo as a tourist center.

Rainier's mood hardened after a fence-mending visit to de Gaulle in which he was offered France's unconditional support in his problems with Onassis. Since Rainier's—and Monaco's—ambitions had been curbed, de Gaulle could afford to be magnanimous. Henceforth French officials referred to Onassis as "an undesirable presence" in Monaco. Rainier made use of this new Franco-Monacan entente by launching his next offensive in the form of a "declaration" to the editors of Le Monde. The prince's high style contrasted oddly with the banal nature of some of his complaints. Much was made of Onassis's reluctance to install floodlights on the principality's tennis courts.

Onassis's behavior, the prince maintained, could only be explained by his being "above all a speculator" devoid of any real concern for his adopted country. "Monsieur Onassis often repeated to us that gambling was immoral," the prince continued. "That is one point of view. But we do not know whether financial speculations are less immoral than gambling which is regulated strictly according to the law." Whatever his behavior elsewhere, Onassis had not shown any speculative financial interest in Monaco—in fact, the opposite had been the case. It was Onassis's conspicuous lack of interest in increasing the value of his investments in the principality that had incurred Rainier's disfavor. Such niceties, however, were obscured in the heat of the battle. "The only solution," the prince concluded, "appears to be a test of force. My government and myself are resolved upon it."

The most obvious option open to Rainier was nationalization, an arrangement that worked well in France, where the state retained a gambling monopoly that was well-administered and highly profitable. But the situation in Monaco was rather different, since gambling was the

200

principality's major industry. Monacans who owned shares in the SBM formed defense committees to protest any move on Rainier's part that might lead to their expropriation. The project was abandoned in favor of a scheme concocted by Jean-Charles Rey, a Paris lawyer who was also Rainier's brother-in-law. The state would create 600,000 new shares in the company, thus acquiring a clear majority. Beyond this it would offer to purchase any other shares which the existing shareholders wished to dispose of at a price fixed halfway between the high and low points of SBM shares during 1966.

The charm of this device was that it ostensibly conserved the private status of the SBM while granting Rainier effective power to do what he wished with it. The shareholders' organizations unambiguously described the proposed legislation as a *"loi gangster,"* and Pastor resigned his official post in protest. When Onassis was told about the scheme, he exclaimed that Rainier must be joking.

But the prince was in earnest. The decree was drawn up and passed. Onassis's appeal against the legislation as unconstitutional was rejected by the supreme court. A few days later Onassis received a check for 39,912,000 francs ($10 million) for his 500,489 SBM shares.

His main complaint in later years was that the shares were worth far more than he received. "We were gypped," he remarked laconically. But his real grief was personal. He had been the most powerful man in Monte Carlo and then had been deposed. He kept away from Monaco until the last months of his life, when he made a valedictory visit. He was ill and lonely and wished to efface the unpleasant memory of unsettled quarrels.

Rainier was invited to dine with him on the *Christina.* "He never bore grudges," the prince explained later. "That was a very fine trait."

14
BEARING GIFTS TO GREECE

ARISTOTLE ONASSIS was never a great reader of books, but he was fascinated by classical mythology. He was particularly interested in the legend of Ulysses, the ancient Greek king who, after years of catastrophe, wanderings, trials, and ultimate triumph, returns to claim his island kingdom. To Onassis, the parallels between himself and the mythological hero were clear. But after World War II, there seemed to be no reason for such an idealized homecoming for the real wandering Greek.

Still in the throes of its own civil war, Greece was not much interested in the personal destiny of Aristotle Onassis. The rebuffs he had received over the Liberty ships and T-2 tanker proposals were a clear indication of his low standing among his compatriots. When, in 1946, he acquired ten elderly Canadian frigates for $750,000, Onassis proposed to the Greek government of the day that he spend $4 million on converting them into passenger ships to ply the interisland Aegean routes. All he asked for was a monopoly. The government did not even bother to reply to the offer.

By the 1950s the situation had changed dramatically. The political climate in Greece had improved, and some of the more thoughtful politicians began to address themselves to the problems of development. They were struck by the fact that the richest and most enterprising

Greek businessmen all seemed to be expatriates. Their success provided a useful quota of stories in the Greek press of the Greek-boy-makes-good variety, but their impact on the Greek economy was negligible.

Constantine Karamanlis, who became prime minister in 1955, did not think that this should necessarily be the case. He was known as a dynamic, if conventional, visionary, and that reputation rested largely on his ability to cut Gordian knots. Once, when he had been responsible for the public transportation system of Athens, he had promptly terminated a long-standing bureaucratic dispute about its future by the simple expedient of sending squads of workmen to rip up the trolley tracks, thus scoring high on incisiveness but low on sensitivity. Now his solution to Greece's economic problems was equally simple. Massive investment was the answer, and where better to fish for it than among the shoals of wealthy expatriates? Men such as Onassis and Niarchos and all the other shipping magnates, who had little or no involvement with the Greek economy, were seemingly awash with funds and might prove susceptible to appeals to their patriotism.

First, Karamanlis needed to consolidate his political position. He had become prime minister upon the death of his predecessor, and his parliamentary majority was too tenuous for long-term planning. In the elections of February 1956, his right-of-center National Radical Union party was returned with the overall parliamentary majority he wanted. By way of marking the opening of a new era, he appointed the first woman to hold a ministerial post in a Greek government. Then he invited Aristotle Onassis to lunch.

The invitation was not unexpected. Karamanlis had already let it be known that if he won the elections, he would be anxious to do business with expatriates. Onassis had intimated that an approach at the prime-ministerial level would be well received. Only past experience and perhaps consciousness of his new international status made him sensitive to protocol, for Onassis was always ready to talk business. Some of his staff felt that he got as much pleasure from talking business as doing it. One former aide referred to this side of Onassis's character as "his voyeur instincts," another said "he was like a sponge for new ideas." Of the ideas which Karamanlis threw out over lunch, the one which excited Onassis most was his proposal for a new national airline.

It was no secret that the existing state-owned airline, TAE, was a shambles. With its associate lines, it possessed only thirteen DC-3s (Dakotas) and one DC-4, and the only international service it could muster was a once-a-week run to Paris and London. It seemed doomed to perpetual loss. What Karamanlis wanted was a profitable airline of international stature. This was not a preposterous ambition: Greece was well situated at an international crossroads, and any national carrier could rely on the considerable market of emigrant Greeks returning home on holiday, particularly from North America. If Greek shipping was an international success story, then why not Greek aviation? What was needed, said Karamanlis, was the right man in charge. Who better than Onassis? Why not scrap TAE and create an entirely new Onassis-owned company?

Onassis liked it. The prospect of being the only man in the world to own a national airline was practically irresistible. Moreover, planes, like ships, were reassuringly mobile assets. He told Karamanlis that, if he cared to submit his requirements, then he would do his best to propose something attractive.

As Karamanlis pressed on with his informal contacts, it soon became clear that there were two projects which the expatriates found the most tempting—the airline and a proposed ship repair yard—and that there were two front-runners for the contracts: Onassis and Niarchos. Onassis later liked to claim that he had submitted the best proposals for both jobs and that Karamanlis was acutely embarrassed at the prospect of having to give everything to one man. The prime minister begged him either to cooperate with his archrival or at least have the grace to make a present of one of them to Niarchos. This is what he did, said Onassis, and Niarchos's Skaramanga shipyard on the outskirts of Athens was the result of his magnanimity.

The recollections of those concerned with the adjudication are slightly different. There was very little to choose between either offer for either project. If anything, Niarchos submitted the better offer for the airline, while Onassis had the edge with his proposals for the shipyard. The airline contract, however, was the first to be awarded. Ministers and civil servants went through each man's proposals clause by clause, awarding points. A decisive factor in the voting was the attitude of Andreas Apostolidis, the Minister of Coordination, a high post which carried overall responsibility for economic development and which traditionally went to the number-two man in any Greek government. Apostolidis, a tough, blunt old politico, had taken a personal liking to Onassis, whom he regarded as the epitome of the rough-hewn, vibrant, self-made man. He had taken an equally strong aversion to Niarchos, whom he regarded as a stuffed shirt and the darling of the meddlesome royal family. Under Apostolidis's forceful influence, the adjudication found in favor of Onassis by half a point.

A few weeks later, the rival proposals for the construction of the shipyard were considered. Onassis again emerged the winner, with somewhat more justification; and he was quite correct in suspecting that this did not suit the prime minister at all. For as far as Karamanlis was concerned, an immediate financial return to the state from these concessions was of secondary importance. He was taking a longer, three-stage view in which the scenario went: (1) tempt back a few big names, with concessions which were initially favorable to them if necessary, so that (2) the rest will rush to follow, resulting in (3) the long-term profitability of all the contracts for the state and the galvanizing of the Greek economy. At stage one, it made no sense to give everything to the same man. He persuaded Niarchos to improve one or two points in his offer, for the sake of appearance, and then awarded the contract to him. It was widely bruited at the time that Karamanlis was also under severe pressure from Queen Frederika to find in favor of her friend and protégé, Niarchos. But that was not the decisive factor, for when the next big concession came up—for an oil refinery in northern Greece—the award went to Tom Pappas, the Boston Greek, despite the fact that both Onassis and Niarchos had submitted proposals which were at least as good.

Onassis inherited TAE, its fourteen planes, and 856 employees under an agreement which he signed with the Greek government on July 30, 1956. He christened the new company Olympic Airways. It had a twenty-year monopoly over all Greek civil aviation, including the handling and refueling of foreign airlines, and started operations on April 6, 1957. Soon afterward, Niarchos formed Hellenic Shipyards and proceeded to construct the yard at Skaramanga. Both deals were regarded as feathers in the cap of the new Karamanlis government, but the hoped-for stampede to invest in Greece never materialized. As this and Onassis's later skirmishes were to demonstrate, international capital could be attracted to the precarious political and economic climate of Greece only by concessions which a large body of Greek public opinion found unacceptable. Patriotism alone was not enough for the expatriates.

No sooner had he signed than Onassis used every opportunity to extract still more favorable revisions. He once said that when he had been hesitating in the first place, wondering whether or not to take the concession, another Greek millionaire of Anatolian origin had urged him on with the words, "Don't worry, Ari, sign! Sign anything! Don't even bother to read the contract! You can always get it revised the next day." Whether or not the story is true, that is precisely what Onassis did. The haggling process continued for as long as Onassis owned Olympic, and, more often than not, he got his way.

Olympic under Onassis was controversial from the moment of its conception. His standard reaction to criticism was never to debate openly the points at issue but to instruct his legal and publicity machines to trundle out statistics supposedly demonstrating the phenomenal growth of the airline, contrasting this with the burden that the Greek railways imposed on the state. But, in comparison with other major international airlines, the performance of Olympic was not impressive. Between 1956 and 1967, a decade of considerable growth in international aviation, Olympic did not even succeed in doubling the passenger-miles flown. Nor was it a popular airline with the traveling public, who were irritated by the usually unexplained and seemingly arbitrary cancelations, diversions, and delays of Olympic planes. They were not the only ones who sometimes wondered for whose benefit the airline was being run.

Onassis never created a modern, streamlined business corporation with a clean chain of command or effective intercommunication among employees. He never had a private secretary to handle his airline affairs. His "office" was a tattered old notebook wrapped in rubber bands and filled with phone numbers. He would conduct his business from wherever he happened to be, and no major decisions could be made without him. This was one of the reasons for Olympic's appalling labor relations, particularly with the militant pilots' union. In fairness to Onassis, there was much bloody-mindedness on the pilots' side. Egged on by those employed by foreign state-owned airlines, the pilots chose to find the whole idea of an airline being owned by one man morally unacceptable. Their disputes with Onassis tended to become symbolic tests of strength, regardless of the immediate grievances.

Onassis's personal handling of industrial disputes did nothing to calm the waters. He once described the airline as "a hobby enterprise," but it was a hobby that he found absorbing. His staff was not convinced that this was a good thing. Time and again Onassis would sit in shirt-sleeves, sweating profusely, trading insults with the pilots' leaders until his anguished executives would succeed in maneuvering him out of the room. Outside they would argue that he should play the big boss, retire upstairs somewhere and leave the dirty work to them. When they had a possible peace formula, they would, of course, bring it to him for approval. For a while it would work; then, just as the negotiations were beginning to make progress, the door would burst open and in would storm Onassis shouting, "I'll be a cuckold if I haven't got rid of the airline by tomorrow!"

206

The mediocre performance and poor labor relations of the airline were not the only grounds for criticism—there was also the astonishing string of concessions which Onassis managed to wring from the government. These included: two extensions of his monopoly, ultimately to the year 2006; exemption from corporate taxes; exemption from landing charges in Greece; compensation for charter flights by foreign airlines into Greece from Europe and a ban on transatlantic ones; compensation by the government for any losses incurred by unofficial or illegal strikes; compensation for losses on transatlantic flights; the right to rent planes from overseas Onassis-owned companies instead of purchase them; the right to export profits; government loans of 100 million drachmas ($3.3 million at the time) at a ridiculous interest rate of 2.5 percent; and the right to import capital goods without paying customs duty.

There was also what Onassis called "my salvation, my key to escape." This was clause 25a of his frequently revised concession to operate Olympic, which allowed either side to terminate the agreement on six months' notice without giving any reason. In games of dare and double-dare with the government, it was a useful threat to have in reserve. In March 1965, while doing battle with the government of George Papandreou, he explicitly threatened to use the escape clause. "I feel like a woman who has given birth," he exclaimed at the time, after a celebratory night out. But as soon as he heard that there were others ready and willing to take over Olympic, he eagerly reassumed responsibility for the airline.

It was, however, a technique that was bound to create enemies. One of the most powerful of these became Air Marshal George Doukas, a former head of the Greek Civil Aviation Authority. Doukas submitted a report on Olympic to the government in August 1967. It appeared to be a highly damaging document alleging numerous failures by Olympic to honor its obligations or to act in the national interest and characterizing Onassis as "a cancerous growth on Greek society. . . . His credo consisted of having no feeling of being bound by his signature, and of buying people and favors by the classic method of corrupting consciences." Doukas described Onassis's method of extracting concessions as exhibiting, "even under the most charitable of interpretations, the culmination of an entirely brigand-like hunger, the absolute negation of any moral element in his dealings, and the base insolence of his approach."

Onassis sued for defamation of character, the only time he ever did so, and it emerged that Doukas's indictment was thin on concrete facts

207

(though those he produced were in the main correct) and faulty in its deductions. Doukas eventually withdrew the allegations, and the case was dropped. It did, however, produce some fascinating courtroom exchanges.

> JUDGE: Do you have profits from Olympic?
> ONASSIS: After the first two years we've gained something. Just a few drachmas, however.
> JUDGE: Then why do you keep Olympic?
> ONASSIS: What should I do? Throw it in the sea?
> JUDGE: These things are not logical. If it is not making progress, why is it continuously expanding?
> ONASSIS: We are trying to lose less.
> JUDGE: I don't understand you. This is not logical.
> ONASSIS: There is no logic in business. With logic I would not be where I am today.

Onassis clearly enjoyed the exercise in mystification, but the complexities of his airline business were far from being accidental. For Olympic Airways under Onassis was not unlike the creation of some maverick astronomer who, refusing to concede that the earth revolves around the sun, is thereby obliged to create ever weirder, more convoluted, and perilous mechanisms in order to make everything agree with his highly personal view of the cosmos. Onassis had approached Olympic with two unshakable convictions: should the red revolution come (and the chances of it have always seemed fair-to-good in Greece), there would be nothing to grab if someone had a mind to nationalize the airline; and Olympic should at all costs avoid the appearances of profitability, which could only make the government reluctant to grant future concessions. These convictions gave Olympic its underlying business logic. By their very nature they were not ones that he could readily impart to the authorities or the courts.

One of the basic problems that these self-imposed limitations presented was how to acquire aircraft. Normally this should not have been a major difficulty—Greek governments have traditionally been generous in underwriting projects deemed to be in the national interest. But taking out a government loan would have involved the kind of accountability Onassis found so repugnant, and it would almost certainly have meant that any assets acquired with the loan would have to be located within reach of the government. That was precisely what Onassis was determined to avoid. The alternative was to raise money on the international money market, but here again Onassis was hamstrung by his own manias.

It is virtually impossible for a company to borrow more than three times its net worth, and in Olympic's case this was a meager $1.5 million. The obvious solution was to float a stock issue, but Onassis refused this option because he was determined to keep his assets on Greek soil to a minimum. Onassis's consequent unwillingness to add to the elderly prop-driven fleet he had inherited was the principal reason for Olympic's unimpressive performance in the first decade of its existence. He muddled through by means of "subordinated loans" from other Onassis companies abroad, such as Ionian Ltd, which effectively guaranteed loans much larger than Olympic would otherwise have been able to raise. The airline thus acquired two British Comet jets and, in 1965, three Boeing 707s. But there was a limit to the amount of money which could be raised in this manner.

When the prestige-conscious military dictators seized power in 1967, Onassis found himself under severe pressure (not least from the impact of the Doukas report) to turn Olympic into a major international carrier operating a sizable jet fleet. Five Boeing 727s and two 707s were strongly indicated at a price of $54.1 million. The problem for Onassis was how he could conceivably raise that sort of money without floating a stock issue.

Onassis adored such conundrums. If they did not exist he sometimes felt obliged to create them. "Time for our gymnastics," he would cry to the Olympic top management if things were quiet. "Now, let's imagine the government has invoked clause 25a . . . what is our next move?" And so the day would pass pleasantly in war games. Making money in itself was no longer enough, unless it also constituted an affirmation of his own genius. Working out how to buy $54 million worth of airplanes for an airline which did not have the ability even to *borrow* the money was the sort of challenge Onassis thrived on.

The solution he finally hit upon and induced the government to accept was entirely his own creation. "I always say I went to three universities—London University, Athens University, and Onassis University," says Tryfon Koutalidis, now head of the legal department at Olympic and one of those who marveled at Onassis's solution. It went like this: Olympic Airways, though a Greek company, was the wholly owned subsidiary of Victoria Financiera Panama, of which Onassis was the sole shareholder. Onassis duly created another Panamanian corporation, Aircraft Leasing Company. This functioned as a consortium financed 70 percent by the First National City Bank, 15 percent by Boeing, and 15 percent by yet another Onassis company in Panama. (He had several which he trundled out for this and subsequent Olympic deals, among them Sociedad Maritima Miraflores Ltd, Ionian Ltd, Armadora Aristotelis Panama, and Condor Financiera Panama.) Aircraft Leasing then bought the planes from Boeing and leased them to Olympic Airways for ten years. All the Onassis organization had to put up was $8 million (15 percent), and none of the money went anywhere near Greece. Olympic Airways paid the rental in 120 monthly installments to Victoria Financiera, which then passed on the requisite amount to Aircraft Leasing. It was then remitted, without deductions, first to First National City, until its 70 percent was paid off with interest, then to Boeing until they had their 15 percent, and then to the Onassis financing company.

When intimations of the deal leaked out (the precise details have never been revealed before), Onassis's critics jumped to what seemed the obvious conclusion: he was renting the planes from himself for a whopping profit, thus insuring that Olympic Airways lost money, while he raked it in tax free in Panama. He was simply milking the hard-pressed Greek economy for his own personal profit.

Onassis was able to rebut these charges to government investigators, though in public he always preferred to lie steadfastly, asserting that the planes *belonged* to Olympic. The rental Olympic pays today for the seven planes is $60,000 each a month, which compares favorably with the price on the charter market. Even if the rental were not a fair one, Onassis would and did argue, the idea that he could rob Olympic in Greece to pay himself in Panama was ludicrous as long as both Olympic and the Panamanian companies were wholly his, and as long as Olympic neither paid taxes nor received subsidies. They were both his pockets, so how could moving assets from one to the other possibly be construed as improper? It was the truth, but not the whole truth.

The least defensible aspect of the deal was what happened to the planes at the end of the ten years. Again, Onassis was able to answer with complete truth, they did not immediately end up in his pockets but with First National City. If they had been acquired by Olympic on a lease-purchase plan, then they would of course have become an asset of the airline. Onassis did not explain the personal reason why he wished to avoid this. His explanation to the investigators was that the credibility of Greece—politically and economically—was so low in the eyes of international financial institutions that he would have had trouble raising *any* money to lease the planes, let alone on such advantageous terms, if the lease had stipulated that the planes were to revert to Olympic at the end of the ten years. What would happen, therefore, was that Aircraft Leasing and its planes would revert to First National City. What Onassis did not say was that immediately after that they would revert once more —to his own company, Victoria Financiera, which thus got the planes and their $8 million back with interest.

Onassis's often reiterated claim that he never received a drachma in subsidy for Olympic from the Greek government was perfectly correct. Olympic received no subsidies because Onassis did not want them. He did not want them because the receipt of subsidies involved the opening of his books. Concessions were much more convenient, and these could be best obtained by pointing to a dismal annual balance sheet. During his eighteen years of proprietorship, Olympic Airways showed a profit during only three years, and these were explained by Onassis as being the result of capital transfers within his empire.

This did not, however, imply any great munificence on his part. Olympic's "losses" were almost invariably outweighed by profits in other Onassis-controlled companies, whose existence was dependent on the airline. George Theofanos, who was appointed president of Olympic Airways by the government after Onassis's death, explained that "most of the planes and buildings belonged to and were leased from other Onassis companies. I have no doubt that Olympic was very profitable— for Mr. Onassis. The complicated system [of interlocking companies] he had created meant that he personally could not lose money."

Onassis made only one serious error in the concession game. Ironically, it was the concession that aroused most public criticism—Olympic's exemption from taxes. It had come about as a result of his original negotiations with Karamanlis when the airline had first been proposed. Onassis had explained his antipathy for tax collectors and his aversion to people riffling through his books. "Never mind," Karamanlis had said. "Will you settle for a percentage of turnover instead—not much, something quite nominal?" "Of course," Onassis had replied, appreciating Karamanlis's need for some return and that the establishment of turnover did not involve any indecently deep probing of the accounts. "How much had you in mind?" Karamanlis suggested 2.5 percent, and Onassis had promptly agreed.

Olympic's first few years of operation were at a genuine loss. It was then that Onassis appreciated his rashness in offering a percentage of revenue in exchange for tax exemption. One did not pay taxes when

211

suffering losses. Onassis, for the first and only time in his life, was seized by an overwhelming desire to be liable for tax. He went to confess this to Karamanlis, sincerely pleading to be treated like everyone else. For once Onassis was outmaneuvered. Karamanlis, realizing that Onassis's accounting techniques could make Olympic a profit- or loss-maker more or less at will, refused his request for "equal treatment." He did, however, offer to reduce the percentage of the take to .5 percent and facilitated a 100-million-drachma, low-interest loan from the public coffer to compensate for past "overpayments."

Although Stavros Niarchos lost the opening battle for Olympic, he never abandoned the war. Indeed, one consequence of Niarchos's and Onassis's "return" to the Greek economy was a new level of absurdity in their rivalry. The Greeks were forever cracking jokes about it. One of the better stories had it that Onassis paid a visit to Dr. Christiaan Barnard, the pioneer of heart transplant surgery, in Cape Town, South Africa, and returned to Greece sometime later with a new heart. The operation cost him, so the joke ran, $1 million. Scarcely had he set foot in Athens when Stavros Niarchos was seen boarding a plane for South Africa. Some weeks later he arrived back in Greece, and it was not long before Onassis was on the phone with him.

"How did it go, Stavros?" asked Onassis.

"Fine. And what's more, he charged me only $500,000."

To Niarchos's surprise, Onassis took this quite calmly.

"And so he should have," came the reply, "considering he gave you *my* heart."

In reality, whenever Onassis, as a negotiating ploy, threatened to abandon Olympic, Niarchos would offer to take it over. His offers were invariably accompanied with letters of guarantee from foreign banks, a potent inducement since money in foreign banks always impresses Greek politicians more than money in Greek banks. The Niarchos camp also maintained close links with Air Marshal Doukas. When Onassis's monopoly was extended until the year 2006, Niarchos challenged the decision in the courts. The concession, he claimed, should not have been renewed prior to its expiration, and then only as a result of an open competition. His suit was rejected on the grounds that he had suffered no material damage as a result of the new concession and that, whatever his present interest in Olympic, there was no evidence that he would still be interested when Onassis's original concession expired.

A more rarefied level of farce was achieved by the plot to thwart Onassis's plans for a prestigious new headquarters for Olympic Airways.

212

Onassis had his eye on what was, without doubt, the most desirable development site in Athens—the corner of Syntagma [Constitution] Square, opposite parliament and the Hôtel Grande Bretagne, once the site of the Athens police headquarters. It was a narrow site of 1,300 square meters, and whoever rebuilt it was obliged to landscape it with flower beds. Thus it was not regarded as economical for a hotel, so the previous owner had offered it as embassies to the Italian and the Yugoslav governments, which declined the offer. The owner had subsequently died, bequeathing his site in a manner complex enough to guarantee lucrative employment for Athenian lawyers. He left 15 percent to his niece and divided the rest into 10- and 5-percent units, which he left to such varied institutions and persons as two municipalities on his native island, the Athens Home for the Blind, the Parnassos (a philological association), the Navy and the Air Force Funds, and two lawyers.

Onassis had succeeded in buying out only one of the lawyers before Niarchos, getting wind of his plans, snapped up the other. Score: Onassis 5 percent of the site, Niarchos 5 percent.

Onassis beat Niarchos to the Home for the Blind's 10 percent, but Niarchos lodged a protest with the Home's board of governors on the grounds that he was prepared to offer more. The board then called for bids, and Onassis shrewdly submitted one for one drachma more than anyone else might offer. Niarchos cried foul, and the board reconsidered the matter. "Being composed mainly of Salonika University professors who commuted regularly to Athens on Olympic Airways," said a Niarchos man, "they opted for Onassis." Score: Onassis 15, Niarchos 5.

The Navy Fund, which had been following the proceedings with keen interest, then decided to auction their share of the site. Bidding started at 64,000 drachmas ($2,112) per square meter. The Niarchos side learned that Onassis had given his men a bidding ceiling, which they guessed was 75,000 drachmas ($2,475). Since the bidding was required to go up by not less than 1-percent increments, the Niarchos men cautiously maneuvered their offer to 74,000 drachmas, which meant that the Onassis men could not top it if their deduction was correct. It was. Niarchos then rapidly snapped up part of the niece's share and all the remaining shares, save that of the Air Force Fund and another 5 percent which the niece kept for sentimental reasons. Score: Niarchos 70, Onassis still only 15.

Before he could do anything with his prize, Niarchos had to fight a two-year court battle to oblige the other owners, Onassis included, to sell. The court ordered a compulsory auction of the entire site on March

213

8, 1970, winner to take all. To the consternation of the Niarchos men, Onassis did not appear to be represented. Instead, representatives of the Seamen's Pension Fund (NAT) turned up, and started bidding vigorously for the site. The Niarchos team had an open line to their boss's aerie in Saint Moritz and were under orders to get the site at all costs. The men from the NAT, seemingly oblivious to their determination, continued to force the price ever upward until even Niarchos began to have second thoughts. Only the nagging suspicion that the NAT might be a front for Onassis—that he had made a deal with the seamen which would give him the entire site after all—held Niarchos to his resolve. Now it was the turn of the men from the NAT to start sweating, which they did with repeated requests for recesses so that they could consult amongst themselves. Finally, at 116.1 million drachmas—roughly $3,600 per square meter—they caved in. The site was Niarchos's at last, for a record price. Niarchos might well have wondered who in fact had been the winner, since Onassis had made a handsome profit at his expense. For a while he toyed with the idea of erecting an office building, but his interest in the site died with his pyrrhic victory. At least he got his money back by selling the site to the National Bank of Greece for 120 million drachmas. Onassis built the new Olympic Airways headquarters elsewhere.

Onassis had made more than a business decision when he acquired and set about creating Olympic. He had committed himself in some ill-defined way to the country of his distant ancestors. For Onassis, the compulsive bird of passage, this initially meant little more than alighting on Greek soil more often than he had in the past. He came to regard Ithaca, the legendary island-kingdom of Ulysses, as his adoptive home. Costa Gratsos was an Ithacan, and Pericles Dracoulis had been one, too. Just as genuine islanders in the shipping fraternity favored their kin, so Ithacans held a high percentage of the jobs Onassis had to dispense.

When the *Christina* cruised from Monaco, it ended up, more often than not, in Greek waters. Ithaca was Onassis's favorite port of call, with famous friends in tow. Churchill was taken to Ithaca, Garbo was greeted there by church bells and volleys of rifle salutes. Callas was taken there, too. Onassis increasingly felt the emotional call of Greece. Like the traditional shipowners, though he was not one, he wanted somewhere to belong, somewhere to return to when it was all over—somewhere, although he would never have acknowledged the fact, to die.

Onassis was always what the Greeks call "mankas," an urchin or a street arab, who responded to the directness of the peasant Greek character and the simple worthies who greeted him in Ithaca with far more spontaneous pleasure than he did to the Riviera jet-setters. Mixing with the Riviera set was a confirmation of his success, but there was something in Greece which he came to recognize as home. Alexis Minotis, Greece's leading actor and a lifelong friend of Onassis, has said, "What I liked about him was that he always remained poor in his heart and in his behavior. He never had the presumption of the rich and the snobbish." Yet Minotis candidly admits the other, paradoxical side of his friend's nature by never doubting for one second that if he had not also made a success of his life, their friendship would never have survived. "Although he was a simple man, he had this 'manie de grandeur.' He had this passion for being distinguished and exceptional. That was why all his friends had to be important. He was very proud of his friendship with Churchill, always brought him into conversations: 'As the great man once told me.' . . . I don't think that even he realized that by flattering the memory of Churchill he was really flattering himself."

Perhaps the most fascinating question about Onassis's character is the extent to which he was a Greek. It was a question that often preoccupied Professor Yanni Georgakis, the man whom Onassis eventually appointed managing director of Olympic Airways. Of all Onassis's Athenian acquaintances, Georgakis—a witty, patrician intellectual—was the most intriguing. They had met and become friends when Georgakis was rector of the Panteios Graduate School of Political Studies in Athens, having been introduced by Costa Gratsos. Their first business link was made on the night of King Constantine's wedding in 1964. On their way back from a reception at the palace, Onassis asked Georgakis to take over as his representative at Olympic Airways.

"But I know nothing about planes," protested Georgakis.

"Never mind," said Onassis. "You'll learn."

On the following morning Georgakis accepted the post and began a close association that lasted until Onassis's death. He never ceased to be fascinated by the personality of his employer. Georgakis believes that Onassis had a chameleonlike quality. "In Greece he behaved like a Greek, in England like an Englishman. He had this facility for adaptation. When he was in an international forum among international ethics, then he was superb, dignified and controlled. In Greece among Greeks he adopted the conduct of the market place." Which is perhaps another explanation for Onassis's occasionally hysterical style of conducting the business of Olympic Airways.

As his flirtation with Greece progressed, so did his interest in Greek culture, history, and theology. His talk was no longer merely of business and ships, with an occasional foray into international affairs. "Men of practical experience do not usually like things which have no practical application," says Minotis, "yet Onassis kept something human. He would converse on matters which were not concrete, which had nothing to do with business, and he had a good ear for philosophy and the poets. He had an artistic temperament." Onassis's enthusiasm for intellectual discussion, coupled with his lack of book learning, led him to develop some bizarre theories. Professor Georgakis remembers a duel he and Onassis fought for several years over Saint Basil the Great, who had come from Cappadocia, where Onassis's father was born, and who is one of the Four Fathers of the Greek Orthodox church.

Onassis argued "in an arbitrary way" that Saint Basil was clearly the first bishop of the Orthodox Eastern church. Georgakis protested that that was impossible since Saint Basil was not born until the fourth century. Onassis, undaunted by this information, developed his argument. Was not Saint Basil's Day January 1, the first day of the year? Was not the Greek name Basil derived from the Greek word for *king?* It stood to reason, therefore, that Basil was the first bishop. "He only became reconciled to the historical facts about Saint Basil shortly before his death," recalls Georgakis. "We also spent several years over his contention that there was no difference whatsoever between religion and metaphysics, that they were one and the same thing."

This interest in the loftier side of life, which burgeoned with Onassis's triumphal entry upon the Greek scene, very nearly resulted in his committing a major act of philanthropy (he was responsible for but one or two minor ones in his lifetime). One evening, when he judged Onassis to be in an expansive mood, Minotis mused how marvelous it would be if the ancient Theater of Dionysus could be restored. The theater, which once seated fourteen thousand people fanning up the walls of the Acropolis, was in an advanced state of decay with only the first few rows of seats intact.

"How many ships do you own?" asked Minotis.

"Leave me alone," grunted Onassis, not at all deceived by the innocence of the query. "You are always talking about theaters."

"And you are always talking about ships," parried Minotis. "How may do you own?"

"One hundred seventeen, at the moment."

"And how much is a ship worth?"

216

"Bah, leave me alone."

But Minotis persisted, extracted the information that a ship might be worth $7 million, and asked why Onassis could not simply assume that one had sunk and spend the money on restoring the theater. What was a mere $7 million if it were spent on restoring the spot where Europe had been born? asked Minotis rhetorically, warming to his theme. It was there that the works of Sophocles, Euripides, and Aeschylus had been performed for the first time. It had been there at the time of Pericles. "There can be a plaque," continued Minotis, "saying, 'Aristotle Onassis restored this.' That plaque will be there for all time. A tanker can sink or rust. What is $7 million—one tanker—to achieve immortality?"

Minotis, as always, had judged his audience skillfully. Onassis, not at all averse to the offer of immortality, swallowed the bait and threw himself into the scheme with his usual enthusiasm for new projects. But there was a snag. The law forbade the restoration of antiquities where the end product would be less than 25 percent ancient Greek; and not only was there a very small amount of the theater still standing, but much of that consisted of Roman, Byzantine, and Frankish additions to the original ancient Greek structure. Onassis, never one to let such minor technicalities impede a project, then embarked with Minotis upon a further round of lobbying with the bureaucrats for a change in the law and for a more modest restoration to seat three thousand. Karamanlis, who was still prime minister, was sympathetic, but in 1963 he fell from power, and his successor, Papandreou, was not enthusiastic. The project was abandoned.

Onassis's search for an emotional home continued. He already owned two houses in Greece. They were next door to each other in the Athens seaside suburb of Glyfada, beneath the approach path of the planes landing at Athens airport. (Ironically, his other Athenian haunt, the night club Neraida, was beneath the usual takeoff path on the other side of the airport, and the performers sometimes had to stop singing because of the noise.) He had installed his sister, Artemis, in one house, and used the other as his own Athenian pied-à-terre. Artemis managed his household affairs, and his household staff consisted only of an occasional cook, a kitchen boy, and two maids. When he had guests, they were usually obliged to stay next door with Artemis.

In seeking a more appropriate Grecian ambience, Onassis could hardly fail to be stimulated by the example of Niarchos. He, too, was spending much more of his time in Greece and had acquired his own island—the five-thousand-acre Spetsopoula, next to the popular tourist island Spetsai in the Saronic Gulf, some fifty miles from Athens. He was developing it with somber good taste. It would have its own harbor, heliport, and go-cart track. A lodge was being built up in the woods, paths were being constructed for pleasant rambles, and a five-mile-long road was being laid around the island. The original "manor" house was being expanded and modernized, and there would be three new guest houses nearby. Much of the coast was wild and rocky, but on the one beach suitable for bathing every modern convenience was being installed. In the village by the harbor, where the permanent residents lived, would be the pheasant hatcheries and hunting-dog kennels; for it was Niarchos's intention to turn his island into a hunting paradise (he was later to import mouflons, a species of wild sheep).

In the summer of 1963 Onassis learned that the island of Skorpios was for sale. It was four hundred acres in size, modestly priced at $110,000, and had a view of the mountainous north end of Ithaca. Skorpios was rocky and barren, though it supported magnificent olive trees from which the two semipermanent residents who harvested them managed to produce fifteen thousand kilos of prime olive oil a year. In his mind's eye Onassis could already see the island covered with such luxuriant vegetation as cypresses, walnuts, almonds, and bougainvillea, and serviced with a road and harbor just like Niarchos's. There was nothing that money could not put right. Onassis had found his island kingdom.

In the fall of 1964 Onassis proudly displayed his island to Maria Callas. In this romantic setting Onassis decided to provide his beloved with a ship. It was a decision that was to cause a great deal of aggravation.

15
AN UNLUCKY SHIP

PANAGHIS VERGOTTIS was one of Onassis's oldest friends. They had first met in London in the mid-1930s when Onassis was beginning to make his way in the tanker business. The Vergottis family, which came from the Ionian island of Kephalonia, had been in ships for generations. Vergottis was a cultured man, a bachelor, and a complete anglophile. He ran his shipping business from an office in London and lived at the Ritz Hotel.

He was sixteen years older than Onassis but always found refreshment in the younger man's company. Over the years their friendship deepened. When Onassis threw his famous party for Maria Callas at the Dorchester Hotel in July 1959 to celebrate her appearance at Covent Garden, Vergottis was among those invited. Some months later Onassis introduced him to Callas as "one of my dearest friends, if not the best I have." In time, a close friendship developed between Vergottis and Callas, his wide knowledge of opera and the arts making for an easy intimacy.

There was not, on the surface at least, any competition between Onassis and Vergottis over Callas. Vergottis was already in his early seventies, and the attention he bestowed on the opera star was essentially paternal. Callas enjoyed the company of both men and turned to them

219

for advice. If anything, the relationship between Vergottis and Onassis was strengthened as mutual concern for the temperamental diva gave it an added focus. The problem arose when they tried to give that concern an economic basis.

The story, as related by Onassis, began in the summer of 1964. For some time he and Vergottis had been worried about how best to secure Maria's financial future. Her greatest asset—her voice—was one that must inevitably decline in value over the years. She had some capital, but not a great deal by the standards of Greek shipowners. There was a strong probability that she would outlive them both. They wanted to protect her and insure that she would be able to live, in spite of inflation, in the extravagant style to which she had become accustomed. The solution was thought to be a ship. Madame Callas enthusiastically endorsed the idea.

In September 1964, Vergottis found what looked like the ideal vessel on a visit to Spain. He telephoned Onassis, then on the *Christina* anchored off Skorpios, with news of his discovery. The 27,000-ton *Artemision II* was in the last stages of construction at El Ferrol, Spain. There was another interested buyer, but it was still possible to purchase it. The asking price was $3.9 million. Shortly afterward the two men met with Maria on the *Christina* and decided to make an offer. They set up a Liberian corporation, Overseas Bulk Carriers, to operate the ship.

After some haggling, a price of $3.4 million was agreed on—20 percent as a down payment, the rest to be paid on an eight-year mortgage. It was agreed that Vergottis would handle the basic acquisition through his company, Vergottis Ltd. Madame Callas forwarded $168,000 to Vergottis to purchase a 25 percent holding in Overseas Bulk Carriers. The plan was that Vergottis should take up another 25 percent interest, while Onassis would initially take up 50 percent. Then it was understood that he would make a gift of 26 percent to Callas. The opera star would thus wind up with a 51 percent majority holding.

Negotiations for the purchase of the *Artemision* were effectively concluded on October 31, 1964. On the same day, Callas, Onassis, and Vergottis met for dinner at Maxim's in Paris to celebrate their newfound commercial intimacy. Although the share division that would control the ownership of the vessel had not yet been put in writing, Onassis remembered Vergottis making a point of congratulating Callas on becoming a shipowner. It was a happy occasion.

Then things started to go radically wrong.

Before the shares could be allotted, Vergottis began to act oddly. On her maiden voyage to Japan, the *Artemision* developed some minor technical faults. To Onassis they seemed like no more than teething troubles, to be expected in any new ship. To Vergottis they seemed more alarming. "She is an unlucky ship," he told Callas.

Vergottis suggested that she would obtain greater financial security by converting her $168,000 investment into a loan to the company, paying her 6.5 percent interest. Onassis did not much like the proposal, but as he understood that Callas would retain the option of changing the loan back to a straight investment at her discretion, he went along with it. In February 1965 there was another celebratory meal in Paris, edgier than the previous occasion but still basically amicable. Onassis, meanwhile, directed that twenty-six of his shares be given to Callas and the remaining twenty-four donated to his nephews. Technically, his interest in the *Artemision* and Overseas Bulk Carriers was at an end.

Six months later, in August 1965, Callas came to London to comfort Vergottis after the death of his brother. Vergottis handed her the first six months' interest payment on her $168,000. Shortly afterward they had a dramatic falling-out over an issue totally unrelated to the ship.

Vergottis had earlier consulted her about a proposal by a German company that wanted her to star in a film of Puccini's opera *Tosca.* Vergottis was very much in favor of the project, but Onassis was not so keen. In September, Callas withdrew from the film. The German producers asked Vergottis to intercede with the superstar on their behalf. Vergottis telephoned Callas, and they had words. Both took offense. Callas wrote a mollifying letter to Vergottis in an attempt to repair the relationship. Vergottis did not reply.

In November 1965—a year after that first euphoric dinner at Maxim's —Callas asked Vergottis Ltd. to convert her unsecured loan into twenty-five shares in Overseas Bulk Carriers, in accordance with the verbal option given by Vergottis. But Vergottis replied that no such option existed and that her claim was unfounded.

Onassis then reentered the lists on Callas's behalf and demanded that Vergottis hand over the shares. His gallantry was not appreciated. One meeting in the dining room of Claridge's ended with Vergottis brandishing a bottle of whisky and shouting, "Get out of here or I'll throw it at you!" Vergottis adamantly refused an offer to have the dispute arbitrated privately by a lawyer or a shipping expert. He told Onassis that if he thought he had a case, he should take it to court. Onassis did.

The case was heard by Mr. Justice Roskill in the Queen's Bench Division, London, starting on April 17, 1967. It provided a feast of copy

221

for the newspapers and some light entertainment, but it was essentially a dismal occasion. Onassis and Callas sought specific compliance with an oral agreement relating to ownership of the *Artemision*. To effect this, they asked that the court direct Vergottis to issue 25 percent of the shares in Overseas Bulk Carriers to Madame Callas.

Callas, wearing a white turban and scarlet dress, sat beside Onassis in the well of the court. The first day made it clear that their privacy was about to be subjected to its greatest public test. In his opening statement on behalf of the plaintiffs, Sir Milner Holland underlined the mood of the participants in the action. "I am sorry to say that Mr. Vergottis said that if either Mr. Onassis or Madame Callas dared to appear in the witness box they would be faced with a great deal of scandal, both in court and the press. It is perhaps natural that Mr. Onassis stigmatized that as blackmail and unnatural that Mr. Vergottis laughed. The breach between these two gentlemen and between Madame Callas and Mr. Vergottis has not been healed from that day."

Inevitably the Callas-Onassis relationship received a thorough airing, though its relevance to the facts of the case was not always apparent. On the first day, Peter Bristow, counsel for Vergottis, attempted to elucidate the connection between the plaintiffs when questioning Onassis.

> COUNSEL: After you got to know Madame Callas did you part from your wife and did Madame Callas part from her husband?
> ONASSIS: Yes, sir. Nothing to do with our meeting. Just coincidence.
> COUNSEL: Do you regard her as being in a position equivalent to being your wife, if she was free?
> ONASSIS: No. If that were the case I have no problem marrying her: neither has she any problem marrying me.
> COUNSEL: Do you feel obligations towards her other than those of mere friendship?
> ONASSIS: None whatsoever.

Callas was subsequently asked about her marital status. "I may answer that immediately," she told counsel. "If I go to America and have a divorce I can marry anyone. In Italy it would not be valid. Everywhere else it would be valid." "Do you regard yourself as a single woman?" "In Italy, no. Elsewhere—yes."

Asked about her relationship with Vergottis, Callas replied, "Until that September [of 1964] I had the great joy of considering him more than my father because I never had a father or a mother virtually. I was very happy and he knew it, and he considered me his greatest joy. He

222

was very proud to travel around and participate in my glory." She had cherished the association with both the men in the case. "Since I separated from my husband we have had many difficulties and he [Onassis] has been advising me. As Mr. Onassis has children and a family of his own I have taken advantage of Mr. Vergottis who has offered himself and whom I consider as a father."

The cross-examination of Onassis produced some lively exchanges, giving him a chance to demonstrate his ready wit. When it was implied that he had turned Callas against Vergottis, he observed, "Madame Callas is not a vehicle for me to drive; she has her own brakes and her own brains." Probing the origins of the *Artemision* deal, counsel suggested that there was evidence that the ship was not on the market when Vergottis first made an approach. A sale had already been arranged subject to charter. "That is nothing to do with it," said Onassis. "When Mr. Vergottis told me she was on the market it meant that she had not been sold. So long as a girl is not married she is free."

Counsel then adroitly tried to use the metaphor against its inventor. Referring to the celebratory dinner at Maxim's over the ship's purchase, Bristow suggested that "if the ship is on the market until the lady is married, your dinner was before the wedding because the deal had not gone through." Onassis, as adeptly, replied, "No. The marriage was announced and all we wanted was the doctor's certificate. It was just subject to inspection and we knew it was really ours when the sellers accepted our offer."

Asked to give his interpretation of Vergottis's motive, Onassis said, "I think he started regretting that he missed the opportunity of owning 100 percent of the ship himself, secondly he missed the opportunity of owning 50 percent of the ship. He was sorry and crying in his heart over spilt milk and he was trying to save out of that spilt milk as much as he could." Callas, more charitably, did not offer any explanation for the breach. "I cannot explain this," she told the court. "I usually must have an explanation. It is my nature and this is good for the work I do, but I do not have an explanation."

Both Onassis and Callas gave their evidence boldly and confidently, with no more than differences of detail between their stories. They were good witnesses and needed to be. Vergottis's defense was simple but strong. He claimed that he had gone into the *Artemision* deal on a simple fifty-fifty basis with Onassis. There was nothing in writing to indicate that Callas's financial contribution entitled her to a 25 percent share in the vessel. The main document before the court was his letter

223

to Callas, dated December 21, 1964—less than two months after the purchase—in which he acknowledged the receipt of her $168,000 "representing unsecured loan which will be repaid within 12 or 24 months at your option plus interest." Interest had been paid on that loan. As far as he was concerned, there had been no suggestion that the $168,000 should purchase shares until after the row over the *Tosca* incident in August 1965.

Vergottis spoiled it all by his performance in the witness box. Unlike his opponents, he had no gift for public speaking. He was old—almost seventy-eight—and sick. His doctor was with him throughout the trial. The dispute had evidently corroded his spirit as well as affected his health. What came across most strongly was his unconfined bitterness against his former friends. It was sad to see a man so reduced. When asked about the business arrangement between the parties, Vergottis said, "I had no idea Mr. Onassis was giving his shares to his partner, Madame Callas. When we had a lunch meeting in Paris and Onassis said, 'Why don't you give her the other 25 shares?', I thought it was a joke. To give 25 shares to a prima donna for nothing at all I should have —I must have—my head examined." He agreed that there was nothing legally wrong with Onassis distributing his own shares how he wished, "but morally there was. I might have given shares to Onassis's adversary, who he hates, Mr. Niarchos. Would that have been right?"

As his evidence unfolded, it became apparent that Vergottis saw himself as the victim of a conspiracy. At one stage, Sir Milner Holland asked, "Is it pure coincidence that the [$168,000] which you say was a loan happens to be just the sum appropriate to a 25 percent shareholding?" Vergottis replied, "Not coincidence. I am now convinced that he had it in mind in order to trap me. I have heard so many things after this that it would make your hair stand on end—the things he has done and how he started. I have been to Greece and investigated lots of things. He is black in his heart." To a suggestion that the loan document had been fraudulently contrived to deprive Callas of a legitimate shareholding, Vergottis responded with some dignity, "I have not reached the age of seventy-seven to perjure myself or to fabricate documents."

But perjury there must have been, the only question being on whose part. In his summation after a ten-day hearing, Mr. Justice Roskill faced the issue squarely. "There is no escape—one could wish there were— from the fact that by one side or the other, perjury has been committed. If the defense is right there can be no doubt that Mr. Onassis and Madame Callas have put their heads together, if I may be forgiven using the term, to 'frame' Mr. Vergottis. If the plaintiffs are right there can be no doubt that Mr. Vergottis has deliberately broken a bargain with the plaintiffs and then lied, and lied more than once, in order to escape the consequences of that breach. There is no half-way house."

He found that the case had "many of the elements of a Sophoclean tragedy." After reviewing the disputed facts, he concluded, "I formed a wholly favorable view of Mr. Onassis and Madame Callas, but take an unfavorable view of Mr. Vergottis, reluctant as I am to say that of a man of his age and standing. His whole attitude in the witness box gave the impression that he had in truth stood on his rights not only that he might see Madame Callas and Mr. Onassis cross-examined at length as to the relationship between them, but that he might use the opportunity of going into the witness box to make such venomous remarks about them as he could slip in before he was stopped by counsel or myself. He made an unfavorable impression upon me and I have no hesitation in holding that the plaintiffs' story is true and defendant's untrue."

Judgment was given for Onassis and Callas with costs, estimated at $84,000. Onassis was less than gracious in victory. Asked by a reporter why the action had come about, he said, "I would say a little bit old age, stubbornness, and greediness, and emotionalism. Or perhaps that should be greediness, stubbornness, and old age." Later, and more reflectively, he described the verdict as a "humiliation of an old friend which I bitterly regret."

Vergottis appealed. Examining the trial evidence in January 1968, the court of appeal was less impressed by the plaintiffs' case. Lord Denning, master of the rolls, sitting with Lord Justice Salmon and Lord Justice Edmund Davies, found that Mr. Justice Roskill had "misdirected himself" in holding that "a wicked motive of greed and avarice" pervaded Mr. Vergottis. They found no evidence of such a motive and were more impressed by the "seeds of misunderstanding" in the case. They were also impressed by the fact that the key documents supported the view that the $168,000 put up by Madame Callas was a loan. Lord Justice Salmon commented, "It seems hardly likely that in 1964 Mr. Vergottis would have set about making false documents for the purpose of cheating two very famous people, one his oldest friend and the other a person he regarded as his daughter. . . . I am certainly not to be taken as having formed a view that Mr. Vergottis is necessarily right, but merely that his case was not sufficiently considered in the judgment." Their lordships ordered a new trial.

Onassis promptly appealed against this decision to the House of

225

Lords, the highest court in the land. On October 31, 1968, the law lords found for Onassis, upholding Mr. Justice Roskill's original judgment by a majority of three to two. Explaining the majority view, Lord Dilhorne stated that the trial judge had been essentially right in his argument that the decision should turn on the credibility of the witnesses in court, and that he had approached this task with the greatest care. Lord Pearce, entering a dissenting opinion, made what seemed a more valid point. The demeanor of the participants in such actions could, he felt, be highly misleading. The class of case where love had turned to hate, where old friends wondered in amazement how they could have been friends, presented special difficulties not present under normal commercial conditions. There was little that either side was not prepared to say about the other by the time the case came to trial. In such an atmosphere, even more attention than usual should be paid to documentary evidence.

As far as he could determine this evidence was on Vergottis's side. He felt that it was not possible to conclude the case fairly without weighing the evidence against Vergottis's having concocted with fraudulent intent the letter of December 21, 1964, which outlined the loan arrangement. At that time there was no overt hostility between any of the three parties involved. Lord Pearce's opinion, supported by Lord Wilberforce, was some consolation for Vergottis but not much. He had lost.

His bitterness endured to the end, although by the time the action was over Onassis had separated from Callas and had married Jackie Kennedy. The two men frequently found themselves in the same dining room at Claridge's, but neither managed to break the angry silence between them. After the court case Onassis flamboyantly announced that he would give $84,000 to "some English charity." One of Vergottis's last private acts was to donate $420,000 for a school in Kephalonia, the Vergottis Public School for Merchant Marine Captains. A few days after his return from Greece, he fell ill in his suite at the Ritz and died.

16
THE SUPERSHIPS

FOR MOST OF HIS CAREER as a shipowner, Onassis proudly boasted that no sailors' lives had been lost on his ships. Given the scale of his operation and the fact that most of his fleet sailed under flags that did not enforce the highest standards of seaworthiness, this was a considerable achievement. There was luck involved—his ships were never employed on the pitiless Atlantic run during World War II—but there was also judgment. Onassis always argued that a better than average fleet enabled a shipowner to weather economic as well as climatic storms.

On June 9, 1966, Onassis was obliged to face the fact that his ships had no built-in immunity. The *Al Malik* was loading crude oil in Caracas, Venezuela, when an engine-room explosion ripped through the vessel, setting it on fire. By the time the blaze was brought under control it was discovered that two of the crew had been killed and six more had been seriously injured. The precise cause of the explosion was never discovered. Those who were superstitious explained that the *Al Malik* had originally been associated with the ill-starred Saudi Arabian venture and that the bottle used to christen her had broken only on the third attempt.

The stain on Onassis's safety record did not affect the build-up of his fleet. He was already poised to enter the next stage of development in

227

oil transportation, which produced the kind of huge carriers that now dominate the business. Onassis was not the first into the new supertankers—known in the trade as VLCCs (Very Large Crude Carriers)—but he, and of course Niarchos, were among the first independents to grasp their potential.

The great leap forward in tanker construction started in the mid-1960s under the impetus of the massive increase in transportation requirements. By 1968, some 475 million tons a year were imported into western Europe by tanker—an eightfold increase since 1950. The credit, if that is the word, for initiating the new technology belonged primarily to Shell International. Tanker tonnage almost doubled in the four years from 1964 to 1968. More importantly, the size of the new vessels was often four times that of those they were designed to replace.

Several factors combined to make the VLCCs economically and technologically feasible. It was more than the simple application of the economics of scale to the basic dimensions of a ship—length, beam, and draft. Long before the advent of VLCCs, owners and builders could do the appropriate calculations: if the dimensions of a 20,000-tonner were *doubled,* the new ship would have *eight* times as much carrying capacity. But the new ship would be so heavy and of such draft that it would be incapable of berthing at any of the main terminals.

The move from fleets in which the largest ships ranged from 45,000 to 70,000 tons to fleets dominated by 170,000- to 210,000-tonners was primarily made possible by advances in steel technology. The introduction of high-tensile-strength steels meant that lighter and thinner plates could be used. At the same time, improved corrosion control systems made it possible to reduce the extra steel thickness previously required to allow for corrosion of the tank walls. Following detailed research work, the ship classification societies rewrote their rules regarding the permitted length of cargo tanks so that fewer transverse bulkheads were required and, as a result, less steel weight.

One consequence of this was that each of the large center tanks in a 210,000-ton supertanker could actually hold more oil than an entire 16,500-ton T-2 tanker—the ship which had played such an important role in the immediate postwar development of the business. The 210,000-tonner had only fifteen cargo compartments as against thirty or more in the smaller ships. Many of the new superships were built with the navigation bridge and all accommodations aft, thus eliminating the midship castle structure and further reducing weight. All this substantially increased the cargo capacity.

228

Developments in propulsion plants was another important factor. The increase in power required for a VLCC was proportionately much less than the increase in carrying capacity. Whereas a very small crude carrier of around 33,000 tons had a power unit developing some 13,000 shaft horse power, the 210,000-tonner's was only 27,500. Driving a single propeller, geared steam turbines were supplied with steam from a single, high-efficiency boiler instead of the two parallel boilers installed in the older ships. The use of a large single boiler (with a small emergency one in reserve) gave more latitude to the designer and simplified remote control of operations from the bridge.

The high degree of automation on such vessels also dramatically reduced the number of crew members and thus the total bill for their wages, though individual members were expected to demonstrate a higher level of skill in return for higher pay. An 18,000-ton tanker in Shell's fleet in the early 1960s needed a crew of forty-two; the first 210,000-tonner Shell received needed only thirty-two.

Onassis watched developments at Shell and at Gulf Oil, another supertanker pioneer, with interest. At first, according to Gratsos, he was inclined to skepticism. The bulk of Onassis's new ship orders in the early and middle 1960s were still in the 50,000- to 60,000-ton bracket, though the *Olympic Fame*, finished in 1965, bordered on the 100,000-ton class. A year later, Onassis took the plunge in style with an order announced with his now customary flourish to the New York press. He had just placed an order in Japan for vast tankers of the 175,000- to 200,000-ton class. They would be among the biggest in the world, said Onassis. With the 700,000 tons of smaller ships he already had on order, the size of his fleet would soon increase more than 50 percent to an estimated 4 million tons. "It is my rule in business," he told the reporters, "to be the buyer, never the seller."

Some of the older Greek shipowners were frankly distressed by the new technology. Manuel Kulukundis, for one, felt that the automated behemoths destroyed some of the romance of the business. They seemed efficient enough, but there was no aesthetic that could pronounce them beautiful. Onassis does not appear to have been moved by such considerations. In any event, obedience to the iron law of survival would have rendered them irrelevant: Niarchos also was ordering 200,000-tonners from Japan.

They were both just in time. The prevailing depression in freight rates since the late 1950s meant that shipbuilding prices were comparatively low. The supply of ships had consistently run ahead of demand. Onassis

229

and Niarchos were among the last owners to benefit from this in a big way before the Six-Day War between Israel and the Arabs in June 1967 provided the impetus for a further transformation of the industry. The moment the Suez Canal closed again, demand for tankers to carry crude around the Cape of Good Hope to Europe went up even more dramatically than it had in 1956. The Worldscale Index, which stood at 30 in May 1967, rocketed to 225 immediately after the war and remained around 100 until the end of the year.

Onassis had ships free of long-term charters and did well out of the postwar boom, though his profits were less spectacular than they had been in 1956. The main beneficiary of the Six-Day War was an enterprising Norwegian tanker man, Hilmar Reksten. It is part of shipping legend that Reksten—a formidable spot-market gambler—was actually on his way to file bankruptcy papers on June 5, the day the fighting began. "People were calling me broke," Reksten recalled later, "but I was in the best position of any owner. I had 1.7 million tons on the starting line." After the war was over, he was advised by a New York shipbroker to put up a statue to Nasser in his garden.

All the independent owners were operating in a superb seller's market. Immediately after the Six-Day War, the rate for tanker charters soared. The basic rates went from about $6.50 per ton before the Suez Canal closed to $30–$31 afterward as major companies like BP, Texaco, and Agip scrambled for spare capacity. Sample profits for independent owners in July 1967 were $1 million for a 30,000-tonner making two consecutive Persian Gulf–Europe trips and up to $2.4 million for a 70,000-tonner. A 120-day voyage around Africa used to gross about $4,500 a day before the war; the postwar rate was around $35,000.

One immediate consequence of these economics was a renewed demand for elderly tankers. In July 1967 only thirty-one tankers were laid up, and the majority of those were built around 1945. "Almost any tanker which has engines inside it and can be put in class and has a crew is either commissioned or is commissioning," said a London tanker broker. Owners were bringing ships out of lay-up, and ships were appearing which, in the words of a Baltic Exchange man, "I thought had been scrapped years ago."

The Egyptian "scorched sands" policy that involved scuttling vessels in the Suez Canal to halt the Israeli advance insured the continuation of the tanker boom. There was inevitably a limit to the number of old vessels that could be pressed into service. The case for a massive increase in supertanker tonnage became irresistible. The startling economies of

230

scale these ships offered became apparent as soon as oil started coming around the cape. Shortly before the war, it cost a shipowner $3.29 per ton to carry crude in an 80,000-ton tanker from the Persian Gulf to Europe via the Suez Canal. A 200,000-tonner going the long way around after the canal had closed was carrying oil at $2.40 per ton. Freight rates, by contrast, had escalated from $2.95 a ton prewar—at which most owners were losing money—to as much as $26 a ton immediately after the canal closed. They remained around the lucrative $9.50 level more than a year later.

The next generation of tankers would be built with a view to remaining on the cape run whether the canal opened again or not. In the following two years, more than three hundred ships of the 200,000-ton-plus class were either ordered or brought into service. Gulf Oil had the first of six 326,000-tonners working by the end of 1968. Onassis placed orders in Japan for another six VLCCs, bringing his supertanker fleet to ten—about 2.5 million tons in all. Niarchos launched a parallel building program designed to add a million tons to his seventy-four-vessel fleet.

Before the war, Niarchos had been considering selling off a substantial portion of his tanker fleet. The two reasons cited by shipping experts were the predictability of the market, which made the business less interesting, and his problems with US tax authorities. In 1966, the Internal Revenue Service obtained a judgment against six of Niarchos's American-based corporations for $25 million in back taxes and interest. The IRS established that for the preceding sixteen years Niarchos's US corporations chartered vessels owned by them to two Panamanian corporations also owned and controlled by Niarchos—Companie International de Vapores Ltd. and Greenwich Marine Corporation.

This device, according to the US authorities, enabled Niarchos's empire to minimize its corporate tax liability since the American companies' charter rates were substantially less than the reasonable, prevalent rates in the shipping industry. In fact, after the Panamanian companies had obtained the charters, they had subchartered the vessels to third parties at rates which, in some cases, were more than double those of the original charters with the American companies. The government's case, therefore, was that the Panamanian corporations were shams designed to place much of the charter income beyond the reach of the IRS.

At one stage, Niarchos was reportedly more than ready to sell two-thirds of his fleet to the New York-based Marine Transport Lines for a figure in the neighborhood of $200 million. Had it gone through, it

231

would have been the biggest shipping deal of all time. After the Six-Day War, Niarchos had no further problems with the IRS, and his fleet was definitely not for sale. His rivalry with Onassis in the main arena of contention—shipping—continued unabated. "In business," Onassis once said of his former brother-in-law, "we cut each other's throats, but now and again we sit around the same table and behave—for the sake of the ladies."

The one area where Onassis scored consistently over his rival was in his relations with the press. Helen Vlachos, the Athens newspaper publisher, once described him as "the top public relations genius in the world, and he concentrates on one client—himself." Niarchos, for the most part, preferred to keep reporters at a long-arm's length, though he often issued lengthy press releases to state his point of view or justify his actions.

Onassis was frankly contemptuous of this technique. On one occasion, while relaxing in the Hôtel Grande Bretagne in Athens, Onassis boasted to a group of journalists about his willingness to talk to anyone. "I always answer the phone, even if I have to get out of my bathroom," he told them. "I am always accessible to the press. I am not like some people who sit on top of the Himalayas." All the Greek journalists recognized the allusion to Niarchos, who spent a great deal of time directing his business from his villa in Saint Moritz. At the same time, even the fact that they were drinking Onassis's scotch did not fully convince them of Onassis's "accessibility." They knew that reporters rarely got a chance to obtain either his telephone number or information on his whereabouts. Calls usually went through his private Cerberus, Amalia Hatziargyri, his confidential secretary at Olympic Airways headquarters in Athens. To discover the truth about Onassis, local newsmen had to tap sources ranging from the maid at his Glyfada house to the crew of the *Christina*. Occasionally, news agency correspondents, harassed by competition, had to use devious means to obtain information. One agency had a standing arrangement with the switchboard on the island of Lefkas through which all the Skorpios calls were channeled.

It was not Onassis's accessibility that won him the affection of newsmen but his amiability once cornered and his refreshing lack of pretense. He also could respect professional guile even when its consequences were not to his immediate advantage. Bryan Wharton, an outstanding British news photographer, remembers a time when he was stalking Onassis with Denis Craig, a reporter from the William Hickey column of the

232

London *Daily Express*. Their assignment was to get a picture-story on Onassis and Callas together. Onassis was staying at Claridge's while Callas was booked into the Savoy. The newsmen decided to stake out Claridge's and judiciously distribute a few pound notes to members of the staff for information on Onassis's movements.

After spending most of the day in this way, Wharton became convinced that the staff was retailing intelligence on *his* movements back to Onassis. "I later discovered," he says, "that Onassis had put out the word that he would double any tips from newsmen for information on their whereabouts." Toward midnight, the newsmen decided to pull a double-bluff operation. Walking past a member of the lobby staff who they suspected was Onassis's main intelligence gatherer, they complained loudly about the tedium of the day, the obtuseness of news editors, and the need to get home quickly for a good night's sleep. Once outside, they hailed a taxi and, after telling the driver to circle the block, had him park fifty yards from the entrance to the hotel. Sure enough, within fifteen minutes Onassis and Callas came out and started to walk arm-in-arm down the street. Wharton leaped out of the cab and got his picture, which was featured in the *Express* the following morning. Later, Denis Craig managed to secure a formal interview with Onassis and was complimented on his part in the photo-snatch operation.

Niarchos could never establish such an amiable relationship with his pursuers, though for a brief period in the mid-1960s he eclipsed his rival as a topic of gossip-column interest. The reason had more to do with sex than ships. Charlotte Ford, the elder daughter of Henry Ford II, was twenty-four years old when she met Stavros Niarchos in Saint Moritz in January 1965. She and her sister were distressed about the recent breakup of their parents' marriage. Niarchos, then fifty-six and the father of four children by Eugenie, displayed paternal concern.

On December 14, 1965, Eugenie Niarchos appeared in a civil court in Juarez, Mexico, and requested that her marriage of eighteen years be ended on the grounds of incompatibility of character. A decree was granted within five minutes. Two days later, Charlotte Ford and her lawyer flew to Juarez from New York. Niarchos arrived from Canada, and they were married by a civil judge. The groom was eight years older than his new stepfather. Charlotte later recalled that when her father first learned of her intended marriage "he nearly had a heart attack." The 50-carat diamond ring valued at $500,000 that Niarchos bestowed on his young bride was referred to in the Ford family as "the skating rink."

It was a curious marriage. After the ceremony they flew to Switzerland and moved into the Palace Hotel in Saint Moritz. Eugenie remained nearby in the neighboring Niarchos villa. Charlotte was pregnant and did not choose to ski. Niarchos and his ex-wife were nonetheless frequently seen on the resort's highest run, nicknamed *"piste* Niarchos." All three frequently lunched together at the Corviglia Club. After three months, later described by Charlotte as "the only married life I knew," the new Mrs. Niarchos flew back to New York and the Sutton Place triplex to await the arrival of her baby. All Niarchos's previous children had been born in the United States. Charlotte gave birth to Elena in May 1966, and Niarchos flew to New York to be by her side. He stayed on for the christening a few weeks later before returning to Europe.

Niarchos's marital affairs naturally made him the object of intense press speculation. It may have been this phenomenon which caused him to act out of character in his relations with the media. In the summer of 1966 Michael Braun, an able young American reporter, was given the red-carpet treatment around the Niarchos empire. His series of articles, which appeared in the London *Observer* in November 1966, provided one of the few intimate glimpses of Niarchos vouchsafed to the outside world.

Braun was shown over Niarchos's yacht, the *Creole,* with its "first sea-going telex, developed for Niarchos by the Dutch Post Office." He inspected the Spetsopoula residence and its "radio room with the only known scrambler telephone in Greece" and commented on the "nearly [$300,000] worth of direct teleprinter links" between Niarchos's offices in London, New York, and Paris. Niarchos, he reported, was about to become the first European to own a Magnetax, a machine developed by Xerox which could produce copies of a document at two separate places by means of a radio telephone—"very useful for clinching contracts."

The purpose of all this apparatus had nothing to do with any fascination with gadgetry per se. It was essential for the instant transmission of Niarchos's will to his seven hundred aides and employees around the world. Niarchos would consult them, but in the end only he could make decisions. "Our kind of business must be controlled by one individual because you need very fast thinking," Niarchos told Braun. "I can make a decision on anything in minutes. If I had to spend all my time convincing colleagues, I would not have time to fight competitors."

Although Onassis was mentioned only in passing, a very clear idea of the fundamental difference between the two men emerged. Whereas Onassis, in his business dealings, tended to rely on flair and instinct

234

combined with a prodigious memory, Niarchos was a master of orderliness and system. Both were energetic individualists operating in the same sphere, but the thought processes that went into their decisions were radically different.

In March 1967, Charlotte made another trip to Juarez. Shortly afterward she and Niarchos issued the following statement to the New York press: "Charlotte Ford Niarchos and Stavros Niarchos who were married in Mexico in 1965, were divorced today by decree of a Mexican court. The proceedings, commenced by Mrs. Niarchos on the ground of incompatibility of temperament, were not contested by Mr. Niarchos.

"A separation agreement had previously been reached on amicable terms. The sole purpose of this agreement was to make provision for the maintenance, education and custody of their only child, Elena Anne Niarchos."

Charlotte was subsequently interviewed by Booton Herndon for his book, *Ford*, the unofficial biography of her father. Herndon reported that Charlotte had been in love with Niarchos and had no regrets about the marriage. Asked why the marriage had broken up, she replied, "He drove me nuts. My ex-husband is not a happy man. He can't relax. He has no office, his office is with him wherever he goes. I found out that he was married to his telex machine. It's as simple as that."

The escapade with Charlotte Ford had no visible effect on Niarchos's standing in the shipping community. He was reunited with Eugenie, to no one's very great surprise. They did not remarry because, according to a Niarchos spokesman, his fourth marriage to Charlotte had always been null and void in the eyes of the Greek Orthodox church. The church did not forbid divorce, but it allowed a man only three marriages. Niarchos continued to meet Charlotte, with every appearance of friendliness, to discuss their daughter's future. Eugenie's accommodating ways earned her a reputation for saintliness that must have imposed a severe strain. She acted, said a friend, "like a heroine straight out of a Victorian novel."

Beside the Niarchos-Ford liaison, the continuing story of Onassis and Madame Callas lost much of its glamour. Most of the impediments to their marrying had long since disappeared, but of a wedding there was no sign. In March 1966 Callas renounced her American citizenship and became a naturalized Greek citizen the following month. Under a Greek law passed in 1946, no marriage that was not performed under the aegis of the Greek Orthodox church was legal for Greek citizens. Thus Callas's marriage to Meneghini was void everywhere but Italy, and she was free

235

to marry Onassis if she, and he, pleased. There are those who believe to this day that Onassis and Callas were married—and soon after divorced—in Las Vegas, but we could find no evidence that a marriage ceremony took place.

Those who knew both Onassis and Niarchos intimately were fascinated by how two men could have so many interests and obsessions in common and yet be so different. The unkindest reflection on Niarchos was that he was "like Onassis without the personality." Yet Helen Vlachos, who liked Niarchos much more than Onassis, said of him, "Stavros is one of the few genuinely boring clever men I have ever met." She remembers evenings on Spetsopoula that were as soporific as "any Sunday school gathering." The sharpness of Niarchos's mind rarely overcame the monotony of his discourse. He would talk *at* people rather than *to* them. He also made the mistake of assuming that whatever was on his own mind was of riveting interest to his company.

Vlachos believes that he was in some ways corrupted by the desire to appear more formidable than Onassis. Niarchos genuinely believed that he was more solid, more serious, and richer than his rival and wanted the world to accept his self-estimation. Without the example of Onassis, she felt that Niarchos might have developed into a patriotic and protective benefactor of his country. As a newspaper publisher, Vlachos also saw a great deal of Onassis. In her book, *House Arrest,* she provides an engaging portrait of a typical encounter with the shipowner.

> "There is a Mr. Onassis at the entrance," a rather diffident secretary would inform me, "and he says he wants to see you. . . ."
>
> "Tell him to come right up."
>
> I did not doubt that it would be Ari Onassis. It was his very clever way of making an immediate and indelible impression on the porter, on the liftman, on anyone who chanced to be around. He tried it every time, and it often worked, as the hall porter did not expect such a humble approach, or simply had never seen him in person, and did not recognise him from his photographs.
>
> "Why don't you ring up before coming, like a sensible man?" I would ask him each time. "How did you know I would be here?"
>
> "Well I would have tried again," he would say, with a slow pleasant, carpet-vendor's smile, "that is all."
>
> And he would sit and talk and be pleasant, friendly, informative. Also, most of the time, hungry and thirsty. "Do you have any bread and cheese? I am starving."
>
> This, conveyed to the office canteen, created an effusion of hospitality.

236

Whole chunks of cheese arrived accompanied by whatever foodstuffs could be found on the premises, and while members of the staff and visitors came and went, Onassis would munch contentedly, offering the picture of a simple, carefree man, different from those exasperatingly busy magnates, always pressed for time. He wanted to meet everybody, he usually overstayed, as if being inside a real newspaper office was the most exciting thing in the world.

His reason for the visit was sometimes clearly stated, sometimes not even hinted at. It could be just talk, or some information about an accident on the Olympic Airways, or an invitation for an excursion, or just nothing. He felt like coming, and he came, and he always left an excellent impression.

Vlachos enjoyed the meetings with Onassis, yet was inclined to distrust his deepest motives.

Onassis wanted publicity, needed publicity, used publicity. Always a taker, never a giver, he used credit more than anything else, and his publicized connections with the great were the keys that opened all doors, that brought him in contact with the top bankers, the important businessmen, the millionaires, the moguls. From then on he relied on himself— on his cleverness, charm, persuasiveness—to bring off the most difficult and complicated deals.

Another shrewd intimate of the two men over a long period was the British diplomat Sir John Russell. His preference was for Onassis, though he detected qualities in Niarchos that others were inclined to overlook. He and his wife, Aliki, a former Miss Greece, first met the shipowners socially in New York in the mid-1950s when he was head of the British Information Service. They used to sail with Niarchos off Long Island, and Sir John felt that the great shipowner was at his best at the helm of his own yacht. "Niarchos was far closer to the sea in a romantic sense than Ari, for all Ari's rubbish about having salt water in his veins and so on. Stavros loved the sea for itself, but for Ari it was just something on which his tankers sailed." On shore, he found Niarchos less impressive. The regular Niarchos circle was characterized by Sir John as being largely composed of "yes-men and yes-please-women."

Onassis, by contrast, was a natural listener. "He loved hearing other people talk about something they knew about, and he never forgot anything," recalled Sir John. "He used to ask me a lot about British policies in the days when I was with the foreign office, not for his own purposes but just because he liked to hear me discussing it." At the same

237

time, Sir John felt there was an affinity between the two men despite their many differences. "Neither of them could afford to cut the other completely out of their lives, personal or business. It was often them against the world, Lloyd's, or the established Greeks. Ari was often very sarcastic about Niarchos. But you'd be surprised how often they were cooperating, or at least talking."

The possibility of an "authorized" biography about Onassis had frequently been canvassed, but Onassis had always refused. In 1967 he was again approached by Willi Frischauer, the Austrian-born British journalist. They were already well acquainted as Frischauer had previously written a number of sympathetic articles about the Greek shipowners and their families. Onassis, however, was still sufficiently unenthusiastic about the idea of a biography to offer Frischauer $50,000 *not* to write the book. Frischauer took mock offense, saying he could not honorably accept such a bribe as "I am too old to accept money for not writing." Onassis laughed and agreed to collaborate. "If I have to be raped," he said, "I might as well lie back and enjoy it."

For Frischauer, it was the beginning of a hectic year jumping on and off planes all over the world as he pursued his subject. During all-night sessions at Claridge's they would squabble "like an old married couple" over the accuracy of Onassis's recollections. Frischauer quickly discovered that Onassis was a vivid but erratic raconteur. On one occasion he consulted the *Congressional Record* to establish the precise dates of Onassis's arrest in 1954 and when he sent the cable saying he would make himself available to the American authorities. He already had some dates from Onassis, but they did not seem to be correct because they would have placed him in New York when the cable was sent—whereas the point of the story was that the cable was sent while Onassis was in Europe and therefore outside US jurisdiction. When Frischauer told Onassis that his dates must be wrong and cited his source, Onassis raged: "I'm not wrong. It must be the *Congressional Record* that is wrong."

At other times when Frischauer would question a fact or an interpretation, Onassis would level the accusation, "I know it. You are in the pay of Niarchos." For the writer, it was an exhausting but lively venture. Its high point came toward the end when Frischauer was invited to Athens to check over the final draft of the biography. The plan was that Frischauer should stay in the Hôtel Grande Bretagne and be taxied to and from Skorpios each day in Onassis's Piaggio. Frischauer, a man of considerable bulk, accordingly fitted himself out in the latest beach wear for an Aegean idyll.

On the first day he was inclined to travel light. Leaving his gear in the hotel, he presented himself at Athens airport in his London suit. The Piaggio was out of order. Onassis then arrived with an immediate solution. An eighty-six-seater DC-8 was wheeled out to fly him and Frischauer to Aktion, a military base near Skorpios. From there they took a boat to Skorpios, where Frischauer sweated it out for the next two weeks in his pitifully rumpled suit. Callas was also on the island and obviously put out by Onassis's absorption in the story of his own life. He was always late for meals. On such occasions, Frischauer recalled, the great diva fluttered around "like an irritated suburban housewife."

Frischauer's biography, *Onassis,* was published in 1968 and became a best-seller in the United States, where Onassis had reasons—both public and private—for wanting a well-burnished image. While researching the book, Frischauer had stumbled on the fact that Onassis and Jackie Kennedy were becoming more than just good friends. With hindsight, Frischauer was inclined to think that one undisclosed but powerful reason for Onassis's ready collaboration on the project was his desire to furnish Mrs. Kennedy with a heroic account of his life and times.

Niarchos, meanwhile, was experiencing a tragic loss. On June 13, 1968, the fourteen-year-old Liberian-registered *World Glory* broke her back and sank in heavy seas off the eastern coast of South Africa. Twenty-four of her crew were lost, including her captain, Dimitrios Androutsopoulos. From the confused recollections of the ten exhausted survivors, it appeared that the *World Glory* had been overwhelmed by a succession of gigantic "cape roller" waves peculiar to that dangerous stretch of the Indian Ocean. The ship's electrician had seen the wave which had finished the *World Glory.* It was about seventy feet high, he estimated, and it had lifted the tanker loaded with Kuwaiti crude clean out of the water—as the wave had passed under the ship, the bow and stern, heavily laden with oil, had been left totally unsupported. At that moment, the radio officer felt a violent shudder run through the ship. Then he saw a crack three or four inches wide opening up across the width of the main deck. "I couldn't believe my eyes. It was opening and closing with the movement of the vessel."

Another massive cape roller then lifted the bow sharply up from the water. The stricken ship—once the biggest tanker in the world at 46,500 tons and the flagship of the Niarchos fleet—began to break in two with the terrifying sound of wrenching metal. As the two sections broke apart, oil poured into the sea and was ignited by sparks from the tearing steel.

239

A few days after the news broke, the Greek press raised the possibility that the tragedy had been caused by some structural defect or weakness in the *World Glory*. "How could this fourteen-year-old tanker break up so easily?" the Athens newspaper, *Acropolis*, asked. "Was it the hurricane that broke its skeleton . . . or was it an explosion that ripped its bowels for some unknown reasons?" There was similar speculation in other newspapers. When the survivors' accounts clearly ruled out an explosion, attention began to focus on the possibility that the *World Glory*'s welded plates had given way under a ferocious battering.

The *World Glory* had been one of a series of twenty tankers built from more or less identical designs by Bethlehem Steel. After she was lost, the American Bureau of Shipping (ABS) did an exhaustive survey of all her sister ships, searching for any common pattern that might help explain the disaster. It produced nothing. The *World Glory* was the only ship in the series to have been lost in a storm. After similar inquiries, the ABS had often issued new guidelines for owners and shipbuilders, but there was nothing to say in this case. Its conclusion seemed to be that whatever had happened, it must have been specific to the *World Glory* alone.

The first formal inquiry into the tragedy was carried out by the South African authorities. Oil from the *World Glory* had spread into a slick covering some one hundred thirty square miles off South Africa's coast. The oil had approached to within a couple of miles of some of the finest beaches and nature reserves. A dozen ships and several aircraft had been used to break up the slick with detergents, and the South Africans were interested in who was going to pay for this. The possibility of having to sue the *World Glory*'s owners led them to take full statements from all survivors, but the principal objective was to establish what had happened *after* the ship broke up, not why it should have split so suddenly.

The Liberians, however, were primarily concerned about the condition of the *World Glory* when she was lost, and a Greek maritime lawyer was appointed to make preliminary inquiries. There was no dispute about the background facts in the case. The *World Glory* had been given an A-1 rating for insurance purposes by the ABS only nine months previously. There was no suggestion of navigational error by Captain Androutsopoulos, an experienced master. The last loading plan he had filed on the fatal voyage appeared to be perfectly in order.

The Liberian "preliminary" investigation lasted eight weeks and accumulated a stack of papers two feet high. But the bulk of its material was, like the South African inquiry, drawn from the recollections of the ten survivors. The lawyer found it very difficult to obtain any other

240

documentation. The *World Glory*'s log and other papers were, of course, at the bottom of the sea. Nothing he received from the owners added much to the sum of knowledge. The Liberians concluded that with so much of the crucial evidence lost forever, there could be no grounds for a full-scale court inquiry.

But there is one set of surviving papers relating to the *World Glory* which the Liberians had not heard about but which came to light during the research for this book. These are the standard forms on which the master and chief officer of every tanker periodically report to the owners about the condition of the bulkheads and heating coils in the ship's cargo tanks (crude oil is normally heated to facilitate its carriage). A former employee of the Niarchos group who regularly handled such reports has confirmed their authenticity.

The relevant sequence of reports began in November 1967, shortly after Androutsopoulos took command of the *World Glory*. On the cargo tank plan provided, Androutsopoulos noted that a number of small cracks and fractures were visible amidships on interior bulkheads. The plans depicted the tanks in rows of three across the ship—port, center, and starboard. In the bulkhead dividing tanks seven-port and seven-center, there was a crack six inches long and three inches wide. This and every subsequent report was signed by Androutsopoulos and counter-signed by his first officer, Stavros Ananiadis.

The next report arrived in London three months later, in February 1968. The crack between tanks seven-port and seven-center was now three feet long, and a new fracture of the same length had developed in the bulkhead separating tanks seven-center and seven-starboard. In his report, Androutsopoulos noted that both the cracks—which ran along the welded seams joining the metal plates—had been rewelded when the *World Glory* underwent a major survey in the middle of 1967. But they were now "leaking a lot."

There were other small fractures elsewhere, but Androutsopoulos seemed concerned only about the two big ones in tank seven. "They make ballasting and tank cleaning operation very difficult, creating un-necessary work and the use of pumping equipment," he wrote. "We tried all means of repair but in vain." Over the next month, these cracks increased another twelve inches to four feet. In April, when the *World Glory* reached the port of Mina Al Ahmadi in Kuwait, another report was sent to London. The cracks in tank seven were now five feet long. Attempts had been made to repair them with Cordobond, a sealing compound.

Early in June 1968, Androutsopoulos reported that the two cracks in

241

tank seven now measured six feet. Both were leaking badly again. It was the last form received from the *World Glory*. Twelve days later she split in two almost exactly along the line of tank seven. Captain Androutsopoulos was washed from the bridge, and his body was never recovered.

We brought these reports to the attention of the Liberian authorities, but they did not consider them adequate grounds for convening a court of inquiry so long after the event. We also showed them to two independent marine experts, who also felt that they did not provide a sufficient explanation for the disaster—most old tankers develop cracks, and those in the *World Glory* provided a cause for concern but not alarm. To this day, her sinking remains one of the unsolved mysteries of the sea.

17
THE PRESIDENT'S WIDOW

THE ARTISTS, MUSICIANS, AND FRENCH CUISINE brought to the White House by Jacqueline Bouvier Kennedy lent an aura of social emancipation and elegance to the Kennedy years. If it was style rather than substance that Jackie imparted to the New Frontier, that elusive quality was nonetheless integral to its success. John Kennedy sometimes acknowledged as much. "I am the man who accompanied Jacqueline Kennedy to Paris," he told the press after a brilliantly successful state visit to France in 1969, "and I have enjoyed it."

Charles de Gaulle, a connoisseur of personal as well as national destiny, was fascinated by her. "What do you think of her?" de Gaulle privately asked his minister of culture, André Malraux.

"She is unique for the wife of an American president, sir," Malraux replied.

"Yes, she's unique," said de Gaulle. "I can see her in about ten years from now on the yacht of a Greek oil millionaire."

Within two years of this uncanny prediction, Jackie was a guest of Onassis on the *Christina*. Within eight years she was honeymooning with him on the yacht.

De Gaulle had been impressed by Jackie's wit and intelligence, but what struck him most forcibly was her ornamental quality. It accounted for much of her public success and no small part of her private distress, for it had been acquired at great cost—both emotional and economic—and was no less costly to maintain. The passage of time had chipped much of the sentiment from the Kennedy marriage, revealing a husband who regularly and enthusiastically "cheated" on his young wife. In furthering their ambitions—his political, hers social and artistic—it was a marriage of wonderful convenience. As a celebration of intimacy, it was not impressive.

According to Ben Bradlee—then a *Newsweek* correspondent, Kennedy confidant, and occasional referee in presidential domestic disputes—Kennedy was as angry about the purposes for which Jackie spent money as the actual sums involved. The Kennedys had never skimped where their political ambitions were concerned, but Jackie's inability to explain such expenses as $40,000 on "department stores" was a rather different matter. "Is there such a thing as Shoppers Anonymous?" the president once asked.

According to her former secretary, Mary B. Gallagher, Jackie spent $121,461.61 on family expenses in 1962—$21,000 more than the president's annual salary. It is difficult to resist the conclusion that Jackie's passion for collecting—clothes, objects, ambiences, and people—was a substitute for some deeper emotional need. Most chroniclers of Jackie's life and times have either sedulously ignored her profligacy or else treated it as a tic of personality. It was, however, central to her character and her class.

The Bouviers were respected, if not especially prominent, members of old New York society. Michel, the first American Bouvier, was an infantryman in Napoleon's army who escaped to Philadelphia, where he prospered as a businessman. Later Bouviers staked out dubious claims to a French aristocratic lineage commensurate with their growing wealth. Jackie's father was John Vernou Bouvier III, a stockbroker whose meridional good looks, accentuated by regular use of a sunlamp and continental clothes, earned him a number of nicknames, including Black Jack, the Black Prince, and the Sheik.

His relationship with his daughters, Jackie and Lee, was unusual. Jack Bouvier was never able to make the transition from social adventurer to devoted husband. A compulsive gambler, he lost most of his money during the depression and drifted away from his wife, Janet, who in 1942 married Hugh Auchincloss, a reticent, ruddy-faced Washington stock-

The rival. Stavros Niarchos makes a point.

Niarchos and his wife Eugenie, on board his yacht, the Creole. Eugenie died in 1970 on Spetsopoula, Niarchos's private island, after suffering physical injuries and taking a large quantity of barbiturates.

Niarchos and Charlotte Ford on honeymoon. In 1965, at the time of their marriage, Charlotte was twenty-four, Niarchos fifty-six. After a child was born they obtained a divorce. "I found out he was married to his telex machine," Charlotte explained. Niarchos returned to Eugenie.

The Beautiful People. Onassis with Elizabeth Taylor and her then husband Richard Burton at the Venice film festival.

Island kingdom. Onassis bought Skorpios in 1963 for $110,000. He laid down six miles of road and built a farm and two houses. The island was planted with trees brought from all over the world by his tankers.

The first lady, Onassis, and Franklin D. Roosevelt, Jr., her "chaperon," on board the Christina, *summer 1963. Jackie enjoyed the cruise but the American public did not.*

Jackie, John-John, and Caroline on Skorpios the day before the wedding, October 1968.

The "wedding of the century." Jackie and Onassis are showered with flower petals outside the chapel of Panayitsa ("Little Virgin").

Invasion fleet. Some four hundred photographers and newsmen clustered in hired boats off Skorpios. Their shouts and screams could be heard throughout the wedding service. Those who swam ashore were allowed to join the party in their wet clothes.

Jackie at sea, off Skorpios, 1970.

Belfast mud. In 1970 the Onassises visited Northern Ireland in an attempt to acquire the Harland & Wolff shipyard.

Blue movie. Mel Finkelstein, New York Daily News photographer, attempts to take a photo of Jackie emerging from I Am Curious (Yellow). Finkelstein explained that Jackie "flipped" him over her thigh. The doorman said he tripped over his equipment. Ari was watching the end of the movie and missed the action.

Meet Santa. The Christmas card Ron Galella sent to the Onassises featured Ari and the paparazzo in a scenario entitled "The Payoff." The document was submitted in court as evidence of Galella's harassment of Jackie.

Peace On Earth

GOOD WILL TOWARD MEN

☆

RON GALELLA
NEW YORK, N. Y.

☆

PAPARAZZO

"Daddy O and Jackie O" going out to dinner with friends in Rome.

Coming out. Christina Onassis in Paris on her way to the "Vampire Ball" organized by playboy Gunther Sachs for his birthday.

Cutting loose. Christina celebrates her twenty-first birthday with her husband, Joseph Bolker, age forty-eight, in Los Angeles. The couple were, in Bolker's words, "subjected to extraordinary pressures." Christina went home to her father soon afterward.

Father and son. Ari and Alexander Onassis.

Fiona von Thyssen. In her own words, she was Alexander's "mistress, mother, and priest confessor."

Fiona and Alexander in Switzerland.

Alexander Onassis shortly before his death in January 1973.

The last rites. Onassis receives Greek premier George Papado-poulos's condolences on the death of Alexander.

The last hurrah. Onassis with Peter Booras and Costa Gratsos, prospecting for an oil refinery in New Hampshire, January 1974. The venture foundered on local opposition.

Onassis on his way into the American Hospital, Paris. Six weeks later, on March 15, 1975, he died of bronchial pneumonia.

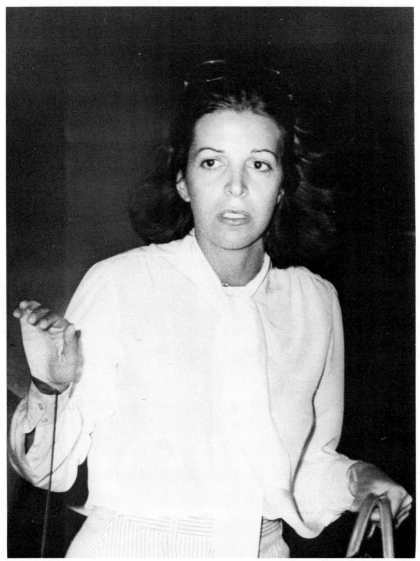

Sole heir and survivor, Christina Onassis, January 1976.

broker with the physique of a Scots Guard. Bouvier did not conceal his dislike for the Auchinclosses and felt compelled to compete for his daughters' affections.

His methods were money and attention. No matter how bleak his fortunes, he maintained horses and charge accounts for his daughters. At Bouvier gatherings in East Hampton, Long Island—according to the family biographer, John H. Davis, a cousin of Jackie's—he "had the typically Latin habit of complimenting his children to their faces. . . . 'Doesn't Jacqueline look terrific?' he would say. 'Girl's taken all prizes in her class this year . . . and she's the prettiest thing in the ring to boot.' " He imposed his distinctive view of male-female relationships on his daughters. His own view of women was simple: Once they had given in to his advances he was no longer interested in them. A woman's aloofness was, conversely, a measure of her desirability. He would continually admonish his daughters never to throw themselves at anybody, to be reticent and play hard to get. The uncertain state of the Bouvier fortunes gave this counsel an economic as well as a sexual significance.

The novelist Gore Vidal, a perceptive and sometimes waspish observer of the Bouvier sisters, later maintained that "they'd been brought up to be adventuresses. Their father had it in mind for them." Vidal had a tenuous family connection. His own mother, after separating from his father, was married to Hugh Auchincloss before he moved on to become the stepfather of Jackie and Lee.

Black Jack's pride in his daughters amounted to an extension of his own narcissism. They were possessions he took pleasure in displaying. Their appearance as teenagers in an East Hampton club or a French restaurant in Manhattan inevitably made them the center of attention. The sisters thought being with him was "fun"—a striking contrast to the staid home environment of the Auchinclosses. The roles they acquired in Black Jack's company were the ones they would impose on the world. Jackie, in particular, combined an impenetrable personal reserve—accentuated by her parents' divorce, which she took as a personal humiliation—with a distinctive histrionic inclination. Ill at ease on a one-to-one basis, she shone in crowds. In 1947 she was nominated Debutante of the Year by Cholly Knickerbocker, the society columnist. Her Bouvier relatives were confused by how the "shy and sensitive" Jackie could enjoy being on center stage. It was a confusion the rest of the world would later learn to share.

It was Lee who showed the earliest signs of fulfilling the promise of social adventure Black Jack had bequeathed to his daughters. Her first

245

marriage to Michael Canfield, a well-connected publisher, took her to London and a life-style she adhered to, even after the marriage had been dissolved, by becoming fashion editor of *Harper's Bazaar*. Magazine assignments increased her familiarity with the European rich and famous. In 1959 Lee married Prince Stanislaus "Stash" Radziwill, an exiled member of the Polish nobility who had more than compensated for his family's ill fortunes by adroit participation in the postwar London real estate boom. To the cachet of an old name, Princess Radziwill could add the perquisites of new wealth, a picturesque manor house near Henley-on-Thames, Turville Grange, and a functional but profitable office building named Lee House. While covering the Paris fashion scene, a fellow reporter inquired how he should address her since her marriage. "Princess Lee will do," she said.

Prince and Princess Radziwill became acquainted with Aristotle Onassis shortly after the breakup of his marriage with Tina. Lee took to Onassis more readily than did Stash—so much so that the celebrated Washington columnist, Drew Pearson, wrote that Onassis had ambitions of being the brother-in-law of the president of the United States. Meneghini, Maria Callas's fretful husband, went on record with the opinion that Onassis had deserted Maria in favor of Lee Radziwill.

Lee provided the original connection between Onassis and Jackie. In the summer of 1963, while she and Stash were dining with Onassis in Athens, it was mentioned that the recent death of Jackie's third child, Patrick Bouvier Kennedy, had thrown her into a deep depression. Onassis suggested a recuperative Aegean cruise. When Lee telephoned her sister with the proposal, Jackie immediately accepted.

The president was less enthusiastic. Onassis's earlier well-publicized problems with the US government made him a less than desirable host. An Aegean cruise might well expedite Jackie's convalescence, but it was no prescription for votes in the next year's presidential election. There ensued a brief and embarrassing minuet. When Onassis, with creditable bigheartedness, agreed it might be better if he were not present on the cruise, it was Jackie who insisted he come, if only as an "act of kindness," and it was her sense of social propriety that prevailed. Franklin D. Roosevelt, Jr., then undersecretary of commerce, was induced against his better judgment to accompany Jackie as "chaperon." A mixed cast of celebrities was assembled, including the Radziwills and Princess Irene Galitzine, the dress designer. The yacht set sail from Piraeus.

The cruise was a success, marred only by periodic breakdowns in the *Christina*'s telecommunications system, which made it difficult for

Jackie to speak to her husband—an inconvenience she overcame with a series of ten-page letters written each night in her stateroom. Onassis was initially discreet to the point of invisibility, declining to accompany his guests ashore when the ship stopped at Lesbos. Jackie sent the indispensable Roosevelt to inquire why he was "hiding away" and let it be known that she would henceforth appreciate his presence as a guide and companion. When the yacht reached Ithaca, Onassis resumed his customary role as host, diverting the ladies with his idiosyncratic interpretations of Greek myth and the story of his turbulent youth.

Onassis's appreciation of Jackie was apparent in the number of gifts he lavished upon her, which exceeded not only his habitual standards of hospitality but also those the other guests received. It was something that Lee later recalled when she wrote to the president about the cruise. Jackie had been laden with presents, she complained, while she herself received only "three dinky little bracelets that Caroline wouldn't wear to her own birthday party." When the president's wife returned to the White House on October 17, a member of the staff said, "Jackie has stars in her eyes—Greek stars." She also had trouble with the press.

The American newspapers had commented freely on the gaiety of the cruise, sustained, as one put it disapprovingly, by "a sixty-man crew, including two coiffeurs and dance bands." A Republican congressman made a speech in the House criticizing the presence of Roosevelt on the *Christina* since he was in a position to influence relations between Onassis and the US maritime authorities.

The adverse public reaction to the cruise became a topic of animated conversation at one of the White House domestic sessions attended by Ben Bradlee. Jackie was contrite about involving Roosevelt in the affair but spoke up warmly for Onassis, whom she described as "an alive and vital person who had come from nowhere." Kennedy was understanding but anxious to avoid any further embarrassment. He revealed that he had informed Onassis, through one of his aides, that he would not be welcome in the United States until after the 1964 election. He also played on what he described as "Jackie's guilt feelings" by using this occasion to invite her to come on his campaign trip to Texas the following month. Jackie, clearly anxious to make amends, had responded, "Sure I will, Jack."

Onassis was in Hamburg launching a tanker when he learned of John Kennedy's assassination in Dallas. He immediately flew to Washington as one of the few nonfamily guests in the White House. His presence did not provoke much in the way of public comment, but he did figure in an intriguing anecdote related by William Manchester in his book *The Death of a President*. On the evening after the funeral, wrote Manchester, "Rose Kennedy dined upstairs with Stash Radziwill; Jacqueline Kennedy, her sister, and Robert Kennedy were served in the sitting room. The rest of the Kennedys ate in the family dining room with their house guests, McNamara, Phyllis Dillon, Dave Powers and Aristotle Socrates Onassis, the shipowner, who provided comic relief of sorts. They badgered him mercilessly about his yacht and his Man of Mystery aura. During coffee the Attorney General Robert Kennedy came down and drew up a formal document stipulating that Onassis give half his wealth to help the poor in Latin America. It was preposterous (and obviously unenforceable), and the Greek millionaire signed it in Greek." Onassis's imposed role as jester to the mourning court of Camelot was not deemed of any particular significance at the time, though it did establish his affability in a difficult social and emotional situation.

For Jackie alone among the Kennedy clan, Onassis shortly became more than a joke in dubious taste. The question of why she took him seriously and ultimately married him can be answered by her inability to evolve a stable relationship with the world as a young widow. Prior to her husband's death, she had enjoyed the privacy she required through the apparatus that effectively insulates the president from the American people. Her conduct in the days after her husband's death was superb. And it is a tribute to her enduring capacity to elicit interest and sympathy that her poise immediately made her into an American folk heroine.

Much of the interest she aroused was innocuous, but some of it was not. For Jackie, the distinction became irrelevant when she discovered that she could no longer control the flow of information about herself. The strategy of qualified reclusiveness she adopted was rational but doomed to failure. Her periodic appearances inflamed her public's wish to know more; her subsequent withdrawal was taken for disdain and provided a justification—to the press, at least—for satisfying the public's presumed desire to know more about her.

To a great extent, those who are famous stay that way because the press keeps them in the public eye. Thus they are usually happy to accommodate information-hungry journalists. In some circumstances, however, this tacitly understood arrangement breaks down because of unusual pressures. Such was the case with Jackie. The public's need to know, as interpreted by the increasing number of Jackieologues, went far beyond a desire to publish the minutiae of her daily life. Previously a model of American womanhood, she became something of a privately

248

financed but collectively sponsored social experiment. What she would do next became a question of consuming interest, and her every action was presumed to carry with it an indication of her ultimate intentions. Ironically, most of the people who wrote about her assumed, probably correctly, that her fans did not really want her to do anything which would alter their preconceived notion of her as the courageous young widow walking behind her husband's coffin.

Never fully at home in Washington, she moved with the two children to a duplex on Fifth Avenue in New York. As far as men in her life were concerned, she adopted the expedient of seeking safety in numbers. Many of them were conveniently and safely married, and they were put on display at the rounds of lunches at the Côte Basque and at the cultural gatherings which it was customary for a woman of her class and interests to attend. Her escorts included composers (Leonard Bernstein, Alan Jay Lerner, Gian-Carlo Menotti), politicians (Averell Harriman, Robert McNamara, Franklin D. Roosevelt, Jr., Richard Goodwin), writers (Arthur Schlesinger, Jr., Truman Capote, John Kenneth Galbraith, George Plimpton, Randolph Churchill, Paul Mathias), foreign aristocrats (the Duke of Alba, Count Dino Pecci-Blunt), a banker (André Meyer), and an actor (Anthony Quinn). Onassis's occasional visits to 1040 Fifth Avenue, although duly noted, aroused no conspicuous interest.

By 1968 the Jackieologues seemed ready for further developments in the action. She had been widowed long enough to have revered her husband's memory, and matchmaking for Jackie became an easy, and readable, option for any gossip columnist with a gap to fill. Among those presumed to be more than simple decorations for her arm were film director Mike Nichols and Jack Kennedy's former deputy secretary of defense, Roswell Gilpatric. Neither was deemed entirely suitable by the severe votaries of the Kennedy legend. There was, however, a presumed front-runner who seemed to have all the right attributes. The influential newspaper *Woman's Wear Daily* expected an imminent announcement of Jackie's engagement to the English aristocrat and diplomat Lord Harlech, who had been Britain's ambassador in Washington during the Kennedy years.

Harlech was forty-nine, widowed, cultured, and the possessor of a large but unassuming estate in Wales. He was also tall, dark, and handsome. He had known Jackie since 1960 and had accompanied her on a trip to Bangkok and Phnom Penh in 1967. What were known as "diplomatic circles" looked favorably on the liaison.

While the newspapers were writing about Harlech as "Jackie's rumored husband-to-be," the Kennedy family was privately bracing itself for the news that Jackie's old friendship with Onassis had ripened into love and that they might be married. Although the Kennedys appreciated the strains imposed on her by the constant press speculation about her emotional life, none of the family welcomed the prospect of such a match. Bobby Kennedy, the member of the family to whom Jackie had grown closest since her husband's death, was particularly upset. His attitude was partly explained by the fact that he was running for president in 1968.

In the spring of 1968 Jackie accompanied Onassis on a brief cruise in the Caribbean. Although the gossip columnists deemed it insignificant, the Kennedys were persuaded that Jackie had already chosen her next husband. As long as Bobby was on the campaign trail, it remained a closely guarded secret. When he was assassinated in Los Angeles in June 1968, the relationship between Jackie and Onassis was still delicately balanced. Onassis initially feared that Jackie's grief at her brother-in-law's death might postpone the idea of marriage. He was relieved to find this was not the case after a visit to the Kennedy home in Hyannis Port, Massachusetts, in Jackie's company. The other Kennedys, however, including the matriarchal Rose, were still nervous about their relationship. As a Catholic, Rose was most concerned about her daughter-in-law's suitor being Greek Orthodox and divorced.

When Teddy Kennedy, the oldest surviving brother and now effectively the head of the family, learned of Jackie's firm intention to marry, he called Onassis on the *Christina* and proposed that they might "get together" to talk things over. Onassis suggested Skorpios as a suitable meeting place. "As I did not expect a dowry," he later explained, "there was nothing to worry about."

An August issue of *Newsweek* contained a picture captioned "Jackie and Teddy en route to Greece," but there was no hint in the brief story that accompanied it of the real nature of their business on Onassis's island. As far as the American public and press were concerned, Onassis was still not a serious contender in the marriage stakes.

One of the high points of the Kennedys' Ionian expedition was a "bouzouki party" aboard the *Christina*. Among those on board was Nicos Mastorakis, an enterprising Greek reporter who insinuated himself into the group as a sort of social director. He recalled the party as follows.

> Jackie is standing at the door. She is resplendent, wearing a flame-red blouse with a check scarf around her neck and a long, checked, gypsy-style

250

skirt. The Greek sun has bronzed her. She is a sweet woman who watches the world with interest and smiles to everybody with the same warmth and without pretense. Onassis introduced her. She squeezes our hands warmly and to each she says something kind. I was the lucky one. She said, "So we'll hear you sing?" I say, "Of course," and I know I am lying. Teddy comes in. He holds a blonde goddess by the shoulders. He is wearing a light pink shirt and matching scarf.

The indications are that the party will be explosive. The musical evening begins with pepper tips, red ripe tomatoes, spinach puree, black caviar and liquor. Teddy drinks ouzo, permanently. Jackie prefers vodka at first . . . the two French bar tenders of the *Christina* move about like robots.

A crooner sings and Jackie is rapt with fascination. From time to time Onassis . . . translates with whispers in her ear the words of the song and she stares with those big eyes. The bouzouki music reaches its peak and Teddy gets up and tries to dance. . . . Teddy returns to his ouzo. Onassis loves one particular song:

> These are bitter summers
> And you have taught me to spend them with you
> And the sky was filled at dawn with dead doves

The laughing face of the Greek Croesus framed by his ashen-gray hair darkens as he hears these words. His eyes cannot betray him easily behind those thick glasses. But the drooping corners of his mouth show that the "bitter summers" remind him of too much. A short time earlier, when we admired him for his simplicity, he had said, "Am I not a son of the people too?" The band-leader replied, "Yes, but a son with cash."

Mastorakis later received a harsh lesson in the perils of covert journalism when Jackie saw him taking a photograph of her flushed brother-in-law. His bag was searched, the film removed from his camera. "If you dare hurt me," Kennedy said, "I'll see you never find another job in Greece." The rest of the band covered for Mastorakis, and Onassis restored a semblance of good humor to the gathering. Later, mellowed by more ouzo and the band's ample repertoire of Onassis's cherished Latin numbers, the party-goers let Mastorakis photograph them. But this mood of tolerance was short-lived. When Mastorakis returned to Athens he was arrested, his film was confiscated, and his story heavily censored.

There was a more serious side to Teddy Kennedy's visit to Skorpios. He discussed the couple's intentions privately with Onassis. Onassis later told his biographer, Willi Frischauer, that Kennedy began by making an oblique attempt to dissuade him from the match. Kennedy warned that the marriage would "not be popular" politically and that Onassis might find it difficult becoming the stepfather of the late president's children.

251

When Kennedy perceived that Onassis was unmoved by these difficulties, he ventured, "We love Jackie." "So do I," said Onassis sharply, "and I want her to have a secure and happy future." Kennedy indicated that if the marriage took place, Jackie would lose the $150,000 annual income she received from the Kennedy trust. The conversation then moved briskly to the specifics of dollars and cents. It was, Onassis perceived, a tacit admission that whether the Kennedy family liked the idea of the marriage or not, they were not going to place any obstacles in its way.

The arrangements made on Skorpios later aroused much speculation. Christian Cafarakis, a former steward on the *Christina*, contended that a document containing 170 detailed clauses was signed by both parties before the marriage. A premarriage contract was signed, but it bore no resemblance to the one described by Cafarakis, with its titillating stipulations of separate bedrooms and provision that Jackie should not be obliged to produce children.

The actual document was a simple formulation of the financial conditions attached to the match by both sides. In Onassis's case, some form of contract was made necessary by the peculiar stipulations of *nomimos mira*, the body of Greek law that required a husband to leave at least 12.5 percent of his wealth to his wife and 37.5 percent to his children. The law was strictly enforced, making it impossible for a Greek to disinherit his family. If a Greek died intestate, the figures were doubled, the wife receiving 25 percent, the children 75 percent. Onassis required Jackie to waive her rights under *nomimos mira*. To make this arrangement watertight he later persuaded the Greek government to pass a law recognizing the validity of this action, provided it was also valid in the spouse's country of origin. If this was a favor to Onassis, it was also, by common consent, overdue reform. Many Greek fortunes had been lost by marriages to citizens of other countries.

In return for this concession, Jackie received $3 million for herself and $1 million apiece for her two children. The agreement also spelled out the settlement eventually incorporated into Onassis's will—after his death, Jackie would receive $150,000 a year for life. It was a businesslike agreement, but it did give some indication of Onassis's attitude toward Jackie. He was prepared to protect her financially, meet her considerable expenses, and make sure that in the case of his death she would be significantly better off than when he had married her. But he was not prepared to make her part of his family at the expense of those he considered his rightful heirs.

252

In mid-August, Doris Lilly, the *New York Post*'s sprightly gossip columnist, went on the popular "Merv Griffin Show" and said that Jackie Kennedy and Aristotle Onassis would marry. She did not know when, but she knew they would. The bases for her deduction were not impressive—her own highly developed intuition, an anonymous source, and random scraps of information. Her antennae had picked up the first signals in the spring, when she learned that Onassis and Jackie had dined with Margot Fonteyn, Rudolph Nureyev, and Onassis's daughter, Christina, at Mykonos, a Greek restaurant in New York. Jackie had lost an earring, and Lilly had recorded the search for it in her gossip column. The Merv Griffin audience was not impressed by Lilly's facts or her deductions. She was vigorously booed. When she left the television studio the crowd which had gathered outside subjected her to further abuse and demanded to know where she had gotten her "lousy information."

In September, Onassis buttonholed Lilly's colleague, Earl Wilson, in El Morocco and "put the record straight." As a result of this encounter, Wilson wrote comfortingly, "We think we can tell you with comparative assurance that Aristotle Onassis is not likely to be marrying Jackie Kennedy or anybody else. . . . 'Ari' had a drink or two with Maria [Callas] just before she flew back to Paris yesterday. . . . The night before he had dinner with Jackie. . . . He feels he's 'not worthy of either of them.' His friends are a little offended that columnists keep harping on his friendship with Jackie, trying to make a romance out of it; their family friendship goes back several years. Onassis furthermore says to his friends that he doesn't expect to marry again for the simple enough reason: He's already been married."

The reasons for preserving secrecy were threefold. On Onassis's part there was the need to let Maria Callas down gently. On Jackie's there was the need to explore the implications of the marriage with the Vatican. This was being done through Cardinal Cushing of Boston, an old family friend who had officiated at her wedding to Jack Kennedy. On both their parts there was the need to round off the details of the premarriage contract. But by now the "secret" was known by too many people for effective security.

Reporters on the *Boston Herald-Traveler* were following up a tip that Jackie was interested in marrying "some guy from Argentina"—information which had been gleaned from a sharp-eared waiter in a fashionable Washington restaurant. They spent several frustrating weeks exploring the credentials of eligible Argentinians before they ran a check on

Onassis. The reference library quickly revealed that the famous Greek was still legally a citizen of the Argentine. Further checks with intimates of the Kennedy family provided the newspaper with its scoop of the year.

On October 15, 1968, the *Herald-Traveler*'s front-page story upgraded the Jackie-Onassis rumors to hard news. The newspaper confidently expected a marriage announcement in the near future. There was still nothing official from the Kennedy family, but the paper had questioned Cardinal Cushing about the rumors, and he could not tell a lie. It was too strong a "leak" to stanch with a little urbane misinformation at El Morocco. Besides, Onassis was in Athens for most of October, engaged in delicate business discussions with the Greek military dictator, George Papadopoulos. Jackie called Onassis with the news that the secret could not be contained much longer. She thought they should marry quickly.

Professor Georgakis, the only person in Athens fully acquainted with Onassis's plans, received an early morning summons to the Glyfada villa. Onassis was sitting in his pajamas by the telephone. He told Georgakis that Jackie insisted the marriage take place with the utmost speed. Georgakis noted that Onassis seemed to agree. They discussed possible places for the ceremony. Onassis's first choice was the American embassy, and, although Georgakis warned him that Greek marriages had to be performed in churches to be legal, he was nonetheless induced to try to "fix things up" at the embassy. "Supposing," Georgakis asked a US official, "a distinguished Greek should wish to marry a distinguished American widow. Could they for reasons of speed and modesty do it here?" The official only repeated what Georgakis already knew to be the case. When he was informed, in confidence, who the happy couple were, he "hit the roof."

It was decided that the chapel on Skorpios was the most suitable place since Jackie was insisting on the sort of privacy that only the island could provide. Onassis was reconciled to a Greek Orthodox service, but he demanded that Georgakis find some way of minimizing the impression of barbarous exoticism it might have on the Kennedy children. Georgakis was urged to find a priest "who could speak some English, you know, and not have too long a beard." This, too, presented difficulties, because the hirsute and unilingual bishop of Lefkas, whose diocese included Skorpios, had already cast himself in the role. After several rounds of ecclesiastical negotiations, Georgakis secured the services of one of the Athens University chaplains.

The news of the marriage was a shock to Onassis's immediate family.

Artemis alone reacted with unequivocal enthusiasm. By nature a match-maker, she considered Jackie the "number one," a bride worthy of her beloved brother. She later took it upon herself to insure that the heavens smiled upon the union by placing charms under the mattress of the nuptial bed. Onassis's children—Christina, then eighteen, and Alexander, twenty—were appalled. Both had nourished the hope that their father might one day remarry their mother, whose marriage to the Marquess of Blandford did not seem destined to last. Onassis had occasionally mentioned this possibility to his son, but it seems to have been a device to reassure the boy rather than a real intention. On the day he broke the news of his firm decision to marry Jackie Kennedy, Alexander rushed out of the house with Christina and spent the rest of the day driving aimlessly and at great speed around Athens in his Alfa Romeo. It was only with the greatest difficulty that he was persuaded to attend the wedding.

The marriage was officially announced in New York at 3:30 P.M. on Thursday, October 17, by the curious expedient of a message from Mrs. Auchincloss relayed to the press by Nancy Tuckerman, Jackie's social secretary. Miss Tuckerman said, "Mrs. Hugh D. Auchincloss has asked me to tell you that her daughter, Mrs. John F. Kennedy, is planning to marry Mr. Aristotle Onassis sometime next week. No place or date has been set for the moment." There were notably anodyne expressions of goodwill from the Kennedy family. At six o'clock in the evening, Jackie, smiling and clutching her children—Caroline, age ten, and John-John, seven—made her way through the crowd outside 1040 Fifth Avenue into a waiting limousine. At John F. Kennedy Airport she was joined by a number of relatives, including two of her sisters-in-law and one of her nieces. Ninety passengers were bounced off the scheduled Olympic Airways flight to Athens to make way for the bride-to-be and her entourage.

The reaction of the American public to news of the match was decidedly unenthusiastic. The objections to Onassis could be easily summarized: he was too old, too foreign, too small, too dark, and too rich. An anonymous Bronx wit remarked that Jackie's choice of husbands reflected the change "from a Greek God to a goddam Greek." It was observed that Onassis was shorter than his fiancée—5 feet 5 inches to her 5 feet 7—but taller "when he stands on his money." A Kennedy aide was quoted as saying, "She's gone from Prince Charming to Caliban." Comedian Bob Hope joked, "Richard Nixon has a Greek running mate —now everybody wants one." A psychiatrist, interviewed by the *Chi-*

cago Daily News, suggested that the former first lady was marrying "a grandfather figure."

The New York Times sent an enterprising reporter, Judy Klemesrud, out on the streets to sample the "vox pop" in Jackie's neighborhood. She came back with the following report.

Very few of those questioned in Times Square, Rockefeller Center, Central Park, and on Fifth Avenue seemed to think that Mrs. Kennedy's engagement was her own business.

Miss Ann Farber, 70 years old, of the Bronx, a retired bookkeeper who was watching the skaters in Rockefeller Center, said: "I'm terribly disappointed. She could have done better. To us she was royalty, a princess, and I think she should have married a prince. Or, at least, someone who looked like a prince."

Peter Moraites, 45, manager of the Pantheon, a Greek restaurant at 689 Eighth Avenue, was one of the few who seemed overjoyed at the news. "As far as I'm concerned, this is the greatest thing that ever happened," he said. "Everyone in the Greek community is enthused. Onassis ate here in 1952, and I think he's a great man. As far as religion is concerned, this is a step in combining Catholicism with the Greek Orthodox religion."

Rubin Gralla, 55, of Brooklyn, who has been a cab driver for 33 years, said: "There's an image about Jackie. I think of her as a lady, a lady. You know what I mean, somebody who's above the other people. Now that she's marrying this fellow, I think: she's going to lose some of the shine. She's no longer on her pedestal. You wouldn't have had this uproar if she had married Lord Harlech. But I think this Aristotle is going to be a good husband. He has the maturity. He'll count to 100 before he loses his temper."

"Everyone in my office is shocked," Miss Gloria Saunders, a 38-year-old secretary from Brooklyn, said as she came out of Saks Fifth Avenue. "That's all we talked about today. She should have married an American businessman or someone connected with the arts. She certainly doesn't need the money."

Captain Charles Brown, 32, of New Orleans, an Air Force pilot who was vacationing in New York, said he had another man in mind for Mrs. Kennedy. "I was pulling for the Prime Minister of Canada [Pierre Elliott Trudeau]," he said. "He's single, and it would have given her the chance to be a First Lady again."

Several long-haired teenagers sitting around the Bethesda Fountain in Central Park indicated favor of the marriage.

"It's Jackie's life, and she should do what she wants to with it," said Lorelle Heacock, 16, of Manhattan.

256

Another, Amel Rush, 17, of Dobbs Ferry, N.Y., didn't say much. He just played The Wedding March on his harmonica.

Europe was less charitable than the kids in the park. "Jackie, How Could You?" asked a headline in Sweden's *Stockholm Expressen*. In Paris, *Le Monde* commented severely, "Jackie, whose staunch courage during John's funeral made such an impression, now chooses to shock by marrying a man who could be her father (Onassis is 23 years her senior) and whose career contradicts—rather strongly, to say the least— the liberal spirit that animated President Kennedy." In Italy, the magazine *L'Espresso* took a dim view, commenting on "this grizzled satrap, with his liver-colored skin, thick hair, fleshy nose, the wide horsy grin, who buys an island and then has it removed from all the maps to prevent the landing of castaways; and, on the other hand, an ethereal-looking beauty of 39, renowned for her sophistication and her interest in the fine arts, and a former First Lady at that." *Il Messagero* headlined the news: "John Kennedy Dies Today for the Second Time." *La Stampa* asked piteously, "Jackie, Why?" In Germany, the headline in the mass-circulation *Bilt-Zeitung* was "America Has Lost a Saint." Naturally, the thoughts of Maria Callas were solicited, and she was quoted as saying, "She did well, Jackie, to give a grandfather to her children. Ari is as beautiful as Croesus." Later she observed, "First I lost my weight, then I lost my voice, and now I've lost Onassis."

The Catholic church also was not disposed to forgiveness, although Cardinal Cushing spoke up bravely for Jackie's right to happiness with the man of her choice. The official view was later expressed in the columns of the Vatican's *L'Osservatore della Domenica*. "Mrs. Kennedy" knew the laws of the church, the form of marriage with Onassis made her "a public sinner," and she was therefore barred from receiving the sacraments.

Onassis had few public friends, but those that seemed well disposed to the marriage made an intriguing mix. Elizabeth Taylor was one of them. She and her fifth husband, Richard Burton, had enjoyed Onassis's hospitality on several occasions, and she had found him charming, kind, and considerate. She thought that Jackie had made an excellent choice. Another warm endorsement came from Roswell Gilpatric, who had once been on the short list of Jackie's most favored suitors. "She once told me," Mr. Gilpatric said, "that she felt she could count on [Onassis]. It was an attribute she looked for in all her friends. One of the things she is looking for for herself and her children is a private life—not being in

257

the public eye all the time—and he can afford to give her that privacy and protection." Gore Vidal was not kind but eminently concise. "I can only give you two words," he told a reporter when asked to comment on the match. "Highly suitable."

On the face of it, Vidal's evaluation sounded like simply a bitchy remark. The only obvious thing that Onassis and Jackie had in common was their heavy smoking. Yet they had important complementary qualities. At the simplest and most obvious level, this could be reduced to the fact that Jackie was one of the world's most expensive women and Onassis had one of the world's largest personal fortunes. In 1968 his worth in money and assets was reckoned to be $500 million. That does not imply that Jackie desired Onassis for his money, rather that marriage to someone who was not exceptionally, perhaps excessively, rich was not a feasible option.

At another level, the disparity in their ages appears to have been an advantage rather than a hindrance. It had not been a serious obstacle as far as the marriage of Jackie's sister to Prince Radziwill was concerned —Stash was twenty years her senior. It is entirely reasonable to adduce the two sisters' relationship with their father as an explanation for their predilection for older men. Onassis was everything that Black Jack had wanted to be but never quite became. Of all Jackie's suitors, he best evinced her father's quality of elusive attraction and combined it with something of key importance that her father never could provide—the promise of security. The irrepressible Doris Lilly made a similar observation when she wrote, with refreshing disregard for psychological jargon, "Jackie . . . always seemed to have been attracted to older men, possibly because you don't have to shoot them in the legs to keep them home at night."

On yet another level, their ideas were in harmony. Jackie, through no fault of her own, had been imprisoned in the political mythology of the Kennedys which, in American terms at least, was to the left of center. Yet she had never been much interested in the minutiae of politics even during her years in the White House. She was, like Onassis, essentially apolitical. She valued her position as first lady for the degree of privilege it conferred. She could be both prominent and secure from unwanted intrusions. Onassis's bizarre and archaic kingdom—with its island stronghold, its fiefs on the sea and in the air, and its luxuriously appointed ambassadorial outposts in Paris, New York, and Athens— seemed capable of offering comparable prerogatives. If the transition from Camelot to Skorpios required a leap of the imagination, the route

258

linking the two kingdoms was nonetheless plain for anyone who cared to look.

It took the wedding itself to demonstrate that the protection Onassis could provide was by no means foolproof. Onassis was in a downtown bar when the official announcement of his marriage reached Athens. He got a good night's sleep at Glyfada, and he was rested and cheerful for his first confrontation with the press as Jackie's fiancé when he arrived at Athens airport with his sister and a secretary. "I am going to marry her tomorrow or within three days at the most," he said expansively. "I can't say exactly because I must see and talk to her." He said the honeymoon would be spent on Skorpios "unless Jackie wants to make a tour of the Mediterranean on the *Christina.*" He brought the conference to a close with: "I have so many family problems to settle on my head. Please leave me alone and give me your blessing."

He had already taken steps to insure that privacy would be maintained. Even the pilot of Jackie's plane had been kept in the dark as to his final destination until the last moment. The newsmen who smelled out the remote airport of Andravida, 192 miles west of Athens, where Onassis's own DC-6B met his bride's incoming 707, were locked up in an airport waiting room. Those intrepid ones who did get telephoto shots of the scene on the tarmac had their film confiscated by the police. They did not miss much. "Welcome, darling," said Onassis to Jackie with a chaste kiss. "Did you have a good trip?" She smiled: "I had a wonderful trip and it's a wonderful day." The party walked across the runway to the smaller plane which flew north to the air base at Aktion, whence they were shuttled by helicopter to Skorpios.

Meantime, some two hundred fifty journalists, all eager to cover "the wedding of the century," homed in on the tiny fishing village of Nidri on the island of Lefkas, less than two miles from Skorpios. They hired a fleet of caiques and besieged Onassis's island. On the afternoon of October 19, the eve of the wedding, Jackie agreed to a brief press conference. She made a valiant attempt to touch the newsmen's hearts, saying, "We wish our wedding to be a private moment in the little chapel among the cypresses of Skorpios, with only members of the family and their little children. Understand that even though people may be well known, they still hold in their hearts the emotion of a simple person for the moments that are the most important we know on earth—birth, marriage, and death."

Regrettably, perhaps, none of her listeners was being paid to respect the privacy of this particular marriage. That evening, thirty-six photographers approached the island disregarding all signals and warnings from the *Christina*. They hit the beach amid the whirr of movie cameras and the rapid-fire clicks of Nikons and Leicas. The crew of the *Christina* launched a counterattack which would certainly have developed into a bloody fray if Jackie had not summarily ordered a retreat. This episode induced the Greek government to reinforce the island guard and ban all non-Onassis shipping beyond an arbitrary 1,000 meters from the island's shores. In practice, this was impossible to enforce.

An agreement was reached with the press which allowed four newsmen to attend the ceremony. This took place at 5:15 P.M. on October 20. One of the journalists allowed in was Mario Modiano, Athens correspondent of *The Times* of London. He gave us this account of the wedding, performed by Archimandrite Polykarpos Athanassiou resplendent in gold brocade and assisted by three cantors:

> The tiny chapel of Panayitsa ("Little Virgin") set among bougainvillea and jasmin was packed with relatives from both sides. Jackie looked drawn and concerned. She wore a long-sleeved, two-piece ivory chiffon lace dress with pleated skirt. Her hair was secured with an ivory ribbon. The groom looked slightly off-key in a blue suit, white shirt and white tie—the sort of thing Onassis loved to wear. Caroline flanked the couple holding ceremonial candles, dazzled and serious. Jackie's glance kept turning anxiously towards Caroline. The Onassis children seemed grim.
>
> Artemis, Onassis' sister, was sponsor (koumbara). She placed on the heads of the couple delicate leather wreaths shaped as branches with lemon buds and connected with a white ribbon. As the priest chanted, she changed them crosswise three times. Then the rings were placed on their fingers and exchanged three times. A silver-bound goblet was handed to each to kiss and they both drank from a goblet of red wine. Jackie stood watching the priest intently, who at one point translated the service in English for her benefit: "The servant of God, Jacqueline and I, in the name of the Father, the Son and the Holy Spirit," he chanted. When the priest started Esiah's dance, Jackie grabbed the priest's hand, then Ari's hand and they sauntered around the altar to mark the end of the ceremony. There was no holding of hands, no kiss when it was over. Jackie seemed oblivious of her second husband but terribly aware of Caroline. Later, on the *Christina*, the closest she came to showing affection was to take his arm. Their hands never touched. One observer said; "It was like a business transaction."
>
> A sullen secret serviceman with a PT-109 tie clip looked very grim as the Lady from Camelot emerged in the steady autumn drizzle, not with her rich Greek husband, but clinging to John Kennedy's daughter.

Showered with flower petals, they headed in the wrong way and had to be brought back to the open-sided mini jeep. She got into the front seat and put Caroline on her lap and held her tightly. Her sister Lee and her own daughter sat in the back with a sullen John who never smiled, and never lifted his head. Onassis took the wheel and drove away towards the *Christina* in the harbour one mile away.

The quiet wedding was often marred by shouts and screams from scores of journalists aboard hired fishing boats who were not allowed to land. A few of them jumped into the sea and were finally allowed to join—in soaking clothes—the group of tolerated "pool" journalists and cameramen flown in by Olympic, who came to be known as the "champagne pool." Otherwise the press was kept out of the church (an earlier attempt to confine them to another part of Skorpios while the wedding was taking place, having been defeated by Alexander who shepherded the pool to the chapel in his jeep). Jackie who seemed terrified of the photographers insisted that there should be no pictures inside the church. Later, aboard the *Christina* they agreed to pose for photographers while the journalistic fishing-boats came alongside and there were screams of "O-na-sis, O-na-sis" until the shipowner and his bride agreed to pose for them too.

The pool journalists were invited for pink champagne in the yacht. The couple responded to good wishes with a laconic "Thank you." They did not know what their honeymoon plans were. Jackie had a blank look and a fixed smile on her face. The only time she reacted was when AP photographer Jim Pringle introduced himself. She looked startled and said: "Are you Irish?" and giggled. Then getting impatient with the press, they returned to the drawing room where relatives and friends had gathered. As the reporters glued cameras and noses on the windows, the curtains were drawn abruptly.

Among the many messages of good wishes Onassis received on that day, was a cable from a New York nightclub offering to despatch its troupe of belly-dancers to Skorpios, free of charges, for the entertainment of the guests.

18
THE DICTATOR'S
HONEYMOON

DAWN BROKE OVER SKORPIOS the next morning bustled by gale-force winds and driving rain. From their boats the press corps scanned the swirling seascape with binoculars in the hope of descrying symptoms of a conventional honeymoon getting under way. There were none. Nor, it seemed, did the celebrated couple have any intention of putting the newsmen out of their misery by revealing their next move.

There were the inevitable alarums and excursions and wild reports. Excitement was generated by the news that an unscheduled Olympic Airways Comet jet was trying to land at Aktion. Calm returned when the jet was beaten back by the storm and when it was learned that the plane had come only to airlift the bride's guests to Paris. These, including the Kennedy children, were later evacuated via Athens airport. The honeymooners then announced that they had planned to fly to New York but that the weather had prevented their leaving. There were reports that they were, variously, to go on safari in Mozambique, cruise on the *Christina*, and be made president and first lady of Greece. What Onassis actually did as soon as the weather lifted was leave Jackie swimming and sunbathing in Skorpios while he went to Athens to do business with the Greek military dictator, George Papadopoulos.

On the afternoon of October 24, 1968, the two men were to be found in the back seat of the dictator's limousine as it purred through the streets of the capital, flanked by a massive police escort. There they initialed a ten-point agreement in principle whereby Onassis would undertake a ten-year, $400 million investment project—the biggest in Greek history. It was to become known as Project Omega. "On that day," says one of the men most intimately connected with Omega, "Onassis was the sun king. He had everything."

On November 1, Onassis interrupted his honeymoon once more to return to Athens to unveil Omega at a press conference. It would, he announced, include the construction of an oil refinery with an annual capacity of seven million tons of crude by 1972, an alumina refinery and an aluminum smelter with a power station to fuel them both, plus "parallel investments" still the subject of negotiation but probably involving shipyards, an air terminal, and sundry tourist projects. The solemnity of the occasion was to some degree undermined by reporters hungry for more personal revelations. Most of their news editors were more interested in boudoir secrets than in oil refineries. The conference ended abruptly when a journalist inquired, "When do you and Jackie plan to fly to New York?" "What has this got to do with what we are talking about?" snapped Onassis, who then stormed out followed by a scrambling train of photographers.

He rejoined Jackie, who had flown to Athens to cast an absentee ballot for the US election in the presence of an official from the American embassy. "With her airline connections, there is no doubt but that it will get there in time," cracked an "embassy spokesman." The spectacle of Onassis's new wife voting while he was cozying up to a regime that had dispensed with the electoral process and other basic civil liberties was not very edifying. Only the most unreconstructed cold warriors could entertain the idea that Papadopoulos might be in any sense a friend of freedom by acting as a buffer against the encroachment of communism in the Mediterranean. And even for them, his effectiveness seemed suspect. His regime had conspicuously failed to exhibit some of the supposed saving graces of dictatorship. The trains still did not run on time and, unlike Franco in Spain, Papadopoulos had not succeeded in convincing foreign investors that he could be relied upon to run a tight and efficient ship of state. The attraction of Onassis was thus twofold: he was a potential investor and, particularly after his marriage to Jackie, also a valuable public relations coup. The disenfranchised Greek democrats were not amused. Helen Vlachos, the newspaper publisher, later wrote in her book, *House Arrest:*

263

With the coming of the Colonels the worst traits of both the top star shipowners, and of all the discreetly following tribe, came out into the open. Their grabbing instincts were sharpened by the Great Junta Sale. Greece was being offered at cut prices, genuine bargains to be secured in exchange for a friendly pat on uniformed backs, the Greek flag devalued below the lowest-priced Panamanian or Liberian, taxes waived, laws forgotten. . . . In a world of vacillating values and acute ambitions, past friendships, however high-level, were forgotten or put aside "for the duration." Allegiances to ideals, democracies, freedoms and rights were dismissed as naive and unrealistic. Greece was now what is called a "fence-less vineyard," and they all flocked to pick the fruits.

It was a harsh indictment though not unfair. Onassis did end up glamorizing one of the most unlovely regimes in Europe. Yet it had all begun with good, even honorable, intentions.

The genesis of Omega went back to the prejunta days. With the acquisition of Skorpios in 1963, Onassis began to groom himself for the role of the returning hero. Soon he was manifesting symptoms of an urge common to many Greeks who have made their fortunes elsewhere—the desire to "do something" for Mother Greece. Among those whose brains he decided to pick was George Pappas, a consulting mining engineer whom Costa Gratsos had introduced to him in an Athens nightclub. One day in 1965, over lunch in the Glyfada villa, Onassis asked Pappas what was now the routine question: did he by any chance know of any worthwhile investment projects a man could undertake in Greece?

Pappas did. The demand for refined petroleum products in Greece now outstripped the country's refining capacity. As a result Greece was importing not only crude oil but also an increasing amount of refined products from the Soviet Union. To pay for the crude and refined products, Greece was shipping half a million tons of bauxite a year to Russia. Bauxite, the ore from which aluminum is made, is one of the few raw materials which Greece possesses in anything approaching abundance. In those days it was worth $5 a ton, which meant that Greece was sending Russia $2.5 million worth of bauxite a year. But if that bauxite could be converted into aluminum before being exported, it would be worth twenty times as much, or $50 million. What stood in the way of aluminum production was the cost of the vast amounts of electric power which were needed. So, Pappas explained, the trick was to build not just an alumina refinery (which converts bauxite into alumina) and an aluminum smelter (which turns the alumina into alumi-

264

num) but a power station and an oil refinery as well. Now, if Greece were to export aluminum instead of bauxite and were to take payment in crude oil only, it would make for an awful lot of crude. Enter the refinery, which would refine the crude and thus remedy Greece's shortfall in refining capacity. Furthermore, the petroleum products could be sold on the Greek domestic market. The by-products of the refining process could be used to fuel the power station, thus producing enough cheap electricity to operate the aluminum smelter and completing the magic, and potentially very profitable, circle.

Onassis was so instantly captivated by what he later described as "the internal logic" of Pappas's idea that within fifteen minutes he was on the phone to his office with the instruction to "get me an appointment at the Russian embassy." At eight o'clock that evening Onassis excitedly outlined the scheme to the Russian commercial counselor, Aram Pironzian, pressing him for an early response from Moscow. Shortly after he had returned home, well satisfied with the day's events, Onassis received a phone call. It was from a senior officer in the KYP, the Greek secret police. Could Mr. Onassis clarify a report which had been received from Greek and American agents that he had been seen at the Russian embassy that evening? Onassis, scarcely able to suppress his amusement, was able to assure him that he had no desire to defect.

Within ten days a team of Russian officials was dispatched to Athens to negotiate with Onassis. They did not seem disposed to drive a hard bargain and agreed to the proposal in toto except for the proviso that, instead of taking everything as aluminum, it would be half in alumina and half in aluminum. Onassis was invited to visit Leningrad in the *Christina* and was inclined to accept. The package was then put to the Greek government, which joined in the enthusiasm.

Then the government fell and was replaced by the first of a series of caretaker governments, which were eventually to be toppled by the colonels. With bigger worries than Omega on their minds and nervous about the political repercussions of dealing with the Soviet Union, the caretaker cabinet quietly shelved the plan. But Omega retained its magnetism for Onassis.

Onassis did not respond with any great enthusiasm to the military coup d'etat which ousted the democratic government of Greece in April 1967. His own political beliefs were hazy, though he was inclined to think of himself as a liberal at heart. He was naturally an anticommunist, but that, as has been seen, did not preclude his doing business with the Russians. The traditional dividing line in Greek politics had been between the Venizelists and the royalists, although neither group had a political party named after itself. The distinction went back to World War I, when Venizelos had set up a government in Thessalonika while the king ruled from Athens. Venizelos and his army had been pro-Allies and also fiercely committed to wresting Smyrna from Turkey. Since those days, the distinction between the two rival camps of Greek politics —which is as much social as political—has become blurred to foreign eyes and anachronistic in the view of many young Greeks. Still, the Venizelists are generally considered republican and progressive, the royalists traditional and reactionary. By this criterion Onassis was, and frequently proclaimed himself to be, a Venizelist. His rival, Niarchos, was a royalist.

Above all, Onassis considered himself a realist. He was most attracted to the dictum that the government was best which governed least, particularly when it came to irksome restrictions and taxes. All things being equal, he preferred to operate in places where the basic freedoms were respected but were not essential. For Onassis, democracy was a convenience, never a passion. In the uncertain months after the military coup, the realistic thing for any businessman to do was to wait and see which way the political wind was blowing. This was precisely what Onassis did.

The key to everyone's uncertainty was King Constantine. He had the power to confer some semblance of legitimacy on the coup, but he held himself aloof, neither condemning nor condoning it. For this reason, both the junta and its enemies wooed him assiduously. As an interim measure, a civilian prime minister, Constantine Kollias, was installed, with Papadopoulos as "minister to the prime minister." Onassis was in no hurry to acquaint the new regime with the "internal logic" of his pet project, but as the owner of Olympic Airways he was obliged to have some dealings with the government of the day.

Onassis's first serious contact came in the summer of 1967, when he learned of the existence of the damaging report on Olympic Airways prepared by Air Marshal George Doukas. Onassis promptly demanded an interview with Kollias to clear his name. It was not, according to sources inside Olympic, an amicable encounter. When Onassis stormed into the prime minister's office to demand an explanation, he found Kollias intent on playing an unsubtle game. He refused to discuss the Doukas report, saying merely, "Ah, yes, we have this dossier, but first there are other matters to discuss." Kollias then embarked on what Onassis regarded as a crude attempt to blackmail him into undertaking certain projects in which the advantages for the government were far greater than for himself. As Onassis was approaching the boiling point, Papadopoulos entered the room. When told the circumstances of the argument, he appeared to take Onassis's side. "Mr. Onassis is quite right, Prime Minister. This is most unfair," said Papadopoulos. "If there are accusations against him, they must be looked into and he must be given the opportunity to present his side of the case."

Onassis told his executives at Olympic that he was thrilled by the blunt honesty of Papadopoulos's intervention. He did not find out until years later that Papadopoulos had also been anxious to use the Doukas report as a lever. At the time, Onassis thought he had found a good friend in the new government. Still, he kept his distance from the somber ideals of what the colonels had come to describe as "the revolution." In private he would sometimes refer to the new leaders as "a bunch of crooks." It was not until the emergence of Papadopoulos as overt prime minister after King Constantine's unsuccessful countercoup of December 1967 that Onassis, in his own words, "went amongst the wolves."

When Papadopoulos assumed power, his old job as minister to the prime minister was taken over by Michael Sideratos, a right-wing lawyer and an old acquaintance of Onassis. There is no doubt that Papadopoulos and his accomplices then had a genuine, if not particularly firm, intention of broadening the political base of the government by luring back prominent and, they hoped, complaisant democrats who had fled abroad at the time of the April coup. Onassis had shown his goodwill by offering the government, through Sideratos, a couple of hundred free Olympic Airways tickets for prospective candidates to fly home to discuss the matter with the junta. Sideratos returned the gesture by promising to fix a formal meeting between Onassis and Papadopoulos.

When the big day came there was considerable trepidation in the Onassis camp. Nobody could be entirely sure that Papadopoulos was not a puppet, manipulated by faceless men whom it would be more circumspect to woo. Onassis's executives at Olympic, nervous about the threat posed by the Doukas report, advised extreme caution. When Onassis arrived at Papadopoulos's office, the dictator was closeted with Hadjipateras, then the head of the KYP, and Roufougalis, the man who was shortly to replace him. The three men were discussing the budgeting and reorganization of the secret police, with a mind to insuring a better surveillance of the regime's numerous opponents. As the meeting ended, Onassis was ushered in. He was nervous and uncertain about the importance of the two strangers with whom he was suddenly faced. Were these perhaps the puppet masters? But nothing rallied Onassis quite like an argument, and he was promptly granted one when the two KYP men ganged up on him, asking what he was doing employing a man like Professor Yanni Georgakis as his right-hand man at Olympic. "What do you mean?" retorted Onassis, suddenly in command of himself. "If you mean that he is a liberal, then I come from the same political school. If you have anything concrete against him, then tell me and I shall listen." The two men had nothing concrete. "In that case," said Onassis, "it is my privilege to choose whom I work with." As the KYP men left, they caught the beginning of Onassis's opening gambit with Papadopoulos. "Mr. Prime Minister," he was saying, "I am a businessman and a shipowner, but in my heart I remain an ordinary Greek. If my country needs me, I am ready to help."

It was Omega, cleaned up to remove the Russian involvement, that Onassis offered. Papadopoulos had the intelligence to appreciate that his only hope of retaining power over the long term was a healthy economy. He was desperate for investment and eagerly accepted Omega. At that moment he would probably have sold the Acropolis, if necessary. For the sake of appearances, it was decided to extend an invitation for tenders to build a third refinery. Greece already had two—the Esso-Pappas refinery in Thessalonica and the state-owned Aspropyrgos refinery, currently being operated by Niarchos. The beauty of this ploy was that any other bidders, in their innocence, would simply offer to build and operate another refinery. When it came to opening the bidding, however, the the government would be able to announce that Mr. Onassis—that well-known benefactor of Greece—had offered a comprehensive investment program of which the refinery was but part and which was altogether far more advantageous to Greece than the rival proposals. Tenders were invited for February 1968.

In the ensuing months the relationship between Onassis and Papadopoulos deepened to an extraordinary extent. One of Papadopoulos's closest associates during the Omega period believes that the austere colonel was, despite himself, seduced by the pure glamour of Onassis in his self-created role as the modern Ulysses. The dictator reacted to him much as a fan would toward a pop singer or a football star. "Remember," the associate has said of Papadopoulos, "he had been the poorly paid, unattractive soldier—brighter and more ambitious than most but still living in the barracks and following from afar the exploits of the founder member of the jet set, who had once been a poor Greek like him."

Onassis's fund of fascinating and slightly risqué stories about the Beautiful People were infinitely beguiling to the petit bourgeois dictator.

The fascination of Papadopoulos for Onassis was more difficult to comprehend. The explanation favored by those who most frequently saw them together was that Onassis was seduced by the vision of power. "For Onassis," said one of Papadopoulos's ministers of the Omega period, "Papadopoulos was the incarnation of power. Anatolian Greeks, who have lived under Turkish despotism, are more susceptible to naked power and its nuances than mainland Greeks and have a greater respect for the holders of power. Power in the hands of one man—there is something metaphysical about it. It is as if you were to be offered an evening's discourse with God. Even an atheist would accept. For someone like Onassis, Papadopoulos was a repository of power on earth." The former minister also believes that the two men recognized each other as "in a way coming from the same cell." For, just as Onassis had no board of directors or shareholders to impair his freedom of action, so Papadopoulos, unlike any other major politician Onassis had met, had dispensed with the irritants of a parliament and an electorate. Professor Georgakis's cryptic analysis was: "It was Onassis's first encounter with political power at its source, or what he thought was its source. He got excessively close." There were flattering intimations that he might share in that power. Onassis told friends that Papadopoulos had asked him to join the government but that he had refused. He was nonetheless flattered to have been asked.

On the economic front, however, Onassis's rapport with Papadopoulos seemed complete. When Omega was publicly unveiled in November 1968, the joke among Onassis's staff in Athens was that their boss was the only man who could enjoy two honeymoons at the same time—one with Jackie, the other with Papadopoulos. In neither case did the honeymoon lead to a full and satisfying marriage. The relationship with Papadopoulos was the first to show signs of stress.

The Omega team, only half a dozen men at the time that the project was announced, occupied half a floor in the Olympic Airways office in Syntagma Square in the heart of downtown Athens. Onassis used this office space as his own Athens business headquarters, uprooting the buying and accounts department of Olympic in order to accommodate his latest project. On the day he had interrupted his honeymoon to fly to Athens to sign the agreement with Papadopoulos, he had whirled through the Omega offices radiating his usual smiles and cheerfulness.

269

A few days later, just before the *Christina* was to sail on her official honeymoon cruise, the Omega team had flown up to Aktion for a brief conference with their leader, who had come across from Skorpios by speedboat. He had seemed a changed man. He had become more authoritarian and was flushed not so much with happiness as with triumph at having married the widow of President Kennedy.

All the Omega team had noticed the change, and all were, in varying degrees, worried. On the plane back to Athens they bandied ribald explanations, speculating upon the strains for a sixty-two-year-old man of marrying a beautiful and relatively young woman. Perhaps, they conjectured, he had taken drugs to improve his performance and their side effects had altered his behavior, making him more peremptory.

Something else was troubling them, too. Onassis, they had learned, had extracted a concession from Papadopoulos which had little or nothing to do with Omega and which could only delay the project since Onassis was adamant that it should be the team's number-one priority. The Niarchos concession to operate the Aspropyrgos refinery had ended, though he continued to run it on an interim basis for 9 percent of the profits. Onassis had persuaded Papadopoulos to turn the refinery over to him for operation until his own refinery was built. It would enable Onassis to establish himself in the Greek petroleum market without delay and, as he freely confessed to the Omega team, it would upset Niarchos. Both were high-priority objectives, and Onassis had offered to waive all profits on the operation of the refinery in order to achieve them. Onassis was due to take over Aspropyrgos on January 1, 1969. For the next two months Omega was forgotten while the team worked on the minutiae of the takeover. There was what seemed like an unnatural lack of reaction from the Niarchos camp. Niarchos, it turned out, was choosing his response with elaborate care.

The Omega agreement between Onassis and Papadopoulos was studiedly vague, being essentially a declaration of intent containing virtually no specifics on the where, when, and how of the project. The job of adding flesh to the bones of the agreement was given to the Ministry of Economic Coordination, headed by Nicholas Makarezos, one of the original troika that had led the military coup. During the early months of 1969, Makarezos officials met with the Omega team, frequently led by Onassis, on a regular basis. Nerves on both sides rapidly frayed. One of the government negotiators recalls Onassis's style.

> It was quite impossible to pin him down to specifics. He had a mentality which was a combination of a Greek merchant and an Oriental bazaar

seller. When he came into the office all the perfumes of the Orient would waft in behind him. For him, bargaining was a bazaar. One day he would accept three or four government points, then he would be rigid on the remaining six or seven, but we would ultimately agree, going some of the way to meet him. But the next day he would be back, wanting to haggle over the first four points again, but refusing to budge an inch on the others.

He would not delegate. There were men on his side, Georgakis and Cokkinis, for instance, who were qualified to discuss matters in a reasonable way with the government, to see our point of view, and to accept certain essential conditions. If he had left things to them we would have signed within two months.

The type of quibble with which Onassis could hold up negotiations for days occurred over Omega's retailing of gasoline in Greece. There would be gas pumps with the Omega sign on them. Onassis insisted that, should he have a mind to build an Omega gas station in some spot that might take his fancy, the government would guarantee to purchase the site on his behalf. In vain did the government men plead that this was quite ludicrous—what if he wanted to build a petrol station on the Acropolis or in the middle of Syntagma Square? Onassis, refusing to see the point, stormed out in a rage.

The main sticking point, inevitably, was money. The problem facing the officials was this: if they gave Onassis a deal on which it would be easy for him to raise money, then it would, almost by definition, be a bargain which was bad for Greece. If, alternatively, they pushed too hard, Onassis might pull out with consequences that, after so much euphoric advance publicity, could only be damaging for the regime. Onassis did not help matters by insisting on government guarantees for the loans he needed. To no avail the government men wailed that this had not been the idea at all—it was Mr. Onassis who was supposed to be making the investment, and if the government had been prepared to guarantee the financing of the project then there would have been little point in involving Onassis in the first place. By way of rejoinder, Onassis said that exemption from profits tax and import controls would also be essential during the early years of the project. After one session, a member of the Omega team told his boss, "You don't want a contract. You want a license."

Some members of the Omega team began to suspect that Onassis was losing his enthusiasm for the aluminum plant which was the cornerstone of the original idea. The refinery—and the lucrative oil transportation contract which went with it—seemed to be what really interested him,

271

despite the fact that, according to everybody's calculations, the aluminum project would be highly profitable. A partner was needed to provide most, if not all, the know-how and some of the capital for the aluminum plant. Onassis dickered first with Reynolds and then with Alcoa, the American aluminum giants, and in both cases, in the words of one of his team, "blew it." It was almost, he says, as if Onassis's *folie de grandeur* made him feel that all he needed to offer prospective partners was the honor of doing business with him. He would offer Alcoa only a minority partnership with a 49 percent stake in the aluminum project, "and you don't make offers like that to Alcoa. Alcoa is the king of aluminum." What, Alcoa asked reasonably, did Onassis know about aluminum? All the same, they made what seemed a conciliatory counterproposal: each party would take 49 percent, with the balance of 2 percent to be held by a mutually trusted third party such as First National City Bank. Onassis refused to contemplate even this marginal surrender of control. "After his marriage," says the member of the Omega team, "he started to lose his feeling of what was feasible. A businessman needs this to succeed. He cannot stubbornly insist on the unfeasible. There might have been no shortage of foreign businessmen who were happy to come to Greece to dine with Ari and Jackie, but there were none who could do business with Onassis when he was in this frame of mind."

Difficulties inside the Omega team were mirrored by dissension within the Ministry of Economic Coordination. The government men lacked experience in negotiation, for the colonels had purged the civil service of many of its ablest officials. As a result, they were less firm with Onassis than they might have been and, in the private opinion of the Omega negotiators, often gave too much away. Two such concessions were a ban on the construction of any further refineries and a ban on the existing French-owned Pechiney aluminum plant's increasing its output for the duration of Onassis's ten-year agreement. (Pechiney, getting wind of this proposal, promptly upped their output before the ban could be enforced.) The apparent irresolution on the official side only served to increase Onassis's appetite for further concessions. Irritation with Onassis was rapidly translated into exasperation with Papadopoulos, who had landed the ministry with the problem in the first place.

For his part, Papadopoulos could not understand why the negotiators were wasting so much time talking. As the affair dragged on, it became clear that for Papadopoulos the publicity value of the project was far more important than anything else. "He totally failed to understand that the project was so vast that the minutiae were not minutiae," explains one of his negotiators, "that if you knock a trifling two cents per kilowatt off the price of electricity it comes to millions in the end."

On March 8, 1969, Niarchos launched his counteroffensive, offering to build the third refinery and undertake other major investment projects. Niarchos claimed that his proposal was worth $100 million more than Omega in investment potential. Both Makarezos and his deputy at the ministry, John Rodinos Orlandos, were inclined to agree. As evidence of his seriousness, Niarchos attached to his offer a draft for $20 million on Crédit Suisse. He proposed that the colonels tear up their agreement with Onassis and put the whole project up for bids, with his own offer as the starting point for other competitors. It was, if nothing else, a shrewd spoiling operation.

The first consequence of the Niarchos intervention was political rather than economic. It gave the heavily censored press a golden opportunity to attack the junta under the guise of economic fair comment. Overt criticism of the colonels was dangerous if not impossible, but it was possible to editorialize on the pros and cons of Omega and, once they were announced, on the Niarchos counterproposals. Criticism of Omega naturally implied criticism of Papadopoulos since he had publicly nailed his colors to the Onassis mast. One of the most outspoken critics of Omega from the moment it was announced had been John Marinos, editor-director of *Oikonomikos Tachidromos*, the *Wall Street Journal* of Greece. "I was convinced from the outset," he says, "that Omega was not in the best interests of Greece and that Onassis foresaw a scenario whereby Papadopoulos would lean on the Greek banks to give him the necessary finance. I was trying to protect our money. But the fact also was that it was a perfectly risk-free way of attacking the junta." In this the press was fueled and encouraged by leaks from Papadopoulos's opponents within the junta, particularly Makarezos.

When the Niarchos counterproposals were unveiled, Makarezos went on record with his opinion that such a contest was "for the good of the nation." Yet two days later, on March 10, the government announced that it was all too late—agreement had been reached with Mr. Onassis, and the contracts were even then at the printers. Onassis held a triumphal news conference in which he lashed out at the "attempt made in recent days by those who were beaten in the original international competition." He described a suggestion that he might cooperate with Niarchos as "a joke in bad taste." But the government excuse that it was too late to scrap the agreement with Onassis, or even that agreement had in fact been reached, was a lie. Niarchos knew it was a lie. So did Onassis. The difference was that Onassis believed that it was a lie only in fact but not in spirit and that Papadopoulos had every intention of standing by his commitment to Omega.

Niarchos's next move was a statement, issued through his Athens office on March 15, to the effect that the government's decision to stick to the Onassis project would cost the country $150 million over the next ten years, since he had offered to supply the new refinery crude oil at $2.50 a ton less than Onassis had. The Greek press joyfully repeated the allegation on its front pages, along with Niarchos's challenge to Onassis to debate publicly the merits of their respective proposals so that it could be established which one was the more beneficial for Greece.

Onassis fired off his reply two days later as he was leaving Paris to fly to the Canary Islands with Jackie on vacation. Niarchos should look to the beam in his own eye, Onassis said, since he had made excessive profits of $100 million out of his ten-year concession on the Aspropyrgos refinery, which Onassis was now running on a nonprofit basis for the benefit of Greece. Niarchos, he continued, was merely trying to wreck Onassis's investment program because he wanted this lucrative concession back. Again the Greek press carried the slanging match as their front page story, asking for full details of the two offers to be made public so that the Greek people could judge them for themselves. The junta promptly slapped a ban on all press comment, including statements by Onassis and Niarchos.

The next stage of the battle was conducted behind closed doors. For the government was much more interested in the Niarchos counter-proposal than it had indicated in public, and the temptation to play the two rival shipowners off against each other proved irresistible. A team was set up in the Ministry of Economic Coordination, under the leadership of Rodinos Orlandos, to determine whether Niarchos's offer was a significant improvement on Omega.

Onassis continued his cultivation of Papadopoulos. He would often dine at the dictator's home before moving on to more informal company in the early hours at Athens nightclubs, where he would alternately brag about the affairs of state that he had discussed and moan that all you ever got to eat *chez* Papadopoulos was beans and onions. Onassis might have found the dictator's life-style austere, but his fellow colonels were not so sure. Under the influence of Onassis, Papadopoulos was beginning to develop what some considered show-business tendencies and an exaggerated sense of his own importance. So, too, was Roufougalis,

Papadopoulos's chief of security, who could be seen most evenings in the hotter Athens night spots in the company of the more flamboyant members of the business community, including, as often as not, Onassis himself. He was, he used to explain only half apologetically, keeping an ear to the ground in these difficult times.

In April 1969, at the suggestion of Roufougalis, Onassis put at the disposal of Papadopoulos and his family a sumptuous villa at the seaside resort of Lagonissi, twenty-five miles from Athens. Onassis had originally acquired it at a cost of $195,000 for his half sister, Callirhoe, whose marriage was breaking up. Papadopoulos took up residence after certain security measures had been made, among them an escape tunnel with a secret entrance behind a sliding bookcase. The rental, a modest one of 20,000 drachmas ($660) a month, was formally paid by Evangelos Vamvakopoulos, a major in the KYP and the official tenant. The natural suspicion among opponents of the regime was that Onassis had "given" the villa to the dictator.

"It is bad and it will look worse," Professor Georgakis told Onassis when advising against the Lagonissi villa gesture. Other aides also argued that the affair would be equally handy ammunition for Papadopoulos's rivals within the junta. There was also the wider issue as to the wisdom of the links Onassis was forging with men whom he had previously characterized as "crooks." He responded to one such suggestion by saying, "These people are not going to disappear overnight. They are here for a long time. Don't indulge in wishful thinking."

Meantime, Onassis's relations with the men in the Ministry of Economic Coordination progressed from bad to appalling. One of the potential contractors referred by the ministry to Onassis made what seemed an immodest proposal. Their conversation included what could have been construed as an offer to "fix" the deadlocked Omega negotiations. All it needed was a sum paid into a certain Swiss bank account. That, at least, was what Onassis told his aides it sounded like. He insisted that the matter should go straight to Papadopoulos, who found the whole episode amusing. "Can't you see?" he said. "It is all the Turks." Honor and tempers were satisfied by the hapless contractor's being dragged off for interrogation by the KYP, though with no conclusive result. The episode only served to further sour the relationship between Onassis and the ministry.

Having completed the study of the Niarchos counterproposal, Rodinos Orlandos submitted to Papadopoulos for consideration a thirteen-page memorandum marked "strictly confidential." He began with a reference to Omega and reviewed the "lengthy and laborious negotiations" of his team, "throughout which [they] were faced with the well-known stubbornness of one of the leading Greek business experts." Rodinos Orlandos pointed out that, as a result of the intervention of Niarchos, "a new situation is created, entirely different from the former one." Niarchos's offer to supply crude oil at an appreciably cheaper price than Onassis ($11.80, cargo insurance, and freight per metric ton as against $14.32) made his "incontestably" the better offer.

Rodinos Orlandos was of the opinion "that not only the economic, legal, and ethical aspects of the matter compel the examination and consideration of the new offer, but the political aspects argue in its favor." His grounds for this judgment was based on an assessment of the forces backing Onassis and Niarchos. The memorandum sought to explain how Niarchos could undercut Onassis so dramatically, whereas none of the petroleum majors had been able or willing to do so when Omega had originally been put to tender (they had all offered precisely the same rate). "It is unthinkable," Rodinos Orlandos continued, "that a single businessman, even one of the stature of Mr. Niarchos . . . would risk direct conflict with the vital interests of his 'employers' by offering crude petroleum at a price far below those dictated by the latter, i.e., the Petroleum Majors."

The answer, he was convinced, was that Niarchos was "working not in isolation, but on the orders of a powerful commander." What they had on their hands was not simply a conflict between Onassis and Niarchos but a battle for Greece between British and American oil interests, with the two men playing "the classic role of 'men of straw' contributing ships and a sizable grudge to the conflict." Onassis was clearly working with British Petroleum. In Rodinos Orlandos's judgment, Niarchos was backed by Esso (Standard Oil of New Jersey), whose contract at the Thessalonica refinery was due to expire in 1976. "It is," Rodinos Orlandos concluded, "especially useful for us to be conscious of the possible extent of the conflict, and the eventual means by which it may be quelled. I feel, Mr. President, that the key to the 'clearing' of the whole matter is offered by Mr. Niarchos . . . [a] competition, the starting point being his offer."

It took Papadopoulos six weeks to conclude that he had to go along with the opinion expressed in the Rodinos Orlandos memorandum. On May 19, first Onassis and then Niarchos were summoned to bring their respective teams to meet Papadopoulos and his ministers and to be told what they already knew. Niarchos's proposals for a fresh round of tenders

276

for the third refinery and other assorted investments had been accepted.

The difference between the two men's business manners was striking. Onassis, excitable and blustering, would rarely let his own men get a word in edgewise, even if it were on a subject they knew far more about than he. "*I* did not say that, Mr. Onassis did" had been an often heard plea from Onassis experts when, in the absence of Onassis himself, they had been confronted with what the government men understood to be their viewpoint on something. Niarchos, altogether calmer and composed, did not sully his hands with the details but turned them over to the appropriate technocrat on his team. The consensus among the government men was that they would rather pass the time of day with Onassis but preferred doing business with Niarchos.

When the international competition to build the third refinery closed, four bids had been submitted. It was immediately clear that those from Onassis and Niarchos were the best. Assisted by a French and a Swiss oil expert, a three-man committee was assigned to the job of picking the winner. All they could conclude was "if this happens the Niarchos offer is best, if that happens the Onassis one is." Once again the rivals heaped abuse upon the scales. Niarchos offered the government a cash loan to build the aluminum complex itself, if it preferred. Well, if that was what the government wanted, wrote Onassis, he would make the loan in gold ingots. Niarchos responded by saying that only underdogs proposed gold and that financial circles were beginning to ask why on earth Mr. Onassis was collecting gold bars. In September 1969 the committee threw up its collective hands in despair and decided it could not decide.

On September 20 the junta, again using a lie to mask its confusion, declared the competition null and void on the grounds that there had been irregularities in both submissions. There had been stand-up rows between Papadopoulos and the pro-Niarchos faction inside the government, and it was clear that it was a political as much as an economic decision that was being made. If Papadopoulos feared for his power base, all the colonels were nervous about Niarchos's royalist connections. The left had been brutally crushed by the torturers and the informers. Resistance to the regime had been virtually eliminated. But they all knew that, if a countercoup ever was mounted, it would be from the royalist side. The junta accordingly intimated that it was now seeking a "Solomon-like" solution with each of the two millionaires to get a small refinery, provided they went ahead with their other investments. And that, more or less, was what was agreed.

On March 13, 1970, Onassis signed an agreement for what was now

277

a $600 million project, including the third refinery and the aluminum complex. Its terms were less advantageous to Onassis than the original agreement with Papadopoulos, but it seemed, at the time, a more rooted commitment. Niarchos took longer to agree on the terms by which he would once again take over Aspropyrgos, which, suitably enlarged, was to be his prize. In the end he agreed to spend $200 million on enlarging its capacity and another $100 million on other projects, notably the enlargement of his own shipyards at Skaramanga.

For a few weeks, Onassis achieved the unique distinction of popularity with the colonels and international liberal opinion alike. With Omega signed and apparently sealed, he gave support to the moves calculated to free the Greek communist composer, Mikis Theodorakis, whose fame in the West rested on the music he had written for the film *Zorba the Greek*. In April 1970 Theodorakis, now a sick man, was released and allowed to go into exile in Paris. The main architect of his release was Jean-Jacques Servan-Schreiber, the millionaire leader of the French Radical party, who had undertaken a one-man mission to the colonels. Servan-Schreiber was a guest on Skorpios, and Onassis helped smooth his passage to the appropriate colonel. He also helped in the secondary problem of securing a passport for Mrs. Theodorakis. It was scarcely enough to make him a liberal hero, but it helped to preserve the notion that he might still be a liberal at heart.

Onassis, however, became embarrassed when Servan-Schreiber heaped public praise upon him and sought his support for the release of other political prisoners in Greece. On April 29, in an interview with the Athens newspaper *Eleftheros Kosmos*, he primly admitted having met with Servan-Schreiber on three separate occasions and went on to say,

I was informed about the meeting of Prime Minister Papadopoulos and J.-J. Servan-Schreiber through Professor Georgakis. At the third meeting I had with Mr. Schreiber, I expressed my views on his requests for my intervention in the release of Theodorakis and other political prisoners. I told him not to take advantage of the Greek premier's generosity and kindness. "You must be crazy to ask for the release of those who have been convicted by Greek court decisions. To release those who planted bombs! . . . Mr. Schreiber, above the freedom of individuals stand the freedom and independence of our nation. When these two are endangered, it is justifiable to sacrifice some of the people's freedoms. We, the Greeks, cannot tolerate any intervention which hurts one's feelings for the freedom of the nation. I cannot understand why you are in such a rush. You are acting like a bull in a china shop."

278

On the same day, in Paris, Theodorakis emerged from the hospital and gave a press conference in the Hôtel du Palais d'Orsay. It was a big day for the international left. The conference room was packed with reporters. Among those on the rostrum were such celebrities as Yves Montand, Melina Mercouri, and Georges Moustaki, as well as representatives from the three main Greek resistance organizations. Theodorakis emphasized the extent of his recovery by reaffirming his left-wing allegiance and warning against the futility of pinning progressive hopes on persons like Onassis, "an enemy of the people."

Within a few weeks, the human implications of Onassis's business activities were again in question on another continent. For a period, the government of Canada was inclined to perceive him as a serious enemy of its people.

19
CRUDE OIL AND WATER

CRUDE OIL IS one of the most complex chemical compounds known. And although its components vary from one geographic area to another, it is generally true that crude can poison, smother, burn, coat, taint, mutate, and cause cancer in marine plants and animals. It can also consume vast quantities of oxygen, to the detriment of anything that lives on or beneath the sea.

Oil is the single biggest polluter of the sea. It gets there in a variety of ways—from the "casual" spillage or leakage which occurs with *every* tanker as it sails, from the deliberate dumping of tank slops (normally as much as 1 percent of the oil clings to the sides of the tanks after emptying), and from disaster spillage. In May 1973, the Ocean Affairs Board of the US National Academy of Sciences estimated that at least 1,370,000 tons of oil find their way into the sea each year from *routine* operations. Another 350,000 tons or so get there by accident.

International anxiety about pollution of the seas is more than fifty years old. In recent years the responsibility for expressing this concern on a global basis has rested with the Inter-Governmental Maritime Consultative Organization (IMCO), an offshoot of the United Nations based in London. IMCO wields influence rather than power. Even when its recommendations are ratified by the flag nations most directly con-

280

cerned, IMCO is devoid of any enforcement or punitive authority. That remains the responsibility of the flag nation itself, which may or may not follow IMCO's recommendations.

Aristotle Onassis was no worse than many other shipowners in seeking those flags which imposed the least possible constraint on his operations, but he was certainly no better. In seeking those laws which were the easiest—and cheapest—to obey, he was pursuing an inexorable economic logic. And where Onassis went, other ostensibly less maverick operators soon followed. Although flags of convenience—"ships of easy virtue," as British seamen used to call them—aroused the fury of the more powerful maritime unions in America and Europe, they had become, by 1970, central to the operations of some of the largest oil corporations.

From less than 1 million tons in 1950, the Liberian-registered fleet had swollen in twenty years to almost 35 million gross tons—about 16 percent of the world's total. Oil tankers comprised 19 million of that figure. Roughly half the Liberian tanker fleet was owned by Greeks while the rest was owned by Americans, including such corporations as Esso, Gulf Oil, and Texaco. Liberian registration allowed exemption from such US registration requirements as that the tanker be built in the United States and that the crew be paid American wages, which averaged double those of most other nations.

Moreover, Title 35 of the 1956 Liberian Code of Laws conveniently states that "income derived by a Liberian corporation owning a vessel registered in Liberia . . . is exempt from Liberian income tax." One American shipping man estimated that the saving in operating costs on a tanker of 80,000 tons amounted to $1 million a year when it was registered under a flag of convenience instead of under the United States flag.

By 1970 the process of buying the most desired flag of convenience —Liberia's red, white, and blue ensign with single star—had become ridiculously simple. Most of the 1,800 vessels using it had never even dropped anchor in a Liberian port. All that was needed was an application form, forty-eight hours to complete the transaction, and a fee of $1.20 per net ton plus an annual tax of ten cents per ton.

Onassis invariably became angry when it was suggested that he used Liberian and Panamanian flags for his ships because of the relaxed attitude of these countries to such matters as safety regulations, working hours, pay, and crew qualifications. The greatest attraction of flags of convenience, he insisted, lay not in the supposed lack of such regulations

281

but in the absence of useless red tape which hampered the efficient operation of his fleet. He was damned if he would be told precisely how many men he must carry on every ship or which job was to be reserved for nationals of a particular country. His ships, he argued, were as safe and efficiently run as those under any of the "traditional" flags. He claimed that his crews were as well qualified as any and better paid than most. He preferred to say that his fleet operated under "flags of necessity." On one famous occasion, he told viewers of the British current affairs program "Panorama" that the way to get ahead was "to make the inconvenient convenient rather than the reverse." Britain could once again become a great shipping nation if she adopted laws along the lines of those favored by the "Panhonlib" countries (Panama, Honduras, and Liberia).

In terms of safety and marine ecology, the statistics suggest that this would have been an exceptionally poor idea. Despite the fact that many of the most modern vessels came to be registered under Liberian and Panamanian flags, the overall tanker safety record of those countries was horrifyingly bad.

Just how bad was revealed in a survey conducted by the Tanker Advisory Service (TAS), an independent fact-finding organization based in New York. In 1974, TAS produced an analysis of tanker losses over the preceding ten years and noted that the seas were becoming increasingly unsafe—the rapid growth of tanker tonnage was eclipsed by the more rapid growth of tankers totally lost. During the decade, 124 tankers had been lost by the fifteen nations with tanker fleets averaging more than 1 million tons. Of those, exactly half had been flying either the Panamanian or Liberian flag.

For Liberia, the losses represented .57 percent of its total tonnage; for Panama, it was .53 percent. Losses for the more traditional maritime nations were as follows: Denmark and the Soviet Union, none; Japan, .03; Germany, .08; France, .10; Britain, .13; the United States, .17; Sweden, .28; Norway, .40; and Greece, .52. On the basis of these figures, it is difficult to avoid the conclusion that the flight to flags of convenience, which Onassis pioneered and preached, made the seas more dangerous and, consequently, more polluted.

A Shell survey of forty serious tanker accidents (not its own) in which there was a major spillage indicated that a frequent cause was that "people made silly mistakes." Such mistakes were most likely to occur on ships with crews that were underqualified, overworked, and underassisted—that is, on ships flying flags of convenience which had less rigorous manning standards.

Onassis could, and sometimes did, argue that it was the minority of convenience flag operators who gave the industry a bad name, but that was begging the question. For it was Onassis and the other major operators themselves who made the whole enterprise economically viable, lending an aura of respectability to the "cowboys" and the more irresponsible owners. Moreover, Onassis was not above using the flags of convenience to escape the wider ecological problems of his business.

It was Onassis's practice, and that of most bulk cargo carriers, to hide the real ownership of his fleet in a thicket of separate corporations. This enabled him to have it both ways. For when he was raising money, the total number of ships controlled by his various companies was acceptable as collateral. At the same time, limiting the assets of each company to one or two vessels insured that his empire would never be seriously threatened by the occasional calamity which was an occupational hazard of owning ships.

Onassis had cause to be grateful for these business methods when the oldest ship in his fleet became one of the loss statistics. On the morning of February 4, 1970, the 11,000-ton Liberian tanker *Arrow* ran squarely aground on Cerebus Rock in the middle of Chedabucto Bay, Nova Scotia. The *Arrow* was fully loaded with Venezuelan crude, which began to seep from her forward tanks soon after she grounded. Prevailing winds and currents carried the oil onto the fine beaches along the bay. Four days later, the *Arrow* broke in half on the rocks, spilling more oil into the sea. The stern section then sank in deep water, carrying with it about a third of the *Arrow*'s total cargo. Gale-force winds spread the floating oil around other bays in the area before a huge slick eventually drifted out to sea. By then, about 11,000 gallons of crude had seeped out of the *Arrow*, and Canada's worst oil spill had assumed catastrophic proportions. Much of Chedabucto Bay's spectacular coastline had become heavily polluted.

Although the *Arrow* had been carrying a relatively nontoxic form of crude oil, the impact of the spill on local wildlife was cruel. Thousands of sea birds were to die in misery, their feathers coated with oil, and other marine life suffered severely. The local clam industry was virtually wiped out that year, and hundreds of fishing boats and tackle were affected.

The Canadian government set up a special task force—Operation Oil —to coordinate efforts to clean up the mess at a cost of almost $4 million. It also began a formal inquiry into the circumstances of the grounding of the *Arrow*. It was the first exhaustive investigation of an oil spill since the British government's report on the wreck of another Liberian-registered tanker, the 12,000-ton *Torrey Canyon*, which went aground off the Scilly Islands early in 1967 with devastating results for the adjacent coastlines. It soon became apparent that much about the *Arrow* was worthy of investigation.

Initially, it proved extremely difficult to find *anyone* who would admit to responsibility for the ship. The job of heading Operation Oil was given to Dr. Patrick McTaggart-Cowan, director of the Science Council of Canada. When the oil was being pumped out of the *Arrow*'s submerged stern, McTaggart-Cowan anxiously tried to locate the ship's hull designs to insure the safety of the operation. Eventually he managed to find a New York telephone number for the ship's agents. The first person he spoke to promised to call back. Two days later, still without the hull designs, McTaggart-Cowan telephoned again. His first contact, he was told, had "gone abroad." The man he spoke to this time denied any knowledge of the *Arrow*. When McTaggart-Cowan, now desperate, tried to contact *him* again, he too was "abroad." In the end he got the original designs from the *Arrow*'s builder, Bethlehem Steel.

The first objective of the inquiry was to discover why the *Arrow* had steamed at almost full speed and in adequate visibility smack into the only rocks within a dozen miles of open water. The inquiry managed to elicit the information that the *Arrow*'s echo sounder had been out of order long before her master, Captain Anastassopoulos, had taken command, and that it had never worked during his tenure; that her gyro compass was prone to periodic failures—it had once been out for three days' sailing and was generally several degrees out of true even when it was functioning; and that the ship's radar, which had been giving trouble on voyages before the *Arrow*'s last trip, was on the blink again as she steamed into Chedabucto Bay.

Anastassopoulos was not an impressive witness. He testified that a lawyer representing the *Arrow*'s owners had come on board shortly after she had grounded and carried off the ship's original log and all the rest of its official papers. The Canadians managed to secure what they were assured was a true copy of the log, but they quickly discovered that there were no entries at all showing what course the *Arrow* had been steering in the final hours before the accident. Anastassopoulos said he had been too busy to write up the log. A government lawyer suggested that an entry made immediately before the grounding had been erased. What had been written there originally, he asked? Anastassopoulos could not remember.

The inquiry found that the loss of the *Arrow* was the fault of Captain Anastassopoulos. It rejected his evidence about poor visibility at the time

284

of the accident, concluding that it had been possible to see more than five miles. It also rejected his claim that a change in marker buoys, of which he had not been informed, caused him to set a false course. In spite of the known defects of his navigational equipment, it concluded, Captain Anastassopoulos had failed to keep a proper lookout at the crucial moment. The blame lay squarely on him for "improper navigation . . . while proceeding at virtually full speed through waters unfamiliar to him."

The question then became one of whether the Canadians could recover the cost of Operation Oil. The *Arrow*'s registered owners, Sunstone Marine of Panama, had been described as an Onassis-controlled corporation by the oil company whose cargo she had been carrying when she grounded. The Canadian press promptly concluded that since Onassis was the *Arrow*'s real owner, he should be made responsible for the damage she had caused.

This was more easily said than done. Groping their way through Onassis's corporate jungle, the government lawyers' hope of finding a flesh-and-blood owner seemed an ever more unlikely prospect. The *Arrow* had been operated by Olympic Maritime of Monte Carlo on Sunstone's behalf. She had been chartered to Standard Tankers of the Bahamas, who in turn had chartered her to Imperial Oil of Canada. To get the sort of proof of ownership that would stand up in court, the lawyers had to start by discovering who owned Sunstone Marine. An extract from the testimony of Marinos Costoletos, representing Olympic Maritime at the inquiry, conveys something of the difficulties confronting them. The number of ships operated by Olympic varied literally from day to day, Costoletos explained, but it was generally between sixty-five and sixty-seven. Each ship was registered with a separate company. Sunstone Marine was, like the others, owned through shares by someone else.

> LAWYER: Who owns the . . . shares of Sunstone?
> COSTOLETOS: I don't know.
> LAWYER: Would you describe the ships managed by Olympic Maritime as the Onassis fleet?
> COSTOLETOS: They have been referred to as the Onassis fleet in the press. . . . I cannot say whether the fleet is owned by Onassis or not.

The lawyers could get no closer to discovering the truth behind the "post-office-box corporation" in Panama. Sunstone's bearer shares were held anonymously. To establish proof of ownership—and contingent legal liability—the government would have had to demonstrate in court that the stock certificates were actually in Onassis's possession at the time of the accident and had been for some time. But even that would probably have been no more than a Pyrrhic victory. For the *Arrow* was Sunstone's only asset: when it sank, there was nothing left to seize in lieu of damages.

The chagrin of the government lawyers was increased by the realization that the success of their own case against Captain Anastassopoulos had worked against them. His incompetence had been so amply demonstrated that it would have been difficult—impossible, they finally concluded—to argue simultaneously that Sunstone, as owners, should bear the fundamental responsibility for the disaster. It was a point which Sunstone evidently appreciated. Maritime law, as a general principle, distinguishes between negligence—normally the fault of the master— and gross negligence. In normal conditions, the owners of a ship can be held responsible for the consequences of an accident only if gross negligence is proved. In the case of the *Arrow*, this meant that the Canadians had to establish that the grounding occurred because of faults in the ship's navigational equipment of which the owners were aware.

In order to evade such findings, Sunstone had to be sternly critical of the unfortunate Captain Anastassopoulos, going so far as to maintain at the inquiry that his sworn testimony about poor visibility had been entirely false. The government's chief counsel found these unusual tactics distasteful. "The owners," he said, "are willing to make a sacrificial goat of their own captain and ruin his career to protect themselves from the responsibility of providing a ship with defective equipment."

The two foreign governments involved with the *Arrow* adopted positions of studied neutrality. The Greek Department of Merchant Marine, which had issued Captain Anastassopoulos's certificate, wanted nothing to do with the inquiry. It was, a Greek government spokesman declared, a matter between Canada and Liberia. Liberia, as the country of registration, sent a representative to the inquiry, but he did not give evidence, and there was no formal investigation by the Liberian authorities. The Canadian government finally gave up its efforts to prove Onassis responsible and turned, instead, to what amounted to an "unsatisfied judgment fund" for the tanker business. Run from London, Tanker Owners Voluntary Assumption of Liability Plan (TOVALOP) was financed by contributions from shipowners based on the size of their fleets and on the frequency with which they had recourse to the fund. The maximum amount TOVALOP could hand out fell well short of the total cost of

286

Operation Oil. The Canadian government eventually received only $950,000, leaving it to the Canadian taxpayers to pay the balance of $3 million.

A scientific perspective on the whole enterprise was given to the Canadian press by Dr. McTaggart-Cowan, the exasperated chief of Operation Oil. "This flags of convenience business," he said, "is one of the sloppiest damn things I ever saw. If the commercial airlines ran their business like the tankers do, you'd be crashing a DC-8 every week, and the world would say stop it." Onassis's ability to distance his name from the *Arrow* disaster contrasted intriguingly with his boldness in defense of his name in another area. On June 27, 1970, less than four weeks after the *Arrow* ran aground, the *International Herald Tribune* carried an advertisement for an enterprise called The Shipowners Fund, Inc., of Panama and Luxembourg (SFI). Its purpose was to encourage the public to invest in the shipping business where "fabulous accumulations of wealth" were possible through the operations of the fund. A starting capital of $10 million was required; shares were available at $5,000 each. "N. Onassis, Chairman/President" appeared prominently at the top and bottom of the advertisement.

"N. Onassis" was Nicholas Onassis, Aristotle's cousin. He was also a native of Smyrna, and one of his earliest jobs as a young man—he was eight years younger than Aristotle—had been helping at the Athens end of Onassis's tobacco business. Subsequently, he had served as an apprentice captain on one of his cousin's vessels, the *Onassis Maria*, before emigrating to Argentina. After the war he had settled in Montreal, where he had built up a substantial real estate business. The cousins had not kept in regular touch, but they had, according to Nicholas, talked about the SFI before the advertisement appeared.

Yet, within a week of its appearance, another advertisement, full-page, appeared in the *Herald Tribune*. This boldly announced: "Olympic Maritime S.A. as general agents for the A. S. Onassis Group of shipping companies wishes to announce that this shipping group HAS NO CONNECTION WITH 'The Shipowners Fund' managed by the Shipowners Fund, Inc., N. Onassis Chairman/President, Luxembourg. That Mr. N. Onassis is not and has never been employed by or associated with the A. S. Onassis Shipping Group." A similarly worded message was also placed in the advertising columns of the *Wall Street Journal* and the *Financial Times* of London.

According to Nicholas Onassis, this advertising campaign had a devastating effect on his efforts to set up the SFI. After receiving 400 replies to his original announcement, all interest suddenly evaporated. Instead of $10 million, the SFI raised only $25,000, and Nicholas lost money as the enterprise was liquidated. He attempted to obtain redress through the New York courts and stated in his suit that Aristotle Onassis, "who is undoubtedly the A. S. Onassis mentioned in the disparaging advertisements" is one of the "most powerful and mysterious figures in the entire world. . . . However, in a manner typical of his shadowy and worldwide operations in the past, he has not acted in his own name, but instead has acted in the name of other legal identities which cannot be traced or identified, since he is apparently able to operate beyond the licensing and taxing laws of the United States and other jurisdictions."

It was a pathetic episode, with evident faults on both sides. It emerged from the legal documents that Aristotle Onassis had indeed sanctioned and approved the "disassociation" campaign without first contacting his cousin and without any apparent grounds for doubting the bona fides of his venture. It also emerged that Nicholas Onassis lacked the kind of shipping experience that could inspire real confidence in his investors. Even so, the overriding impression was that the Onassis Group had wielded a sledgehammer to crack a nut.

After the case, which Onassis successfully defended, the cousins ceased to have any further contact. Nicholas Onassis still lives in Montreal, though in more straitened circumstances. The memory still rankles. "When I saw my cousin's ads," he told us, "I could have shot him."

Yet Onassis's problems with the *Arrow* and the SFI were mild in comparison with those experienced by his great business rival. By the time Niarchos got around to signing his part of an investment agreement with the Greek government on May 30, 1970, he was involved in an inquiry into the circumstances of his wife's sudden death.

20
AN AEGEAN TRAGEDY

EUGENIE NIARCHOS, the sister of Onassis's ex-wife, Tina, died in the early hours of the morning of May 4, 1970, on Niarchos's private island of Spetsopoula. She had suffered physical injuries and had taken a large quantity of barbiturates. She was forty-four years old.

Niarchos gave an account of the events leading to his wife's death in statements to the Greek investigating authorities. He said that on the evening of May 3 there had been some tension between Eugenie and himself. Over dinner they had discussed an impending visit to the island by Elena, his daughter by Charlotte Ford. Elena was four years old, and he thought it likely that her mother would insist on accompanying her on such a visit. He was disposed to allow this. Around 9:30 P.M. he received a call from America. He talked for almost twenty minutes with Charlotte Ford and Elena. They agreed that Elena.should come to Spetsopoula for the months of July and August and that Charlotte should come for ten days. Eugenie had entered the room while the telephone conversation was in progress but had left abruptly.

After the telephone call Niarchos had gone to bed, but at 10:25 P.M. he decided to go to his wife's room to further explain the situation. He found her on the bed wearing a nightgown. Her eyes were closed. When he spoke to her she did not move. He assumed she had taken a larger

289

than necessary dose of sleeping pills. He shook her vigorously and slapped her in an attempt to revive her. She slipped to the floor. He took her by the neck and lifted her upward. He then took her by the shoulders. She fell a couple of times as he was trying to lift her back on the bed. Finally, he succeeded.

He phoned the telephone operator of the villa and asked for some strong coffee to be sent up. He also asked him to contact his personal valet, Angelo Marchini. When Marchini arrived they tried to force the coffee between his wife's clenched teeth. Her pulse rate was then sixty-five. It descended to 19. Around 11 P.M. he spoke to his sister, Maria Dracopoulos, in Athens and asked her to call a doctor as he suspected barbiturate poisoning. She immediately contacted the Skaramanga shipyard doctor, Panayotis Arnautis. He did not call the nearest doctor, the elderly Spyridon Georgopoulos on the neighboring island of Spetsai, because he suffered from asthma and did not like to travel on patrol boats, and besides a doctor could come by helicopter from Athens just as quickly.

Dr. Arnautis arrived at Spetsopoula around 12:25 A.M., immediately gave Eugenie a massage, and then proceeded to inject a serum. While doing so he realized she was dead.

Niarchos told the authorities that his wife had been "grieved" by his behavior earlier in the evening but added that he had not been uncivil. He also revealed that Eugenie had left a note. The first part, written clearly in red pencil, read in English, "For the *first* time in all our life together I have begged you to help me. I have implored you. The error is mine. But sometimes one must forgive and forget." Then, semilegibly in ball-point pen, some more words had been added in a violent scrawl: "26 is an unlucky number. It is the double of 12. 10 b of whisky." In one of his statements, Niarchos recalled his contributions to the Greek economy, placing particular stress on the agreement he had just concluded with the colonels and adding this curious postscript: "Now my antagonists pour accusations and gossip against me . . . and try to destroy what I have made for the good of Greece, I repeat, 'for the good of Greece.' "

Onassis, in his dual role as rival and relative of the deceased, could hardly remain indifferent to the affair. There is every indication that Onassis's immediate reaction to Niarchos's predicament was unsympathetic.

The immediate postmortem examination of Eugenie's body was conducted by Dr. Georgios Agioutantis, professor of forensic medicine at

Athens University, and Dr. Demetrios Kapsakis. Dr. Kapsakis was director of the Department of Forensic Medicine in the Ministry of Justice and had achieved international notoriety in 1968 as an expert witness for the Greek colonels before a hearing on torture charges at the European Commission on Human Rights in Strasbourg. Their report, completed on May 12, listed fourteen injuries on Eugenie's body. They included a bruise on the left eye and swelling on the left temple; an elliptic hemorrhage on the right side of the neck; three parallel smaller bruises on the left side of the neck above the collarbone; injuries to the skin below and the fibers of the muscle; a hemorrhage to the left of the larynx; a two-inch bruise on the abdomen with internal bleeding and bleeding behind the diaphragm in the region of the fourth and fifth vertebrae; bruises on the left arm; bruises on the left ankle and the left shin; a bruise on the ring finger and a tear on the little finger of the left hand. The doctors concluded that these injuries were commensurate with "old-fashioned attempts at resuscitation." Death, in their view, was caused by an overdose of sleeping pills.

Constantine Fafoutis, the Piraeus investigating magistrate who was handling the case, promptly ordered another expert examination of the body. Two other doctors recorded their findings in June and suggested that "the collapse and death of Eugenie Niarchos" was caused by her physical injuries. In their view, the concentration of Seconal found in her body—two milligrams barbiturate in a hundred cubic centimeters of blood—could not have produced a fatal effect.

In an effort to eliminate the contradictions, Fafoutis set up another tribunal of experts. This included the four doctors who had previously examined the deceased plus two more Athens University professors and two experts nominated by Niarchos. The eight wise men eventually agreed on the following conclusion: "The injuries found on the body were slight, and Eugenie Niarchos was already in a comatose condition when they occurred. They did not contribute to the fatality which was partly due to the effects of Seconal and partly to the action intended to revive the deceased."

The tribunal's finding was welcomed by those with responsibility for the Greek economy. When a new dry dock—the Eugenie Niarchos—was opened at Skaramanga, the economic minister, Nicholas Makarezos, attended as guest of honor. He told the assembled workers, "We are confident that the inspirator and creator of this shipyard will face the blows of fate with the same courage which enabled the ancient Greeks to triumph over the power of death."

Fafoutis, however, continued to pursue his inquiries. He still felt there were too many unanswered questions about the case. On August 21, 1970, he produced a lengthy analysis of the evidence, setting out his reasons for rejecting the suicide hypothesis. He then formally recommended the institution of proceedings under Article 311 of the Greek penal code "against Stavros Niarchos, son of Spiros, born in Piraeus, resident in St. Moritz, Switzerland, temporarily at Spetsopoula, age sixty, shipowner of Greek nationality and of Greek Orthodox faith." Fafoutis urged that Niarchos should be tried for "inflicting injuries leading to the death" of his wife on the night of May 4. If convicted, Niarchos could receive a prison sentence of five to ten years.

Fafoutis's recommendation was immediately referred to the Piraeus high court, which had the final say on whether Niarchos should be charged. Three judges studied Fafoutis's submission and the other evidence before rejecting the proposed indictment. They declared that the evidence showed that Eugenie Niarchos had committed suicide during the night of May 3 to 4. Fafoutis had until October 3 to contest the decision, but he raised no further objections. The official case was closed, and although further attempts were made to revive it, none were successful.

Onassis's attitude toward the affair underwent a radical change when Fafoutis called for Niarchos's arrest. Something like a modest "rapprochement" between them can be dated from this point. Yet, in the end, it was not the vision of his rival's humiliation that shocked Onassis into relenting. Like so many sworn enemies, it seems that the two men had reached the catalytic point at which it dawned on them that they had more in common with each other than with the spectators who were egging them on and that continued combat could only result in their both being the losers. At the same time, there were family pressures that dictated moderation. Onassis's son, Alexander, who was close to his cousin, Philip Niarchos, asked his father to refrain from doing anything that might embarrass his uncle. Arietta Livanos, Onassis's former mother-in-law, remained a staunch supporter of Niarchos despite the loss of her daughter. Her other daughter, Tina, Onassis's former wife and now Lady Blandford, had Niarchos's two younger children to stay with her in England. Like her mother, Tina would say nothing against Niarchos. Indeed, the tragedy on Spetsopoula seemed to draw them closer together. Onassis began to appreciate that Niarchos's plight was causing unhappiness to people who were also dear to himself.

292

At this stage of his career, Onassis's views on life and how to succeed in it were much sought after. The spectacle of a man who had come from obscure origins to become beloved of some of the most beautiful women in the world and deferred to by the most powerful men was naturally arresting. He appeared not only to have the secret of how to make money but also to have mastered the more subtle art of being able to enjoy it. Unlike Samuel Smiles or Dale Carnegie, he never seemed inclined to codify his self-help philosophy for the benefit of the struggling masses. He did, however, assist one reporter in assembling "My Ten Secrets for Success." They appeared in the October 1970 issue of an American publication called *Success Unlimited*.

1. Take care of your body. Make yourself as good as you can. Don't worry about shortcomings. Look at me. I am no Greek god but I did not waste my life in crying because I wasn't born good looking. Remember nobody is as ugly as he thinks he is.

2. Eat lightly and stay away from the wines and rich food when you have a job to do. Spending several hours at the table in the middle of a working day is the best way to shorten your life.

3. Wait until evening, when you have more time and the day's labor is finished. Then enjoy a good meal with friends, and never talk business while you eat.

4. Exercise and keep yourself trim. The basic yoga exercises help immensely, both mind and body. And if you can manage an hour or two of judo every week, it frees you of all your complexes.

5. Keep a tan even if you have to use a lamp. To most people a tan in winter means only that you have been where the sun is, and in that respect, sun is money.

6. Once you have taken care of your physical appearance, establish a successful way of life. Live in an elegant building—even if you have to take a room in the attic—where you will rub shoulders with wealthy, successful people in the corridors and on the elevators. Frequent luxury cafes even if you have to sip your drinks. Soon you will learn that many people with money are very lonely.

7. If you are short of money, borrow it. And never ask for small loans. Borrow big but always repay promptly.

8. Keep your troubles to yourself and let people believe you are having a wonderful time.

9. Don't sleep too much or you'll wake up a failure. If you sleep three hours less each night for a year, you will have an extra month and a half to succeed in.

10. If you aspire for success, do not squander your time reading about

293

things others have done. It is better to get on living your own life than to concern yourself with what others have done.

This rule applies strongly to all the stories about me, Jackie and my friends. If a quarter of what reporters have written about me were true, I would already be ruined, abandoned, and so depressed by my misadventures that I would be on the point of shooting myself.

It must be said that Onassis did not observe all his own axioms. He did discuss business over the evening meal, and there is no record of his being a particular enthusiast for yoga or judo. Yet, at all stages of his life, he did contrive to keep fitter than most of his peers in the business world. In cities he would always prefer to walk rather than take a cab or limousine. When on board the *Christina* he would make a point of going for two long swims in the sea every day.

More curiously, he omitted from the list what was undoubtedly the real clue to his success in his early and middle life—the courage to take risks. One reason for this may have been that this was the very quality that he was in the process of losing.

The first real evidence of this came in his deteriorating relations with the Greek authorities. In November 1970 a fresh wrangle over the Omega agreement erupted between Onassis and the colonels. If there were those who suspected that it was not the aluminum project which really interested Onassis, nobody doubted that the feature of the agreement which had most excited the shipowner was the clause which gave him the exclusive right to transport all the oil the new refinery would use in his own ships. This no longer looked so enticing. The relevant part of the freight contract fixed the rate at $3.30 a ton from the Persian Gulf to Greece for the duration of the Omega agreement. At the time of signing, that was a good rate. But for the rest of that year freight rates soared until, in November, the going rate for the voyage was $8.50 a ton. Onassis, perhaps understandably failing to point out that what he lost on Omega oil transport he would be making hand over fist on spot charters, howled that he would be ruined. He demanded a revision of his agreement and insisted on government or Greek bank guarantees as collateral against the foreign loans he still needed in order to realize Omega.

Once again the junta was split by Onassis's antics. Makarezos argued that he should be told to go to hell, and Papadopoulos, suspecting that Onassis might welcome the opportunity, argued in favor of an accommodation. Yet despite his attachment to Omega, the dictator's arguments on behalf of Onassis were becoming cooler. Onassis failed to appreciate

294

that the bargaining methods that served so well in negotiating ship charters or extracting concessions for Olympic were wholly inappropriate for a massive, capital-intensive industrial project. This failing, combined with his inability to delegate important decisions, distressed even his greatest admirers. Omega was becoming Onassis's monomania. "One of the most tragic things," recalls Professor Georgakis, "was to see this most enchanting and fascinating of men becoming a bore. He became obsessed with subjects, constantly repeating himself, constantly returning to them and distorting them. In the end he bored even Papadopoulos. He ground on and on about Omega, wrote him letters, often twenty-four-page ones, often daily, all about Omega, alternately pleading and accusing."

On this occasion Papadopoulos could only take the edge off the controversy. Onassis was obliged to drop his demand for guarantees, and backpedaled on the matter of freight rates to the point where he was insisting that all he wanted was the right to appeal, not an immediate revision. When he was curtly required by Makarezos's ministry to fulfill his side of the agreement by producing a $7 million cash guarantee by December 11 or regard the contract as null and void, Onassis did so, with twenty-four hours to spare and with bad grace.

Thwarted in his search for government-backed finance, Onassis turned east in the hope of finding someone to shoulder the risk. The Russians again reacted positively to his feelers, and Professor Georgakis was dispatched as emissary extraordinary to Moscow to see what could be arranged. He was well received. The Russians had no qualms about doing business with the junta and offered Onassis virtually unlimited credit, equipment, and know-how. Unfortunately, the colonels, conscious of their dependence on American military and economic support, were obliged to veto the Soviet initiative as politically undesirable. But the problem was not simply one of high finance.

The peasants who owned the land in Megara, where Onassis proposed to locate his industrial site, decided to revolt. The system of land tenure in Greece, as any foreigner who has ever built a holiday villa knows to his cost, is complex. Fathers divide their property among their sons and often bestow portions of it upon their daughters by way of dowry. On the 2,500 acres which Onassis said he needed there were no fewer than 1,500 families and 150 poultry farms, not to mention 57,000 fruit trees. The compensation Onassis was proposing to pay for the land was fair only if one did not take into account the difference between its value for subsistence agriculture and its value for a giant industrial complex.

The peasants themselves had no intention of ignoring the extra development value of their land and vociferously contended that they were
being robbed. Hundreds of them invaded the Athens courthouse where
a judge was fixing compensation rates. The police were called in, and the
four peasant ringleaders arrested. They were later released without being
charged.

In March, Onassis announced that Omega would come to a halt (it
had not exactly started) unless the colonels agreed to a revision of the
contract. He was now claiming that increased oil prices were compounding his prospective ruin and that he stood to loose $1,000,000,000 on
the deal.

Despite the hike in oil and freight rates, Onassis's position was not
nearly as desperate as he painted it. His agreement on the price he would
receive for refined products was regulated by the following formula. It
would be (1) the price of crude, plus (2) the fixed freight rate, plus (3)
six dollars per ton. Item one, the price of crude, was variable, so the hike
in oil rates was neither here nor there. Item two, the fixed freight rates,
did seem a temporary misfortune, but such are the vagaries of the market
that within two years—as Onassis himself should have known—they
would have been profitable again. Tom Pappas, the Greek-American
millionaire who owned what was then the only other refinery in Greece
apart from Aspropyrgos, was working on virtually the same price formula
and had no complaints. Item three, the six dollars per ton, was itself
subdivided into two dollars for amortization, two dollars for refining
costs, and two dollars for profit. Of these, only the refining costs were
vulnerable to inflation, and even a 100 percent wage increase would have
eaten into the six dollars to the tune of only one dollar.

The real problem was that Onassis's proposed power station would be
obliged to provide a considerable amount of surplus electricity to the
national power grid at what was threatening to become an unprofitable
rate. Even so, all those concerned with the Omega negotiations on both
the Onassis side and the government side were quite convinced that the
whole package—the refinery, the aluminum complex, and the freight
deal—would give Onassis a handsome profit if he had the nerve and the
will to see it through. That was now seriously in doubt.

There was one last extraordinary attempt to save the situation—a
proposal that Onassis and Niarchos should pool their resources as co-
equals in a new company to see Omega through. The shuttle diplomatist
responsible was Rodinos Orlandos, who, despite the fact that he had
resigned from the government, had remained on reasonable terms with

Onassis and Niarchos. The ex-minister had a summer home on the island of Spetsai, a few minutes by helicopter from Spetsopoula. Onassis had dropped by for drinks one day, and Rodinos Orlandos had mentioned the idea of the joint company. He had appealed to Onassis's paternalistic and dynastic instincts. Both men, he argued, were getting old and had children on the brink of maturity, and they should be thinking in terms of creating something for their future instead of wasting their energies competing. Onassis said gruffly that "Niarchos will never agree, of course," but, provided every precaution was taken, he had no objection to Rodinos Orlandos's broaching the subject with Niarchos "for the sake of the children." Niarchos was agreeable.

It was, of course, only the familiar agreement in principal, and the two men continued to avoid a meeting, but Rodinos Orlandos and their employees hammered out something which they felt was concrete enough to put to Papadopoulos. The dictator refused point blank to countenance the scheme, still feeling that he had everything to gain by keeping the two rivals at each other's throats and everything to lose by their cooperation. In vain Rodinos Orlandos argued that, since the joint venture would proceed broadly along the lines of the two men's existing contracts, Greece had already profited from their rivalry and should now do the same from their cooperation.

Omega was abandoned in November 1971. The government agreed to return Onassis's $7 million guarantee in return for a promise that he would drop any claim for damages. Onassis still retained a wistful hankering for the refinery. When it was once again put out to tender in January 1972, both he and Niarchos submitted separate bids. They were rejected. Onassis then proposed a partnership to one of the winners, the banker Stratis Andreadis. That too was rejected. Later still, Onassis called a consultant on the Andreadis team and inquired about the prospects of buying the concession. Onassis said of Andreadis, "He is a banker. What does he want with oil?" "When you had it you didn't want it," observed the consultant. "Don't you understand," said Onassis, "I don't like to lose."

It is difficult to gauge the importance of Onassis's role in Greek politics. Despite the restoration of democracy in Greece, there are still hidden areas of the junta's history. Several of those whom we interviewed for this and the preceding chapters had close links with the junta. They are understandably reluctant for the Greek public to be reminded of those links or to condemn former colleagues, some of whom are now in jail. We did, however, find among them a large measure of bitterness about the Onassis-Papadopoulos connection. In their minds it played a significant role in the downfall of the junta.

In considering this possibility, it is necessary to recall that Papadopoulos himself fell from power in November 1973 as a result of a bloodless putsch by other junta members led by Dimitrios Ionnidis. Those who replaced him were, if anything, more incompetent, and their culminating folly was the Cyprus adventure of July 1974 in which President Makarios narrowly escaped assassination and was replaced by a junta puppet, Nicos Sampson. Turkey promptly invaded Cyprus on the grounds that the junta was about to take over the island, and Greece and Turkey squared up for war. Not only had the colonels led their country to the brink of war, but it transpired that they were incapable of fighting it. The army (which is supposed to be the strong point of military dictatorships) proved to be even more maladministered than the country, and the "mobilization" of the inadequately equipped men was a shambles. The colonels handed over the mess to the democrats.

Onassis, of course, was no militarist, but his significance for Greek politicians lay in the events that brought the architects of the Cyprus adventure to power. One former government minister referred specifically to the odor of corruption which surrounded what Helen Vlachos termed the Great Junta Sale. "Onassis was like a red flag to a bull in the eyes of many of the younger idealistic officers," he said. "His life-style and friendship with Papadopoulos was to them a betrayal of the ideals of the revolution. It was one of the things which gave the man with the gun [Ionnidis] his chance."

Onassis's failure to realize Project Omega may not have been accidental. Despite his superlative talents as a shipowner and, to a more limited extent, as an airline proprietor, he never did manage to establish any serious land-based business enterprise. This was not for want of trying or opportunity.

Even before his marriage to Jackie, Onassis was much sought after as a sponsor of major projects, and it was his pleasure to discuss their practicality. When the flow of incoming ideas faltered, he would ask Gratsos or George Moore, his banker at First National City in New York, to think up some more. The projects they discussed girdled the globe—mining in Alaska, mineral extraction in South Africa and Australia, pipelines in Suez, holiday developments in the Caribbean. Onassis would sometimes fly off on "feasibility studies" and come back refreshed by the expedition but too conscious of the problems to proceed any further. "From 1959 onwards, he had the ability," says Moore, "to throw

298

money out of the window, but he possessed a hard core of caution which stopped him doing it."

The same constraint seems to have impeded any impulse toward large gestures of charity. Onassis's son, Alexander, frequently urged his father to spend some of his millions on good works. Possibilities were discussed but always deferred. George Moore thought the reason was that Onassis's wealth had become central to his sense of self and that the idea of giving it away struck him as an admission of defeat. "It wasn't any absence of generosity on his part," recalls Moore. "He was in fact very kind to friends who needed help. But he could never get really interested in the notion that he should systematically use his wealth for philanthropic purposes."

There was one notable exception to this pattern of caution. It originated in an idea that had been obsessively discussed by Onassis over a long period—a shipyard of his own. The quest went far beyond the feasibility stage but ultimately collapsed for reasons that offer an intriguing insight into his limitations as an industrialist.

The search for a shipyard of his own had taken Onassis—or more accurately, had taken long-suffering executives like Kurt Reiter—all over the world examining one prospect after another. Over the years Reiter had accustomed himself to the role of enthusiastic devil's advocate, scuttling proposals in Holland, France, Greece, and Japan. Now he was frankly puzzled by Onassis's determination to get into shipbuilding. It might look like textbook business expansion, Reiter argued, but Onassis of all people should understand that shipowners and shipbuilders were essentially in an adversary relationship. How, for instance, would the contract price be fixed on an Onassis supertanker to be built in his own yard?

Onassis's most determined effort to realize the dream of having his own shipyard was made in Belfast, the capital of Northern Ireland, Britain's most troublesome province. In 1970 he had two 250,000-ton supertankers in construction at the Belfast yard of Harland & Wolff, a company with a history stretching back over a century. Onassis already had a 25 percent shareholding in the company, but despite the modernity of its facilities—the yard was reckoned the best-equipped in Europe —it had fallen on hard times. Orders were scarce and labor relations were appalling. As the prime industry in a province torn by sectarian strife between Protestant loyalists and Catholic republicans, it was the focus of extraordinary tensions.

For the loyalists the yard was not simply an economic force but also

299

a talisman of Protestant authority in Northern Ireland. For the republicans in the IRA it was a continuing reminder of the low status of Catholics under British rule. Of the yard's work force of ten thousand men, only 5 percent were Catholic, mostly holding down the more menial jobs. Seven times in its history the yard had experienced severe riots in which the Catholic minority had been driven from their jobs, the latest one having occurred on June 29, 1970. With the British army out in force and many of the basic civil liberties suspended, it had been a long, hot summer all over Northern Ireland.

In September 1970 Onassis persuaded Jackie to accompany him on a bizarre public relations exercise. While edgy British army patrols crisscrossed the hostile city, Onassis, Jackie, and Alexander arrived in Belfast in a sleek black limousine to do the honors at a new $100,000 social club for employees of the Harland & Wolff shipbuilding group. Jackie was wearing a dark blue knee-length coat and matching dress and dark glasses. A posse of security men held back the press. Inside the club, Jackie chatted graciously with the workers over a buffet lunch and Onassis presented a check for $12,000 to the committee. Onassis and Alexander were presented with shillelaghs, and Jackie was given a gold-plated key to the club's front door. Ceremonies complete, the trio hastened back to the airport, where Onassis's executive jet was waiting. An indignant statement from Harland & Wolff denying that the "purely social" visit had anything to do with the company's serious financial problems naturally strengthened the impression in Belfast that Onassis was keen to take over the business. A month later it was official: Onassis was to make an offer. "We're worried about that Greek!" one shop steward told a reporter. "If he ever takes over, in no time Jackie will have the yard full of Papist foremen."

Onassis responded by turning on the charm. Shortly before Christmas, he invited seven key union men from Belfast to come and talk things over in London. When fog caused the diversion of the flight from Belfast, Onassis sent his jet off to collect them. In the meantime, he and two national union leaders sat down to a lunch of smoked salmon, roast beef, and orange soufflé washed down with champagne. "We talked of everything," Onassis informed a reporter, "of politics, the arts, music and philosophy." When the weary Belfast men eventually turned up, just in time for an equally splendid dinner, Onassis suggested they should put up at Claridge's for the night as his guests. Talks began again over breakfast the next morning. Back in Belfast, the union men were uncommunicative about their discussions, though one did indicate that the beds in Claridge's were a trifle too soft for his liking. They were all,

300

nonetheless, impressed by Onassis's capacity to match them drink for drink. What they did not know was that Onassis's own "scotch" was poured from a bottle that contained cold tea.

Onassis's overall plan called for him to spend $5.9 million acquiring 49 percent of Harland & Wolff's shares and about another $7.8 million to complete various steelworking facilities. When he was in control, he promised, there would be more supertanker orders for the yard from his own organization. All he wanted in return was for the government to write off Harland & Wolff's $12 million losses on existing orders taken on fixed-price contracts. The proposal, as local shop stewards pointed out, was not quite as munificent as it appeared. Two of the three supertankers Onassis had ordered were then being built in the yard, and Harland & Wolff stood to lose substantially on both ships because wages and material costs had risen considerably since the contract was signed. Onassis, as he had every right to, had consistently refused to renegotiate more favorable terms for the group. That meant that a sizable chunk of the debts he wanted written off by the government were, in fact, on his own business. If he got the yard, the government would in effect be paying him for his own ships.

That was not all. The two ships had cost him $20.3 million each when first ordered. On the buoyant tanker market late in 1970, they were now worth at least $33.4 million each. All that was not a bad return for an investment of $14 million, particularly when the price included the world's biggest building dock—it could handle ships of up to one million tons—in which a great deal of public money had been invested.

The local shop stewards, banking on the government's commitment to keep the yard open, were inclined against the offer. At the same time, there were powerful figures in the British government and the national union leadership who wanted the Onassis bid to succeed—for all its flaws, his offer was reckoned better than those made by two other interested parties, the Swan Hunter Group and the Norwegian shipbuilder Fred Olsen. There was no mistaking Onassis's determination. He told Frank McFadzean of Shell that he was eager to shape up the company and make it great again. How? asked McFadzean. Well, Onassis said, he would start by sending in a hundred fifty of the best Japanese technicians he could find. "Like hell you will," McFadzean replied, aghast at the notion of what their impact might be in a situation already fraught with racial bigotry. But if some of Onassis's ideas seemed unrealistic in the context of Northern Ireland, he had two enormous advantages to offer—money and guaranteed orders.

The British civil servants involved could appreciate these advantages, but they also had to take into political account the xenophobic mood in the shipyard itself. They played for time. Onassis, exasperated at the delays, rashly allowed his impatience to surface in print. The London *Daily Express* ran a story under the headline "Full speed ahead or I'm quitting warns angry Ari." Meanwhile the deteriorating security situation in Ulster hardened the mood in the shipyard. Much as some government ministers wanted to get Harland & Wolff off public money, the risk of provoking another bitter clash with the yard's hard-core Protestant workers became too great. In March 1971 the British government decided to reject the Onassis offer and render further support to the existing management of Harland & Wolff. As one perceptive journalist put it, "It was an emotional verdict based on the special social circumstances of Belfast."

Onassis was cruising on the *Christina* when the formal announcement was made. He was resigned to failure by then. It was just as well that he was spared the final indignity of hearing the epitaph pronounced on his hopes by an exultant Protestant lay preacher in a mission hall off Newtonard Road in Belfast: "We give thee thanks, O Lord, that the hand of the foreigner has been taken from the throat of Ulster and that our shipyard shall remain always Protestant. Amen."

21
THE LIMITS OF
SUCCESS

ONASSIS AND JACKIE had been married for just three days when the famous American interior designer, Billy Baldwin, received an overseas call to his New York office.

"The *Christina* is calling Mr. Baldwin," said a thickly accented male voice.

"This is Mr. Baldwin."

"One moment. Madame Onassis."

There was a series of clicks and some static before Jackie's breathless voice came on the line.

"Billy, I need you. I need a friend. How soon can you come to see me?"

Baldwin, who had previously decorated Jackie's Washington and New York homes, said he could come immediately. He was later to provide in his book, *Billy Baldwin Remembers*, one of the few authentically intimate accounts of the Onassises' early married life-style. It was his first visit to Greece, and his finely tuned aesthetic sensibilities were fully receptive. The Jackie he found was in girlish good spirits. "Billy," she said, before he sat down to eat at the Glyfada villa, "you are about to have your first experience with a Greek lunch. I will kill you if you pretend to like it."

303

After lunch Onassis announced "a treat"—a helicopter trip to Skorpios, then on to the *Christina*, where Baldwin was to take up residence. The *Christina* struck the fastidious designer as the "epitome of vulgarity and bad taste." His own stateroom abounded in pink taffeta and gold finishes; the bathroom was solid pink marble. Though, "for all its vulgarity, the room was fantastically comfortable."

Baldwin had no reservations about his host. Several women had previously told him that Onassis was the most charming man they had ever met, and he could see why. Jackie seemed radiant and delighted with herself in her husband's company. Baldwin had never seen her so "free."

Pleading fatigue after his long journey, Baldwin retired early on his first evening aboard the *Christina*. In the morning he awoke to find a bag of toothsome candies, cakes, and Turkish delight on the chair inside his door. They were a sample of the treats he had missed from the night before. There was also a note from Jackie: "Billy, you missed your midnight sweets—and the houris have been kneading unguents all day long. . . . After the zenith of the moon and our evening prayer, which is sweetened by Turkish delights, we have a dainty feast, and since, O cruel Allah, you could not share it, before we find la Belle aux Bois Dormant we drop these sweetmeats by your couch, to make voluptuous the dawn for you. Mme Suleiman le Brillant."

Baldwin's job was to produce designs for a house on Skorpios that was being converted to Jackie's taste. Onassis was prepared to leave everything to his new wife. "This house I want to be a total surprise," he said. "I trust you and I trust Jackie and I don't want to know anything about it." His only request was that there should be a long sofa by the living-room fireplace "so I can lie and read and nap and watch the flames." For Baldwin it was a rushed but highly agreeable commission. There were even compensations on the *Christina*. Baldwin was shown Onassis's study, which he found magnificent—very masculine, very personal, and full of books. It almost "made up for the horror of the rest of the ship."

On his trips around Skorpios with Jackie, Baldwin detected some sharp differences of taste between the newlyweds. In a uniquely beautiful clearing near the top of the island, Jackie revealed that her husband had plans to build a villa. She told Baldwin coolly, "I think he has in mind something like the Trianon at Versailles or some kind of domesticated Acropolis. As far as I'm concerned, there will never be a house here." But Baldwin's most vivid impression was of the strength of the bond between them. One evening he was sitting by her side, working on his

304

designs, when the sound of Onassis's Piaggio became audible in the distance. Jackie got up, stood on the end of the *Christina*'s diving board, and was bathed in the glow of a spotlight in the nose of the plane. Baldwin thought it was like Wagner's *Tristan and Isolde*—corny, but ultimately convincing. The same was true of Jackie's words: "I heard the splash of the landing. Thank God he's safe."

Baldwin completed his commission just before Christmas. Back in New York, he received a cable from the newlyweds a few weeks later. "Happy New Year," it said, "and congratulations on the Erechtheum [a Greek temple] of Billy, which we are now enjoying. Love, Ari, Jackie."

Although Jackie and Ari were happy together, even at the outset of their marriage there were hints of the tension that would strain their natural sympathy for one another. The abrupt manner in which Onassis broke off his wedding celebrations on Skorpios to do business with the Greek junta was a sign of things to come. While working in the Omega office in Athens during his interrupted honeymoon, Onassis noticed that one of the consultants was leaving early. He asked where he was going. "From time to time," came the reply, "you need some rest." "Ah," expounded Onassis, "you are a happy man. You go to play when you want to. You are not *obliged* to play."

Onassis's life with Jackie rapidly came to seem predictable only in its irregularity. There was a perfunctory Aegean cruise, then the couple went their separate ways—Jackie to Turville Grange, her sister's country home in England, and Onassis to Paris. A photograph of him dining with his old friend Maria Callas at Maxim's promptly spawned the first generation of rumors of divorce. The fact that they had a genuine reason for meeting each other—to conclude business arrangements left unresolved by the litigation with Panaghis Vergottis—was not mentioned in most press reports of the encounter.

Onassis joined Jackie at Turville Grange, but the visit was not a huge success. Never adept at the sort of skills required for English country weekend parties, he caught a cold and retired to his room to nurse it while Jackie sauntered through the winter woods with Rudolph Nureyev and Margot Fonteyn. The party was enlivened by the presence of an uninvited guest who made off with $12,000 worth of Lee's jewelry. He was later apprehended with the help of a photographer who had been hiding on the grounds and had taken a picture of the interloper climbing up a drain pipe.

Jackie returned to New York by herself, and Onassis returned to Paris.

305

While she was observed fox hunting in Peapack, New Jersey, and visiting the graves of her late husband and brother-in-law, Onassis was once again making the rounds of his Paris haunts. He even threw a party at Régine's nightclub. They spent Christmas together aboard the *Christina*.

In January 1969 the couple was together in New York but soon separated again, Jackie for Hyannis Port, Onassis for Paris and Skorpios. The pattern continued through February and March. Jackie contented herself with a New York season leavened by periodic forays to Palm Beach and Switzerland, where Lee was undergoing treatment in a sanatorium to increase her weight. Ari spent much of his time in Paris, where the press zealously logged his appearance at nightclubs with Elsa Martinelli while overlooking the attendance of Ms. Martinelli's husband. He was also much in demand in Athens, where the Omega project was boiling along. His visits to New York were brief, his nights out in the company of his wife were the object of much public attention. At P. J. Clarke's, a Third Avenue bar, Jackie was followed to the ladies' room by a throng of curious women. Only during April, on an eight-day cruise aboard the *Christina* from the Canary Islands to Trinidad, did the couple enjoy any real intimacy.

Onassis's view of his new status was expressed with characteristic terseness. Asked if marriage had changed his way of life, he replied, "Not at all. . . . What do you expect me to do?" Even so, he was obviously elated at the exclusive social occasions he attended with his wife. Gardner Cowles, the publisher of *Look*, attended a dinner in Manhattan given by David Rockefeller in honor of the newlyweds. Onassis's manner was unusually muted. "He was happy to stay in the background, basking in his wife's social radiance," recalled Cowles. "One had the sense of a man who felt he had accomplished something prodigious and was proud of it."

There could be no doubt about Ari and Jackie's affection for each other. A friend recalled one of their anonymous nights out at Elaine's, the hangout of New York's literary community. They had their distinctive private jokes, like any other couple—Ari tried to stop his wife from smoking by grabbing at her pack of cigarettes every time she reached for it. After dinner he hailed a cab and amused his guests by arguing with an aggressive driver, ultimately persuading him to take five passengers when he was only allowed to take four. "They seemed to have a very good thing going," the friend recalled.

In his rare moments of home life, another Onassis was apparent. He took an immediate liking to John-John and Caroline Kennedy, which was instantly reciprocated. The simpler side of his nature, which had always responded to young children, was fully engaged. There were walks in Central Park, visits to Shea Stadium for the World Series, even games of musical chairs aboard the *Christina.*

Initially, Jackie satisfied the protective and possessive side of Onassis's nature. "She is like a diamond," he explained revealingly, "cool and sharp at the edges, fiery and hot beneath the surface." In the first few months of his marriage, the nature of the compact between himself and Jackie was the essence of simplicity. "Jackie is like a little bird that needs its freedom and its security," he said, "and she gets them both from me."

Her appetite for good things increased. The Upper East Side of Manhattan, with its department stores and boutiques, is something more than one of the world's most elaborate consumer centers. It enforces the taste of the rest of urban America, and so the purchases of the rich and famous are of more than passing interest. Jackie is estimated to have spent $1.25 million in the first year of her marriage on clothes, most of it on Madison Avenue. True, the figure is based on nothing more precise than the sums quoted by the boutique owners themselves and so is open to deep suspicion. Yet there can be no doubt of the scale and seriousness of her shopping expeditions. Her visit to a store often produced among the staff and other shoppers a reaction verging on hysteria, which was intensified by the speed and variety of her purchases. Spring of 1969 was the high watermark of her activities, and when *Woman's Wear Daily* labeled her the "retailer's best friend," it caught the appropriate feverish note. "Jackie O continues to fill her bottomless closets," the paper reported. "She is making Daddy O's bills bigger than ever with her latest shopping spree. She is buying in carload lots."

Jackie had always loved to shop. What was different about this phase of her acquisitiveness was that it seemed compulsive, exceeding even the lavish standards of the wealthy circles in which she moved. She bought dresses and jewels by the dozens. If a designer had a little blouse she fancied, she would order it in every color it was made in. It seemed unlikely she ever wore many of the clothes she bought.

Onassis had more than encouraged the emergence of Jackie the Super-spender. During his courtship he had showered her with bracelets and rings. As a wedding present she received a million dollars' worth of heart-shaped ruby earrings and a matching ring the size of a raspberry that covered her entire knuckle and had to be removed when she used the telephone. For her fortieth birthday there was a forty-carat diamond

307

ring ("much finer than Elizabeth Burton's stone," ventured a jewelry expert) and a pair of earrings designed by Onassis himself. These represented the Apollo 11 moon landing, with which Jack Kennedy had been involved: a moon and an earth of twenty-two-karat gold, encrusted respectively with rubies and diamonds and sapphires and diamonds, were linked together by a chain of space ships, also in gold. Jackie wore the contraption on only one occasion—its excessive weight made it impractical for regular adornment.

Onassis was rarely at a loss when asked to justify his wife's appetite for things. "God knows Jackie has had her years of sorrow," he once said. "If she enjoys it, let her buy to her heart's content." To a reporter in Paris he said, "There is nothing strange in the fact that my wife spends large sums of money. It would be abnormal if she didn't. Think how people would react if Mrs. Onassis wore the same dresses for two years, or went to second-class beauty salons, or rode around in a family-type automobile. They would immediately say that I am on the verge of bankruptcy and that soon my wife will be forced to work to earn a living." A more metaphysical idea was contained in his thought that "if women didn't exist, all the money in the world would have no meaning."

Although Onassis took genuine pleasure in giving people things, his gifts were rarely made in a spirit of undiluted altruism. He usually expected something in return. There is no evidence that he gave much deep thought to the question of what he required from Jackie. She was a possession he took pleasure in displaying. In one sense her capacity to adorn his name and person was in itself a sufficient source of satisfaction, at least for a time. The spending had another function. It provided a link between them during their long separations. A diligent student of their peripatetics calculated that during their first year of marriage they had been together for 225 days, apart for 140.

Gore Vidal pronounced on the early stages of "the marriage of the century" in uncharacteristically glowing terms: "Onassis is dynamic and protective, and I think that is what Jackie needs. Not so much physical protection, but a certain kind of warm fatherly affection. Though she's independent, she's very brittle. She needs someone who will give her a thicker lining. I think Onassis is doing this for her. Jackie is very happy with Onassis—perhaps more so than with her first husband. . . . John Kennedy was wrapped up in himself and his career. She was like another room at the White House—almost a prisoner. Can an omnivorous, rich businessman of sixty-four find happiness with an attractive woman of forty? The answer is YES!"

Yet, despite their evident affection for each other, the marriage never seemed to develop that organic quality that characterizes the most happy unions. They satisfied important needs in each other but probably not the most basic ones. It is difficult to see how they could, given the diversity of their concerns and endeavors. Jackie took her responsibilities as a mother very seriously, and this dictated that she should spend most of her time on the East Coast since John-John attended school in New York, Caroline in Massachusetts. Onassis's most time-consuming business concerns were in Greece, and his children, though grown up, preferred to spend most of their time in Europe.

A series of minor disputes brought home to him the fact that his wife had a strong will that was often at odds with his own. Onassis complained about the expense of the Skorpios house, for which he had so eagerly made her responsible. Some television sets had been installed for Jackie in ignorance of the fact that the island was beyond the range of conventional signals. Many of Jackie's decorating ideas did not please him, most notably the removal of the allegorical friezes on board the *Christina*—his past, he felt, was being eroded. Jackie neglected the farm he had created on Skorpios, with its Arab stallions and Shetland ponies. She was "always reading," he complained.

Such pinpricks might not have assumed such importance had it not been for the attentions of the press. One almost certainly unlooked-for consequence of their marriage was the shedding of the last vestiges of privacy. Journalism, as an astute Australian reporter, Murray Sayle, once remarked, is often like "blind man's buff played with straight razor blades." It seemed for a while as if all the sharpest razor blades in the business were bent on dissecting Onassis's marriage. Not only were there more Jackie-watchers than previously, they were also more ruthless in their methods. This was not just because they had to be in order to penetrate the cordon Onassis tried to throw around his wife's private life. There was also a "new Jackie" to replace the old, without the residual defenses imposed by respect for her widowhood. Accordingly, the paparazzi went to some lengths to provoke Jackie into dropping her smiling mask of timidity.

For a while, the Onassises' uninvited contacts with the press were characterized by a kind of exasperated good humor. A case in point was the night of July 31, 1969, when Onassis held a pink champagne party at his favorite Athens nightclub to celebrate Jackie's fortieth birthday and banned photographers from the premises. "It was first light, about 5 A.M., when the vigilance of assorted doormen, waiters, and toughs started flagging," said one of the eager throng of ostracized photographers. "Then we broke in." "Have you no God?" Ari asked, laughing as he and Jackie found themselves surrounded by the familiar faces behind the clicking cameras and flashing strobes. "Why do you keep chasing us?" he asked, as he offered them champagne and food. "Why do you keep running away from us?" asked one photographer. "Ah, but that is my trick," Ari said. "If it was too easy to take our pictures, none of you would have bothered."

The problem was more serious in New York, a city where privacy is literally priceless. On the afternoon the couple spent watching *I Am Curious (Yellow)*, an erotic Swedish film, Jackie left Ari to enjoy the last scenes by himself. There was later some doubt as to the precise nature of the melee that ensued on the sidewalk outside the movie theater. A crowd of photographers was present, including Mel Finkelstein of the *New York Daily News*. "It looked as if she was going to say something," Finkelstein recalled. "Then she reached for my hand as though we were going to shake hands. Then she took my right wrist with her right hand, and very slowly and deliberately brought her other hand under my left elbow. She put her left leg out and flipped me over her thigh." The theater's doorman suggested that Finkelstein, in his efforts to position himself for a camera shot, had become entangled in his equipment and tripped over himself.

A more serious embarrassment occurred in February 1970 when a cache of personal letters from Jackie to her former escort, Roswell Gilpatric, was discovered and offered for sale. Despite Gilpatric's protests that the letters had been purloined, their contents were reproduced in American newspapers and magazines. The final letter, enclosed in an envelope bearing the return address *"Christina,"* was written during Jackie's honeymoon cruise and mailed from Greece on November 13, 1968. It read:

> Dearest Ros—
> I would have told you before I left—but then everything happened so much more quickly than I'd planned.
> I saw somewhere what you had said and I was very touched—dear Ros —I hope you know all you were and are and will ever be to me—
> With my love,
> Jackie

The publication of the "Dear Ros" letters, though glossed over as unimportant, seems to have widened the gap between the two partners.

310

Onassis, for his part, appears to have felt less inhibited about his continued friendship with Maria Callas. In May 1970 Henri Pessar, a diligent Ari-watcher, reported that Onassis spent four successive evenings at Maria Callas's apartment on avenue Georges Mandel, leaving between 12:30 and 1 A.M. each night. Lest there should be any mistake about the significance of those meetings, the press was encouraged to come to Maxim's on May 21, where the famous lovers would be happy to pose for photographs. Jackie arrived in Paris the next day and spent the following evening in a tête-à-tête with Onassis at the same table in the same restaurant. Again photographers were welcome to preserve the event for posterity.

Maria Callas may have been less than enchanted by her role in this small drama. Four days later she was admitted to the American Hospital at Neuilly. Her presence there was ascribed to "sinus troubles." A nurse, however, told the press that she had arrived in a coma induced by an overdose of sleeping pills.

Three months later Onassis flew by helicopter to Tragonisis, the island belonging to the Embiricos family, with whom Maria Callas was staying, and presented her with a pair of 100-year-old earrings. Under a big beach umbrella, he gave Maria a kiss on the mouth. He also kissed Maria's poodle. A photographer, offshore in a small boat, recorded both displays of emotion with a telephoto lens. His pictures were sold to publications on both sides of the Atlantic. Callas was quoted in the press as saying, "I have great respect for Aristotle, and there is no reason for us not meeting here since Mr. Embiricos is a mutual friend." Jackie, still in New York, was moved to put in a prompt appearance in the Aegean. As *Time* magazine put it, "Responding like a dalmatian to the fire bell, Jackie flew to Greece, to Onassis, to the yacht *Christina*, and to squelch rumors."

The most resourceful Jackie-watcher was Ron Galella, a free-lance photographer who by his own estimate earned $50,000 a year from his encounters with his beautiful prey. His attitude to the "world's most famous couple" was graphically expressed in the Christmas card he sent his friends (including the Onassises) in 1970. Galella was featured receiving a gift from a bearded Santa Claus. Beside them was a theatrical placard with the inscription "The Payoff, starring Aristotle Onassis as Santa and Ron Galella as the Paparazzo."

After an incident in Central Park which ended with Galella's being hustled away while trying to photograph John-John, the combatants resorted to the courts. Jackie sought a permanent injunction to keep the photographer 200 yards from her Fifth Avenue apartment and 100 yards from her person anywhere else. Galella counterclaimed, seeking $1.3 million in punitive damages for "false arrest, malicious prosecution, and interference with his livelihood as a photographer."

When the case eventually came to trial in 1972, it became the most popular off-Broadway show in town and raised a number of significant legal points. The First Amendment, with its unequivocal stress on the public's right to know, seemed to favor Galella's suit. Jackie was a "public figure," and Galella's slides, which were shown in court, established beyond reasonable doubt that he had been harassed by the Secret Service agents who accompanied John-John and his mother on their walks in Central Park. Jackie's case rested on the assertion that the photographer had inflicted "emotional distress" by his constant surveillance. This, too, could be inferred from some of Galella's pictures, most notably one which featured a rear view of Mrs. Onassis sprinting across Central Park meadow to avoid Galella's attentions.

In his testimony, Galella asserted that Jackie was "snobbish and cool" but "the number one cover girl in the world." He only wished she wouldn't wear sunglasses because that reduced the selling price of his photographs. The court heard evidence on "the Ron Galella smile," which had been evolved in desperation. Jackie testified, "I try to keep smiling, to keep my head up . . . because I believe he wants to provoke me into an unusual position." The extent of her ordeal was explained by Jackie's lawyer, Simon Rifkind, who countered Galella's suggestion that his client represented "the American dream" with the claim that the photographer had made her life into a nightmare.

While the case was lumbering through the New York courts—logging up a transcript of 4,700 pages—more summary justice was being meted out in Greece. In February 1972, Nikos Koulouris, one of the most aggressive Skorpios-watchers, was taken to court in Lefkas and sentenced to six months' imprisonment on four charges related to his attempts to take pictures on Skorpios. He was found guilty of endangering the landing of the Piaggio, which was bringing in Mrs. Onassis, by maneuvering his motorboat across the landing route, and of insulting behavior. The local police officer told the court that Jackie, whom he had seen after the incident, had been frightened and shaken. "She told me: 'I am scared of this man. He is dangerous,'" he said. A witness for Onassis said that Koulouris had pelted John-John with stones and had then taken pictures of him as he was throwing the stones back. "Mr. Onassis is thinking of giving up Skorpios because of Koulouris," said the witness.

312

"He has become the shadow of Mr. and Mrs. Onassis and won't leave them in peace. Mrs. Jackie Onassis is very upset with the defendant, who has made her life unlivable."

Shortly afterward the livability of Jackie's life was further enhanced by a legal decision in New York. The judge there ruled that Ron Galella's activities had indeed violated her privacy and granted her the injunction she desired. The appeals court, however, was less sure about the merits of her case. A year later it reduced to a mere twenty-five feet the distance Galella was obliged to keep from Jackie. Her triumph was ultimately one of principle alone. Galella more than overcame the temporary setback to his career with a best-selling book and a series of lecture tours in which he lamented Jackie's fall from grace.

Onassis, though vigilant in his defense of Skorpios, was not much involved with his wife's attempts to defend her own privacy in New York. When the bill for Jackie's legal costs in the Galella affair was routinely forwarded to him, Onassis refused to pay. He told a reporter that he had "nothing to do with the damn thing." Jackie's prestigious and expensive law firm—Paul, Weiss, Rifkind, Wharton and Garrison —was reduced to the undesirable expedient of suing its own client for the recovery of costs. Jackie complained to her friends that her husband was "cheap." In the end, a check for $235,000 was sent. "Everyone is happy now," Onassis remarked casually.

But not very. In the summer of 1972 Onassis dined with Elizabeth Taylor in Rome and splashed a glass of champagne into an importunate photographer's face. Jackie was not amused and protested that "the children had seen news reports" of the incident. "I am ashamed of you," she told Onassis, who passed on this piece of information to a columnist. His own gallantry and his wife's supposed mean-spiritedness thus became a matter of public record.

A new level of grotesquerie was achieved when Jackie was photographed in the nude while preparing to bathe off Skorpios. The resulting full-frontal portfolio was printed with the title "the billion-dollar bush." At a New York cocktail party John Kenneth Galbraith, the economist and Jackie's occasional erstwhile escort, got off a polished one-liner with Mrs. Onassis: "I didn't recognize you with your clothes on."

Onassis himself rose to the occasion with a pantomime of his own. While cruising on the *Christina* off the coast of Sardinia he spied a photographer going about his stealthy business onshore. He had himself rowed to the beach, where he dropped his swimming trunks and shouted to the photographer, "Now it's my turn!" The end product was subse-

313

quently well displayed in *France-Dimanche*—though, out of deference to public sensibilities, the aging tycoon's crotch was airbrushed to appear hidden in a shadow thrown by a nearby tree.

The joke, like most good jokes, was Onassis's way of dealing with anguish. He was surrendering to the fact that his marriage to Jackie was, on one level, global property. He had some control over its disposal but not much. At the same time, as the world's most famous displaced person, he was almost obsessively concerned with the world's evaluation of his activities, and that was not always flattering. Late in 1970 Fred Sparks, a Pulitzer Prize-winning journalist, produced *The Twenty Million Dollar Honeymoon*, a book purporting to give a detailed account of Jackie and Ari's first year of married life. It was not a good book, nor was it particularly well researched, but it did explore some sensitive areas. Onassis was shocked by the book's picture of him as the indulgent squire of a gold-digging hedonist. Beneath his exhibitionism there had always been a core of vulnerability. The suggestion that his wife's spending was a surrogate for other needs was particularly wounding. If she was indeed "emotionally malnourished," as the review of Sparks's book in *The New York Times* suggested, the failure was in part his. Sparks's volume was soon accompanied in the bookstores by *The Fabulous Onassis: His Life and Loves* by Christian Cafarakis, a former mess steward on the *Christina*. Cafarakis claimed to have seen the Onassises' legendary marriage contract of 170 clauses. Those he quoted seemed designed to keep Onassis in his place. He also dwelt on Jackie's spendthrift habits. Onassis approached his own biographer, Willi Frischauer, and promised to help him "strictly unofficially" if he would undertake a biography of his wife that rose above the level of keyhole journalism. (Frischauer did eventually produce a sound biography of Mrs. Onassis, but it was not published until eighteen months after her husband's death.)

Although the attentions of the press and publishing houses greatly magnified the problems of the marriage, they were surmountable. What could not be overcome was the weight of their respective pasts, which drove them first gradually, and later inexorably, apart. In his biography, *Jackie*, Frischauer laid great emphasis on the shadow cast by John F. Kennedy. As a former first lady, Jackie was still greatly in demand for the various ceremonies which commemorated the late president's life and career. They were also important to Jackie, not so much for herself but as a method of establishing an identity for her children. Such events, however, put a severe strain on Onassis, whose manhood was firmly based on the need to be a hero in his own legend. They were a constant

314

reminder of the fact that his wife's charisma had more to do with her dead husband than her living spouse. If the problem was self-induced, it was nonetheless real. The demands Onassis made upon his women were both complex and self-contradictory. They had to be satisfactory vehicles of self-promotion and adoring females; and they also had to simultaneously accept his engulfing protectiveness and withstand his massive ego. Jackie was better equipped than most to deal with the man but hopelessly unequal to the problems presented by his family. Certainly, it could be argued that she fulfilled the contractual obligations implicit in their original union. The trouble was that Onassis began to change the rules of the game. He was worried about his children and, perhaps for the first time in his life, needed the support and strength of a real wife. Since both Alexander and Christina insisted on perceiving Jackie as an interloper who had deflected their father from the cherished possibility of remarriage to their mother, the new Mrs. Onassis was in no position to be very supportive to her husband. Indeed, her very existence further complicated the already complex problems of communication between Onassis and his children. For Christina, her stepmother was *e kyria* ("madame"), for Alexander she was "the geisha."

Christina seemed the more immediate problem. Her face, even after her nose had been bobbed, gave evidence of real strength of character, but she could not escape the consequences of a rootless upbringing. Never an eager student, she learned dancing under Margot Fonteyn and was educated at a series of expensive finishing schools in New York, London, and Lausanne, Switzerland. She emerged a good linguist but with no real sense of place. In her late teens she divided her time between London—where her mother lived—Lausanne—the home of her maternal grandmother—Paris, Monaco, Athens, and New York. Her contacts with her father, both before and after his marriage to Jackie, were erratic but intense.

She was his "pet," and nothing she wanted was ever refused her. But his generosity had its limits—what he gave her either had to be asked for or to be offered out of his own largesse. When she purchased a color television set for her Monte Carlo apartment Onassis was furious, ostensibly about the extravagance. Yet only a few weeks earlier he had bought her an emerald necklace worth a dozen television sets. The episode, though apparently trivial, reflected his immense possessiveness. Christina was never allowed to grow away from her father. When in desperation she did manage to break away, Onassis was both hurt and irate.

Onassis's possessiveness even extended to choosing Christina's husband for her. His mistake was to underestimate how much of his own temperament his daughter had inherited. Paradoxically, Christina's admiration for her father made it difficult for her *not* to stand up to him. "How could I fall in love when I have a father like mine," she once remarked. "As soon as I meet a boy, I immediately compare him with my father, and my father comes out best. Whenever we go to a nightclub together, he makes everything come alive."

Onassis wanted the best marriage for his daughter, but to him "best" had economic overtones. The Goulandris family controlled four separate shipping enterprises, including more that 130 vessels valued at a total of $2 billion. They owned yachts, islands, race horses, and soccer teams. Peter Goulandris was twenty-three years old, personable, and good-looking. His mother was a member of the still richer Lemos family. A male offspring of a Goulandris-Onassis union would become the Croesus of Greek shipowners, linking in his person three of the largest Greek shipping empires in the world. Once it had taken shape in Onassis's mind, the match, like any other business arrangement, became a foregone conclusion. The possibility that Christina might not wish to marry anyone for a while, let alone a Goulandris scion, seems never to have occurred to her father.

Up to a point, Christina complied with her father's wishes. She liked Peter and was often seen in public with him. On five separate occasions she agreed to marry him. Each time, however, she canceled the engagement party. Discreet pressure exerted on her father's behalf by Artemis the Matchmaker and later by Jackie was to no avail. Christina would not be moved.

She spent more and more time in Monaco, the furthest she could get from her father without actually cutting loose. It was the one place she knew he would not follow her—since his troubles with Rainier, he had not set foot in the principality. It was there, at the swimming pool of the Hôtel Métropole, that she met Joseph Bolker, a forty-eight-year-old realtor from Los Angeles.

Bolker was small, dark, silver-haired, and wore steel-rimmed glasses— an Onassis without the aggressiveness, the sense of humor, or the paunch. He was a teetotaler and a nonsmoker, and although he had been divorced some years previously, he seemed the epitome of the earnest and puritanical North American male. He had raised four daughters and had amassed a modest fortune erecting single-family homes in southern California. He had come to Monte Carlo under the auspices of the Young Presidents Association, an organization that existed to further the

316

aims of its sober, upwardly mobile members. He liked to swim to keep in shape. He was also a good and patient listener.

On their first meeting at poolside, Bolker found Christina "a very poised young lady." On their second arranged meeting he was surprised to find out she was so young. He was also surprised to discover her surname. Further meetings led to her opening her heart. She told Bolker she was sick of Europe, the rootlessness of her existence, her family and her father, which prompted Bolker to feel that Onassis was a "lousy father." Christina told him she wished to come to California, and he did not rule out the possibility. Nonetheless, he was not altogether pleasantly surprised when she appeared on his doorstep in Los Angeles without having told her family where she had gone.

His instinct was to do the decent thing. When Christina refused to tell her family where she was, he called her mother in the south of France. Tina, according to Bolker, suggested they should either get married immediately or go their separate ways. "Ari will never give his consent to any man," she said. The worst thing they could do would be to allow the situation to drift. Alarmed by this view of events, Bolker gently told Christina that it might be best if she went back to Europe. Christina became hysterical: "What's wrong with me? Aren't I good enough for you?" she shouted, and dashed out of the room. Bolker found her in the bedroom in an emotionally overwrought condition and rushed her to a hospital.

They were married on July 29, 1971, in Las Vegas. Onassis, who was on Skorpios celebrating Jackie's forty-second birthday, was informed of the event by telephone. "He was furious," a guest remarked: "He did not try to hide his anger. The news exploded like a bomb on the island." Onassis's displeasure soon found concrete expression. For the next six months the couple were, in Bolker's words, "subjected to extraordinary pressures."

Without any evidence, Onassis promptly took the darkest view of Bolker's motives. First, he made it absolutely clear that as long as Christina stayed married, she would never receive a penny of the trust established for her and Alexander after Onassis's legal settlement with the US government in 1955. This was easily done, since three years previously Onassis had reserved the right to continue the trust, which then had assets of $100 million, throughout his children's lifetime and to make whomever he pleased its beneficiaries. The move had been designed to accommodate the possibility of further demands on his estate by Jackie, but it could now be used to assert his will over Christina.

317

The role of his first wife, Tina, in the whole affair became an increasing obsession with Onassis. She had recently filed a divorce suit against the Marquess of Blandford, and Onassis not unnaturally concluded that any "advice" she may have given to her daughter was connected with her own plans for the future. She had been spending an increasing amount of time looking after her Niarchos nephews and nieces. In September it became apparent that this was more than simple concern for her late sister's offspring. Tina spent a highly publicized two weeks with Stavros Niarchos at a Breton seaside resort. Niarchos took the saltwater cure each day. Although the maître d' at their favorite restaurant never saw them holding hands, he deduced from their general intimacy that they were "very much in love." On October 22 they were secretly married in Paris, the only relative present being Tina's mother, Arietta. Alexander and Christina Onassis were informed of their mother's remarriage by registered mail.

At the best of times such news would have distressed Onassis; as it was, it drove him wild. Alexander, who was also furious, suspected that Tina had facilitated Christina's marriage to make her own less difficult, and he told Onassis so. Onassis's inflamed imagination seized on the makings of a conspiracy. Tina first denied and then admitted that she had met with Bolker prior to the marriage. Onassis deduced, again without evidence, that she had provided a financial incentive for the match. To get the facts, he ordered one of his staff to have Bolker's telephone tapped.

The results did not support Onassis's suspicions. By now, Bolker was alarmed by the family passions he had unwittingly aroused. The stress, he said, was "tearing Christina apart," and he did not feel able to protect her. Costa Gratsos flew out to California and found him "quite a gentleman." By mutual consent, a break was made when Christina flew to London to see her doctor. She then called her husband to say she was coming home "regardless of her father's demands" and asked him to organize a twenty-first birthday party for her on December 11 at a French restaurant in Beverly Hills. The party was a gloomy occasion: Bolker had already lost hope. He hid his disappointment philosophically. "She is a young woman," he said, "and should not be alienated from her father."

In this cruel and ugly situation both Bolker and Christina achieved a measure of simple dignity. In February 1972 Bolker started divorce proceedings—under California law a declaration of irreconcilable differences was enough for dissolution. Christina observed, "He may soon be just my ex-husband, but he will always be my best friend. I am too Greek and he is too Beverly Hills. That's really the trouble." The divorce became effective in May 1972. By then she had become partially reconciled with her father, though her relations with Tina remained uneasy.

Jackie was evidently upset by the dark passions which stirred within the Onassis family, both because of their intensity and because they made her feel like an outsider. She was also concerned about the impending breakup of Lee's marriage to Prince Radziwill. In some ways Jackie was as much a victim of circumstances as the unfortunate Joseph Bolker had been. The whole business had been conducted far beyond the range of her tightly controlled emotions. Her instinct was to bury pain; the Onassis instinct was to let it rip. This was hardly Jackie's fault, but it did not prevent Onassis from giving vent to his feelings of frustration with his wife. His fury was as vehement as his earlier generosity had been exaggerated. "My God, what a fool I have made of myself," he told friends when asked about his wife. He felt he had been deluded, and the realization was painful. Jackie, he asserted, was "coldhearted and shallow."

He felt cheated in his marriage and betrayed by his family, among whom he still included Tina. He seriously began to believe that his luck might be deserting him.

It was in this mood of depression that he experienced the greatest disaster of his life.

22
LOSS OF CONTROL

THE MOST IMPORTANT HUMAN BEING in the world for Onassis was his only son, Alexander. For a Greek, any Greek, a son is a significant portion of himself. The fishing boat is built, the house is bought, the vines are sown not just for the immediate needs of the family but for the future of the son. The son is his guarantee of immortality. For Onassis, with so much to bequeath and with an ego so overpowering, his son represented his own imperishable destiny.

The symbolic importance of Alexander to his father did not insure a comfortable relationship. Onassis never did manage to evolve a clear idea of how to bring up the heir to his vast fortune. Even before his parents' divorce, Alexander had been a shy, introverted child with few acquaintances of his own age. It was not as if Onassis were an overprotective father, rather the contrary. Onassis's own experience seemed to affirm the validity of the hard-knocks school of child rearing. "Aggression," says Professor Georgakis, "was his idea of education." Alexander never had a bodyguard and was allowed to swim in the sea from the *Christina* from an early age. If Onassis had a theory of child management, then immersion at the deep end played a large part in it.

Alexander demolished his first speedboat at the age of nine when he gave it full helm at forty-five knots "just to see what happened" (it

320

somersaulted three times but fortunately threw him out on the first one). At the age of eleven he had written off his second speedboat by colliding with one of the *Christina*'s metal lifeboats.

Onassis's own inner conflicts were often expressed in the way he treated his children. At times he could be harsh and impatient—"I've told you to do it, so do it," he would say—but these moments alternated with others when their every escapade was bathed in waves of admiration. His main contribution to Alexander's development was his concept of the excellence and the importance of being an Onassis. He successfully indoctrinated the infant Alexander with the idea that he was something apart, that the rest of the world was populated with beings who had their price, most of whom would seek his company only for his money and because he was an Onassis. Alexander and his sister accordingly grew up in an atmosphere of luxurious privation. Their only relaxed relationships were with crew members of the *Christina*. They possessed no real friends, only employees.

Yorgo Zakarias, the youngest crew member of the *Christina*, was closest to Alexander. Yorgo had been sixteen and polishing the brightwork when Alexander, then eight, had started talking to him one day, asking who he was and where he came from. Alexander was always interested in the welfare of the crew members—he had been overcome with remorse when his impetuosity with the speedboat had landed one in the hospital—but Yorgo believes he was singled out because he was the youngest. Soon, being a companion to Alexander when he was on board became Yorgo's unofficial job. Alexander's passion then and always was mechanical things—first toys, electric cars, and electric boats in the swimming pool and then real boats in the sea. The pair would spend hours dismantling machinery and radio equipment and then putting it back together. Onassis himself showed little direct interest in the boy, although he did help teach him to swim. Later, Alexander began to manifest a lively interest in girls as well as machines. Yorgo remembers an occasion when Alexander, then about fifteen, read that Brigitte Bardot was aboard a yacht in Cannes. "Let's go and see her," he said to Yorgo. They took a speedboat and raced along the coast from Monaco to Cannes, located Bardot's yacht, and proceeded to drive around it in circles until it began to rock drunkenly in their wake. Bardot appeared at the rail hurling insults until Alexander, well satisfied with the expedition, ordered a return to base.

At age sixteen, Alexander failed his exams at the lycée in Paris after a dilatory academic career. Professor Georgakis was dispatched to Paris

321

to talk some reason into him. "I was surprised at the maturity and the subtlety of judgment of this young man whom I was really meeting for the first time," he recalls. "He knew his father like a coin collector knows the two faces of an old, battered, and much treasured coin. But in those days he was very bitter about him, because he had neither the time nor the system for the boy." Georgakis failed to convince Alexander that exams were worth working for. He was pulled out of school and set to work in the Monaco office. His father explained, "If you are not going to study then I'm not going to pay for you to stay on at school." Alexander later regretted the early abandonment of his studies—they might have provided him with a means of independence from his father —but was not particularly regretful at the time.

His parents' divorce heightened his introspection. Both were inclined to use the children as long-distance pawns in their own game of emotional chess, betraying confidences that they might let slip if they could be used against the other. Alexander felt that Tina was particularly treacherous in this respect. He learned to keep his private thoughts and feelings to himself. Originally, he had held his father very much to blame for the divorce because of the Callas episode. Later he was not so sure. He learned that his mother, too, had been unfaithful, thus stinging Onassis into what might be fairly called a male chauvinist revenge.

Once he was old enough to appreciate such matters, Alexander realized that women posed a peculiar problem for his father. Even in his sixties Onassis still maintained a healthy sexual appetite. He could not gratify it on casual affairs with pickups or with prostitutes without attracting unwelcome publicity. Alexander recognized this need for a woman, though he wished it could be Tina. He was upset by his father's marriage to Jackie, not simply because he did not care for Jackie but because it was yet another example of his father's insensitivity to the children's feelings. He was particularly incensed at being "used" at the wedding to create a semblance of family unity by his presence. "I didn't need a stepmother," he said sometime after the ceremony, "but my father needed a wife." For Callas—or "the singer," as he called her— he had a sneaking regard and recognized her as a worthy companion and adversary for his father. They even had a couple of reasonable conversations.

By the time Onassis married Jackie, Alexander had already achieved a degree of emotional independence from him through a relationship with a woman old enough to be his mother. The Baroness Thyssen-Bornemisza was a lovely and complex woman. She was the daughter of a British rear admiral and, as Fiona Campbell, had achieved international fame as a fashion model. She married Baron Thyssen in 1955 and had two children, Francesca and Lorne. They were divorced nine years later. When she met Alexander Onassis in the winter of 1967, she was thirty-five years old and he was nineteen. For the next five years she was, in her own words, "his mistress, mother and priest confessor."

When Fiona first met Alexander, she encountered a temperament that remarkably combined withdrawal with arrogance. In appearance he was very like his father, though slimmer and slightly taller. He was also nearsighted and wore heavy, horn-rimmed glasses. His father had succeeded in indoctrinating Alexander with an exaggerated concept of his own importance, yet at the same time he had hammered his personality into the ground until there virtually was none. Alexander had few friends and none with whom he could have a reasonable conversation about anything other than machinery. He found it difficult to talk with people and was utterly at a loss with someone as domineering and bombastic as his father.

Yet it was clear that Ari, in his own way, was very fond of his son and that Alexander admired his father in return. Aristotle Onassis and Howard Hughes were the two heroes of Alexander's cosmos, but he admired them for their achievements, not for what they were. Nothing embarrassed Alexander more than his father in full extroversive flow. He was ill at ease in the Onassis business circus of sitting up all night drinking and driving bargains. Sir Frank McFadzean, then managing director of Shell, recalls one such meeting: "Alexander hardly said a word, he seemed uncomfortable when his father was letting his hair down, certainly the very opposite of Ari with his great knack of relaxing in the company of virtually anyone."

Alexander found it difficult to convey the tension of his relationship with his father, even to someone as close to him as Fiona. She could not understand why he went to the most extraordinary lengths to avoid meeting him, even having squads of doctors lined up to testify that he was unfit to travel to wherever he was ordered to put in an appearance. When the phone rang, she knew immediately when it was Onassis by the expression of wilting horror on Alexander's face. "It is impossible to *talk* to him," Alexander wailed. In the end he started tape-recording their phone conversations to show her why.

They consisted of Onassis in monologue, either haranguing or needling his son. The needling might take the form of Onassis starting a telephone conversation with a rendition of "Singing in the Rain." He would pause at the end of a verse and ask a question relevant to the song —"How's the weather at your end?"—and, without waiting for an answer, break into the next verse. It would be several minutes before Ari finished his act and Alexander would have a chance to break in, and when he did, it would be with monosyllabic replies or grunts of affirmation or denial. More often it would just be Ari screaming reproach and abuse, with Alexander holding the phone away from his ear, apparently not even listening until the tirade ended. Onassis never bothered to conceal his disapproval of his son's affair with the baroness.

Alexander felt he was trapped, eternally enmeshed in the Onassis business machine. He had no salary but an allowance. If he wanted a new car, he had to ask Ari. If he wanted a day off or even to go away for the weekend, he had to ask Ari. If he displeased his father, the money tap would be promptly tightened. He did not dare leave the office for an hour in case his father phoned, though in Monte Carlo at least he alleviated the problem by rigging the phones and training the operators so that, when Onassis called, he did not know whether he was talking to Alexander in the office or in his flat on the floor above. Only once in five years did he manage to get away for two weeks' holiday with Fiona without "something coming up." He managed this by extracting a written promise for a fortnight's leave from his father and even then was mildly surprised when Onassis did not attempt to renege.

The irony was that everything Onassis did to Alexander was done with a view to grooming him for the succession, and that most things he did were counterproductive. His egocentricity made it impossible for his thinking on the subject to moderate a simple belief that the best person to inherit the empire of Onassis was Onassis. What he wanted of Alexander was for Alexander to be like him. It solved every conceivable problem. Still, he was able to perceive the necessity of firing Alexander's interest in the family business and to make concessions in that area, if necessary. It became clear that aircraft were Alexander's consuming passion, whereas ships never would be, at least at the level of pushing markers around a map of the world in Monaco. Onassis gave him Olympic Aviation to play with. It owned a fleet of small planes which provided scheduled services to the smaller Greek islands, an air taxi, and local charter service. Alexander did rather well with the company, demonstrably better than his father was doing with Olympic Airways, but Onassis seemed more inclined to pique than pride. "Never forget," he grunted, "Olympic is only the leaves of the tree. The roots are the ships."

Their relationship contained all the terrible antinomies of a love affair. One tirade against his son ended with the accusation "and you didn't

324

call me to wish me 'happy New Year.' " Alexander always referred to his father's proudest possessions with mocking irony: the *Christina* was "the tub," the Piaggio "a heap of junk." Yet his respect for his father always outweighed his exasperation. According to Georgakis, "Alexander could penetrate the tycoon facade and understand all the dreams and paranoia of the man. You cannot love or respect a man who has no center. Alexander could see the center."

The central dilemma of their relationship was that Onassis wanted to create in his son something that no parent can bestow but can only help to emerge—a sense of independence and sureness of self. Onassis had achieved his own by the dramatic expedient of breaking with his father and most of his family. Yet Alexander could not rebel because he had convinced himself, or allowed Ari to convince him, that his father held all the cards. He had no qualifications which would allow him to get another job of consequence. Because of his poor eyesight he could never get a commercial flying license and earn a living as a pilot. The shipping business was divided into Ari's friends and Ari's enemies. Neither would be likely to give him a job if he walked out.

The tension in Alexander was expressed in the way he would drive. Miraculously, he had never had a serious car accident. Passengers found the most disconcerting aspect of his driving technique his refusal to slow down for corners. He loved the winding *corniche* (cliff road) between Monte Carlo and Cannes and rarely made the journey without collecting a ticket for speeding. Alarmed for his safety, Fiona Thyssen talked him into trading in his Ferrari for a relatively sedate Mercedes.

Fiona was convinced that there was nothing both Ari and Alexander wanted more than to *talk* with each other. Instead they had maneuvered themselves into a situation where it was only possible for Ari to talk *at* Alexander. As she listened to the tapes of their conversations on the phone, she became more and more convinced that Ari was desperately trying to provoke a reaction from his introverted son. She reckoned that Ari would have enjoyed it if Alexander had talked back, calling his father a son of a bitch as Ari himself would have reacted to such treatment. In the same way, she suspected that Ari, though he professed total opposition to their affair and wanted a sixteen-year-old virgin from another shipping dynasty as his daughter-in-law, would have been privately delighted had Alexander defied him and married her. Onassis was, she felt, so desperate for proof of what he could recognize as "guts" in Alexander that even the wrong marriage would have been a price worth paying.

Under prompting from Fiona, Alexander began to voice his opinions

325

to his father both on personal and business matters. It was a slow process, and Onassis would rarely follow his son's advice, but he started to listen if only to disagree. There were those at Olympic, where Alexander was very popular with the staff, who even hazarded the opinion (though not to Onassis) that the son was more in touch with the realities of modern business than the father. Alexander felt that his father's "Tarzan-style" approach to business problems was no longer effective in a large bureaucratic organization.

Developments elsewhere in the family aided the tenuous emergence of real communication between father and son. Alexander had always shared his father's antipathy for Stavros Niarchos. When he met Fiona Thyssen, she had been a friend of the Niarchos family for some years and a regular visitor with her former husband to Spetsopoula. Alexander had given her a "them or me" speech. Fiona had written to Eugenie Niarchos explaining that she was sorry, she was in an impossible position, and she was also in love. It had to be Alexander. When Alexander's mother, Tina, became Mrs. Niarchos, he was, if anything, more upset than his father. Their shared horror at Tina's supposed defection to the other side brought the two men closer together. More important, Onassis also began to share Alexander's cool opinion of Jackie.

In September 1972 they enjoyed a night out in Athens of the kind that Jackie abhorred. Among others, they took on Elsa Martinelli and Odile Rodin, the widow of Porfirio Rubirosa, in a crockery smashing competition of prodigious dimensions. After their evening of revelry, the headline in an Athens newspaper ran: "Olympic Plate-smashing Record Goes to Onassis." The fact that the Greek government had previously outlawed plate-smashing as a barbarian practice offending "the noble traditions and mores of Greek society" gave the event an added piquancy. There was never any prosecution, though there was plentiful photographic evidence of Aristotle and Alexander Onassis's enjoying each other's company while smashing a lot of plates.

Alexander's increasing self-confidence may have been related to his having decided what to do with the next stage of his life without consulting his father. He had come to the conclusion that the only answer was to get the academic qualifications he lacked. Fiona, who encouraged him in the project, undertook to provide a financial safety net (she was moderately wealthy in her own right), and a whole floor had been set aside in her Swiss home where he could have lessons and pursue his studies to university level.

Alexander did not tell his father of his intention, but they did meet

326

to discuss—and agree on—increasingly important subjects. He went back to Fiona exhilarated after a meeting with his father in Paris on January 4, 1973. He had secured agreement on two issues that were important to both of them. Onassis had promised to replace the Piaggio aircraft, which Alexander regarded as dangerous, with a helicopter. The plane, though nominally part of Olympic Aviation's fleet, was used almost exclusively for ferrying Onassis and his guests between Skorpios or the *Christina* and the mainland. Alexander was distrustful of amphibians in general and had once hit a log while landing the Piaggio in a storm off Saint Tropez. Alexander was pleased by his father's mild acceptance of the safety arguments. He was also pleased by his father's admission that his marriage to Jackie had become pointless. They discussed the practicalities of a divorce and how much Onassis money should be settled on her.

On the evening of Sunday, January 21, 1973, Alexander in Athens spent an hour and a half talking on the phone to Fiona in London. They made arrangements to meet in London the next evening. Alexander explained that he had one important job to do before flying on to see her. His father had announced his intention of taking the *Christina* across to Miami, and he wanted the Piaggio on board with a trained pilot (the helicopter which was to replace the Piaggio had not yet arrived). Unfortunately, the regular pilot of the Piaggio, Donald McGregor, a former BOAC captain, had been grounded while recovering from the effects of an eye operation. An American pilot, Donald McCusker, had been recruited, but though experienced with amphibians, he had never flown a Piaggio before.

Alexander had devised an ingenious solution to the problem of how to train McCusker as quickly as possible. As the boss of Olympic Aviation, he was qualified to check McCusker's suitability as a charterer. He therefore intended to take him up in the Piaggio on the following day to check him out as a legal formality, charter the plane to him, and assign McGregor to travel as a passenger for a week of familiarization flights. On this basis, Alexander reckoned he would be able to fly to London to see Fiona early Monday evening.

During their conversation, Alexander also talked about the crash the previous summer of a British European Airways Trident jet at Staines, near London Airport, in which all on board had died. The causes, which were only now being established with certainty, were a perfect illustration, said Alexander, of his own thesis about aircraft accidents: there was very rarely one single, major reason for a crash; usually it was a matter

327

of a lot of little things building up. He had come to this conclusion earlier when his father's Lear jet had crashed into the sea on a night approach to Nice airport, killing the two Kouris brothers who were piloting it. The wreckage was never found, and the cause of the accident, beyond a strong indication of pilot error, never established. Alexander had admired the Kouris brothers and felt a personal responsibility in that they had been coming to collect him. He and Fiona spent two weeks scouring the beaches of the Cap d'Antibes in a vain search for traces of wreckage. In the end Alexander had concluded that it had probably been a combination of circumstances: the younger, less experienced brother making his first night landing in tricky conditions at one of Europe's more difficult airports, a navigational error, and, perhaps, someone pulling the wrong lever at the wrong moment.

Alexander was usually as careful in planes as he was maniacal in cars and speedboats. As a pilot he always flew by the book, although he had been known to fly rescue missions to collect urgent hospital cases from the smaller islands in weather no other Olympic pilot would fly in. The reason for his sobriety in planes was, apart from his vivid appreciation of the risks, due to his desperate eagerness to be accepted as an equal by the men he most admired: the professionals. It was one of the great disappointments of his life that he would never be able to qualify as a commercial pilot because of his poor eyesight, and he was one of the unfortunates who was unable to wear contact lenses.

McCusker, the new pilot, was tired. He had spent the previous afternoon and night traveling from his home in Ohio to Athens, where he had arrived at 8 A.M. on Monday. He and McGregor had spent much of the day sitting around fortifying themselves with coffee, waiting to hear what the plan was. It was his first taste of what it meant to be a personal pilot for Onassis. The reason Alexander had had to recruit from outside was because there were no regular Olympic pilots who cared to volunteer for the job. None of them wanted to be up at all hours waiting upon the whims of their boss, more often than not far from home. They preferred the unglamorous but secure rostering of commercial flying when a man and his family knew when he would be where.

Since McGregor was an integral part of the training scheme, Alexander asked him to accompany McCusker and himself on the first flight. The subterfuge meant that both McGregor and McCusker needed tickets for the flight to keep everything legal. These were issued by Olympic, listing their takeoff time as 3:15 that afternoon and their destination as "Athens local." The intention was to do a few sea landings

328

and takeoffs between the nearby islands of Aegina and Poros and then return to base.

When the trio got to the Piaggio, they discovered that nobody had the preflight checklist—the list of safety checks which a pilot is required to make before takeoff. Alexander, anxious to avoid any further delay, felt that he knew the plane well enough to go through the checks from memory, and besides there was also McGregor in the back who knew the plane equally well and who could monitor their checks. Alexander went through the checks to his and McGregor's satisfaction, explaining the procedure to McCusker. Alexander sat in the right-hand seat with McCusker to his left. He handed the stick over to McCusker (the plane had dual controls), who taxied the Piaggio to the edge of the runway, where they held, awaiting permission to take off. While they waited, Alexander carried out two more checks—the engine run-up and the "before takeoff" check.

As a departing Air France Boeing 727 hurtled down runway thirty-three, the control tower cleared the Piaggio for takeoff with instructions to turn left once it was airborne, presumably to avoid the wake of the 727. McCusker, who was to pilot the plane, acknowledged the instructions and eased the Piaggio onto the runway. He accelerated to 100 MPH and was airborne. Two seconds later, at less than one hundred feet altitude, the plane banked sharply to the right, hitting the ground with the right float. Still veering to the right, it spun off the runway onto the right wing tip. The plane then cartwheeled in a circle for another four hundred sixty feet, smashing the nose, the tail, and the other wing before coming to rest. When the rescuers reached the wreckage, Alexander's head injuries were such that he was recognized only by the monogram on the bloodstained handkerchief in his pocket.

Aristotle and Jackie Onassis were in the United States. Christina Onassis was in Brazil. Tina and Stavros Niarchos were in Switzerland. Fiona Thyssen was still waiting in London. The news, when it reached them (in Christina's case it was from the radio), could not have been worse—Alexander's right temple had been reduced to pulp, his brain was apparently dead, only a miracle could save him. McGregor and McCusker, though badly hurt, had every prospect of surviving. Alexander was placed in an oxygen tent on a life-support system after a three-hour operation to remove blood clots and relieve pressure on his brain. Despina Papadopoulos, the wife of the Greek dictator, was one of those who spent much of the night at the hospital.

At midnight a neurosurgeon arrived from London. The next morning

Aristotle and Jackie Onassis arrived with a Boston neurosurgeon. A heart specialist came from Texas. Fiona Thyssen arrived from London, and the Niarchoses from Switzerland. By 2:00 in the afternoon of January 23, nearly twenty-four hours after the crash, it was clear that nothing more could be done. Onassis told the doctors to wait until Christina had arrived from Brazil to say "good-bye" to her brother, and then "to torture him no more." Christina arrived later that afternoon. Alexander died at 6:55 P.M.

Onassis's grief was so extreme that at first he refused to bury Alexander. It was not altogether clear what he wanted instead. "In moments of tragedy," says Professor Georgakis, "a volatile character swings into unforeseen dimensions of illogic." His impression was that Onassis wanted the body "deep frozen," organically preserved against the day when brain surgery was sufficiently advanced to restore Alexander to life. In the end, Georgakis, playing Antigone to Onassis's unwitting Creon, was impelled to write his friend an impassioned letter protesting that he had no right to dispose of the soul of his son in this way. Even in this, so ingrained was the habit and so instinctive the reaction, Onassis haggled. He would consent to the burial, but only if it were inside the chapel on Skorpios. Georgakis protested that this was impossible, the church would not allow it, it was a privilege reserved for saints. A compromise was found. Alexander was buried beside the chapel, and an annex was later built to cover the grave.

Onassis was certain that the crash was no accident. So convinced was he that sabotage was the cause that he offered a million dollars to anyone who could prove it: half a million to the informants and another half a million to the charity of their choice.

The Greek courts appointed a team of investigators to establish the cause and to see whether there were grounds for criminal proceedings. Much has been made by conspiracy theorists of the fact that air force men predominated on the investigating team, the implication being that the military dictatorship wished to suppress "the truth." Certainly the investigation was shrouded in the kind of heavy-handed cloak of secrecy which can only encourage such lively suspicions. But the appointment of men from the air force, the only repository of aviation expertise in Greece apart from Olympic, was perfectly normal in a situation where Olympic was an interested party.

When the investigators delivered their report on April 20, 1973, they were unequivocal as to the cause of the accident. The connections between the control column and the ailerons on the wings had been

330

reversed. The effect of this would be that when the pilot gave "left wheel"—as McCusker would have done in obeying the control tower's request to turn left after takeoff—the plane would in fact have banked to the right. Then, when the pilot had taken the instinctive reaction to an unexpected banking to the right, namely the application of even more left wheel, he would only have made matters worse: increasing the right bank and so steering the plane into the ground. This explanation perfectly fitted the behavior of the Piaggio, but McCusker, who had suffered amnesia as a result of his injuries, was unable to confirm or deny that this was in fact what had happened. And it had all been over so quickly that McGregor, in the back seat, had not been able to see what was happening at the controls.

This report, which was still top secret, did little to clarify matters as far as Onassis was concerned. If anything, it provided an added impetus to his unshakable belief in sabotage. Who had crossed the controls, and when? The same question was taxing the imagination of the top management of Olympic, but for somewhat different reasons.

The switch had been made some time between November 15 the previous year and takeoff on January 22. On November 15, an Olympic mechanic had removed the control column of the Piaggio. It had been replaced with a new control column by a different mechanic on November 25. This had been a routine replacement of old parts to prepare the plane for its new certificate of airworthiness (C of A). On January 18, Greek Civil Aviation Authority and Olympic inspectors had spent two hours examining the plane. They had granted the Piaggio its C of A subject to the usual formality of a test flight. This would have involved a pilot taking her up and pronouncing her sound. The fatal flight, therefore, had had a dual function: it had been a C of A test flight, and not only McCusker but also the plane had been on trial.

If Onassis and the Olympic management accepted this report, then at least the Olympic management was faced with two equally unpalatable alternative explanations. Either the controls had been crossed because the Olympic mechanic had installed the control column incorrectly, or someone had been able to spend enough time in the hangar subsequently to undertake the lengthy and skilled job of sabotage. Either explanation added up to some degree of negligence by Olympic. Onassis's offer of a reward had already provoked a furious row at Olympic, with the Olympic men arguing that it was tantamount to admitting to the traveling public that, when they flew Olympic, they were flying planes which were not adequately protected from passing maniacs.

331

There were other, more objective reasons for being unhappy with the official investigation. Its methodology was demonstrably shaky. To take one of the less arcane examples: it is normal practice when examining wreckage after an accident to daub any control links with paint before disconnecting them. This is so that, subsequently, there can be no doubt as to what was connected to what and how at the time of the accident. Yet the vital link, the misconnection which the investigators said had caused the crash, had apparently been painted *after* disconnection by the investigators. It was the mechanic who stood to take the rap who noticed this after the plane had been reassembled: the paint, he pointed out, was *under* the nut which had to be removed to make the disconnection.

What was more, those who had flown with Alexander found it impossible to believe that he had missed anything quite so obvious as crossed controls during his preflight checks or that the inspectors had also missed it five days earlier. McGregor in particular has a vivid memory of the day he first flew the Piaggio with Alexander when he, like McCusker on the day of the crash, was being checked out. McGregor had flown 707s for years. On big aircraft the wings are not visible from the cockpit, so normal practice is to trust to the mechanics and merely check that the controls are "full and free" (not jammed). This is what McGregor did during his preflight checks the first time he flew the Piaggio, and Alexander had pounced upon the misdemeanor. The wings (and hence the flaps and ailerons) were visible from the cockpit of a Piaggio, he pointed out, and McGregor, he insisted, should always perform visual checks. McGregor adds that even on 707s visual checks are always done for C of A test flights: the pilot has someone on the tarmac doing them for him and reporting what the flaps, ailerons, and rudder are doing. He therefore finds it doubly difficult to believe that Alexander did no visual preflight checks that day. But, from where McGregor was sitting in the rear, he himself could not see the wings, and he cannot remember whether or not Alexander did glance back out of the window during the preflight checks. Other people we have interviewed who flew regularly with Alexander find it equally difficult to believe that he omitted the visual checks. But then they also find it difficult to believe that he went ahead, as he undeniably did, without a preflight checklist.

The crisis for Olympic was threatening to become a major one. Not only did it seem probable that the airline was going to have to shoulder some of the responsibility for Alexander's death, but Onassis himself, crushed with grief, had lost all interest in it. He refused to go anywhere near the airport or the offices of the airline. Its whole future, at least as a creation of Onassis, seemed in jeopardy. Onassis's own private sabotage investigation was getting nowhere. The reward offer had brought thousands of tips, mostly from cranks, but all had been painstakingly followed through with no result.

There was one face-saving possibility which Olympic's own flight safety department under Captain Xydis was pursuing. The Piaggio had taken off dangerously close behind the departing Air France Boeing 727. Calculations which took into account the fact that the Piaggio had started its takeoff a third of the way down the runway suggested that it would have reached the area of maximum turbulence created by the 727 only one minute and thirty-four seconds after the larger plane had passed. The most dangerous turbulence is that caused by the rotation of air currents around the wing tips of an aircraft as it begins to experience maximum lift at takeoff. Rather like the wake of a ship, these vortices of spinning air persist for some time after the passage of the plane, and the bigger the plane causing them in relation to the size of another plane which runs into them, then the greater the danger that the smaller plane will be spun around on its own axis like a top. A 727 is a giant in relation to a Piaggio, and the Piaggio, because it had not started its run at the end of the runway, was closer to the heels of the big jet than it should have been. Two minutes is regarded as the minimum safe time lapse in such circumstances. The behavior of the Piaggio also appeared consistent with this explanation, which is the one McGregor himself favors to this day.

The problem with the 727 theory was that it was totally unverifiable. It was condemned to remain a hypothesis by the simple fact that eddies of air—unlike crossed controls, a mechanical failure, or a tape recording of conversations between a pilot and the control tower—are by their very nature impermanent. They do not remain as concrete evidence for an investigator and must be discounted if there is more positive evidence. Besides, the theory did not suit Onassis. It shifted at least some of the blame onto Alexander (he should not have allowed McCusker to take off when he did), and Onassis's conviction that Alexander himself was totally innocent of error was the one coherent element in his sabotage mania. By that stage, recalls an Onassis aide, "he had built himself a whole edifice of suspicions and paranoia, the number of suspects and supposed motives, was almost limitless." The list was headed by the CIA and his business rivals.

The Olympic management asked Onassis if he would commission

an impartial outside investigation in the hope that it would resolve matters one way or the other. Onassis needed little persuading. He was prepared to spend his entire fortune and the rest of his life, if necessary, to find out how Alexander had died. The Boeing Aircraft Company advised him that he could do no better than hire Alan Hunter, a British accident expert. He was on vacation at the time, but Onassis had him tracked down and rushed to Athens under conditions of extreme secrecy. Nobody was to know who he was or what he was doing, and only a handful of people at Olympic ever knew about Hunter's investigation.

Hunter's confidential accident report, dated July 6, 1973, did not tell either Onassis or Olympic what they wanted to hear. Not only were the contents of the report never made public, but its existence was never revealed. We managed to obtain a copy. Hunter produced incontrovertible evidence that the aileron controls had indeed been reversed. The official inquiry had got it right, even if for the wrong reasons and by a less than impeccable procedure. The clincher was something the air force men had missed: a line of small marks on the leading edge of the right aileron which had been caused on impact. These marks aligned precisely with a line of small screw heads which protruded from the undersurface of the wing, facing the leading edge of the aileron. They could only have caused those marks on the aileron if the aileron had been *up* (that is, banking the plane to the right) at the moment of impact. The plane had been driven straight into the ground.

Hunter's report did not presume to establish when the controls had been reversed or by whom. But it did indicate how mistakes could easily happen when a new control column is being installed in a Piaggio. The column controls the ailerons by a system of chains, cables, and pulleys. Chains and cables can only be pulled, not pushed. There are, therefore, two parallel cables running back from the control column—one attached to either end of the control column chain (it was here the faulty connection was made), and one delivering the "left bank" demand to the ailerons, the other "right bank." To bank to the right, a pilot applies "right wheel" (like a motorist turning right). But it is the *left* cable which delivers the command to the ailerons. The report points out, therefore, that

334

when connecting the cable to the chain link a potentially confusing situation exists. When correct

APPLY RIGHT WHEEL = RIGHT AILERON "UP"

BUT . . . . . PULL RIGHT CABLE = RIGHT AILERON "DOWN"

The method used during assembly for deciding upon the "correct" cable was to pull it and watch the aileron before making the connection.

It only requires an understandable lapse for someone to believe that it is necessary to "make the cable do what the wheel must do" for a reverse connection to be made. A cable cannot be pulled. This sort of situation is conducive to human error.

Is this what happened when the Olympic mechanics changed the control column? The mechanics denied the suggestion hotly, and neither Onassis nor Olympic were inclined toward this explanation, which was why Hunter's report never saw the light of day. Yet Onassis's own private sabotage investigation was fizzling out. None of his investigators really believed in sabotage anymore.

Their reasoning was as follows. Nobody, not even Alexander himself, knew he would be in the plane on its next flight until two days earlier. There was no possibility whatsoever that Onassis himself would be aboard the next flight of the Piaggio. It was to be a C of A flight, and the person who would perform it would certainly be McGregor, on his own. It was only because McGregor failed his eye test at the last moment that Alexander was in the plane at all. It was just conceivable that if the saboteurs had been in collusion with one of the handful of people who knew of Alexander's last-minute decision, they would have had time to undertake the lengthy job of clandestine sabotage by reversing the aileron connections. Possible, but very unlikely, and exceptionally risky. More to the point, if they had been that close to Alexander, then they would have known that this particular method of sabotage was stupid because it had no right to succeed. Alexander's reputation for thoroughness was such that a less obvious form of sabotage would have seemed necessary, particularly when it was a matter of a C of A flight after a control column change.

To the end, Onassis remained unable to accept the conclusions of the Greek inquiry and the Hunter report, although Olympic tacitly admitted liability by giving McGregor an ex gratia payment of damages for his injuries. A similar agreement was drawn up with McCusker, though Onassis refused to let the payment for McCusker go through. "Keep the case open," he cried whenever it was suggested that the settlement with McCusker should be made. "Something might still come up."

Nothing ever did. Indeed, what was on the record seemed more than enough: reversed controls, takeoff before air turbulence had subsided, skimping of the preflight procedures, and a new pilot, tired after a night of traveling, flying an unfamiliar plane. There is no reason to believe that Alexander's death was anything other than a tragically perfect illustration of his own thesis on the cause of accidents: usually they are a matter of a lot of little things adding up.

336

23
EXERCISE IN WILLPOWER

THE OVERWHELMING SENSE OF LOSS felt by Onassis after the death of his son was concealed behind a facade of normality. After Alexander's funeral he took to the sea, sailing across the Atlantic from Dakar in West Africa to the Antilles with Jackie, Pierre Salinger, the one-time press secretary of President Kennedy, and Mrs. Salinger. When he was not attending to business, Onassis spent the days arguing with Salinger about journalism and politics. Salinger, who had been involved in both professions, was a lively companion, but he was struck by the detachment of his host.

When the talk turned to personalities, Onassis's opinions were positive enough. "Of his peers," Salinger recalled, "he preferred those who had fought their way ruthlessly to the top, like himself." Yet when Onassis spoke of his own experiences he seemed remote from the story and himself. Salinger felt as if he was speaking about a different person.

Although he ate little, Onassis still took care of his health, swimming twice a day in the *Christina*'s pool. He was tender to his wife and attentive to his guests. Although the subject of his son's death was avoided, there was no doubt of the extent of his grief. Each night, when his guests had gone to sleep, he walked the *Christina*'s deck. Only at dawn did he join Jackie in the stateroom he shared with her.

Onassis spent more time than usual on Skorpios that summer. The "Erectheum" of Billy Baldwin and the farm he had created for Jackie were completed. The trees, shrubs, and flowers his ships had brought from all parts of the world were especially luxuriant. To his guests Onassis seemed almost his usual self—a considerate host and a skilled conversationalist. His relationship with Christina seemed much improved, though he still scolded her about her taste in men and clothes. There were guests on the island the day Christina arrived with Alexander's possessions, which she had brought from Monte Carlo. Onassis was subdued, but he spent the afternoon talking with a visiting archaeologist and his sister, Artemis.

His personal charm remained undiminished. An intelligent young American woman who met Onassis for the first time as a guest on Skorpios soon after Alexander's death told us, "When he talked to you, you had this feeling that he was totally absorbed in the conversation. I think this was genuine and not something put on. There are a lot of people who feel it is their duty to appear interested as hosts but you can see if it is not genuine. I was bowled over."

For all his gregariousness, Onassis remained secretive about his emotions. He never spoke of his grief, though his suffering was plain enough. His insomnia became acute. Where in the past he had stayed up all night out of pleasure, he now did so to avoid sleeping in the dark. When there were guests, he would drink ouzo and sing the nostalgic Spanish and Greek songs he loved. When there was no one, he roamed the island alone, waiting for the dawn. He would spend much of the night outside the chapel of the Holy Virgin, sitting by the tomb of his son.

Old enmities that had once seemed so important now scarcely mattered. Onassis was reconciled with Tina and Stavros Niarchos. In the summer of 1973, they came to Skorpios to visit Alexander's tomb and went swimming together.

When Onassis went to New York, he spent much of his time sitting in Gratsos's office, talking about the past with its simpler verities and more measurable standards of success. He and Gratsos relived the Argentinian phase of their lives—the first ship, the first love, the first million. "He did not really want to live," recalled Gratsos. "He felt cheated and he blamed himself for having been cheated. He felt responsible for Alexander's death. But there was no self-pity at all. There was an extraordinary degree of stoicism in the way he took everything."

Business provided some solace and diversion. The spring and summer of 1973 was a boom time for the tanker business, and Onassis's fleet of over a hundred ships—including fifteen VLCCs of over 200,000 tons—was excellently placed to take advantage of it. The worldwide economic boom enormously increased the demand for tonnage operating out of the Persian Gulf. Spot market rates more than trebled, and supertankers that had been getting $2.5 million for a trip around the Cape of Good Hope were suddenly able to command $8 million or more. After some years of uncertainty about the economics of supertankers—inflation had seriously eroded profit margins on long-term charters—Onassis again became bullish about their prospects.

He decided to plow his profits, estimated at $100 million in the first nine months of 1973, into further expansion. He ordered four more VLCCs from Japan and two ULCCs (Ultra Large Crude Carriers) of over 400,000 tons from yards in France. It was a serious miscalculation. The third Arab-Israeli war and the ensuing Arab oil embargo in October 1973 had a traumatic effect on the whole industry. The increase in oil prices and the subsequent fall in demand plunged the tanker market into the worst depression in its history. Not only were the new ships not needed, Onassis's existing fleet, so stretched in the earlier months of the year, found a third of its tonnage suddenly idle. Spot market rates sank to levels that barely paid the cost of the fuel, and none of the oil majors were interested in taking on additional long-term charters. Onassis eventually canceled the two French ULCCs, losing his $12 million down payment in the process.

Onassis was astounded by the new evidence of Arab determination, but no more so than the rest of the industry. He was also confident of his ability to weather the crisis: where others might go bankrupt, all he had to do was cut back the scale of his operation. A more personal humiliation lay in store for him in rural America. For it was there that one of the ironclad certainties of his business career—that everyone has a price—took its most severe battering.

The people of New Hampshire take seriously their state motto, "Live Free or Die." They are equally proud of New Hampshire's nickname, the Granite State, finding in it an echo of the flinty virtues of their Revolutionary forebears, the first to take arms against the British. It is one of America's smaller states, with a scattered population of under one million. Onassis first set foot there in the winter of 1973, when he arrived to defend his plan to build an oil refinery on New Hampshire's most beautiful stretch of coastline.

The collapse of Onassis's bid for the refinery contract in the Omega project two years earlier had not altered his determination to break into this end of the oil industry. Commercially, it made better sense than ever after the Arab oil squeeze. A refinery of his own would offer Onassis regular employment for his fleet and a strong position in the distribution market, which was contracting with ominous rapidity. With the arrival of the energy crisis, President Nixon had appealed to patriotic Americans to turn down their thermostats and reduce their gasoline consumption.

The idea of building a refinery in New Hampshire was put to Costa Gratsos in New York by Peter J. Booras, a Greek-American and an old family friend. Booras ran a printing and greeting card company of his own in Keene, a sleepy little New Hampshire town, but until the refinery project turned up, his heart was in the Booras Endless Bread System. He had calculated that 15 percent of every loaf was thrown away in restaurants because of their reluctance to serve the customers with end crusts. Booras therefore devised a machine that extruded a continuous stream of dough, baking it by electronically agitating its molecules. No crusts, no waste. He patented his design and waited for the big bread companies to beat a path to his door. He was still waiting when the possibilities of promoting an oil refinery for New Hampshire occurred to him.

Booras enjoyed an acquaintance with New Hampshire's Republican governor, Meldrim Thomson, Jr., who was anxious to broaden the state's economic base. Most of the traditional industries—textiles, shoes, and timber—were in decline. In October 1973 Booras told Gratsos that the governor would smooth the way for a major refinery project. Gratsos had been looking for such an opening in North America. Onassis was pressing him to get a refinery project under way, and he had already sent Robert Greene, an expert from Texas, to look at a possible site in Nova Scotia. Greene had previously worked on the abortive Omega refinery project. Now Gratsos asked him to drop everything and go to New Hampshire. It was, Greene recalls, an unusually succinct briefing—find a site, Onassis wants a refinery there. "Obviously Onassis had the ships, and if he could find somewhere to move the oil to, he could tie them up okay," Greene told us. "But the way Gratsos put it, it was just like ordering a Cadillac."

Gratsos and Booras began crisscrossing New Hampshire in a helicopter. It soon became clear that the state's short but ruggedly beautiful coastline, a major tourist attraction only eighteen miles long, provided the best locations. Greene decided that the ideal site would be on Durham Point, a wooded headland overlooking the fine sweep of Great Bay. Tankers could discharge their cargoes at a terminal built on one of the granite outcroppings known as the Isles of Shoals, ten miles offshore. A pipeline would carry the crude from there to the refinery.

With money provided by Onassis's New York headquarters, a team of real estate brokers, mostly Greek-Americans, fanned out through the selected area, buying options on a wide swath of property. The fewer people who knew what the land was wanted for, the cheaper it would come. Some ingenious explanations were invented for anyone who asked what was going on. Evelyn Browne, a white-haired professor of physical education at the University of New Hampshire, Durham, was one of them.

A man turned up one day at Salty, her 170-acre estate, with an offer on behalf of a "dear friend" who craved isolation. Salty was not for sale, but Miss Browne was ready to listen to offers for another of her properties, Amblers Acres. A few days later, the "friend" arrived with a bid for both Salty and Amblers Acres. "My wife and I have had a walk around and peeked in your windows and we just love your big wide floor boards," Miss Browne says he told her. Assured that there was no question of the land being developed, Miss Browne agreed to sell Amblers Acres. It was to be a legacy for his little boy, the buyer told her, somewhere quiet and unspoiled. "I was relieved and quite cheerful at the thought of selling twenty-five acres . . . for $80,000 to such a nice Greek family," Miss Browne later explained. Other people were told their land was earmarked for an old people's home, a plush beach club, a bird sanctuary. The deception saved Olympic Oil Refineries thousands of dollars. It also earned them undying local hostility when the real nature of the project was revealed.

By the time that an obscure New Hampshire weekly paper called *Publick Occurences*, run by a blacksmith-turned-editor, broke the story, Onassis had spent about $6 million on options for more than 3,000 acres around Durham—almost 20 percent of the area of the town. As rumors and resentment grew, Olympic Oil Refineries was forced to go public. On November 26, police motorcyclists hurtled around the state delivering invitations to a special news conference by the governor in Concord the following day.

Governor Thomson's televised press conference made great play of the impressive figures attached to the proposed refinery: cost, $600 million; capacity, 400,000 barrels a day; hundreds of extra jobs; new tax revenue for the state. Onassis was mentioned only indirectly. Olympic Oil Refineries was described as a major international company "associated with Mr. Onassis." Some journalists present wondered how the company was going to get around the obvious environmental objections to the site on Durham Point, but most concluded that Onassis had sewn everything up before the announcement was made.

The furious controversy which followed Thomson's announcement took Gratsos and Onassis by surprise. The first protest group, Save Our Shores (SOS), was formed and in action within forty-eight hours. Its earliest efforts were received in Durham with enthusiasm. Even so, Onassis's team did not see much cause for alarm. Apart from Governor Thomson, the refinery project also had the unstinting support of William Loeb, then the most controversial—some would say notorious— figure in New Hampshire business and politics. He owned the state's only big newspaper, the *Manchester Union-Leader,* which faithfully reproduced the boss's profoundly right-wing views. Loeb's favorite soapbox was the *Union-Leader*'s page-one editorial column. Beneath a quotation from Daniel Webster—New Hampshire's most famous orator and statesman—to the effect that "there is nothing so powerful as truth," he would excoriate blacks, Jews, homosexuals, radicals, the Kennedy clan, the United Nations, and anyone else considered a threat to civilization as defined by Mr. Loeb. His editorials frequently went beyond the accepted bounds of political exchange—during the Middle East war, one had been headlined "Kissinger the Kike?" When the opposition to Olympic's proposals surfaced, the *Union-Leader* pulled out the stops for Onassis.

The backing of Loeb and Governor Thomson significantly influenced Onassis's tactics. As far as Gratsos and his team were concerned, they had the two biggest guns in the state on their side. Compared with that, the early opposition seemed laughable: a hastily organized bunch of environmentalists, home owners, lobstermen, fishermen, tourist industry operators, and faculty and staff from the university. Most of them came together under the umbrella of SOS, where William Loeb soon had them in his sights. The *Union-Leader* denounced SOS as "professional agin-ers and pseudo-environmentalists."

It was true that SOS was composed of something less than a cross section of New Hampshire. Away from the coastal strip, in big towns where traditional industries were ailing, there was considerable enthusiasm for Onassis's refinery. These were the conservative heartlands of the state, envious of the coast's tourist-based prosperity and resentful of the social divisions that had sprung up between them and the wealthy "liberals" in places like Durham. Booras, Loeb, and Thomson represented, in different ways, this stream of opinion in New Hampshire, and it was really the only one which the Onassis men had encountered until they came up against people like Nancy Sandberg and Dudley Dudley.

Nancy Sandberg was president of SOS, bringing to the job a formida-

342

ble combination of personal charm and organizational skills. She and her husband, Don, a local math teacher, farmed eighty acres inherited from her grandparents. Their handsome colonial house overlooked Great Bay, and at harvest time the Sandbergs sold their vegetables to their neighbors from a broken-down barn. SOS understood that it was going to have to fight the refinery project through the press and television. Nancy Sandberg was a media natural—darkly pretty, fluent, and sympathetic.

Dudley Dudley was an equally splendid asset. Born and bred in Durham, she was a descendant of the celebrated Daniel Webster. Two of her ancestors had been colonial governors in New England. Her husband, Thomas Dudley, contributed a third governor in his blood lines. Dudley Dudley was the first Democratic representative Durham had sent to the state assembly for years. She had come of political age with the great liberal causes of the 1960s—civil rights, the Vietnam War—and had acquired in the process a toughness that was not immediately apparent behind her blond good looks.

One of SOS's first efforts was to present a petition to Governor Thomson, signed by four thousand people, protesting the location of the refinery. The governor was not amused. At local meetings across the state, SOS and its supporters hammered away at what they saw as Olympic's weakest points—above all, the obsessive secrecy ordered by Onassis. "They were just like moles at first," Nancy Sandberg remembers. "Then when they had to come out into the light, they couldn't do it. There were too many questions they thought they would never have to answer." When they did attempt to justify their plan, the result was not always felicitous. Costa Gratsos's letter to an indignant Durham lady was a case in point:

> I cannot agree more with you as to the loveliness of the place.
> My family background, academic education and personal inclinations would make me the last person on earth who would like to desecrate a beautiful landscape. Unfortunately, the evolution of the world since the industrial revolution will inevitably result in the elimination of all that you and I and many other people cherish.
> Humanity has reached the point that urbanization and computerism are essential elements of survival. In other words, today and also in the future we shall have to choose between existence and beauty and it is not difficult to foresee the choice. Ecologically, the modern refineries can be as free of pollution as an apartment building.
> Aesthetically, a modern refinery, when illuminated, looks like a Christ-

mas tree and is not uglier than the modern sculptural masterpieces adorning the streets of the major capitals of the world.

The truth was that Onassis researchers had hardly begun work when *Publick Occurences* blew the whistle on the project. From October until the end of the year, SOS virtually had a clear run. Members planted awkward questions at public meetings and pestered Onassis's spokesmen for information they did not have. The Onassis men chose to view their opponents as primitive reactionaries. It was, one recalled, "like trying to bring electricity to grandma."

There were, nonetheless, some very high-powered experts on the locals' side. The protesters were greatly aided by scientists from two of America's most famous marine biology stations located on the Shoals. Olympic's early investigations had apparently overlooked their existence. Professor Fred Hochgraf, a specialist in pipeline metals at the University of New Hampshire, produced a lengthy report on the danger of oil spills and pipeline ruptures. He calculated that if Olympic's supertankers pumped 275,000 barrels of crude to the refinery every day, at least 3,360 barrels would *routinely* be spilled into New Hampshire's waters. If Olympic pumped half of the refinery's capacity back out to tankers for distribution, another 3,360 barrels of refined oil would leak into the ocean. Hochgraf based his figures on data from operational refineries around the world. A Shoals marine biologist spelled out what this meant. One part per million of crude oil in seawater could kill the larvae of lobsters and perhaps damage the lobster beds irrevocably.

In December, Olympic decided the time had come for a set-piece public relations exercise starring Onassis in person. It turned out to be a disaster from the moment that Onassis helicoptered over Durham en route to a lavish reception in Manchester. Loeb had prepared for his arrival in ebullient fashion. "Welcome to the two Big O's, Oil and Onassis," the *Union-Leader* trumpeted. "He is the nearest thing to Santa Claus New Hampshire will ever see." The communication from Durham was less festive. Huge letters, scooped out by the inhabitants in a snow-covered field, spelled "GET LOST ARI."

"I am not a Greek bearing presents to New Hampshire," Onassis began after Governor Thomson introduced him to the press in Manchester. "The last thing I would like to do is to impose an unpleasant investment on the inhabitants of New Hampshire. Particularly if we bear in mind that the people of New Hampshire are part of the American aristocracy. So, however, every aristocracy needs a kitchen." His thick accent surprised people. Half-hidden behind a bank of microphones, he

344

looked rather small and insignificant. Nancy Sandberg of SOS, who had gate-crashed the press conference, thought Onassis looked desperately old and tired under the television lights, like an aging actor battling through a part he hated. There was some perplexity in the audience as he plodded on with the kitchen metaphor. "All this time for years now, your supplies were coming from very far away—expensive restaurants. If we can produce a refinery clean as a clinic, without any smell and without any smoke, and if we can persuade and convince the experts and the officials of the environment and ecology, I hope we are doing something good for everyone. That's all I have to say."

Under questioning, the sure touch and easy affability which generally marked Onassis's dealings with the press deserted him entirely. When he said he would not impose a refinery on New Hampshire, he was asked if he meant the people or the state. "The state is the people, the people are the state," he answered curtly. The evasion fooled nobody and hardened the mood of the conference. When it was disclosed that Olympic was considering setting up an antipollution laboratory to be operated by the university, a journalist asked if that could be considered a bribe. There was also the inevitable question: If the enterprise was so advantageous to the citizens of the state, why had Olympic's representatives deliberately misled the property owners from whom they bought the options? Onassis smiled. He had come prepared with a prop to deflect the awful question with an awful joke. He held up a bottle of maple syrup, Governor Thomson's customary gift to visitors. "I have something to make a little joke with you," Onassis said. "We said we were coming to Durham to build a distillery for maple syrup. This is made by the governor . . . it's an exclusive syrup produced by the governor without the distillery."

Anne Gouvalaris, a local reporter, was sitting a few feet away. She thought Onassis looked dazed, his body seemed curiously floppy. "He was holding that jug of syrup in his hand with a look on his face that seemed to say, 'What in God's name is somebody as rich as me doing with this idiotic thing?'" Even the press corps felt awkward, and the questions dried up. Anne Gouvalaris buttonholed Onassis before his aides hurried him away. Didn't he think it was unfair, she asked, that because of his great wealth he could come along with offers which local people just could not afford to turn down? Momentarily Onassis came to life. "You don't force with money, my dear," he said. "You seduce."

As a public relations exercise it was a total disaster, though Onassis still appeared to think that it was possible to steamroller the opposition.

He kept telephoning Loeb from places around the world with suggestions that were counterproductive in the New Hampshire context. Loeb told us, "He wanted to hire the biggest law firm in New Hampshire. 'They have fourteen partners,' he'd say. 'They must be the best.' " Loeb and Governor Thomson tried to put Onassis straight. Business did not work that way in New Hampshire, they explained. One lawyer was enough if he was the right man. It was a bad idea to come on like Goliath in a state that provided plentiful opportunities for the emergence of would-be Davids. The right of individual towns to reject policies put forward by the state's central government had been built into New Hampshire politics for two hundred years. Things got done—or undone —at the annual town meetings, a durable relic of pure democracy open to every adult citizen. Now that Durham seemed set to veto the refinery, the question which the protesters were exploiting with considerable skill was whether the Thomson administration would dare to use its ultimate authority to overthrow home rule.

On March 4, 1974, the start of the annual town-meetings week, New Hampshire was subjected to the most intensive public relations barrage of the campaign. The nine daily newspapers published in the state carried an eight-page "supplement" crammed with blatantly prorefinery stories and information. "Don't let a noisy minority Stop Our State," the front page appealed. Inside were the home phone numbers of New Hampshire's 424 state legislators. Readers were urged to call them and solicit their support for the refinery when the state government voted on the issue.

This heavy-handed effort rebounded badly. Many citizens, outraged by the attempt to dress up hard-sell advertising as ordinary news, took Olympic's advice and rang their local legislators—to complain about the advertising blitz and urge a vote against the refinery. One representative in Portsmouth, whose annual meeting was held that day, received 147 calls, all antirefinery. One by one, obscure communities around the state agreed to give Durham the final say on the project; Governor Thomson's hometown, Orford, was among them.

Durham was determined to reject Onassis in style. On March 6 the biggest annual meeting in living memory opened in the Oyster River High School gym. Six television networks covered the event, their lights beating down on Durham's moderator, Michael Joseph, a Lebanese-American who claimed to be the only Arab around with no interest in oil. By a freakish stroke of timing, Olympic had chosen that day to announce that it would, after all, proceed with the refinery over Dur-

346

ham's objections if the state government gave the go-ahead. Voting took two hours, but hardly a soul left the gym. Olympic was defeated as resoundingly as its advisers had feared—144 votes for the refinery, 1,254 against.

Durham's decision was reviewed a few weeks later by the state legislature, and despite Governor Thomson's last-minute efforts to mobilize support, the refinery cause was lost. Dudley Dudley called upon the house of representatives to throw out Onassis just as New Hampshire had thrown out King George III two hundred years before by maintaining the principle of home rule. The house supported her by 233 votes to 109.

It is possible that Onassis's inept performance in New Hampshire was related to the steady deterioration of his marriage. Alexander's death had been the occasion for a brief renewal of tenderness, but it had not lasted. Despite Billy Baldwin's embellishments of the island, Jackie seemed more uncomfortable than ever on Skorpios. Guests sensed that she made an effort to be suitably hospitable for the sake of her husband, but the effort showed. She much preferred swimming on her own or reading. She would occasionally join in the singing and dancing but always seemed a bit stiff and inhibited. The British diplomat Sir John Russell, a Skorpios regular, thought the problem was social—"There was nobody there who had much in common with her, nobody she could be perfectly relaxed with."

New York was her scene, but it was never Onassis's New York of business and bars. They were seen and photographed together when El Morocco opened under new management, but the occasions they could genuinely share were becoming fewer and farther between. In January 1974 they made a trip together to Acapulco, where Jackie had spent her honeymoon with Jack Kennedy. It was not a happy expedition.

Jackie expressed a desire for a house in Acapulco. Onassis prevaricated —he did not want a house in Acapulco and resented what he presumed to be his wife's motives in asking for one. There were arguments on the ground and in the Lear jet on the way back to New York. Jackie lost her temper and said she did not expect anything from him, and he replied that she was not going to get anything. It was in this acid mood that he wrote his will on board the plane.

Greek law is punctilious on the question of wills. They must be written out in the hand of the legator to avoid any suspicion of senility. Nowadays, this stipulation has been reduced to the formality of copying a lawyer's typescript draft, but Onassis's will was entirely his own creation. The document he composed during the six-hour flight subtly wove together the strands of his life. Christina was to be the prime beneficiary but it began with an act of homage to his dead son:

> If my death occurs before I proceed with the establishment of a cultural institution in Vaduz, Lichtenstein, or elsewhere under the name of "Alexander Onassis Foundation," its purpose, among others to operate, maintain, and promote the Nursing, Educational, Literary Works, Religious, Scientific Research, Journalistic and Artistic endeavors, proclaiming International and National Contests, prize awards in money, similar to the plan of the Nobel Institution in Sweden, I entrust and command the undersigned executors of my will to establish such a Cultural Institution.

The problem of Jackie was briskly resolved: "Having already taken care of my wife Jacqueline Bouvier and having extracted a written agreement through notary in USA, by which she gives up her hereditary rights on my inheritance, I limit share for her and her two children John and Caroline to a lifelong income of $150,000 [per annum]." Onassis also examined the possibility of his wife's or her heirs' challenging this disposition. If this should happen, he wrote, "I command the executors of my will and the rest of my heirs that they deny her such a right through all legal means, cost and expenses charged on my inheritance." If it happened that his wife's legal challenge was successful, she was to receive no more than 12.5 percent of the total estate, the least he was allowed to leave her under the *nomimos mira* laws. Whatever distinctive status Jackie had enjoyed during Onassis's life, it would be discontinued after his death. He was prepared to care for her in much the same way he had done for the other women who had crossed his life. That was the least he could do and the most he was prepared to do.

The way in which he disposed of the management of his empire was intriguing. It was clear that the system of anonymously owned companies over which he had retained effective control all his life would not survive his death. He accordingly created two companies—one in which all his assets were consolidated, the other containing nothing but the shares in the first company. Christina, his principal heir, received all the assets in the first company. But she did not receive a controlling stake in the second one; that was left to the Alexander Onassis Foundation.

The device was another variation on the theme of control and ownership which had absorbed Onassis all his life. He wanted to keep his fortune together, but he also did not want Christina to exercise full

348

control over it. The foundation was both more and less than it seemed. Its board of directors consisted of his most trusted aides, who were left $30,000 annually over and above their salaries as long as they continued to work within the organization. If the foundation's Nobel-style functions were left rather vague, the same could not be said about its other duties. It was to run Onassis's business much as he had always done—to reinvest half of its net earnings, never to sell a ship that was capable of turning a profit, never to merge a company with outside interests. The skein of requirements and prohibitions stretched over the void left by the absence of a male heir. In the absence of a foreseeable future for the organization, it was designed to perpetuate the present. The spirit of Onassis would survive through the medium of a committee.

The will also benefited Onassis's relatives and the larger family of "collaborators" surrounding it. His sisters, Artemis, Merope, and Callirhoe, were to receive $60,000 annually for life. Others were rewarded in proportion to their status and loyalty. His cousin, Costa Konialidis, was assigned $60,000 annually for life. Gratsos and Cokkinis were each assigned $30,000 annually, along with Stylianos Papademetrious. Costa Vlassapoulos, another key man in the Monte Carlo headquarters, was assigned $20,000. Apart from the annuities, there were numerous other lump-sum benefactions for low-level staff. Georgia Beta, the chambermaid at the Glyfada house, who later sold her memoirs of her time in that establishment to *Ici Paris*, was awarded $5,000.

Onassis's disposition of the property that was not held by the companies to be incorporated in the master company was equally meticulous. "My yacht, the *Christina*, if my daughter and wife so wish, they can keep for their personal use," he wrote. But it would be expensive, he reminded them. If they did not wish to spend the $500,000 required annually for its upkeep, they should remove "whatever objects of their liking," replace them with copies, and give the ship to the Greek treasury for the use "of every new leader of the Greek state."

Skorpios was the subject of a similar recommendation. If Jackie and Christina were unable to agree on how to use the island, they must give it to Olympic Airlines as a "holiday resort and especially for children's encampments." There was one provision, however. The thirty-acre area surrounding Alexander's tomb must be preserved inviolate as a monument. Onassis named "the mother of my son Alexander, Athina née Livanos-Onassis-Blandford-Niarchos," as the chief executor of his will.

24
VACANCY AT THE TOP

THE AGENCE FRANCE-PRESSE (AFP) in Athens had what almost amounted to an obsession about being first with the news of Onassis's death. They would sometimes file the story first, then check. On one occasion they had Onassis dying in a dentist's chair in the Athens Hilton while the man was soundly asleep in New York. Before he was awakened by a frantic phone call from aides in Athens to ask if he was alive, AFP reported jubilantly that its Hilton report had been confirmed by their man in Geneva. Onassis enjoyed the game and sometimes entered into the spirit of it. After one premature report of his death, he remarked, "It helps to sell newspapers. I didn't deny the rumor. I just walked in the streets."

He had never bothered about his health, which had on the whole been good throughout his life. The suspicion in which he held the medical profession amounted to a sort of superstition. Illness was almost synonymous with death, and to be stricken by the one was to experience the proximity of the other. But by the spring of 1974, Onassis could no longer ignore the prospect of his mortality.

He had felt tired since Alexander's death, and in the beginning his illness was indistinguishable from his normal state of health—he simply felt more tired. When he experienced difficulty in keeping his eyes open,

350

in swallowing food, and in speaking without slurring his words, he finally sought medical advice. He was told that he was suffering from myasthenia gravis.

Myasthenia is classed with rheumatoid arthritis as a disease in which the body turns against itself. Its cause is not known, but its symptoms are brought on by stress, by too much alcohol, and by fatigue. There is a defect in the chemical process at the point at which the nerves and muscles meet, and this prevents the routine transmission of impulses: the body can no longer be made to work. The disease can be contained but not cured; attacks can be minimized by a series of painful injections. The symptoms then disappear, leaving the patient to lead a normal life. Only in rare cases is myasthenia fatal.

Onassis made light of his affliction. He had often hidden his eyes from the world behind dark glasses. Now they served to disguise the only physical evidence of his illness—the tape that attached his eyelids to his eyebrows to keep his eyes open. He appeared in public at the 21 Club in New York, where it was suggested that he was suffering from the results of a stroke. Onassis ignored the suggestion and joked about his illness with his friends. "If I spend as long with my makeup as Jackie," he said, "I could use invisible tape and no one would be the wiser."

In April, Maria Callas discussed her relationship with Onassis on American television. Interviewed by Barbara Walters for the "Today" show, the opera star described Onassis as the big love of her life. She did not, however, regret not becoming his wife because "love is so much better when you are not married." Asked whether she had any bad feelings toward Mrs. Onassis, Callas replied, "Why should I? Of course, if she treats Mr. Onassis very badly, I might be very angry."

Onassis, meanwhile, had embarked on a long cruise with Christina to Monte Carlo, Egypt, and the eastern Mediterranean. He had not been to Monaco since his quarrel with Rainier, and his stay at the scene of his greatest social triumphs was elegiac in tone. He dined with Rainier and Princess Caroline aboard the yacht. Amends were made on both sides. "Although he cheered up during dinner it was all very sad," Rainier recalled. "To have come so far just to end up heartbroken and ill on board this vast yacht with only your daughter for company seemed unfair."

After the cruise, Onassis seriously began to treat Christina as his successor. In normal circumstances he would not have encouraged her interest in shipping. As a Greek, he would not have found the notion of a woman in business attractive; as a tanker owner he would have been

351

skeptical of her chances in a business dominated entirely by men. But he arranged a crash course for her at the New York office and at his ship and insurance brokers. He also took her to business lunches with the oil executives he knew. When she was allowed to attend a boardroom lunch at the British Petroleum headquarters in London she said nothing, in spite of the efforts made by the chairman, Sir Eric Drake, to draw her out. That evening, over cocktails, she was extremely voluble. When Sir Eric asked her why she had been so silent at lunch she replied, "Daddy told me to listen to everything you said and not open my mouth."

In New York, Onassis rarely spent much time with Jackie. He would find pretexts to prolong a conversation with Gratsos as the working day ended. At eight o'clock, when it became evident that he could no longer reasonably justify remaining at the office, he would suggest going to a nearby bar. Gratsos had never been able to match his friend drink for drink. After two whiskies he would make his excuses and leave. Sometimes Onassis went with him, sometimes he moved on to George Moore, his personal banker and friend, who lived on Fifth Avenue. There was more drinking, more talk of the past. When he became hungry, Onassis would raid the refrigerator.

When he referred to the present it was often to complain about his marriage. Neither Gratsos nor Moore were willing listeners. The complaints were banal, that Jackie spent too much money with too little effect. There was a feeling of inappropriateness about his words. They could sense his engulfing misery, but it could only find expression in the most trivial forms. "I don't think he ever knew what he wanted," Gratsos told us. "The difference was that in his last years he knew he would never get it. Behind his gaiety, there was this melancholy, this tortured soul, and a terrible irony. Here was a man who had made himself without his family, who had never had a successful family life because he couldn't or never needed it. And when he did—after Alex's death—he found himself in a position where that was the one thing his enormous wealth could not buy. If you are a moralist you will look at this as an edifying tale. If you look at life as a human being, you will find it tragic. He had climbed to the top of the tree and there was nothing there."

At the end of a long evening in New York, Moore and/or Gratsos would ultimately go to bed, leaving Onassis to talk to their wives. When they retired, he often went on to El Morocco, where he sat at his customary table and spoke to whoever happened to be there. His evening lasted into the next morning. At dawn he would put his guests into a cab outside Elmo's, walk down to Fifty-seventh Street and buy a newspaper, and then walk the remaining mile up Fifth Avenue to his wife's apartment. It was the way he experienced New York when he was still young and hopeful. Angelo Zuccotti, the maître d' at El Morocco, sometimes became concerned about his failure to wear a topcoat. "I'd say, 'Mr. Onassis, look it's cold and the city isn't as safe as it used to be. Take a cab, please.' And he'd say, 'No, I'm just an old man. I don't dress in a fancy way. Nobody will recognize me.'"

In Paris he was most often at Maxim's. Flora Lewis, a correspondent for *The New York Times,* met him there and subsequently cabled a pen portrait to her newspaper.

He sat at his usual table in Maxim's crowded that day with British, American and French social figures who had flocked to Paris for the Grand Prix. Fashionable young women kept coming up to give him a peck on the cheek and one said, "Ari, we're going to be cruising around Skorpios next month. Is it all right if we drop in?"

"Yes, yes," he said, waving her away as he did the others and going on with the stories of his youth which engrossed him. . . .

He was wearing glasses with one dark lens to hide the eye that was unable to keep open because of his ailment, but the other eye gleamed with gusto as he described how he worked nights crawling around fixing wires where the young women operators sat at their switchboards. . . .

He didn't talk much about his famous wife, Jacqueline Kennedy Onassis, who was having lunch elsewhere that day. He talked, with great nostalgia, about the marvelous times he had as an ardent, desperately determined youth. And when a young man walked up to say hello, Mr. Onassis patted his cheek paternally. Then, his dark eye misted for a moment.

An evening that began at Maxim's and continued at the Crazy Horse Saloon in the company of Jacques Harvey, a French journalist, was less dignified. Onassis, who had drunk a good deal, was annoyed when a paparazzo, Roger Picard, flashed a bulb in his face. He summoned Picard into the nightclub and promised him an exclusive picture. Together the two men went down to the men's room. "You can take a photograph of the secret of my success," he said, unzipping his fly and placing his penis on the saucer in which patrons of the cloakroom had placed their five-franc tips. "There you are," he said. "That is my secret, sex and money." He laughed so much at his own joke that he dropped the saucer on the stone floor and broke it.

The one ostensibly bright area of promise in the early summer of 1974 was the fact that Christina appeared to be taking her duties as heir apparent to the Onassis fortune seriously. Onassis's associates in New York were deeply impressed by her ability to pick up her father's traits. George Moore found her "uncannily able to remember everything he had told her, almost as if she had a computer in her brain that had been programmed by Ari." She dressed simply and worked all day without a break for lunch. Her fascination with a variety of playboys of the Western world seemed to be at an end, and she had developed a liking for her cousin, Philip Niarchos. Grandmother Livanos and Tina encouraged the relationship, and Onassis himself expressed interest in a possible union so long as Christina's assets were safeguarded by means of a premarital contract.

Christina, nonetheless, still suffered sharp fluctuations of mood. That summer she was taken into an emergency ward of the Middlesex Hospital in London under the name A. Danoi and treated for an overdose of sleeping pills. As Christina recovered, her mother, who flew over from Paris to visit her in the hospital, went into decline. Tina's marriage to Niarchos had not brought her happiness, and since Alexander's death she had increasingly withdrawn from the world. Her health had never been good, and it was eroded by the large amounts of barbiturates and tranquilizers she took to cure her insomnia and steady her nerves. On the morning of September 10 she died in the Hôtel de Chanaleilles, Niarchos's Paris residence. A doctor concluded her death was the result of an edema of the lung. Onassis was in Paris at the time and went to see Niarchos immediately. The meeting was sad but friendly. Onassis suggested that it might be a good idea to have an autopsy performed in order to counter the rumors of suicide that would inevitably follow the public announcement of Tina's death. Christina arrived in Paris at 4 A.M. the next day, went straight up to Onassis's bedroom, and expressed her own desire for an autopsy.

An upset Niarchos agreed to make a joint statement with Onassis about the autopsy. It acknowledged that it was Christina who had asked for the autopsy but declared that the two families "not only are not opposed to it, but on the contrary welcome the decision." The results of the autopsy confirmed the findings of the first postmortem examination. Niarchos, however, made a statement further explaining his wife's death. She had, he suggested, been depressed ever since her visit to Christina in the London hospital a month earlier. Tina had been "very disturbed morally and physically by this new trial after the death of her son Alexander" and "had never completely recovered."

Onassis did not attend his former wife's funeral. "He's too old, too sick," one of his aides explained. His condition deteriorated drastically. At the end of October, he was admitted to a New York hospital under the name of Phillips for intensive treatment. The cortisone prescribed for him made his face puffy and exacerbated his temper. On his discharge from hospital, he threw a rage when he was kept waiting in the office of his Park Avenue cardiologist. The doctor observed afterward that it was "a cortisone rage." "And when he's not on cortisone?" asked the nurse.

In the fall of 1974 the Olympic Tower, a fifty-two-story skyscraper overlooking the spires of New York's St. Patrick's Cathedral, was formally dedicated. It was a joint development involving both Onassis and the Arlen Realty Corporation. With its 250 condominium apartments and nineteen floors of office space, it was—and remains—Onassis's most conspicuous contribution to Manhattan culture. To make Olympic Tower what the press handouts described as "one of the most secure residential buildings in the world," computer experts had collaborated with security experts to devise a foolproof master system. Owners with valuable works of art could arrange to have each picture or piece of sculpture individually wired, along with their wall safes, to a central computer. Every apartment would have a computer-monitored intrusion alarm. On the building's opening, the press made suitably admiring comments on Olympic Tower's "mixed-use facilities" and Orwellian security devices and suggested that Onassis would probably take up residence there with his wife.

The suggestion was good for business but remote from reality. Onassis's complaints about Jackie to his friends had become increasingly intense. The question of divorce had been raised as far back as 1972, while Alexander was still alive, only to be shelved. Now Onassis determined to do something. He asked Roy Cohn, a lawyer who had earned a certain notoriety in the fifties as one of Senator Joe McCarthy's investigators if he would represent Onassis in divorce proceedings. Cohn agreed, and Onassis secured the services of a private investigator. A "blueprint" for the divorce took shape in the course of a number of meetings at the Onassis offices and at El Morocco.

Only one of the many ideas was actually implemented. Jack Anderson, the syndicated Washington columnist, was startled to receive a call from Onassis's secretary with the suggestion that her boss and he should have lunch together. He had never met Onassis or tried to see him. He took the shuttle to New York, where he was met by a limousine and whisked

355

off to the 21 Club. Onassis was cordial but not particularly forthright. Initially, Anderson could not see what the purpose of the meeting was, though he noted Onassis's evident desire to talk about his wife. "He would make a start on Jackie. 'What does she do with all those clothes. All I ever see her wearing is blue jeans,' he would say. And then he would stop; apparently out of tact, delicacy or reticence."

After lunch, Onassis suggested that Anderson come back to his office. They walked together through the streets, Anderson with a rising conviction that he was "onto something big." At the office Onassis introduced him to a number of his aides, including Gratsos, and then left, pleading another engagement. Anderson, who was a familiar of "deniability" procedures, was convinced that the aides, on instructions, would be more forthright than their boss. And so it turned out.

Anderson was plied with details of Jackie's alleged profligacy with Onassis's money and given the impression that it had soured the marriage. There was no doubt in his mind that it was Onassis's desire to have these details made public. Anderson asked the aides for a definition of the Jackie-Ari relationship. "Total incompatibility" was the reply. Anderson was informed that divorce proceedings were imminent, and he left the office in no doubt that his own role in making them publicly acceptable would not be inconsiderable.

Onassis's divorce plans, however, were interrupted by another unwelcome development in his business interests. Olympic Airways, like other carriers, had had a bad year as a result of the rise in oil prices and the world recession. Unlike them, it had also suffered from the mobilization and near war with Turkey over Cyprus and the collapse of the Greek military junta. The tourists stayed away, with disastrous effects. By December 1974 the airline was no longer capable of generating enough cash to keep its planes in the air. Onassis had never entirely regained his enthusiasm for Olympic Airways after Alexander's death. It was run by Costa Konialidis, his cousin, as an entity separate from the rest of the Onassis interests. For a time, no one dared tell Onassis just how bad things had become; when they did tell him, he decided to handle the affair himself.

His first action was to make new demands of the Greek government —a substantial low-interest loan and exemption from fuel duty. The Karamanlis administration was not impressed. Once again Onassis had miscalculated a basic change in attitude toward him. Karamanlis had been his confidant and friend when Olympic was created, but now the prime minister was in no mood to be bullied into concessions by a

356

multimillionaire who was generally considered to have been closer than courtesy demanded to the military dictatorship. When Onassis instituted a program of cutting back manpower, and his employees struck and were locked out, the government responded by passing retroactive legislation making it impossible for him to fire more than 2 percent of his staff.

Onassis was still in New York undergoing treatment and unable to grasp the extent to which the Greek world had moved on. He invoked the clause that allowed him to relinquish his concession and summarily grounded all Olympic planes and froze all Olympic airlines employees' salaries. It was the sort of move that had worked in the past, and Onassis was surprised and wounded when Karamanlis called his bluff. The government put in its own management team and announced that it would buy the airline.

His activity throughout the rest of December was a caricature of his old dynamic self. Against his doctors' orders he flew back to Athens, ostensibly to supervise the Olympic transition. His negotiations with the government were compulsive. He did not want to lose Olympic, and he used every stratagem to delay the takeover. Many evenings and nights of negotiation were wasted over trivial matters. He was physically exhausted but maintained what seemed like an inexhaustible supply of quibbles. He ruined everyone's New Year by prolonging the business proceedings until almost midnight. His desire not to sign documents to which he had given verbal assent became so transparent that the government negotiators were forced into extraordinary strategies to pin him down.

At one meeting, George Theofanos, the Greek government's choice as Onassis's successor at Olympic, insisted that Onassis should deliver on his verbal agreement and sign the basic takeover document. It was already past midnight. "But there are no secretaries to type up the agreement," said Onassis. Theofanos said he would type it out himself. "I'm too tired," Onassis replied and walked out. The agreement was finally signed on January 15, 1975. Professor Georgakis thought the loss of Olympic also resulted in the loss of Onassis's will to live: "Emotionally and for his sense of grandeur it was the final blow. For once he was not begged to remain."

While Onassis was wrestling with the Greek government, Jackie was occupying herself with a photographic project in New York. She visited a new museum sponsored by the International Center of Photography and lunched with its executive director, Cornell Capa, and an old friend,

357

Karl Katz, the former director of New York's Jewish Museum. She took copious notes of the conversation and wrote them up in succinct, reportorial style. *The New Yorker* happily accepted her article as an anonymous contribution and published it in its second January 1975 issue while concealing the identity of the contributor.

In February she received a call from Athens to say that her husband had collapsed with pains in his abdomen. Onassis's Greek doctors told him he had pneumonia as a result of the cortisone treatment for his other ailments. He experienced an attack of gallstones. There was nothing new about this. His doctor had recommended an operation to remove his gall bladder two years earlier, but Onassis had declined the advice. This attack was more severe, again as a result of the cortisone. Doctors were summoned from Paris and New York. The French liver specialist Dr. Caroli recommended an immediate operation to remove Onassis's gall bladder. The American heart specialist Dr. Isidore Rosenfeld cautioned against an operation. Onassis would never survive it; he was far too weak. He recommended that Onassis should fly immediately to New York and undergo another period of intensive treatment before any decision to operate was made.

Onassis wavered through the first week of February. He was frightened and he knew that neither of the two options outlined by his doctors offered much prospect of his surviving. On Wednesday, February 6, he gave in to the remonstrations of his Paris doctor and agreed to an operation. Olympic's lawyer, Tryfon Koutalidis, called the Glyfada house to speak to Costa Konialidis. By mistake he dialed the wrong number and came through on the extension in Onassis's bedroom. A voice he did not recognize answered. After a momentary confusion, it was established to be that of Onassis. "I have to go to Paris," he said. "I want you to know that I shall die there. Everyone wants me to go but I don't like the idea." Onassis made Koutalidis swear to do a number of things after he was dead. The most important was to continue the fight against Niarchos on Christina's behalf.

Onassis flew to Paris with Christina, his sister, Artemis, and Jackie, who had flown over from New York, for company. Most of his conversation, however, was directed at Dr. Caroli, who sat beside him. As the plane climbed through the clouds, he turned to Caroli and said he felt close to his dead son, Alexander. Later in the flight he said, "You understand, professor, the meaning of the Greek word *thanatos*— 'death.' You know I will never come out of the hospital alive. Well, please practice *thanatos* on me."

At Orly Airport, Onassis refused a stretcher and, against his doctors' advice, insisted on going to his apartment on the avenue Foch. Looking gray and haggard, he walked unaided into the building through a crowd of expectant journalists. Next morning he was driven to the American Hospital at Neuilly, which he entered through a back door. On Sunday, February 10, his gall bladder was removed. A family spokesman said he was "feeling much better." In fact he was suffering from jaundice and had difficulty breathing. He spent the next five weeks in a semiconscious state, fed intravenously and kept alive by a respirator and massive infusions of antibiotics.

His family drew tighter around him during the last weeks, excluding Jackie, whom they had always considered an interloper. Christina refused to share the Onassis apartment with her stepmother and moved into the Hôtel Plaza-Athénée. She spent each day by her father's bedside. Jackie visited the American Hospital each day but otherwise kept up a normal social life, dining out with friends in the evenings. In his moments of lucidity Onassis expressed concern for the future of his family and his business interests. Christina had recently been seeing Peter Goulandris again. She took Peter with her to Onassis's bedside and told him they had decided to get married. Onassis was cheered by this innocent deception.

By the end of February he appeared to be showing slight signs of recovery. Jackie decided to fly back to New York to see her daughter, who was helping make a documentary film on the underprivileged of Appalachia. When she told Onassis, he made no attempt to dissuade her. Christina was under the impression that she would only be away for the weekend. When Jackie called back the following Monday, she was told his condition had not changed. Later in the week he went into a rapid decline, but Jackie did not appreciate the seriousness of his condition. She was still in New York on Saturday, March 15—the day Onassis died with Christina at his bedside.

His death was said to be due to bronchial pneumonia, which "resisted all antibiotics." Dr. Maurice Mercadier, one of his physicians, said that the cortisone treatment had lowered his resistance to infection and had made the pneumonia "uncontrollable."

Jackie arrived in Paris on the day after her husband's death and went alone through the bronze doors of the hospital chapel where he was lying on an open bier with a Greek Orthodox icon on his chest. Christina, exhausted by her father's agony, was under sedation. Two days later the body was flown to Aktion aboard an Olympic Airways 727, accompanied by Jackie, Christina, Teddy Kennedy, and Onassis's sisters. They were joined there by mourners from Athens.

The coffin was placed aboard a launch and ferried across to Skorpios, where the mourners walked slowly up the hill behind it, led by the local priest, Father Apostolous. Christina walked in front with Onassis's sisters by her side. Behind her were Jackie, leaning on the arm of her son, with Teddy Kennedy at her other side.

In the courtyard outside the chapel were seven large wreaths on white tripods. One of them, containing white and pink carnations, pink hyacinths, and white lilies was inscribed, "To Ari From Jackie." The courtyard was ringed with hundreds of white lilies, their pots draped in white velvet. The *Christina* was anchored in the bay with her flag at half-mast. Only a few of the mourners were able to crowd into the chapel for the service. Father Apostolous took as his text one of Saint Paul's Epistles to the Thessalonians, and a small choir sung several verses, including, "I went to the grave and I saw the naked bones, and I said to myself, 'Who are you? King or soldier? Rich or poor? Sinner or just?' "

The coffin was carried outside and placed in a grave of cement and plaster on the side of the chapel opposite from Alexander's grave. After the ceremony, the funeral party walked down the hill to the *Christina*. They were joined on deck by the crew and Onassis's employees. A few months earlier Christina Onassis had said, "Both my father and myself have learned how short life can be and how terribly death can strike." Now she acknowledged her father's death with a wide, embracing sweep of her arms. "This boat and this island are mine," she said in Greek. "You are all my people now."

BIBLIOGRAPHY

Ambler, Eric, *The Mask of Dimitrios.* London: Hodder & Stoughton, 1939.

Amory, Cleveland, *Who Killed Society?* New York: Harper and Row, 1960.

Baldwin, Billy, *Billy Baldwin Remembers.* New York: Harcourt Brace Jovanovich, 1974.

Bender, Marylin, *The Beautiful People.* New York: Coward-McCann, 1967.

Bouvier, Jacqueline and Lee, *One Special Summer,* New York: Delacorte Press, 1972.

Bradlee, Benjamin, *Conversations with Kennedy.* New York: W. W. Norton & Co., 1975.

Cafarakis, Christian, *The Fabulous Onassis: His Life and Loves.* New York: William Morrow & Co., 1972.

Cameron, James, *Point of Departure.* London: Arthur Barker, 1967.

Cash, Kevin, *Who the Hell Is William Loeb?* Manchester, N.H.: Amoskeag Press, 1975.

Curtis, Charlotte, *The Rich and Other Atrocities.* New York: Harper and Row, 1976.

David, Lester, and Jhan Robbins, *Jackie and Ari: The Inside Story.* New York: Pocket Books, 1975.

Davis, John H., *The Bouviers: Portrait of an American Family.* New York: Farrar, Straus & Giroux, 1969.

Dedichen, Ingeborg, and Henry Pesser, *Onassis, Mon Amour. . . .* Paris: Editions Pygmalion, 1975.

Fonteyn, Margot, *Margot Fonteyn: Autobiography.* New York: Alfred A. Knopf, 1975.

Frischauer, Willi, *Jackie.* London: Michael Joseph, 1976.

———— *Millionaires' Islands.* London: Michael Joseph, 1973.

———— *Onassis.* New York: Meredith Press, 1968.

Gage, Nicholas, *The Bourlotas Fortune.* New York: Holt, Rinehart and Winston, 1975.

Galella, Ronald, *Jacqueline.* New York: Sheed and Ward, 1974.

Gallagher, Mary Barelli, and Frances S. Leighton, *My Life with Jacqueline Kennedy.* New York: David McKay, 1969.

Getty, J. Paul, *As I See It: Autobiography of J. Paul Getty.* New York: Prentice-Hall, 1976.

―――― *How to Be Rich.* New York: Playboy Press, 1966.

Giannaris, George, *Miki Theodorakis.* London: George Allen and Unwin, 1973.

Graves, Charles, *Royal Riviera.* London: William Heinemann, 1957.

The Greek Shipping Director, Athens, 1976.

Gunther, Max, *The Very, Very Rich and How They Got That Way.* Chicago: Playboy Press, 1972.

Harvey, Jacques, *Mon Ami Onassis.* Paris: Editions Albin Michel, 1975.

Hawkins, Peter, *Prince Rainier of Monaco.* London: William Kimber & Co., 1966.

Herndon, Booton, *Ford.* New York: Weybright and Talley, 1969.

The International Celebrity Register.

Jackson, Stanley, *Inside Monte Carlo.* New York: Stein & Day, 1975.

Joesten, Joachim, *Onassis.* New York: Abelard-Schumann, 1963.

Kennedy, Rose Fitzgerald, *Times to Remember.* New York: Doubleday & Co., 1974.

Kramer, Freda, *Jackie.* New York: Award Books, 1975.

Lemos, Andreas G., *The Greeks and the Sea.* London: Cassell & Co., 1976.

Lilly, Doris, *The Fabulous Greeks.* New York: Cowles Book Company, 1970.

Lundberg, Ferdinand, *The Rich and the Super Rich.* New York: Lyle Stuart, Publisher, 1968.

Manchester, William, *The Death of a President.* New York: Harper and Row, 1967.

―――― *The Glory and the Dream: A Narrative History of America 1932–72.* Boston: Little, Brown and Co., 1974.

Moran, Lord, *Churchill: Taken from the Diaries of Lord Moran.* Boston: Houghton Mifflin Co., 1966.

Mostert, Noel, *Supership.* New York: Alfred A. Knopf, 1974.

Naess, Erling D., *The Great Panhonlib Controversy.* London: Gower Press, 1972.

Pendle, George, *A History of Latin America.* London: Penguin Books, 1963.

Rey, Pierre, *The Greek.* New York: G. P. Putnam's Sons, 1974.

Robyns, Gwen, *Princess Grace.* New York: David McKay, 1976.

Sampson, Anthony, *The Seven Sisters.* New York: Viking Press, 1975.

Schlesinger, Arthur Jr., *A Thousand Days.* Boston: Houghton Mifflin, 1965.

Sorenson, Theodore C., *Kennedy.* New York: Harper and Row, 1965.

Sparks, Fred, *The Twenty Million Dollar Honeymoon: Jackie and Ari's First Year.* New York: Bernard Geis Associates, 1970.

Stettinius, Edward R., Jr. *The Diaries of Edward R. Stettinius, Jr. 1943–46.* Edited by George C. Herring, Jr. New York: Franklin Watts, 1975.

Thomas, Lately, *When Even Angels Wept.* New York: William Morrow & Co., 1973.

Toynbee, Arnold J., *The Western Question in Greece and Turkey.* Boston: Houghton Mifflin Co., 1922.

Vidal, Gore, *Two Sisters.* Boston: Little, Brown and Co., 1970.

Vlachos, Helen, *House Arrest.* Boston: Gambit, 1971.

White, John W., *Argentina.* New York: Viking Press, 1942.

Woodhouse, C. M., *The Story of Modern Greece.* London: Faber & Faber, 1968.

INDEX

United States Maritime Commission
  (cont.)
  161ff; "trade-out and build" agreement,
  161-62, 165-66
United States Petroleum Carriers (USPC),
  161; and surplus ships deal, 102-3, 106-
  8, 111
USS Edsall, 21, 24

Venizelos, Eleutherios, 13, 36, 266
Venizelos, Sophocles, 72, 75
Vergottis, Panaghis, 40; *Artemision* shares
  lawsuit, 220-26, 305; friendship with
  Callas, 219-22, 224-26; and Onassis, 47,
  219, 224-26
Victoria Financiera Panama, 209, 210, 211
Victory Carriers, 108, 158, 161
Vidal, Gore, 245, 258, 308
Vlachos, Helen: *House Arrest*, 236, 263-
  64, 298; on Niarchos, 47, 236; and
  Onassis, 232, 236-37
Vlassapoulos, Costa, 349
Voulgarides, Yanni, and Manolis, 6-7, 9,
  12, 17, 24

Wadsworth, Edward, 139-40, 143-45, 151
War Shipping Administration, 57
Western Tankers, 161
Westphal, Adolph, 92
Whaling, 103, 115-16; catch seasons, quo-
  tas and species, 117-19, 121-22, 127-30;
  Convention signatories, 118, 119; gun-
ners, 116, 117, 118; national fleets, 116,
  118, 119, 122-3, 127-29, 131; oil price,
  116, 121, 122, 127; Peru, actions against
  Onassis, 124-27
—Onassis operations (1950–56): 115-31,
  156; Eureka, 64-65; flouts IWC rules,
  119-22, 127-30; visits factory ship, 120
Whaling Association, Norwegian, 117-23,
  127-31
Whaling Commission, International
  (IWC), 117, 119, 122, 127, 130
Wharton, Bryan, 232-33
Wilson, Earl, 253
Woman's Wear Daily, 249, 305
World War I, and Smyrna, 12-13
World War II: Argentina, 85; Greek ship-
  ping repercussions, 52, 65-66, 70, 73-74
Worldscale Index. *See under* Tankers, oil

Yachts: *Creole* (Niarchos), 98, 148, 234;
  Deo Juvante (Rainier), 191
—*Christina*, 96, 115, 166-69, 173-75, 190,
  192, 220, 243, 303, 321, 325, 337, 360;
  design and decor, 97-98, 304, 309;
  Onassis-Callas cruise, 182, 184; Onassis-
  Jackie Kennedy cruise, 246-47, 250, 306;
  Prince Rainier cruise, 193; will, disposi-
  tion, 349

Zakarias, Yorgo, 321
Zelenko, Herbert, 162-65
Zucotti, Angelo, 353